Live&Work
IN
AUSTRALIA
AND
NEW ZEALAND

Live&Work
IN
AUSTRALIA
AND
NEW ZEALAND

Elisabeth Roberts
Susan McIntosh

Published by Vacation Work, 9 Park End Street, Oxford
Web site http: //www.vacationwork.co.uk

LIVE AND WORK IN AUSTRALIA AND NEW ZEALAND

First Edition 1995, Fiona McGregor & Charlotte Denny
Second Edition 1999, Elisabeth Roberts & Susan McIntosh
Reprinted 2000

Series Editor: Victoria Pybus

ISBN 185458 213 5 (softback)

Publicity: Roger Musker

Cover design by Miller, Craig and Cocking Design Partnership

Typeset by Worldview Publishing Services (01865-201562)

Printed by William Clowes Ltd., Beccles, Suffolk, England

Contents

Australia

SECTION 1 – LIVING IN AUSTRALIA

GENERAL INTRODUCTION

RESIDENCE AND ENTRY REGULATIONS

SETTING UP HOME

DAILY LIFE

RETIREMENT

SECTION II – WORKING IN AUSTRALIA

EMPLOYMENT

STARTING A BUSINESS

Establishing a new business – Intellectual property protection – Registering

New Zealand

SECTION 1 – LIVING IN NEW ZEALAND

GENERAL INTRODUCTION

RESIDENCE & ENTRY REGULATIONS

SETTING UP HOME

DAILY LIFE

RETIREMENT

SECTION II – WORKING IN NEW ZEALAND

EMPLOYMENT

STARTING A BUSINESS

MAPS

APPENDIX

Preface

This second edition of *Live and Work in Australia and New Zealand* has been revised throughout to assist anyone thinking of going 'down under' to experience a way of life which verges on the legendary. From the perspective of the grey and overcrowded cities of nothern Europe, the tourist-brochure paradises of Australia and New Zealand have an especial allure, and for generations the adventurous and hopeful have headed south to live out the dream. For the short-term visitor, these countries offer a wealth of unforgettable experiences, but for those considering a more permanent move the challenge becomes more daunting. In this book, we have tried to convey something of the sights and opportunities that are there for all to enjoy, and also to bring out some of the difficulties and problems that a newcomer may encounter.

Both New Zealand and Australia are continuing to develop increasing affinity, through economic links, with their Pacific and Asian neighbours. While this may not seem much of a recommendation in the wake of the current Asian economic crisis, emergency recovery measures announced by the Japanese government in late 1998 suggest that prospects may soon improve throughout the Asia-Pacific region.

One sign of Australia's confidence in particular, is the growing tide of republicanism that aims to cut the final constitutional ties between Britain and Australia – a goal that is likely to be achieved early in the next millennium.

Increasingly, both New Zealand and Australia are streamlining immigration procedures to favour young, educated and/or skilled migrants, while still allowing family-linked and humanitarian immigration to take place, albeit under more strictly controlled criteria. Business investors and successful entrepreneurs are welcomed with open arms, and more importantly, financial incentives. This book describes the categories under which you can enter Australia and New Zealand, shows you how to maximise your potential for qualifying and where to get help with your application. Working holiday visas for up to a year give those aged 18-30 an opportunity to combine a holiday with the chance to discover whether they would like to commit themselves for longer.

The popularity of the first edition of *Live & Work in Australia and New Zealand* has proved that Australia and New Zealand still exert a strong pull on Britons and other nationalities who wish to experience the travel, temporary and long-term work, career opportunities, or even retirement prospects offered by these countries. You will find a wealth of practical information on every aspect of travelling and living in the different regions with extensive sections devoted to establishing a home and social life, and to finding the right job in the right place. We hope that it will help you make the most of a culture that will always reward you for 'having a go'. Enjoy it!

Elisabeth Roberts &
Susan McIntosh
January 1999

Acknowledgements

The authors and publishers would like to thank the many people who provided information and assistance in compiling this book. In particular, thanks are due to Geraint Davies of Montfort International and Geoff Taylor of the Emigration Group for their contributions, the staff of Oxford University Computing Services for unfailing technical assistance, and most especially, all those family and friends who offered the moral and logistical support necessary in completing a project of this kind.

Telephone area code changes.
On April 22nd 2000 there are to be a number of changes to certain area telephone code prefixes in the UK. The most important of these is that the current 0171- and 0181- prefixes for London will be replaced by the prefix 020-, followed by 7 for current 0171 numbers and 8 for current 0181 numbers. Also affected will be Cardiff (numbers will begin 029 20), Portsmouth (023 92), Southampton (023 80) and Northern Ireland (028 90) for Belfast; contact directory enquiries for other numbers in Northern Ireland.

In addition, as from the same date the numbers for various special services including freephone and lo-call numbers will begin with 08 and all mobile phone numbers will begin with 07. Telephone operators are planning to ease the transition by running the current 01 numbers in parallel with the new 02 numbers until spring 2001.

Australia

SECTION I

Living in Australia

General Introduction
Residence and Entry Regulations
Setting Up Home
Daily Life
Retirement

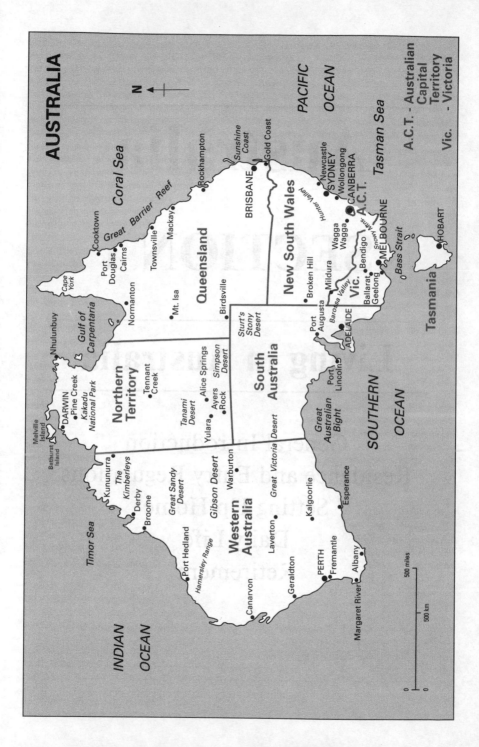

General Introduction

Destination Australia

For several generations, Australia has been one of the world's most popular migration destinations. The promises of eternal sunshine and prosperity, and of freedom from the class-bound traditions of the Old World have proved a magnet both for young, independent travellers and for families seeking a new life. In some cases, they have been disappointed. Australia is not a utopia and, although it is fiercely loved and defended by its citizens, it would not claim to be. Like any other country in the industrialised world, it experiences its share of contemporary social malaise: recession, unemployment, crime, and public corruption have all made their mark in recent decades. Nonetheless, the attractions of good weather (but not *every* day!) and a high standard of living remain as strong as ever, and there has been no decline in the numbers of people seeking to emigrate from Europe and, increasingly, from south-east Asia and other regions.

The days of the 'ten pound Pom', though, are gone. Australia no longer needs to offer inducements to build up its population and skill base, and immigration quotas are now strictly regulated. The application procedure is lengthy, complex, and expensive, with an emphasis on the net gain to Australian society. Whilst the country actively pursues a programme of humanitarian immigration (Australia took, and continues to take, more Vietnamese refugees than almost any other country), most applicants will need to be able to demonstrate financial security and significant professional experience.

Australia's affluence and, to some extent, its complacency, have recently been rocked by the crisis in the 'tiger economies' of south-east Asia. The Pacific Rim is Australia's biggest export market and for more than a decade the country has pursued a policy of 'asianisation', forging close political, cultural, and economic ties with its near neighbours. Today, however, the Australia dollar is plunging with each new fall in the value of the yen, and it is uncertain how long the economy will be able to sustain the growth and low levels of unemployment experienced in recent years.

Nonetheless, many of Australia's greatest attractions remain unchanged. The expansive landscape with its infinite variety, the oceans and waterways which are at the heart of the Australian way of life, and the spacious and attractive cities are all valued and enjoyed. Australian society is refreshingly open and vigorous, the people are friendly, and the ethical cornerstones of equality and freedom are championed in a kind of congenital anti-authoritarianism. Whether you are considering a short holiday or a lifetime's move, you will find that Australians will always be prepared to give you a 'fair go'.

Pros and Cons of Moving to Australia

Australia's climate has always been a motivating factor in the decision of many European migrants to leave their home shores. The warm, sunny weather in most coastal regions allows people enjoy an outdoor lifestyle with an emphasis on leisure. Even hardship looks better when the sun shines, and there are acknowledged health and psychological benefits to living in a favourable climate.

Fruit and vegetables are abundant, fresh, and almost invariably locally grown. There is a huge variety available, including many tropical and exotic fruits rarely seen in Europe, and prices are significantly lower. Meat is particularly cheap and of excellent quality, and there is no risk of BSE infection in Australian beef.

Most Australians live in large, modern cities which compete successfully in the global economy. Australian scientific and technical research lead the world in many areas, and technology, engineering, commerce and banking are now as important to the economy as its agricultural and mining industries. Salaries are not as high as in the UK when converted dollar-to-pound, but with a much lower cost of living, an average wage goes much further. Real estate is very much cheaper and most Australians own their own home, which will be large by European standards. Sydney and Melbourne are the most expensive cities in which to purchase property, and although these cities have a higher population density than others in Australia, residents retain the expectation of a large, detached house with a garden and garage, even in central city areas. Relatively few people live in flats.

In spite of these and other advantages, many immigrants do find certain aspects of Australian life difficult at first. In particular, new arrivals are sometimes painfully aware of their geographical isolation in Australia; homesickness and the prohibitive cost of international air travel occasionally promote a sense of exile. Many are overwhelmed, and it is not uncommon for immigrants to return permanently to their home country within a couple of years.

Although the cost of living is, in general, low, imported goods carry a substantial luxury tax, which may place familiar or favourite brands and items outside financial reach. Local alternatives are always available, but there are those migrants for whom no amount of sun, sea and sand can compensate for an over-priced tin of mushy peas.

Australia is also notorious for its unpleasant insects, snakes and sharks. With the warm weather come flies, swarms of them, and, if you live near freshwater, probably mosquitoes too. It is wise to assume that any spider you encounter is venomous until you learn to recognise those which pose an actual danger. Red-back, funnel web, and trapdoor spiders are all potentially fatal to adults as well as children, and Australians learn from an early age where these are likely to lurk. Even local bushland parks may harbour snakes such as dugites, whose bite will be lethal unless treated immediately. Most Australians know how to apply a tourniquet and suck out venom from a snake bite (and most *never* need to use this knowledge), and it may be reassuring to take a first aid course when you arrive, especially if you have a young family. Sharks live in Australia's coastal waters, and most beaches have an aerial shark patrol, as well as life-savers on duty. Shark attacks are extremely rare and their possibility does not discourage Australians from the beach. Once again, however, it is important to be alert, and born-and-bred Australians do not swim at dawn or dusk, which is known to be the sharks' feeding time.

In spite of these disadvantages, Australia has a cultural vitality and diversity which is invigorating. The population is very cosmopolitan, and this is reflected in the huge choice of restaurants and the range of entertainment available in every city.

From the European perspective, the main pros and cons of living in Australia can be summarised as follows:

Pros
Warm, sunny climate
High standard of living, including better pay
Better work conditions
Low cost of real estate
First class educational facilities and standards
Excellent medical facilities
Multicultural diversity
Low cost of living and high quality produce

Cons
Geographical isolation
Expensive national and international travel
High cost of imported goods
Annoying and dangerous insects and other animals

Political and Economic Structure

Australia is divided into six states – New South Wales (NSW), Victoria (Vic), Queensland (Qld), South Australia (SA), Western Australia (WA), and Tasmania (Tas) – and two territories, the Northern Territory (NT), and the Australian Capital Territory (ACT). The states and territories of Australia each have their own parliaments, capital city, flag, and emblems depicting regional flora and fauna. Australian mapmakers, atlases, and educationalists use cartographic projections which show Australia and the South-East Asian region at the centre of the world map, with Europe to the extreme left and the American continents to the right.

Historical Background

Although archaeological and historical evidence suggests that Australia was first settled over 50,000 years ago by Aborigines, and later mapped by Dutch and Portuguese galleons in the 16th century, Australia's founding mythology centres on the 'discovery' of the east coast by Captain James Cook in 1770. It was Cook who claimed the 'Great South Land' for the British Crown, and 18 years later, in response to a crisis in English jails and a shortage of natural resources following the American Declaration of Independence, the First Fleet arrived in Port Jackson, now known as Sydney Harbour, with 11 ships, 736 convicts, and a contingent of guards. As is well known, the majority of convicts were transported for what now seem petty offences and came from London, Manchester, Liverpool, Dublin, and Glasgow. A total of 160,000 convicts were brought to Australia over a period of 70 years, and many who survived their sentences chose to stay in the country as farmers. The first free settlers, lured by the promise of cheap land and convict labour, began to arrive in 1793, whilst explorers gradually opened up new country, discovering rich grazing land to the west. Wool soon became one of Australia's most important industries, and remains so to the present. The discovery of gold in the 1850s brought a fresh influx of immigrants from Europe, China, and America, and rich gold seams were found at Ballarat, north of Melbourne, and in central Western Australia, at Kalgoorlie. Large copper deposits were found in the York Peninsula in South Australia. Settlements were established in Hobart, Tasmania, in 1803; on the Brisbane River, Queensland, in 1824; on the Swan River, in Western Australia, in 1829; on Port Phillip Bay, Victoria, in 1835; and on Gulf St Vincent, South Australia, in 1836. The capital cities of each state have grown from these sites. In 1900 the colonies, which were previously independent entities, united in order to encourage economic expansion, regulate the postal system, and build a military defence force. The constitution was presented to the House of Commons in 1900 and was signed by Queen Victoria. Australia became the Commonwealth of Australia on 1 January 1901, and this date is known as Federation Day. Australia Day is celebrated on 26 January every year and commemorates the arrival of the First Fleet at Port Jackson.

Government

Australia is governed by three levels of elected government – local, state, and federal – and has been called the most over-governed country in the world. Local government operates through city and shire councils who have responsibility for local amenities, town planning, parks, and pet and vermin control. State governments fund and administer roads, vehicle licensing, the police force, education, and health care (amongst many other departments), while the Government of Australia (the federal or Commonwealth government) takes care of international trade, foreign affairs, and the national treasury. State governments are located in the capital city of each state, and the national parliament is in Canberra, the administrative capital of Australia. Although there are both state and federal taxes, income earners fill out only one tax return per year, remitted to the Australian Taxation Office, which then distributes revenue to the various states to fund their public services.

State and federal governments are run according to the British Westminster system, with two key differences. Firstly, unlike Britain, Australia has a written constitution, inspired by the constitution of the United States; and secondly, Australia's upper house, the Senate (equivalent in function to the House of Lords) is a democratically elected body. The lower house is known as the House of Representatives and its parliamentarians as Members of the House of Representatives (MHR). The legislative power of the Commonwealth of Australia is vested in the Parliament of the Commonwealth. The Queen is Australia's Head of State (under the Australian *Royal Styles and Titles Act* of 1973, her title is 'Queen of Australia and Her Other Realms and Territories, Head of the Commonwealth'), and her representative in Australia is the Governor-General, who has the powers to prorogue Parliament and to dissolve the House of Representatives, and to assent in the Queen's name to a proposed law passed by both the Houses of the Parliament. The Governor-General is Commander-in-Chief of the Australian Defence Forces. In practice, the Governor General's role is largely ceremonial, and there has been only one occasion in recent memory where he has interfered in the democratic government of the nation. This incident, widely considered by Australians to have been an insupportable intrusion of monarchical power in Australian affairs, occurred in 1975 when the then Governor-General, Sir John Ker, dismissed the democratically elected Prime Minister, Gough Whitlam, after backroom manoeuvring by opposition parties. Australia's real political power is held by the Prime Minister, currently John Howard, and the elected representatives of the upper and lower house. The House of Representatives formulates and debates proposed legislation, which is then passed on to the Senate for further reading and eventual ratification. A cabinet of ministers with responsibilities for various portfolios, such as trade and foreign affairs, is appointed by the Prime Minister on election and is subject to frequent reshuffles during the lifetime of a parliament.

State governments are constituted under the same bicameral system as the federal parliament, except in Queensland, which abolished its Upper House in 1992. The lower house of the state parliaments of New South Wales, Victoria and Western Australia is known as the Legislative Assembly, and in South Australia and Tasmania as the House of Assembly. The governments of Queensland, the Northern Territory and the Australian Capital Territory are known as the Legislative Assembly. In each state a Governor acts as the representative of the Queen, exercising prerogative powers conferred by Letters Patent issued under the Great Seal of the United Kingdom, as well as various statutory functions defined by the state constitution and by the Commonwealth *Australia Act 1986*. A Governor of a State assents in the Queen's name to bills passed by the Parliament of the State but acts on the advice of state cabinet ministers.

Australia has universal adult suffrage, and electoral registration and voting in both state and federal elections is compulsory for all eligible persons. In order to qualify to vote, you must be either an Australian citizen (or a British subject who was on the Commonwealth Roll on 25 January 1984), over 18 years of age, and resident in Australia. People who fail to vote in an election are charged and fined (currently $50 for a first offence).

Political Parties

There are six mainstream political parties in Australia: the Australian Labour Party (ALP), the Liberal Party (LP), the Country Party (CP), the National Party of Australia (NPA), the Australian Democrats (AD), and the Green Party. The ALP is traditionally a left-wing party, but has become increasingly centrist, so that it now embraces such previously right-wing policies as privatisation. The Liberal Party is conservative in orientation and is currently the party of government. The Country Party and National Party are also conservative organisations whose power base lies in rural areas, and although they are never likely to hold power in their own right, they inevitably enter into a coalition with the Liberal Party when that party is in government. In many cases, including the current parliament, the Liberal Party holds power only by the consent and co-operation of the NCP. The Greens are active in environmental issues, particularly in states such as Tasmania where development threatens natural wildernesses, and they, together with the Australian Democrats, are usually successful in gaining seats in the Senate rather than in the House of Representatives. A recent ugly development in Australian politics is the foundation and expansion of the One Nation Party, which espouses overtly racist policies. Sadly, the platform of this party appeals to redneck communities in highly conservative outback areas, particularly in Queensland; it is, however, reviled by the majority of Australians, and its leader, Pauline Hanson, is generally considered an embarrassment to the country. The antics of the One Nation Party have caused several diplomatic incidents between Australia and its South-East Asian neighbours, and the government is at pains to stifle its sphere of influence as far as democratically possible. In the federal election of October 1998, the One Nation Party was resoundingly rejected by the electorate and Pauline Hanson lost her seat in the House of Representatives.

Republicanism

Support for a republican Australia has been growing steadily since the 1970s, although it is only in the 1990s that republicanism has taken centre stage in national debate. In 1993, the Prime Minister of the day, Paul Keating, established a Republican Advisory Committttee, which founded its enquiries on the premise of 'when and how' rather than 'if', enraging pro-monarchy factions. Although traditionally the conservative Liberal Party has opposed the formation of a republic (in the 1960s, Liberal PM Sir Robert Menzies was an arch-monarchist), the new Liberal government, under John Howard, has been forced to bow to the public clamour for independence, and a referendum on the issue will be held in 1999. In February 1998, a Constitutional Convention, comprising democratically nominated delegates from all areas of Australian society, was held in Canberra to consider firstly, whether or not Australia should become a republic, and, secondly, which republican model of government should be adopted. The Convention found in favour of the formation of a republic under the 'Bipartisan Appointment of President' model, and subject to a successful referendum outcome in 1999, it is likely that the new republic will come into effect on 1 January 2001. Public support for a republic is high (convention delegates voted 133-17 in favour) and a recent article in the London newspaper, *The Independent*, noted that '(The Queen's) biggest problem will not be if the referendum decides to end her family's reign over Australia since 1788, but if it produces an inconclusive result, leaving her to stay on as a head of state who is not really wanted'.

A new flag, from which the Union Jack will almost certainly be absent, will be designed, probably by public competition, and will be placed before the voters in a referendum before being formally adopted. The Australian national anthem, 'Advance Australia Fair', which replaced 'God Save the Queen' in 1984, will be retained.

The Economy

Australia has a free-market economy which is subject to extensive regulation and tariff controls. Government policy, however, currently favours privatisation and deregulation, and has embarked on the process of reducing the role of government in the national economy over the long term. Many of Australia's industries have already been deregulated and government monopolies in domestic airlines, banking, and telecommunications have been opened up to private competition.

Australia's major trading partners are the USA, Japan, the EU, ASEAN, New Zealand, Hong Kong, China, Taiwan, and Korea. It is one of the world's largest suppliers of coal, iron ore, bauxite, alumina, petroleum, natural gas, gold, wool, beef, cotton, and sugar; however, traditional trading patterns are now changing, with manufactured goods now accounting for over a quarter of exports. Around 60 per cent of Australian exports have gone to East Asian countries in recent years, and thus, the current economic crisis in this region is likely to have a significant impact on Australia's export economy. Exports of goods and services account for around 19 per cent of Australia's national income. Manufactures make up the largest sector of merchandise imports, especially capital goods, transport equipment, and consumer goods.

Manufacturing industry accounts for around 14.5 per cent of Australia's GDP, and has developed behind high tariff walls. Protection is now being reduced to make Australian industry more competitive and export-orientated. Approximately 98 per cent of all manufacturing firms are small businesses. The main industries are chemicals, aerospace engineering, food processing, motor vehicles, iron and steel, paper, woodchipping, and forestry.

Australia's enormous natural resource base has allowed it to develop an efficient and competitive agricultural industry, which contributes around 2.4 per cent to the GDP. Australia leads the world in wool production and is a major supplier of cereals, dairy produce, meat, sugar, and fruit. Over 123 million sheep and 24 million cattle are grazed on the nation's plains and farms (known as stations), which are of a size undreamed of in Europe. The world's largest cattle station, Strangeray Springs in South Australia, comprises 30,028 square kilometres - about the same size as Belgium or Maryland! The export market for Australian wines has grown exponentially in recent years, and fisheries products, especially crustaceans, are exported in large number to East Asia and the USA.

Australia is also a major producer and exporter of energy resources, and is one of the world's biggest producers of minerals and metals. More than 60 different minerals are mined, including bauxite, mineral sands, diamonds, black and brown coal. Mineral ores containing gold, silver, lead, zinc, iron, copper, nickel, tin, manganese, and uranium are also mined in various locations all around Australia. Australia imports its heavy crude oil, but exports light crude and liquefied natural gas. It is also an important producer of precious and semiprecious stones, most notably, diamonds, sapphires, opals, and pearls. Most electricity is produced using coal-fired power stations and Australia's large coal deposits allow it to produce its electricity at relatively low cost. Hydroelectricity is another important source of power and is generated in the Snowy Mountains and in Tasmania. The Australian government has become very environmentally-conscious in recent decades, and strict regulations govern the disposal of industrial waste. Flouting these regulations can result in the forced closure of the business as well as heavily punitive fines. Major mining companies, such as ALCOA, have for many years replanted and landscaped exhausted bauxite mining sites to a level where they are, in many instances, indistinguishable from native wilderness.

Australian science and technology has effected many advances in manufacturing, mining and agricultural industries, and private sector research and development has achieved an increasingly high profile in the last decade. The government has sought to discourage the traditional view of Australia as the 'Lucky Country', replacing it with a new ethos – the 'Clever Country'. The

CSIRO (Commonwealth Scientific and Industrial Research Organisation) is Australia's main scientific body, and its work focuses on industry, the natural environment, minerals, energy, and construction industries. Australia has bilateral agreements on technical co-operation with India, Russia, Germany, China, Japan, Mexico, France, the European Union, and Indonesia.

Trade unionism in Australia is declining rapidly as new information-led industries arise to replace traditional blue-collar ones. Fewer than 50 per cent of the Australian workforce belongs to a union, and in recent years many unions have amalgamated into coalitions in order to remain viable.

Geographical Information

Geography and Topographical Features

Australia is the only country entirely to occupy a continent, albeit the world's smallest. It has a land mass of 7,682,300 square kilometres, is the sixth largest country in the world after Russia, Canada, China, the USA, and Brazil, and is 31 times as large as the United Kingdom. The coastline, which stretches over 36,735 km, encompasses a wide variety of coastal seascapes from the wild surf and dramatic cliffs of the Australian Bight, to the tranquil bays of the South-West. It is bounded by the Pacific Ocean to the east, the Indian Ocean to the west, the Arafura Sea to the north, and the Southern Ocean to the south. The Great Barrier Reef, the largest natural reef in the world runs almost parallel to the Great Dividing Range from the northernmost tip of Queensland at Cape York, down to Fraser Island, approximately 200 kms north of Brisbane. Australia's marine conservation reserves cover more than 380,000 sq. km.

Australia is characterised by the flatness of its topography, and much of central Australia is a giant plateau; its highest mountain, Mount Kosiusko (2228m), is only half as high as the tallest peak on any other continent. The coastal strip is fertile, but it is insignificant in size compared to the vast inland deserts at the dry heart of the continent. This inland region, known as the Outback, is broken by saltlakes, starkly beautiful mountain ranges, such as the MacDonnell Ranges near Alice Springs and the Kimberly Ranges in WA, and by mysterious rock formations such as Uluru (Ayers Rock) and Mount Olga (Kata Tjuta). Deserts such as the Great Sandy Desert, the Gibson Desert and the Great Victoria Desert are barren, unpopulated wastes of red dust, low scrub and spinifex (extremely hardy tufts of spiny grass), which are extremely hot by day and freezing by night. The harshness of this land is sometimes reflected in the names given to geographical features, such as Lake Disappointment in Western Australia.

The Murray River and the Darling River are the main internal waterways of Australia and form the Murray-Darling River Basin. This drainage basin comprises the major part of the interior lowlands of Australia, and covers more than one million square kilometres (around 14 per cent of the country). The headwaters of the Darling, Australia's longest river, are found in the Great Dividing Range, between Queensland and NSW, and finally reach the coast south-west of Adelaide, 3,370 km later. Australia's three largest lakes, Eyre, Torrens, and Gairdner, are located in the interior lowlands of South Australia, and are fed by the rare run-off of heavy rains in the desert. Lake Eyre has been filled only three times this century, and Lake Torrens, only once.

Around 524,000 square kilometres of public land in Australia has been designated as nature conservation reserves, and a further 1.1 million sq. km. is preserved as aboriginal and Torres Strait Islander land.

Other Territories

Australia is responsible for administering seven external territories: Norfolk Island, Cocos (Keeling) Island, Christmas Island, Ashmore and Cartier Island Territories, the Territory of Heard Island, Coral Sea Islands Territory, the sub-Antarctic McDonald Islands, and the Australian Antarctic Territories.

Neighbouring Countries

Australia's nearest neighbour is Papua New Guinea, less than 200 km across the Torres Strait to the north of Cape York in the east. To the north-west of Australia lies the Indonesian archipelago, and, further away, to the north-east are the French Island of New Caledonia, the Solomon Islands, Fiji, Western Samoa and Tonga. Australia's nearest neighbour in a cultural sense is New Zealand, approximately 1,700 kms east of Sydney. Beyond Tasmania, to the south, there is nothing but ocean until Antarctica, and to the west beyond Perth, nothing before the islands of the Seychelles, Mauritius and Madagascar, near the African coast.

Population

The population of Australia is currently around 18 million. Most of this population is concentrated in cities situated in coastal areas, and thus, although population density figures are as low as two people per square kilometre, this figure averages population over the vast inland areas of Australia, and does not reflect Australia's urban environment. Population growth is steady at around 0.8 per cent per year, and the projected population for the year 2010 lies in the region of 21.5 million. Around 95 per cent of Australia's population are of Caucasian descent, a further four per cent are Asian, and a mere one per cent are of Aboriginal extraction. Seventy per cent of Australians are Christians (mainly either Roman Catholic or Anglican). Australia's official language is English, and 98.7 per cent of Australians are functionally literate.

Australia prides itself on its multicultural composition. Its multicultural policies enshrine the right to individual cultural identity, and to social justice regardless of race, ethnicity, culture, religion, language, birthplace, or gender. All Australians, whatever their background, are expected to have an overriding commitment to Australia and its interests, and to accept the basic structures and principles of Australian society. Australia's multicultural policies have gone through three main phases over the decades. Until the 1960s, a policy of assimilation was in place, which drew its rationale from the long-discredited and disbanded 'White Australia Policy'. This policy effectively excluded non-European immigration, but was weakened by attitudinal changes after the Second World War and is now regarded with shame by younger generations of Australians. From the mid 1960s through to 1972, the government adopted a policy of integration, recognising that large numbers of migrants, especially those whose first language was not English, required direct assistance and intervention to help them become integrated into Australian society. Finally, multiculturalism became established as government policy in 1973, and today minority groups are assisted in promoting the survival of their language and heritage within mainstream institutions.

In 1978, a comprehensive review of immigration in Australia led to the adoption of new policies and programmes as a framework for Australia's population development. Three-year rolling programmes were put in place to replace annual immigration targets, as well as a more consistent and structured approach to migrant selection, emphasising the migration of skilled people who would represent a positive gain to the nation. An average net population gain of 70,000 per annum has been forecast through to 2001. Today, nearly one in four of Australia's population were born overseas, and in 1995/96, the number of new settlers totalled 99,139. Of these, 18.9 per cent came from New Zealand, 12.5 per cent from the UK, 5.6 per cent from China, and 5.4 per cent from South Africa. There are around one million British-born permanent residents and citizens in Australia, more than in any other country.

The Aboriginal People and Reconciliation

The Australian and Torres Strait Islander people are the custodians of one of the world's oldest cultural traditions. This tradition is an oral one, in which legal, social and religious structures and customs are transmitted through story, song, and dance. Art plays a central functional, rather than solely aesthetic, role in aboriginal culture, mapping out the Dreamtime (or creational mythology), explaining tribal law, and describing ceremonies and events or historical happenings. Aborigines have traditionally subsisted as hunters and gatherers in small, tribally-based communities, and their unique relationship with the land has enabled them to survive for millennia in one of the harshest environments on earth.

The arrival of British settlers in Australia presaged the beginning of the end for traditional aboriginal culture, and today, their population, which was always small, has been decimated. In the early years of settlement, the British sanctioned the deliberate destruction of the Aboriginal population; and a policy of genocide in Tasmania was effective in murdering every last indigenous inhabitant. Systematic campaigns of extermination, in the form of 'hunting parties', pursued their human quarry in every early settlement, and within three years of the arrival of the First Fleet in Sydney, the Aboriginal population was reduced by two-thirds through imported diseases, accidents and violent death. Aborigines were considered by British settlers to be a sub-human species, and were treated as either animals, scientific specimens, or the subjects of social experimentation. Such attitudes prevailed, to some extent, into the 1970s, and it was not until then that Aborigines were released from curfew restrictions or entitled to the rights of citizenship. The Aboriginal people now suffer from high rates of alcohol dependency, infant mortality, suicide, death in custody, and criminal involvement; their life expectancy is shorter than that of other Australians and they are four times as likely to suffer unemployment. There are very few pure-blood Aboriginal people in Australia today, and aboriginality is defined by ancestry and identification, rather than racial purity. The population of pure-blood Aborigines stands at approximately 10,000, reduced from an estimated 100,000 at the time of the arrival of the first settlers. Although those who remain are now struggling to regain their cultural and historical roots, many feel a sense of fragmentation, isolation, displacement, as well as a deep bitterness towards the successive governments responsible for their near-destruction.

Today, Aborigines have found a new voice and are actively defending and reinstating their rights within society and on their traditional lands. Reconciliation is now the cornerstone of public policy and seeks to foster co-existence, respecting the different rights of people in the same land. In May 1998, a National Sorry Day was held to allow all Australians, regardless of racial origin, to express their regret for the tragic past treatment of the nation's indigenous people. In particular, National Sorry Day, sought to raise awareness of the distressing truths behind the forced removal of aboriginal children from their families well into the 1970s. It highlighted the consequences of this policy in terms of broken families, physical and mental abuse, and the loss of language, culture and connection to traditional lands.

Land Rights

In 1992, the High Court of Australia handed down the Mabo Decision, which recognised that under Australian law, indigenous people had a right in their land, which existed before European settlement and which still exists. This right was called 'native title', and reversed the long-standing legal fiction that the continent of Australia was *terra nullius*, land belonging to no-one, at the time of British settlement. As a result of the Mabo Decision, the Commonwealth Government passed the Native Title Act in 1993, after extensive consultation between the Australian government and indigenous Australians. Past grants of land away from indigenous ownership (for example, to pastoralists) were made valid, in return for the reinstatement of the common law rights of indigenous people according to their traditions, laws, and customs. In particular, Aboriginal and Torres Strait Islander people sought the right to contribute to, if not control, future planning and development on native title land. Native title rights still exist on much Crown land and in national parks, where the traditional owners have maintained their cultural and religious connections. In 1997, the Wik Decision, which was handed down by the High Court following a case brought by the Wik people of Northern Queensland, enlarged native title rights by permitting the right of access to land held under pastoral leases, for ceremonial and traditional activities. Mining companies wishing to operate on land held under a pastoral lease were also obliged to negotiate directly with the native title holders. Although the rights of indigenous people under native title are still limited (native title is extinguished on land held under freehold or ordinary leases), the issue has become a controversial one in Australia, and is generally clouded by fear and misinformation.

Climate

Australia's size means that it encompasses several climatic zones. The more southerly regions have a temperate, mediterranean climate with hot, dry summers and mild, wet winters, while areas nearer the equator are sub-tropical. Northern Queensland and parts of the Northern Territory experience heavy rainfall between January and March (the 'wet'). The seasons in the southern hemisphere are inverted: the summer months are from December to February, autumn is from March to May, winter from June to August, and spring from September to November.

Sun Protection

Australians these days are highly aware of the dangers of their climate. The hole in the ozone layer, which is concentrated over the southern hemisphere, means that more and more ultra-violet rays are penetrating the atmosphere, with an increased risk of skin cancer. The greatest damage is done in childhood, and today everyone is prepared to cover up to an extent undreamed of by British holiday-makers. Factor 15-plus sunscreen should be worn at all times, and many people choose to wear impenetrable zinc cream on their faces (often in fluorescent colours). Most adults and all children wear hats every time they step outside, and clothing often comes with a protection rating, depending on sleeve length, colour, and fabric.

Weather Chart

Average temperature (Celcius), rainfall (mm), sunshine in hours per day

	Jan	Feb	Mar	Apr	May	Jun	Jul	Aug	Sep	Oct	Nov	Dec
Adelaide												
Max	29	29	26	22	19	16	15	16	19	22	25	27
Min	17	17	15	12	10	8	7	8	9	11	14	15
Rainfall	21	11	25	38	58	79	82	69	62	43	29	29
Rainy days	4	4	6	8	12	15	17	17	14	10	8	7
Sunshine	10	10	9	7	5	4	5	6	7	8	9	9
Brisbane												
Max	29	29	28	26	23	21	21	22	24	26	27	29
Min	21	21	20	17	14	11	9	10	12	16	18	20
Rainfall	160	173	140	89	98	70	62	41	33	93	96	126
Rainy days	13	14	14	11	10	7	7	6	7	10	10	11
Sunshine	8	8	8	7	6	7	8	8	9	9	9	9
Canberra												
Max	28	27	24	20	15	12	11	13	16	29	22	26
Min	13	13	11	7	3	1	0	1	3	6	9	11
Rainfall	62	55	53	50	49	39	42	46	51	66	64	53
Rainy days	8	7	7	8	8	9	10	11	10	11	10	8
Sunshine	9	9	8	7	6	5	6	7	7	9	9	9
Darwin												
Max	32	31	32	33	32	31	30	31	32	33	33	33
Min	25	25	24	24	20	19	21	23	25	25	25	25
Rainfall	431	344	316	98	22	1	1	6	16	72	141	234
Rainy days	21	20	19	9	2	1	0	1	2	6	12	16
Sunshine	6	6	7	9	10	10	10	10	10	9	8	7
Hobart												
Max	22	22	21	18	15	13	12	13	15	17	19	20
Min	12	12	11	9	6	4	4	5	6	7	9	11
Rainfall	42	36	37	46	37	29	47	49	41	49	45	58
Rainy days	9	8	10	11	12	11	14	14	14	14	14	12
Sunshine	8	8	7	6	5	4	5	5	6	7	7	8
Melbourne												
Max	26	26	24	20	17	14	13	15	17	19	22	24
Min	14	14	13	11	9	7	6	7	8	9	11	13
Rainfall	49	47	52	58	57	50	48	51	59	68	60	60
Rainy days	8	7	9	12	14	14	15	16	15	14	12	11
Sunshine	9	8	7	6	4	4	4	5	6	7	7	8
Perth												
Max	32	32	29	25	21	19	18	18	20	22	25	29
Min	17	17	16	13	10	9	8	8	9	10	13	15
Rainfall	7	16	15	42	106	174	163	118	70	47	27	12
Rainy days	2	3	4	8	13	17	18	16	13	10	7	4
Sunshine	12	11	9	8	7	6	6	7	8	9	10	12
Sydney												
Max	26	26	25	22	19	17	16	18	20	22	24	25
Min	19	19	17	15	11	9	8	9	11	13	16	17
Rainfall	7	16	15	42	106	174	163	118	70	47	27	12
Rainy days	2	3	4	8	13	17	18	16	13	10	7	4
Sunshine	12	11	9	8	7	6	6	7	8	9	10	12

Sunglasses are not a fashion accessory but an essential item, and you should choose a pair with high quality lenses, such as Raybans. All sunglasses are sold with a removable sticker on the lens indicating the level of ultra-violent rays against which they offer protection, and you should only buy those which screen 100 per cent of these dangerous rays. Sunglasses are available for all ages, from babies upwards; baby glasses come with colourful elasticated straps to keep them in place (but its usually a losing battle). All of the above points apply in winter as well as summer. On the beach, throw away those ideas of a sexy bikini and a great tan. Today, tanning is out, and no-one wears a bikini. Young women generally choose a one-piece swimsuit, and both men and women cover up with T-shirts and hats. Children *all*, without exception, wear swimsuits reminiscent of the Victorian era neck-to-knee bathing costume. These sunsuits are made of UV-resistant lycra and come in fluorescent colours; they have wrist or elbow length sleeves, cover the whole body, and extend to the knees or even the ankles, zipping up at the front, like a diver's wetsuit. They are quick drying and designed for speed in the water, and are generally thought 'cool' by children. If you let your children on the beach in a European-style swimming costume, the under-the-breath tut-tutting all around you will probably drown out the sound of the waves. Australian-style children's swimsuits are available in all surf shops and department stores, as well as, more cheaply, from Cancer Foundation shops in most cities.

A Guide to the States and Territories

Information Facilities

Tourism is one of Australia's most important industries and enjoys an increasingly high profile in the domestic economy. Every capital city has a large and well-supplied Tourist Bureau, and most regional towns have a smaller Tourist Information Office providing specialist and local information. Isolated regions and national parks which are not served by an office will usually have a tourist information point, with maps, general information and points of interest displayed for reference. Most railway and bus stations also have counters where you can obtain information on your journey as well as advice on accommodation, facilities and attractions in the area you are visiting.

The Australian Tourist Commission has an office in London (open from 9am-5.30pm) which will answer your travel queries and assist with itineraries. They also stock an extensive range of pamphlets, maps, and guides, and will forward free literature to you on request. The Australian Tourist Commission has an excellent website at www.aussie.net.au. The Australia Centre at the Australian High Commission in London provides information supplied by all the states except Queensland (which maintains its own office at Queensland House in the Strand, London), including an extensive range of booklets. This office also has a reading room where you can consult up-to-date newspapers from each capital city, including the classifieds pages.

There are many guide books available for every region of Australia, and every type of traveller. The specialist travel bookshop, Stanfords (12-14 Long Acre, London, WC2E 9LP; tel: 0171-836 1321; fax: 0171-836 0189) has a particularly extensive range, and publishes an Australian and New Zealand Book List, available from the above address, or on the internet at www.stanfords.co.uk.

Useful Addresses

Australian Tourist Commission, 1st Floor, Gemini House, 10-18 Putney Hill, London SW15 6AA, tel: 0181-780 2227 or fax: 0181-780 1496.
Queensland Agent General, 392 The Strand, London WC2R 0LZ, tel:- 0171-836 1333 or fax: 0171-240 7667.

WESTERN AUSTRALIA

Capital: Perth.
Area: 2,525,500 sq km (1,515,300 sq. miles) = over 10 times the size of the UK.
% of total area of Australia: 32.87
Coastline: 12,500 km (7,500 miles).
Climate: Average Perth daily maximum temperature in January (Summer) 27°C, in July (Winter) 15°C. Note that there is significant variation in temperatures throughout the state from the temperate South to the tropical North.

Western Australia's huge size (the whole of Western Europe can easily fit into Western Australia with a bit left over) encompasses the whole range of climatic and geographical zones. From the endless white sands and crystal waters of the tropical north, to the arid zones of the Nullarbor Plain, through to the vineyards of the south-west, Western Australia is the Australian landscape encapsulated. Its features include the spectacular Ningaloo Reef, a marine reserve less well-known than the Great Barrier Reef but equally impressive, majestic Karri forests, ancient and massive gorges, and geological formations such as Wave Rock and the Pinnacles (an ancient fossilised forest now standing in a desert landscape). The Stirling and Porongorup Ranges very occasionally see snow in winter.

The State is rich in a wide variety of natural resources, and is a leading producer of iron ore, gold, industrial diamonds, alumina, mineral sands, wool, wheat, salt and forest products. Whilst wheat and wool account for around two-thirds of the state's income from agriculture, Western Australia is also developing more unusual primary industries, farming cashmere and angora goats, emu, and deer. Western Australia's fishing industry produces rock lobster, prawns, shrimp and scampi, which are mainly exported to the USA and Japan. Mineral and petroleum production adds a further $8 billion per annum to the State's economy, and comprises 60 per cent of the value of the State's overseas exports and one third of Australia's total mineral exports.

Since the 1960s, the Western Australian economy has grown faster than that of any other State, with an average real Gross State Product growth of 5.1 per cent. The state's economy is export-based and its overseas trade surplus is more than double that of the rest of Australia. Its major export markets are Japan and the South-East Asian nations, as well as the USA and the EU. Western Australia attracts almost 20 per cent of Australia's total business immigrant intake, including the investment capital that such immigrants bring. More than a quarter of Western Australia's population was born overseas, and it consequently enjoys a broad and cosmopolitan lifestyle. It also has a young population, second only to the Northern Territory, with an average age of 30.4 years. Western Australian medical and health services are considered amongst the best in the world. With a doctor-patient ratio of 1:500, the state is ranked with Norway, Sweden, Finland, Denmark, France and the Netherlands, and is considerably ahead of the USA, UK and Japan. The average life expectancy in Western Australia is high, and currently stands at 74 years for men and 80 for women.

Western Australian education is of a very high standard, both in the public and private sector. With four universities in Perth, five advanced education campuses, and a network of technical and further education colleges throughout the State, Western Australia has world class education facilities, and is a world-leader in certain areas of research, such as wave technology.

Real estate costs are among the lowest in the country, and Western Australians enjoy a high rate of home ownership, with more than two-thirds of all residences being privately owned.

Perth: Perth is the most geographically isolated capital city in the world and has a population of just over one million people. The city is stunningly situated along the banks of the Swan River, and has a relaxed and friendly atmosphere and easy-going lifestyle. The most popular residential areas are built along the river and coastal strip, with suburban sprawl extending inland to the edge of the escarpment of the coastal plateau. Perth summers are very hot, and although the average temperature is only 27°C, the mercury frequently hovers around 40°C for days at a time. The heat is very dry, and as it is not sticky or cloying can easily be dealt with by staying in the shade. In the afternoon, the sea-breeze comes in off the Indian Ocean, and by sunset the weather is usually extremely pleasant. This breeze is known affectionately as 'The Fremantle Doctor', for its remedying effect on the wilting population. Perth is, in fact, Australia's windiest city, and the third windiest city in the world. It enjoys more sunshine and clear days than any other Australian capital and while it also has one of the wettest winters, rains are usually short and sharp, interspersed with cool, sunny periods.

The centre of Perth is dominated by a large park, King's Park, which consists of approximately 1,000 acres of natural bushland, wildflowers, and landscaped gardens. This park is a focus for family life and its various cycle tracks, nature walks, adventure playgrounds, and water features are popular with all sections of the community. King's Park is the home of the state botanical gardens, which features the full array of native flora, and, in September, hosts the Wildflower Festival.

Perth has an active cultural scene, with a permanent symphony orchestra, ballet company and opera company performing year-round at the city's two main arts venues: the Perth Concert Hall and His Majesty's Theatre. The enormous Entertainment Centre hosts large scale popular events and commercial productions, such as the Moscow Circus and ice shows. The Festival of Perth is held every year, and is centred on the venues of the University of Western Australia. Major national and international performing artists in the fields of music, dance and theatre are brought in for the four week event, so that every year, the world's best can be seen on the local stage. In addition, the Festival Fringe offers cutting-edge comedy and experimental theatre and music, and the concurrent film festival screens art movies from around the world. Musica Viva operates a national and international chamber music touring scheme, the largest of its kind in the world.

Perth has an efficient public transport system, and the rail line to the city's northern suburbs is expected to be extended southwards to Mandurah some time in the next few years. City planners are actively seeking to improve public transport to alleviate congestion in the city centre. Long distance commuting is rare in Perth, and most people live within about 20 minutes of their place of work.

The beaches and the Swan River provide a perfect water-playground for Perth's population, and swimming, water-skiing, windsurfing, surfing and sailing are the cornerstone of Perth leisure activities. There are more boats per capita in Perth than in any other Australian city. The other major sports played in Perth include cricket (the Western Australian Cricket Association, affectionately known as the WACA, often hosts One-Day International and Test matches), various codes of football (Aussie rules, soccer, rugby), horse-racing, tennis, hockey, lawn bowls and golf. Basketball and baseball are also increasingly popular.

Western Australia's healthy economy, its growing population, developing industries and technology, outdoor lifestyle, cheap real estate, and prime facilities contribute to a general feeling of well-being, which occasionally borders on smugness, and most locals consider themselves lucky to live there.

Useful Addresses

Real Estate Institute of Western Australia, 215 Hay Street West, Perth, Western Australia 6005, tel: 08-9380 8222; public enquiries, tel 08-9380 8200 (9am-12pm). REIWA produces an illustrated weekly property guide. Copies can be obtained directly from REIWA.

Education Department of WA, 151 Royal Street, East Perth, Western Australia 6004, tel: 08-9264 4111.

Department of Commerce and Trade, PO Box 7234, Cloisters Square, Perth, Western Australia 6850, tel: 08-9327 5666 or fax: 08-9327 5481. The DCT produces a quarterly economic briefing on Western Australian economy.

Business Assistance Gateway, email gateway@commerce.wa.gov.au.

NORTHERN TERRITORY

Capital: Darwin.
Area: 1,346,200 sq km (807,720 sq. miles) = 5.5 times the size of the UK.
% of total area of Australia: 17.52
Coastline: 6,200 km (3720 miles).
Climate: Average daily maximum temperature in January 31°C, in July 31°C. In Alice Springs temperatures vary more widely, as the town lies in the semi-arid central region rather than the tropics. The average daily maximum summer and winter temperatures for Alice Springs are 35.2°C and 20.5°C.

The Northern Territory (also known as 'The Top End') is situated in central northern Australia, to the east of Western Australia. It is bordered by South Australia in the south and Queensland to the east. The Northern Territory's history of development is closely linked with that of South Australia, as in 1863 the British Government handed over control of the Northern Territory to the Colony of South Australia. Within a year, the first sale of land in the Territory was held in Adelaide. In 1869 an expedition led by the Surveyor-General George Goyder resulted in the establishment of a permanent settlement, now known as Darwin. South Australia's control was relinquished in 1901 after Federation, and control over the Northern Territory was held by the Commonwealth Government until 1 July 1978, when the Territory was granted self-government. The powers of government differ from those of other states in name only. Its assembly consists of a single lower house, and its leader is known as the Chief Minister. In 1998, a referendum was held in the Northern Territory on the issue of statehood and it is likely that the Territory will soon become a State in its own right.

The Northern Territory lies within the torrid zone of the Tropic of Capricorn and much of its area is semi-arid. Although its landscape contains Australia's great 'dead heart' of claypan desert, which covers an area 805 km long and 322 km wide, the tropical northern part of the Territory is luxuriantly verdant. These two climatic regions result in a diversity of vegetation within the Territory, ranging from mangrove and freshwater swamps and billabongs (pool or backwater), rainforest, eucalypt and mulga woodlands, to spinifex grasslands, gibber and sandy deserts. There are no major rivers in the Northern Territory's interior, and rivers and creeks flow only after rains in the 'wet' season (October-April). The Todd River, on which Alice Springs is located, is usually dry. The wet season is a period of high humidity, and torrential rain and thunderstorms occur in the transition from the 'dry' to the wet season. These rains often cause flooding, and transport and communications in the Northern Territory can be difficult or even disrupted at times. All of the Territory's major rivers are on the coastal fringe. The Roper River which flows into the Gulf of Carpentaria, is the Territory's largest; amongst other smaller rivers are the Daly, Victoria, Adelaide, Mary, South and North Alligator rivers. The Northern Territory is prone to cylones or hurricanes, the most famous of which, Cyclone Tracy, destroyed Darwin on 24 December 1974. The city has subsequently been rebuilt and is now a modern showcase of urban planning. Houses are constructed to withstand cyclone conditions, and government authorities maintain crisis plans against future disasters.

The remoteness and harshness of the Northern Territory have made it unique in many ways, not the least of which is its relatively tiny population. It has a population density of only one person per nine square kilometres. The population of Darwin is around 80,000 and of Alice Springs, 27,000. Nonetheless, the Northern Territory is currently experiencing the fastest population expansion in Australia. Over the census intervals from 1961 to 1991, the population grew at an average rate of 4.7 per cent per annum, nearly three times the national growth rate. This rate has slowed recently due to changing patterns of interstate migration, but the Northern Territory continues to have the youngest population in Australia, with an average age of 28 years, compared with the Australian average of 34.7 years. Almost one quarter of the Territory's population is identified as Aboriginal, although overall Aboriginal and Torres Straits Islanders account for only 1.5 per cent of the Australian population. More than 50 different ethnic groups are represented in Darwin, and 24 per cent of people speak a language other than English.

Although the Territory is hampered by its distance from major Australian economic and political centres, and by restricted transport and communication links, its economy has experienced a growth rate in Gross Domestic Product (GDP) which has generally exceeded that of Australia as a whole. Its rapid growth can be attributed mainly to developments in mining, especially oil, and to tourism. The abundance of natural resources such as alumina, manganese, gold, bauxite, and uranium, as well as oil and gas, have enabled the Northern Territory to participate substantially in the international market, and the value of exports for the Northern Territory per capita is over three times the national figure.

There are three main interstate highway links in the Northern Territory, the Stuart Highway from Darwin to the South Australian border, the Barkly Highway from Tennant Creek to the Queensland border, and the Victoria Highway from Katherine to the Western Australian border. Although there are road houses along these highways, there are stretches of road which are not serviced for over 280 km. It is always advisable to notify the Automobile Association of the Northern Territory before embarking on an unfamiliar road (especially in the wet season), or before undertaking long journeys over unsealed or unserviced roads. You should ensure that you take supplies of petrol, water and food, and if possible a CB radio. In the case of breakdown or emergency, stay with your vehicle at all times.

The cost of housing varies widely within the Northern Territory. Rented accommodation in Darwin is amongst the most expensive of all Australian capital cities, and suitable properties may be scarce. In recent years the Northern Territory government has encouraged home ownership through an incentive scheme, which includes a deposit assistance grant scheme, and a vendor-finance scheme, with favourable interest rates for the home buyer.

Education has been the responsibility of the Northern Territory government since 1979, and in recent years it has modified its schools' curriculum to reflect the multicultural nature of its classrooms, promoting intercultural understanding and literacy. There are also correspondence schools, known as 'Schools of the Air', which use two-way radio, video and computers, to bring the classroom to isolated students. The Northern Territory Secondary Correspondence School offers an excellent range of secondary courses up to university entrance level for those who do not have access to normal school facilities. Tertiary education in the Northern Territory is usually undertaken through either the Northern Territory University or the University's Insititute of Technical and Further Education which specialises in trade and technical courses. In 1983, the postgraduate research institution, the Menzies School of Health Research, was established at the Royal Darwin Hospital and it is currently enjoying a reputation as a centre of scientific excellence in its field. One of its primary objectives is to assist in improving the health of people in tropical and central Australia. The School has an academic link with the University of Sydney and its students may qualify for the higher degrees of that university.

The Northern Territory Health Services are remarkable, considering the distance and difficult terrain that must be covered. There are modern, well-equipped hospitals in Darwin, Alice Springs, Katherine, Tennant Creek and Nhulunbuy. All hospitals provide general in- and outpatient, accident and emergency services. The Royal Darwin and Alice Springs Hospitals offer a wide range of specialist services and are both special teaching hospitals affiliated with the University of Sydney. A private hospital is also available in Darwin. Mobile services are provided in remote areas, and the Northern Territory government subsidises missions and Aboriginal organisations in the provision of health services. While there are health centres in all major towns and settlements, in extremely remote regions, the Royal Flying Doctor Service (RFDS) and the Aerial Medical Service operate in cases of serious injury or illness. The Patients' Assistance Travel Scheme (PATS) provides financial assistance to people from isolated areas who have had to travel for specialist consultation and treatment. The Northern Territory government also provides mental health services, blood banks, services for the aged, family, youth and children's services, services for the disabled and women's information services, as well as women's refuges and shelters, a Sexual Assault Reference Centre, and the Ruby Gaea Darwin Centre Against Rape which provides counselling, support services and emergency accommodation.

Although the Northern Territory is best known to non-Territorians as one of the world's great wilderness, the capital, Darwin, is a modern city which provides the services and lifestyle expected of any Australian city. Like any other Australian state, the Northern Territory offers a huge range of outdoor activities, including a wide variety of sports, as well as diverse cultural events, including theatre and festivals. In general, the towns are small, uncrowded and have a relaxed atmosphere and a strong sense of familiar community.

Useful Addresses
Department of Employment, Education and Youth Affairs, TCG Centre, 80 Mitchell Street, Darwin, 0801, tel 08-8989 5605.
Department of Asian Relations, Trade and Industry, Ministry of Regional Development, Development House, 76 The Esplanade, Darwin, 0800, tel 08-8999 5210; fax 08-8999 5333; Public relations and marketing, freecall 1800 675 005; Business services, freecall 1800 193 111.

SOUTH AUSTRALIA

Capital: Adelaide.
Area: 984,377 sq km (380,070 sq miles) = four times the size of the UK.
% of total area of Australia: 12.81
Coastline: 3,700 km (2,300 miles).
Climate: Average daily maximum temperature in January 29°C, in July 15°C.
South Australia is situated in the middle of the southern coast of Australia along
the Great Australian Bight. It is bordered by Western Australia to the west, the
Northern Territory to the north, and Victoria to the east. It has a Mediterranean
climate, ideally suited to the production of wine, and vineyards established by
early European settlers are prolific throughout the Barossa Valley. South Australia
produces more wines than any other state or territory in the country. The State has
a population of 1.5 million, or around 8.5 per cent of the total population of
Australia. Most of South Australia's population lives in Adelaide, the capital,
which has a population of just over one million. Adelaide is situated on the River
Torrens, between the waters of the gulf and a range of low hills on the coastal
plateau. The city covers an area of 984 sq km, and stretches 63 km from its
southernmost to northernmost suburbs. The rest of the population is scattered
throughout the state in the major regional centres of Whyalla, Mount Gambier,
Port Augusta, Murray Bridge, Port Pirie and Port Lincoln.
Adelaide: Adelaide's transport system is a well-oiled machine that rarely
experiences breakdown or congestion. This is largely due to the city's first planner,
Colonel William Light, who planned Adelaide with such geometric symmetry that
all major city roads are straight and wide. Adelaide enjoys a unique bus service
called the *O-Bahn*, which is a right-of-way guided transport system on which
commuters are shuttled to and from the city at speeds of up to 100 kmh.
  Most of the housing follows the pattern of single-storey houses on spacious
blocks, ensuring off-street parking and a private back garden. The standard of
homes in South Australia is amongst the highest in the country, and rented
accommodation is up to 15 per cent cheaper than elsewhere.
  Adelaide is an important industrial and scientific centre, and is home to a
rapidly expanding electronics industry. The Advanced Engineering, Electronic
Research and Electronic Surveillance laboratories at the Defence Science
Technology Centre are world-leaders in laser research, and the academic centres of
the Adelaide and Flinders Universities support this research, as well as enjoying a
fine reputation in many other disciplines. The University of Adelaide is one of
Australia's premier universities, and ranks ahead of universities in Victoria,
Queensland, Western Australia and Tasmania in its ability to attract funds through
the Australian Research Grant Scheme. Australia's first planned centre for high-
technology development and manufacture, Technology Park Adelaide, is
integrated with the campus of the University of South Australia. South Australia's
industrial base is supported by vast mineral resources in the form of oil, gas and
other hydrocarbons which are tapped in the Cooper Basin area. Brown coal is
mined at Leigh Creek, and copper, uranium and gold are extracted at Roxby
Downs. Australia's biggest opal fields are at Andamooka.
  South Australia has a warm, friendly ambience, and Adelaide is a rapidly
developing city. It has excellent sporting and entertainment facilities, and a highly
regarded education system. The city has a permanent symphony orchestra, ballet
company, and opera company, and hosts the world-famous Adelaide Festival every
summer. Adelaide offers a very attractive environment with some fine architectural
features, and is known as the 'City of Churches'. The cost of living and real estate
is generally low in South Australia, making it an appealing place in which to live.

Lifestyle

Whether you are a skilled migrant seeking employment or a business person wishing to relocate your family and business to Australia, the State of South Australia WELCOMES YOU.

WELCOME TO SOUTH AUSTRALIA

The South Australian Government is committed to attracting skilled migrants to our State. We offer independent migrants a unique package of services (Immigration SA) that includes, On Arrival Accommodation, Meet and Greet Service and referral to personal consultants.

Information and space technology, manufacturing, mineral and energy industries, commerce, business, health, education and tourism are among the range of sectors which offer opportunities for jobs.

Adelaide is the elegant and exciting capital of South Australia.

It provides the unique mix of city living without congestion and pollution. South Australians enjoy an exceptional quality of life. The cost of living and housing are relatively low and facilities are excellent.

For more information on living in SA contact Immigration SA,
24 Flinders Street,
Adelaide South Aust. 5000
Telephone: 61 8 8226 1944
Facsimile: 61 8 8226 1955
Website:
http://www.immigration.sa.gov.au

Come join us . . . we will help you to migrate to South Australia

Government
of South Australia

Useful Addresses

Immigration SA, State Development, State Administration Centre, 200 Victoria Square, Adelaide, SA, 5000; tel 618-8226 2690; fax 618-8226 3570; Website http://www.immigration.sa.gov.au

The Department of Industry and Trade, Terrace Towers, 178 North Terrace, Adelaide, SA 5000; tel 08-8303 2400; fax 08-8303 2410.

TASMANIA

Capital: Hobart.
Area: 68,331 sq km (26,375 sq miles) = 0.22 times the size of the UK.
% total area of Australia: 0.88.
Coastline: 3,200 km (1,920 miles).
Climate: January 22°C, July 11°C.

Tasmania is Australia's smallest state and is an island separated from the south-east corner of the mainland by the Bass Strait, a shallow body of water with an average width of 240 km. Tasmania's coastline is bounded by the Southern Ocean to the south and west, and the Tasman Sea to the east. Tasmania spans 296 km from north to south and 315 km from east to west at its greatest width. Despite the fact that it is Australia's smallest state, it is, nonetheless, still twice the size of Wales. Tasmania is the only Australian state which does not have a desert region and it is fertile throughout. It is the most mountainous state and one of the most completely mountainous islands in the world. It has the largest rural population in relation to its size of all the Australian states, and is one of the world's most richly mineralised areas. Tasmania is the leading Australian state in terms of the production of minerals in point of value of output per capita, and almost all of Australia's tungsten is extracted from King Island.

Orchard and berry fruits are grown in the south of the state, and due to its high production of apples and its shape, Tasmania is often referred to as the Apple Isle. Industries in the southern region include the Cadbury Schweppes cocoa and confectionery factory, the Electrolytic Zinc Company, the Australian Newsprint Mills, Stanley Works (manufacturers of hand tools such as the Stanley knife), Sheridan Textiles, International Catamarans and the Cascade Brewery, which was established in 1824 and is the oldest brewery still in operation in Australia.

Fishing is the major industry on the east coast of Tasmania, and is based in the ports of St. Helens and Bicheno. Catches include crayfish and abalone. Tasmania has a rapidly developing fisheries industry and now farms salmon and oysters for the international market.

In the north-east of the state, the fertile soil provides ideal farming land. Beef and dairy cattle, wool sheep and prime lambs are all farmed in this region. Market gardening is also important, as it is in the north-west of the state, where vegetable and dairy farming predominate. Other types of farming in the north-west include pig, sheep and poppy farming (to provide oil for pharmaceutical preparations). Manufacturing here is dominated by forest-based industries, whereas in the central northern region of the state industries include the knitting yarn producers Coats Patons, the automotive parts manufacturers ACL Bearing Company, and the aluminium smelter and refinery Comalco. Central and northern Tasmania has developed a viticulture industry, and is the home of the Ben Lomond Ski Fields.

The west of the state is a region of dense forests and mountain ranges, raging rivers and rugged hills, and has a treacherous coastline with many untamed beaches. Mining is the predominant industry in the west, and metal ores such as copper, zinc, tin and iron are extracted here. Much of the south-west region is inaccessible and uninhabited, and contains some of the most spectacular scenery in the world. The south-west wilderness area has been listed by the World Heritage Commission and consists of dense rain forests, scrub, wild rivers, rapids and ravines, and harsh mountains which can only be tackled by experienced bush-walkers.

Approximately 20 per cent of Tasmania is World Heritage Area, and there are extensive cave systems, many of which contain aboriginal cave art.

The central lakes area is dominated by the hydro-electric schemes which produce the state's electricity. Trout-fishing is also popular. In the flatter midland area, sheep farming, particularly for wool, and beef cattle grazing are also important.

Many parts of Tasmania are reminiscent of the green but windswept landscapes of some parts of Scotland and England, and over the decades a large number of British and other European immigrants have settled in Tasmania. The population of Tasmania is currently around half a million, of which two-fifths were born outside Australia, mostly in England, Scotland, and Germany. Tasmania's climate and farming conditions are most comparable to those of the UK, which also helps new British settlers feel more 'at home' than they might in the harsh dry regions of the Northern Territory or the tropical areas of Queensland.

Hobart: Tasmania's capital city is situated in the south-west of the state, 20 km from the mouth of the Derwent River. It is Australia's second oldest city, founded in 1804, and it extends over both sides of the river. To the west of the city lies Mount Wellington (1,269 m), which is usually snow-capped in winter. The city was founded as a penal colony, and was reputed to be one of the harshest prison settlements. Transportation to Van Diemen's Land was as good as a death sentence, and many convicts did not survive. Despite its ruthless beginnings, the city flourished in the mid-nineteenth century thanks to its ship-building, whaling and port facilities. Today, Hobart is more likely to make the shipping news during the famous Sydney-Hobart yacht race held every year commencing on Boxing Day.

In 1869 Tasmania became the first colony in the British Empire to make education compulsory and in 1898 school attendance was made obligatory between the ages of seven and thirteen, expanding to between six and fourteen years in 1912. In 1946, Tasmania became the only Australian state to make attendance up to the age of sixteen compulsory. It now has its own university, the University of Tasmania, as well as numerous colleges of advanced education and a conservatorium of music. Tasmania's main employment sectors are retailing and manufacturing, however, employment is currently depressed and the outlook for young people is considered poor. For over a decade, unemployment has been rising in Tasmania, and it currently has the highest unemployment rate of all states.

Tasmania is becoming increasingly popular as a migration destination. The high standard of education, modern health facilities and cheap housing are all strong attractions, however, the cost of living can be slightly higher than in other states due to freight costs. Although some love the small-community feel of the state, others feel that the sense of isolation which almost inevitably affects new settlers is exacerbated by Tasmania's separation from mainland Australia.

Tasmania's geographical isolation has meant that the state has developed a unique flora and fauna. Tasmania has ten species of mammal not found elsewhere, including the Tasmanian Devil (a carnivorous, nocturnal marsupial) and the 'Tasmanian Tiger' generally believed to be extinct, although occasional sightings are claimed, fourteen indigenous species of birds and two of reptiles. The duck-billed platypus is more common in Tasmania than elsewhere and the Tasmanian mountain shrimp, which is only known outside Tasmania as a fossil, has remained obstinately unaltered and very much alive.

In terms of natural environment, Tasmania is breathtaking, and perhaps feels a little more familiar to the European settler than the harsh, sandy, sunbaked land of mainland Australia.

VICTORIA

Capital: Melbourne.
Area: 227 600 sq km (136,560 sq miles) = 0.93 times the size of the UK.
% of total area of Australia: 2.96.
Coastline: 1,800 km (1,080 miles).
Climate: January 25.1°C, July 14°C, but Victorian, (particularly Melbourne), weather is notoriously unpredictable. Victoria's exposure to frequent cold fronts and southerly winds results in changeable weather patterns, popularly known as the 'Four Seasons in One Day' phenomenon.

Victoria is situated in the south-eastern corner of Australia, bordered by South Australia to the west and New South Wales to the north. Even though Victoria is the smallest of all Australian States, it still offers a wide geographical diversity ranging from the Victorian Alps, which lie on the shared border with New South Wales, fertile wine-growing regions in the Murray and Yarra River Valleys, rainforest in the Gippsland region (in the south-east corner of Victoria) on the Errinundra Plateau, and desert beauty in the north-west inland Mallee region. Victoria has the world's third largest volcanic plain in the Western District. The Great Dividing Range, which forms a spine down the inland 'back' of Victoria and New South Wales, is known as the 'High Country'.

The land on which Melbourne was built was purchased in 1835 from Aborigines of the local Dutigalla clan. The Aborigines had no concept of land as a commodity at that time, and in exchange for their ancestral home they received articles of clothing, 50 pounds of flour, handkerchiefs, knives, tomahawks, looking-glasses and blankets. The driving force behind the founding of Melbourne was John Pascoe Fawkner, the son of a convict. He was a self-educated bush lawyer and established several newspapers. Fawkner sat on the Legislative Council of Victoria for 15 years, where he was an energetic campaigner for the rights of small settlers and convicts, and instrumental in ending transportation. His energy was drawn from his own personal experience of the harsh penal code – he received 500 lashes when he was 22 for assisting seven convicts to escape, and he bore the scars for the rest of his life.

The population of Victoria is currently estimated at 4.5 million, and consists of immigrants from the UK and EU as well as the Middle East and South-East Asia. There are approximately 12,000 Aborigines in Victoria. All of these different ethnic groups give the state a real cultural diversity and have a positive influence on Victorian culture. Melbourne has a population of around 3 million, and other major regional centres include Geelong, Bendigo, Ballarat, Horsham, Mildura, Warnambool, Castlemaine and Shepparton.

Victoria's economy has suffered in the past from industrial unrest and from poor economic government. In an attempt to boost the State's economy, the Victorian Government sponsors successful overseas entrepeneurs and senior executives intending to live permanently in Victoria through the Australian Government's Independent Business Skills Migration Category. Victoria is the site of research and development in the areas of food, paper, chemicals and petroleum, transport equipment, electrical equipment and biotechnology.

The standard of tertiary education in Victoria is particularly high. There are eight universities in the State, as well as numerous technical and further education institutions. The Commonwealth Scientific and Industrial Research Organisation is based in Victoria.

Melbourne: The Population Crisis Committee, based in Washington DC, recently rated Melbourne the world's most liveable city in terms of safety, health, and air quality. Melbourne's location on the coastal plain between the Pacific Ocean and the beautiful Dandenong hills provides a superb living environment, and its cultural and sporting facilities are unequalled elsewhere in Australia.

Melbourne flourished during the great gold rush of the 1850s, and as a consequence became the Australian centre of business and commerce. Today, 15 of Australia's top 25 companies have their headquarters in Melbourne. In the 1880s, Melbourne was known as 'The Paris of the Antipodes', and was the capital of Australia from 1901 (Federation) until 1927, when the capital was moved to Canberra (to avoid in-fighting between Melbourne and Sydney).

Melbourne is one of Australia's leading exporters of computers, engines and pharmaceuticals, and is the location of eight major medical research institutes, including the Walter and Eliza Hall Institute, the home of modern immunology and one of the world's best known medical research centres. Australia's main telecommunications research and development facilities are based in Melbourne, and the city is the site of 70 per cent of Australia's telecommunications production. Melbourne is the second most popular destination in the Asian region, behind Singapore, for conventions, meetings and exhibitions.

The population of Melbourne is a cosmopolitan one and, with nearly 160 different nationalities represented, is one of the most multicultural cities in the world. It has the world's third largest Greek community, behind Athens and Thessalonia.

Melbourne is widely considered to be the cultural capital of Australia, and it enjoys the facilities of a world-standard Arts Centre. The Australian Ballet Company is based in the city. Melbourne is the home of the Australian film industry, and of much of Australian television output (including *Neighbours* and *Home and Away*). The city is Australia's premier shopping location, with an unlimited selection of designer shops and other stores. Melbourne is also host to the nation's biggest horse race, the Melbourne Cup, the Australian Rules Football Grand Final, and the Australian Open at the impressive Koorong Tennis Centre.

Useful Addresses
Business Victoria, 55 Collins Street, Melbourne, VIC 3000, tel 03-9651 999; email helpline@business.vic.gov.au.
Investment Centre Victoria, Level 46, 55 Collins Street, Melbourn, VIC 3000, tel 03-9651 9066.

AUSTRALIAN CAPITAL TERRITORY

Capital: Canberra.
Area: 2,400 sq km (1,440 sq miles) = 0.01 times the size of the UK.
% of total area: 0.0003.
Coastline: 0 (except 35km in Jervis Bay Territory).
Climate: January 28°C, July 11°C.

Canberra was established in 1901, at Federation, to provide a 'neutral' headquarters for the new seat of government. Sydney had threatened to refuse to join the Federation unless the capital was in New South Wales; Melbourne, for its part, considered it had the greater claim. As a compromise, the Australian Capital Territory was established mid-way between the two states, in a move which was, as it was said, acceptable to everyone, but satisfactory to nobody. The American architect, Walter Burley Griffin, won the international competition to design the capital city, resulting in a completely planned city, where even the sites of trees have been carefully selected. The effect can appear sterile, and this sterility is reinforced by the fact that 60 per cent of Canberra's residents are civil servants. The weekend sees an evacuation of politicians back to their state of origin, giving Canberra the reputation for being a dead city. During the week, however, Capital Hill, through which the artificial Lake Burley Griffin cuts, is the hub of the nation's political activity. Canberra is a derivative of an Aboriginal word *kamberra* which means 'meeting place'. Canberra is home to the Australian National University, the Australian Institute of Sport, the Australian National Gallery, and the Australian War Memorial and Museum. Canberra does not have a commercial centre, and its big shopping centres are all located in suburban areas. Instead the city has many parks and recreational areas, and traffic congestion is virtually unknown.

Canberra is an attractive city, although it is much derided by most Australians who find its planned and highly ordered environment less than easy to appreciate. Nonetheless, it has a friendly atmosphere, and is not inferior to other Australian cities, merely different.

NEW SOUTH WALES

Capital: Sydney.
Area: 802,000 sq kms (309,572 sq miles) = 3.25 times the size of the UK.
% of total area of Australia: 10
Climate: The mean January temrperatures along the coast are usually between 18°C and 21°C, but 22°C in Sydney. The plateaux are about 4°C cooler and the temperatures in the plains increase in direct relation to the distance from the sea. Temperatures at the Queensland border are about 27°C to 31°C. The maximum temperature in July is 17°C and the minumum is 8°C.

New South Wales is probably the Australian state most visited by tourists and business people, and is the state which receives most international publicity. This is largely due to its spectacular capital city, Sydney, which in 2000 will be host to the Olympic Games. There is, however, so much more to New South Wales than Sydney, and it is well worth venturing beyond the city limits to explore its diverse regions.

New South Wales is bordered to the north by Queensland, to the east by South Australia and to the south by Victoria. The Australian Capital Territory lies wholly contained within the south-east corner of New South Wales. From Sydney, it is 1,157 km west to Broken Hill, almost on the South Australian border, 908 km north to Tweed Heads which borders Queensland, and 498 km south to Eden, the last sizeable town before Victoria. Within these extremes lie mountain ranges, beaches, fertile farming land, rainforests and arid desert.

The Blue Mountains, 100 km west of Sydney, is a national park containing some of the most breathtaking scenery in the world. Standing at one of the numerous lookouts it is possible to survey hundreds of miles of unbroken, uninhabited bush, and to view the immense rock formations at Echo Point known as 'The Three Sisters'. The area was home to Aboriginal people at least 14,000 years ago, and they have left their mark in the numerous rock carvings and cave paintings. The rugged 250,000 hectare park is composed mainly of sandstone which has been eroded over the ages by rivers and creeks to form dramatic valleys and sheer escarpments.

Approximately 150 km north of Sydney lies the main wine region of New South Wales, Hunter Valley. The Valley is divided into two distinct regions, the Lower Hunter and the Upper Hunter areas. Cessnock, 183 km from Sydney is the centre of the Lower Hunter region, and was originally founded on the coal-mining industry. The area produces some of the state's best wines and famous wineries include McWilliams, Mount Pleasant, Lindemans, Hungerford Hill, Tyrells and Brokenwood. One hundred kilometres further to the north-west is the smaller and less well-known Lower Hunter, home of the renowned Rosemount Estate. Muswellbrook is the centre of this region and is also known for its coal and agriculture.

In the south-east of the state lie the Snowy Mountains, less than a three-hour drive from Canberra in the ACT. Thredbo is a popular ski resort which has hosted various World Cup Ski events; it is possible to take a chair lift to the top of Crackenback and then hike up Australia's highest mountain, Mount Kosciusko which, at 7,328 feet (2241 metres), is less than half the height of Mont Blanc. On the northern side of Mt Kosciusko, in Perisher Valley, lie two of the most popular ski resorts, Perisher and Smiggins Holes. This is Australia's 'alpine country' which, surprisingly, contains more snow covered area than Switzerland. Instead of the pine trees with alpine scenes, be prepared for ghostly eucalypts silhouetted against the snow. The Australian ski season runs from June to October and the snow is usually best between late July and mid-September. Mt Kosciusko is located at the heart of the Kosckiusko National Park, which contains 629,000 hectares of rugged moorland, glacial lakes, caves, the source of the Murray River, Australia's largest waterway, more than 200 species of birds, and an abundance of wildlife including kangaroos, possums and wombats. The Snowy Mountains support seven hydroelectric stations which supply a large proportion of the state's power grid.

The Murray River rises in the Great Dividing Range and flows for over 2,500 km, forming the border between Victoria and New South Wales. From Wentworth in the far west of New South Wales, the Murray continues through South Australia and veers south, entering Lake Alexandrina and the ocean. It is used extensively for irrigation and is crucial to the region's agricultural industries. One of the state's most important agricultural districts is the Riverina which lies along the northern borderlands of the Murray River. Crops as diverse as rice, vegetables and citrus fruits are grown here, and cattle and merino sheep are also important. Albury is at the heart of this fertile region and its population is approximately 37,000. It is a National Growth Centre, established to encourage the decentralisation of industry from major state capitals. Wentworth is important as the heart of the region's irrigation scheme and both the citrus and avocado growing areas.

Broken Hill is one of the state's most easterly settlements, lying almost on the border with South Australia. It is isolated and remote, but nearly 26,000 people live here and it is famous for its silver mines and the Royal Flying Doctor Services. The mining industry has survived, and silver, lead and zinc are still mined in significant quantities. In addition, Broken Hill is the birthplace of Broken Hill Proprietary Limited (BHP), which is Australia's biggest company. In the northern desert region of the state, along the border with Queensland, lies the town of Lightning Ridge, famous for its opal mines. Over 1,000 people from 30 different nations are based at Lightning Ridge, and manage to survive the extreme weather conditions and limited water supply (artesian bore water is the only kind available here) to mine the fields for the highly prized black opals. Visitors are allowed to tour various mines and to fossick (prospect) for the gems.

New South Wales' north coastal region is one of the state's favourite holiday destinations, and the region contains spectacular surf beaches, lakes, rivers, small coastal towns and beautiful inland scenery. Byron Bay, Australia's most easterly point, is considered to be the unspoilt gem of the New South Wales coast. Cape Byron is home to many people who prefer an alternative lifestyle away from the rat-race of the busy cities. Coffs Harbour, closer to Sydney, is a popular harbour and port town, with many top-class tourist resorts. There is plenty of good surf, and it is also a famous yachting centre. Bananas are grown in this semi-tropical area, and the nearby Dorrigo National Park contains rainforest, waterfalls and lush vegetation. Inland from Coffs is the Nymboida River, a popular spot for white-water rafting. Grafton is situated in this area, some 65 km inland, and is at the centre of a region which specialises in both dairy and sugar-cane industries.

New South Wales also controls Lord Howe Island and originally owned Norfolk Island, although this is now a Territory of Australia. Lord Howe Island is a tiny island, 11 km long and 2.8 km at its widest point, some 700 km northeast of Sydney. It has a population of 300 and was listed as a World Heritage area in 1982 because of its soaring volcanic peaks, the world's most southerly coral reef, exceptional birdlife and scenic beauty. Lord Howe Island was first sighted in 1788 and was named after the first Lord of the Admiralty. The numbers of visitors to the island is strictly controlled to protect it from becoming overrun by crowds, and the island's 37 km coastline provides plenty of opportunity for fishing, coral reef viewing and relaxation. Norfolk Island is a much larger and more isolated island, 1,600 km to the east of Sydney. It was first discovered by Captain Cook in 1774 and later became a penal settlement for the colony of New South Wales between 1788 and 1855. Norfolk Island was the home of the Pitcairn Islanders who included descendants of the *Bounty* mutineers. There are still many Pitcairn descendants on the island who speak 'Norfolk', a curious mixture of Tahitian and English. The island has a population of about 2,000, most of whom are involved in either tourism or agriculture.

Sydney: Sydney has a population of nearly six million people, around 60 per cent of the state's total population. The second largest city in New South Wales is Newcastle, on the northern coast 170 km from Sydney, with a population of half a million, and Wollongong, some 82 km south of Sydney, is the third major urban area. The city of Sydney is open and spacious, surrounded on three sides by national parks and on the fourth by 60 km of beautiful and quite spectacular coastline. Sydney Harbour, on which the city is built, has 240 km of foreshore, much of which has remained as it was when the First Fleet made its initial investigative journey up the waterway in 1788. Sydney has been described as 'the best address on earth', although it has its share of the problems associated with big cities, such as pollution, ugly industrial areas, traffic congestion, homelessness, unemployment, drugs and crime. The Sydney Harbour Bridge and the Opera House, which are the most dramatic features of the Harbour, were opened in 1932 and 1973 respectively. In 1988, a re-enactment of the First Fleet entering Sydney Harbour was staged as part of the bicentennial celebrations. The day was perfect and the view included a bank-to-bank flotilla of small pleasure boats, the old 'Coathanger' and Centrepoint Tower in the background, in front of which stood the Sydney Opera House, the sun gleaming off the millions of highly polished white tiles that make up its shell. There is no doubt that Sydney Harbour is simply stunning and that the city is an exciting place in which to live. Even some Australians do, however, tire of the bright lights and relatively fast pace and prefer to move to quieter, calmer and perhaps safer cities each with their own distinctive beauty.

Sydney is one of Australia's most historic cities, as it was into Botany Bay, just south of Sydney, that Captain Cook sailed in the *Endeavour* in 1770. In May 1787 the First Fleet of 1,044 people, including 759 convicts (191 of whom were women) set sail from Portsmouth and arrived eight months later. Unimpressed with Botany Bay's windswept barrenness, the Fleet moved north in search of a more suitable site and six days later the ships arrived at what became Port Jackson, described by Captain Phillip as 'the finest harbour in the world'. Even though Port Jackson was superior to Botany Bay, the first days of the colony were harsh, as crops failed and the anticipated supply ships failed to arrive. Somehow, however, the colony managed to survive and slowly began to grow. Captain Phillip was replaced by Governor Macquarie, known as the 'Father of Australia', in 1810 and over the next 11 years streets and fine new buildings were built. Convict transportation to New South Wales continued until 1840, but free settlers began to arrive from 1819. From 1831 to 1850 more than 200,000 government-assisted migrants streamed into the colony to begin a new life far away from the urban nightmare of Victorian Britain. During the 1850s, goldrush fever brought a new influx of settlers which continued until the end of the nineteenth century, and by 1925 the area around Sydney had a population in excess of one million.

Sydney today boasts Australia's most influential Central Business District (CBD) and most national and international businesses choose to have their major Australian offices in the city. Darling Harbour houses the Sydney Aquarium, Chinese Gardens, Powerhouse Museum and the National Maritime Museum, and is linked to the CBD by monorail. The Rocks is Sydney's most historic area, and much of it has been restored to its former glory. Doyle's Restaurant at the foot of the Rocks is a haven for the seafood connoisseur, with fresh fish a house speciality. There are many beaches around the Sydney area, the most famous of which are Bondi (grossly overrated) and Manly (slightly overrated). The most beautiful, unspoilt and uncrowded beaches lie further north or south of the city. The northern coastal suburbs are particularly beautiful as the coastline is made up of rugged headlands interspersed with long sandy beaches. Most beaches have sea-water swimming pools naturally carved out of the rocky headland, which provide safe, sheltered swimming areas. The beaches of Dee Why, Long Reef, Collaroy, Narrabeen, Newport, Avalon, Whale Beach and Palm Beach are among the most beautiful Sydney beaches.

Sydney is a cultural centre and is home to the Australian Opera and the Sydney Symphony Orchestra, both based at the Opera House. Standing tickets for the opera can be bought for as little as $20, and many agents sell last-minute tickets at half price. Sydney is also home to the Museum of Contemporary Art and the Sydney Observatory. The city's Gay and Lesbian Mardi Gras is an international crowd-puller, as the country's gay, bisexual and transvestite population take to the streets in bizarre and outlandish costumes. The Queen Victoria Building houses many chic boutiques and plenty of bargain shops, but better bargains can be found at Paddy's Markets in Paddington.

New South Wales has many special events during the calendar year. The Festival of Sydney usually takes place in January, as does the New South Wales Tennis Open and the Country Music Festival. The Sydney Royal Easter Show usually occurs between March and April, and the Sydney Film Festival takes place in June, as does the Darling Harbour Jazz Festival. The Rugby League Grand Final is held in Sydney in September. Other major state sporting events include the Tooheys 1000 Bathurst Touring Car Race at Bathurst in October, and the Sydney to Hobart yacht race which commences on Boxing Day every year.

Sydney is one of the most expensive areas in Australia in which to live, but many of the outer suburbs and regional areas are less expensive. Rent in Sydney is very high by Australian standards, but is still markedly lower than current rental rates in London for comparable properties. The state's unemployment rate is average, with a higher rate of unemployment in the city than in country areas. Major employment sectors in the city are commerce (banking, insurance and finance), retail, manufacturing, hospitality and tourism. Agriculture and tourism are the biggest employment sectors in regional areas.

Education and health services are exceptionally good in New South Wales, which is home to many large and excellent tertiary educational institutions. New South Wales currently attracts more new settlers than any other state or territory.

QUEENSLAND

Capital: Brisbane.
Area: 1,725,000 sq km (1,035,000 sq miles) = seven times the size of the UK.
% of total area of Australia: 22.48.
Coastline: 7,400 km (4,440 miles)
Climate: In Brisbane, the average daily maximum in January is 29°C and in June is 21°C. In Cairns, the average daily maximums for the same months are 31°C and 26°C.

Queensland is Australia's second largest state, but has the largest habitable area (defined by rainfall), a staggering 1,554,000 sq km; in contrast a mere 57 per cent of Western Australia is considered habitable (1,440,000 sq km). Queensland is situated in the north-eastern corner of Australia and it is bounded by the Northern Territory to the west, South Australia to the south-west and New South Wales to the south. It stretches from the temperate and densely populated south-east to the tropical and sparsely populated Cape York Peninsula in the north.

Queensland epitomises the image of Australia overseas. With the Great Barrier Reef, the Whitsunday Islands, World Heritage areas such as the Daintree Rainforest and Fraser Island, and a beautiful climate, it is not suprising that Queensland is one of the most popular tourist destinations in Australia. Queensland is known as the 'Sunshine State', and Queenslanders are affectionately called 'banana-benders'. They are also considered to be the rednecks of Australia, and as such are renowned for their very conservative political outlook.

Like most of Australia, Queensland is rich in natural resources. Its four major products are sugar, meat, grains and wool, and growing areas are spread throughout the state. Australia is the world's second largest exporter of raw cane sugar, and 95 per cent of Australia's production comes from Queensland. The State also contains vast mineral deposits, including coal, bauxite, gold, copper, lead, zinc, silver and magnesite. Besides agricultural and mining industries, Queensland's biggest industries are manufacturing and tourism. Queensland's economic growth is significantly higher than the national average, and it has a Gross State Product of 3.2 per cent (compared to a national average of around 24 per cent).

For more than 20 years, Queensland has experienced a consistently higher rate of population growth than the national average. Queensland's population growth can be attributed to overseas immigration (18 per cent), natural increase (35.7 per cent), and most importantly, to interstate migration (46.2 per cent). Queensland, it seems, is the place where most Australians want to live, and more Australians are moving to Queensland than to any other state or territory. An increasingly popular myth is that Australians are moving to Queensland to retire, however, census figures from the Australian Bureau of Statistics show that 31 per cent of Queensland's population lies in the 25-44 year age range, and there is no substance to the perception of Queensland's Gold Coast as the 'Grey Coast'.

Queensland's population is much more decentralised than that of any other state. Its population of just over three million is scattered over major regional centres such as the Gold Coast, Bundaberg, Toowoomba, Rockhampton, Longreach, Townsville, Cairns and Mount Isa, as well as Brisbane, which is home to 1.5 million people.

Until recently, the Queensland Government had a reputation (going back more than 35 years) of ultra-conservativism. For most of those years the state was under the leadership of the Premier, Sir Joh Bjelke-Peterson, and became notorious for its repressive and racist attitudes. Vestiges of this xenophobia remain, and Queensland is the seedbed of the racist One Nation Party, led by Pauline Hanson. Antipathy is particularly directed towards the Japanese who have invested large sums in Queensland property, however, most Queenslanders recognise that Japanese investments and tourists play a significant part in promoting Queensland's healthy economy. The Queensland Government has suffered from allegations of corruption at the highest levels. When the Labour Party was elected in September 1992, its leader, the Hon. W K Goss, became the first Labour Premier in Queensland since 1957. The new government represented the desire of Queenslanders to end the corruption and hypocritical moralising of the old government and make a fresh start.

Queensland's health and education services are broadly comparable with the national standard. Brisbane is home to the University of Queensland and to Australia's first private university, Bond University, established by entrepreneur Alan Bond. The multi-millionare Western Australian, after whom it is named, is now serving a prison sentence for illegal business ventures; however, the university that bears his name is none the less regarded as a centre of excellence.

Most Queensland residents own their own home, and the high standard of living combined with an extraordinary natural environment makes Queensland a popular choice for settlement.

Useful Contact
Department of Economic Development and Trade, tel 07-3224 4254; fax 07-3225 1671.

Getting There

These days, if you want to get to Australia, you have to fly (unless you're Michael Palin). QANTAS is Australia's national carrier, and is legendary for its outstanding safety record, although its reputation for quality and service allows it to charge premium fares. Over 20 international airlines fly direct to Australia, usually to Perth (the nearest point of disembarkation, if you are travelling from the UK), or Sydney. The flight time from Europe to Australia, depending on your route, point of departure, and destination, is likely to be between 19 and 26 hours.

Fares to Australia vary dramatically according to the seasons, and are also affected by special events, such as Christmas. Prices skyrocket in early December, for example, but drop dramatically on the 26th of December, so delaying your departure by a few days may save you hundreds of pounds. The cheapest time to fly to Australia is during the Low Season, from March to June (precise dates differ from airline to airline). Mid Season (or Shoulder), from July to November, and during February, is somewhat more expensive; and Peak Season, from December to January, is really best avoided from a financial point of view, unless you can only travel at that time. Once you have decided when to travel, you should try and book as early as possible – seats fill up very fast, and for flights during the Australian summer may be fully booked as early as July.

Scheduled flights by various national carriers will usually offer the possibility of a stop-over in their home country, which allows a welcome break in the arduous journey at the same time as providing a cheap exotic holiday. Malaysian Airlines, for example, offers a stopover in Kuala Lumpur as well as a free internal flight, so that if you choose, you can fly to the resorts of Penang or Langkawi for a few days. Return fares are usually valid for 12 months, and travel agents are required to request proof of residency if you wish to purchase a one-way ticket. An open-jaw return ticket will allow you to enter Australia via one port and leave from another, however, this type of ticket is likely to be more expensive.

Charter flights, operated by tour companies rather than airlines, are usually the cheapest way to travel to Australia. They won't get you there in much style, but they are ideal for travellers on a budget. Britannia Airways runs charter flights from Manchester and Gatwick during the peak period, from October to March, with several departures each week to a range of cities in Australia and New Zealand. Currently, prices start from £499 in December. The disadvantage of charter flights is that they generally operate on a short-term return basis, so that you are likely to have to return two weeks after arrival. Flights book out very early, and stop-overs are not permitted.

Insurance
Working travellers and those on speculative job finding trips to Australia are strongly advised to take out comprehensive travel insurance. Insurers offering reasonable and flexible premiums include:

Atlas Travel Insurance Ltd.: 37 Kings Exchange, Tileyard Road, London N7 9AH; tel 0171-609 5000; fax 0171-609 5011; email quote@travel_insurance.co.uk

Columbus Direct Travel Insurance, 17 Devonshire Square, London EC2M 4SQ, tel 0171-375 0011; fax 0171-375 0022; www.columbusdirect.co.uk.

The Travel Insurance Agency, tel 0181-446 5414/5; email tia.london@virgin.net
Worldwide Travel Insurance, tel 01892-83 33 38.

Discount Fare Specialists for Australia & New Zealand

Campus Travel: 52 Grosvenor Gardens, London SW1W OAG, tel: 0171-730
8111. Their opening hours are Mon-Fri 8.30am-6.30pm, Thurs 8.30am-8pm,
Sat-Sun 10.00am-5pm. Also see their website at www.campustravel.co.uk.

STA Travel: 86 Old Brompton Road, London, tel: 0171-938 4711 or Oxford
01865-240 547.

These two agencies specialise in student travel and discount fares for the under-35
market. They are particularly helpful in arranging non-standard travel. Both
agencies have offices around the country, particularly in areas with large student
populations (such as Oxford).

Austravel 'The Basement', 152 Brompton Road, Knightsbridge, London, SW3; tel
0171-584 0202. Austravel produces a fares guide which gives price
comparisons between all the major airlines for the year.

Cresta World Travel; 44-6 George Street, Altrincham, Cheshire WA14 1RH; tel
0161-927 7177; fax 0161-929 0433.

Platinum Travel, 52 Earls Court Road, Kensington, London, W8 6EJ; tel 0171-937
5122; fax 0171-937 6279.

Modern Air Travel, 61 Reform Street, Dundee DD1 1SP; tel 01382-322713; fax
01382-201079.

Travelbag, 12 High Street, Alton, Hampshire, GU34 1BN; tel 01420-88724 or
373/375 The Strand, London WC2R OJF, tel: 0171-497 0515.

Travelsavers, 3rd floor, 25-27 Oxford Street, London, W1R 2AA; tel 0171-437
7878; fax 0171-439 9090; email fares@comettravel.demon.co.uk

The Australian Youth Hostels Association (Level 3, 10 Mallett St, Camperdown,
NSW 2050; tel +61 2-612 565 1699; fax +61 2-565 1325), also offers complete
travel packages including accommodation and 12 months coach travel.

Residence and Entry Regulations

The Current Position

Immigration has recently become a contentious policy area in Australia with many people reacting to economic stringencies by calling for an end to Australia's migration programmes. The rationale for this position (that 'foreigners take our jobs') has been proved to be completely erroneous. This has not prevented anti-migration activists, generally operating from a distinctly racist platform, from continuing to dominate debate on the issue in the media. In response, the government has stressed its commitment to Australia as a 'deeply tolerant, fair-minded and generous society' and outlined the benefits of immigration in a recent booklet, *Dispelling the myths about immigration* (available from the Department of Immigration and Multicultural Affairs, or in electronic form, on their website at www.immi.gov.au/package/booklet.htm). The current government recognises that migrants have made, and continue to make, an enormous contribution to Australian society, bringing new ideas, technologies and skills to the nation's economy and skill base. In the context of the globalisation of Australia's economy, migrants' awareness of the nuances of international cultures provides an important asset for its international and domestic competitiveness.

Australia's migration programme is carefully managed, with annual quotas imposed on each area of temporary and permanent residency category after extensive assessment of the current economic circumstances. In 1997-98, 80 000 people were granted entry to Australia on a long-term basis: 68 000 in the Migration programme (family and skilled streams) and 12 000 in the Humanitarian programme, which offers entry to refugees of civil war and human rights abuse. These figures represent a drop (on 1996-97 figures) of 14 000 entrants under the Migration programme (Humanitarian entry has remained the same), a reduction implemented because of concerns about the high, and continuing, level of unemployment among arrivals in certain migration categories. The government's intention is that migration should become more focused on the intake of skilled migrants, although it retains a commitment to bona fide immediate family migrants. The overall intake is small compared to the high levels of the 1980s, when around 140 000 people a year were successful in gaining entry to Australia as permanent residents.

Although racist polemics in the popular press would suggest otherwise, Australia operates an entirely non-discriminatory immigration programme. It is selective on the basis of skills, age and language ability, but is open to anyone in any part of the world, regardless of their country of birth, ethnic origin, race, sex or religion. At the time of the last census in 1996, 23 per cent of the population were born overseas, with 6 per cent (or around 1.2 million people) originating in the UK. In the 1996 intake, British citizens were successful in gaining around 11 per cent of the annual quota of permanent residence visas.

Applying to live in Australia can be a time-consuming and expensive exercise, and a number of migration consultancies offer services which can help prospective applicants with the procedures. Although the Australian consular service, following the collapse of one agency with the extensive loss of clients funds, recently warned applicants that such consultancies cannot 'get round the system' and guarantee success, a reputable firm may ease the pressure and provide valuable advice to those unfamiliar with the migration application process.

Useful Addresses
Challice Emigration: Freepost (NG6151) Newark NG23 5YZ; tel/fax 01636-525903; email wbce.challice@lineone.net. Professional migration consultants.
The Emigration Group: 7 Heritage Court, Lower Bridge Street, Chester, Cheshire CH1 1RD; tel 01244-321414; fax 01244-342288; email theemigrationgroup@ btinternet.com. Professional migration consultants specialising in Australia and New Zealand.
Four Corners Emigration: Freepost NWW 1289, Manchester M22 3FR; tel 0345-419453; fax 0161-498 9889; email UKenquiries@4-corners.com. Professional migration consultants.
Ian Harrop & Associates: P.O. Box 12, Lechlade, Glos. GL7 3YG; tel 01367-860850; fax 01367-860851; email ianharrop@aol.com. London office: 1 Warren Road, London SW19 2HY; tel 0181-540 8448; fax 0181-540 5811. Professional migration consultants.

Entry for Australian Citizens

Travellers holding either an Australian passport, a New Zealand passport, or a British passport with Australian permanent residency are exempted from the requirement to obtain a visa prior to entry into Australia. All other travellers, whether making a short-term visit as a tourist or for business purposes, or a longer stay on a working holiday or as a migrant, must obtain the appropriate visa from their nearest Australian mission before leaving their home country. Visitors who arrive in Australia without a visa are immediately deported and are held responsible for any costs arising from their deportation. If you are in doubt over whether you are an Australian or New Zealand citizen, or whether you have an entitlement to permanent residency, the Australian High Commission, which is responsible for all visa and migration queries, will be able to advise you. In general, if you wish to visit Australia as a tourist you will need a Visitor's Visa; if you are planning to go on a working holiday or to retire, you will need a Temporary Residence Visa in the appropriate category; and if you are hoping to settle permanently in Australia, you will need to be accepted as an immigrant and be granted permanent residence.

Visitor's Visa

To visit Australia as a tourist, you will require a Visitor's Visa, for which you will need Form 48 obtainable from the Australian High Commission and many travel agents. This form can also now be downloaded from the Internet at www.immi.gov.au/forms/48.gif. Visitors' visas are classed as either 'short-stay' (3 months) or 'long-stay' (more than 3 months). Short-stay visas are valid for three months from the date of entry into Australia and must be used within 12 months from the date of issue, whilst the long-stay visa is valid either for entry within four years or for the life of the passport (whichever occurs first). There is no application fee for a short-stay visitor's visa, however, a non-refundable fee of $35 is charged for the longer visa.

Travellers visiting Australia to conduct business of a short-term nature which is deemed not to disadvantage local residents, should also apply for a Visitor's Visa on Form 48. Retired parents of Australian residents are entitled to a Visitor's Visa valid for a period of 12 months. In order to be eligible for this extended visa, you need to provide proof of funds sufficient to support you during the entire period of the visit, although if you intend staying with family or friends for any or all of this time, the level of funds required will be assessed at a lower level than that for a tourist.

The three-month Visitor Visa can be applied for by post, with a processing time of approximately three weeks. Enclose a large, stamped and self-addressed envelope for the return of your documents. Applications can be made in person at the Australian High Commission in London (tel 0171-379 4334), the Australian Consulate in Manchester (0161-228 1344) and the Australian Embassy in Dublin (+353 1 676 1517). The AHC in London can be very busy, especially from September to February, and you should expect a long wait; Monday to Wednesday are generally the busiest days.

It is possible to extend a three-month visitor's visa to one of six months duration whilst in Australia, however, the cost to do so is currently $200. If you wish to stay longer in Australia, it is most important to extend the visa before it expires. The Department of Immigration will deport immediately any applicant who holds an expired visa. You must leave the country on a valid visa and renew it overseas before returning, although some travellers following this procedure have been refused re-entry into Australia despite leaving Australia on a valid visa and renewing their visas in New Zealand or Singapore.

The Visitor's Visa is now being superseded by Australia's state-of-the-art 'Electronic Travel Authority' (ETA) system, which is currently available to UK and US citizens, and in most EC countries. The ETA is an 'invisible', electronically-stored authority for short-term travel to Australia which can be issued in less than ten seconds at the time of making travel bookings. It is claimed that the ETA is currently the most advanced and streamlined travel authorisation system in the world, permitting visitors to be processed in seconds on arrival at their destination. At this end, the advantages include an end to form-filling, queues and embassy visits: the whole process is completed on the spot. ETAs can be obtained from any participating travel agent or from the nearest Australian diplomatic mission. There are three different types of ETA and travellers should make sure that they obtain the one appropriate to their needs: tourists and those visiting family or friends for a period of 3 months or less need a free Tourist ETA (Type V), whilst business visitors need a Long Validity Business ETA (Type BL), which costs $45. Holders of US or Canadian passports travelling on business should obtain a Short Validity Business ETA (Type BS), for which there is no charge. It has recently been reported that some British travel agents are charging as much as £15 to issue a *free* ETA to their clients. The amount of work involved in supplying this visa can in no way justify this charge, and travellers should be alert to this potential rip-off.

Temporary Residence

Visitors intending to enter Australia temporarily for the purpose of work need to obtain a Temporary Residence visa. There are currently 15 different visa sub-classes which are issued according to the type of employment the applicant will undertake in Australia. The temporary residence programme is designed to allow people from overseas to come to Australia for specific purposes, which are expected to provide some benefit to Australia. The focus is on the areas of skilled employment, social, cultural and international relations. The categories for temporary residence visas are as follow:

Exchange (Category 411) Allows visitors to come to Australia to broaden their work experience and skills under reciprocal arrangements by which Australian residents are granted similar opportunities abroad. A letter of invitation is required from the organisation offering the position.

Foreign Government Agency Staff (415) Intended for foreign government officials conducting official business on behalf of their government, where that government has diplomatic status in Australia. This visa category includes staff of the British Council, Alliance Française, Goethe Institute, and Italian Cultural Institute.

Special Program (416) Intended for people visiting under approved programmes for the purpose of broadening their experience and skills. It is generally used for youth exchanges and programmes such as the Churchill Fellowship. A letter of support is required from the organisation.

Working Holiday (417) The Working Holiday Maker Visa aims to promote international understanding by giving young people the opportunity to holiday in Australia, whilst working to supplement their funds. The WHM visa has numerous conditions attached which are explained in the section *Working Holiday* below.

Educational (418) Allows entry of staff to fill academic, teaching and research positions in Australian educational institutions, which cannot be filled from within the Australian labour market. A letter of appointment is required.

Visiting Academic (419) Allows entry of people as Visiting Academics at Australian educational and research institutions, with the intention that their presence will contribute to the sharing of research knowledge. A letter of invitation is required and you may not receive a salary from the host institution.

Entertainment (420) Allows entry of actors, entertainers, models and their associated personnel for specific engagements or events in Australia. Visa assessment will take into account the need to protect the employment of Australians in the industry.

Sport (421) Allows entry of amateur and professional sportspeople, including officials and their support staff, to engage in competition with Australian residents and to improve general sporting standards through high calibre competition and training.

Medical Practitioner (422) Allows entry of suitably qualified medical practitioners. The relevant State or Territory Medical Board must recognise the applicant's medical qualifications as acceptable for practise in that State or Territory. There must be a demonstrated need to employ a practitioner from overseas.

Media and Film Staff (423) Allows entry of foreign correspondents to represent overseas news media organisations in Australia, and television or film crew members or photographers, including actors and support staff, involved in the production of films, documentaries or advertising commercials in Australia which are not being produced for the Australian market.

Public Lecturer (424) Allows entry of specialists and recognised experts to deliver public lectures in Australia.

Domestic Worker (Diplomatic/Consular) (426) Allows entry of domestic workers for diplomatic and consular staff in Australia where Australian Department of Foreign Affairs and Trade supports the entry.

Domestic Worker (Overseas Executive) (427) Allows the entry of domestic workers of certain holders of visas in class 457 long-stay temporary business entry.

A visa of this category will only be granted where it can be shown that the entry of such staff is necessary for the proper discharge of representational duties.

Religious Worker (428) Allows entry of religious workers, including ministers, priests and spiritual leaders to serve the spiritual needs of people of their faith in Australia.

Occupational Trainees (442) Allows entry of persons for occupational training appropriate to their background and/or employment history, for the acquisition or up-grading of skills useful to their home country. A nomination must be provided unless the training is being given by the Commonwealth of Australia.

People who wish to enter Australia on the temporary residence visas listed above must meet the normal health and character requirements for entry. Some applicants may be asked to have a medical examination before a visa will be granted. In most cases, if you have your application for temporary residence approved, you will then be granted a multiple entry visa for the period of the approved stay. If you need a further re-entry visa, you will need to apply to an office of the Department of Immigration and Multicultural Affairs (DIMA).

Students

Australia's student visa programme provides for the entry of overseas students who wish to undertake full-time study in registered courses in Australia. Students have the right to work up to 20 hours per week while their course is in session, however, the intention is that income derived from working in Australia should be a supplement to the main source of funding, and applicants will need to produce evidence of their financial resources when apply for a visa. Students may work without restriction during vacation periods. Recent press reports have suggested that some students entering Australia on this type of visa are deliberately enrolling in a minimal courseload and maximising their working hours illegally. It is likely that holders of student visas will be more closely monitored in future. Secondary school students visiting on an exchange programme must obtain a Student (Temporary) Visa.

Working Holiday Maker

The Working Holiday Maker scheme aims to promote international understanding by giving young people the opportunity to experience the culture of another country. It allows working holiday makers to enjoy an extended holiday by supplementing their travel funds through incidental employment, thus experiencing closer contact with local communities. Australia has reciprocal working holiday arrangements with Canada, Ireland, Japan, Korea, Malta, the Netherlands, and the United Kingdom. Although there are specific arrangements with these countries, the Australian working holiday scheme is applied globally, and applicants from other countries are considered where there might be a benefit both to the applicant and to Australia.

The Working Holiday Maker Visa (WHM) is available to applicants between the ages of 18 and 25 (and in special circumstances, for applicants from arrangement countries, up to age 30). Applicants may be either single or married, but must not have children (even if any children are not in their custody). The visa is valid for 13 months from the day of issue, of which a maximum of 12 months may be spent in Australia. It is best to apply for the WHM visa no more than four weeks before the date of travel, however, if you do not arrive in Australia until some time after your visa is issued, the visa can be 'topped up' to the maximum 12 months at the local immigration office. This must be done approximately two months before the expiry of your visa and currently costs $200.

When you apply for a working holiday visa, you must demonstrate that your main purpose in visiting Australia is to holiday, and that any work you expect to undertake will be solely to assist in supporting you whilst on vacation. You must have a good chance of finding temporary work, and may not enrol in formal studies of any kind. You must also have a return ticket or sufficient funds for a return airfare, in addition to being able to demonstrate £2,000 in funds for your travels (or a parental guarantee for the same amount). If you are over 25 and applying in the UK under the 'special circumstances' clause, you will need to demonstrate that the opportunity to visit and work in Australia will benefit you, and that you are able to offer benefits to Australia in return. A Working Holiday Maker visa usually allows for multiple entry, which means that you may leave and re-enter the country as many times as you like (within the time restriction of your visa). When visa is granted, ensure that it has been stamped 'multiple entry'. You cannot get an extension on a Working Holiday Visa under any circumstances, and must leave the country on or before the expiry date of your visa.

The working holiday scheme is currently subject to quota restrictions, introduced in 1995 to limit the impact of working holiday makers on the job prospects for long-term unemployed Australian residents. In 1997-98, 55 000 visas were issued, an increase of 5 000 on the previous year, and more than half of these visas were granted to UK nationals. A number of factors influence the volume of applications for working holiday visas, such as the strength of various economies around the world, and the popularity of certain kinds of tourism. The staging of the Olympic Games in Sydney in the year 2000 is expected to increase enormously demands for WHM visas during this period, although the number of visas allocated will not necessarily be increased. Some prospective working holiday makers have suffered under the new 'capping' rules, and have had their application for a visa refused after paying for their travel. Travel agents who specialise in Australian travel suggest that one way of avoiding this is to plan to commence the working holiday shortly after the beginning of July, which is the beginning of the annual visa allocation period. Applications made at this time have a good chance of succeeding.

Once in Australia, surveys show that most working holiday makers find temporary or casual employment in farming, clerical and hospitality industries. Fruit picking, bartending, secretarial and clerical work obtained through temp agencies, and labouring are all popular options for travellers, and this work tends to be widely available on a seasonal basis. Most travellers earn, on average, around $300 per week, and, in general, experience three or four different jobs over the period of their visit, holding each for 6 to 8 weeks at a time.

Retirement Visa

Retiring to Australia is a popular option for many people, particularly those with family connections there. It is possible to retire to Australia permanently, but initially you must apply for the Temporary Residence Retirement Visa (category 410). This visa does not officially entitle the applicant to permanent residence but in effect does allow you to stay indefinitely. If your visa is approved it will initially be granted for a period of four years, which may then be extended in two-year increments whilst in Australia. You will not have to demonstrate that you meet health and financial prerequisites on your subsequent applications for extension.

The Retirement Visa is available both to single applicants, and to couples in a married or de facto relationship. You must be at least 55 years of age, have no intention of entering the workforce, have no dependants other than your spouse, and be of good health and character. You must also be able to meet 'Funds transfer requirements' on the day you lodge your application. This means that you should have sufficient funds to maintain yourself (and your spouse/partner, if applicable) in Australia. You need to prove that you have capital for transfer of at least $500,000, or that you have a combination of both capital for transfer of at least $150,000 and a pension or income, or further capital providing an income of at least $35,000 per annum. If you need to sell a house to meet the funds transfer requirements, the Immigration Department requires that the sale be completed within 12 months of the date of your application.

Aged parents and relatives of Australian residents may also be eligible for entry under the Family Stream of Australia's migration programme. For more detailed coverage of visa and other issues relating to retirement in Australia, see the chapter on Retirement later in this book.

Permanent Residence (Migration)

Most applications for permanent residency in Australia are dealt with under one of several categories. These are: Family Stream Migration, which entails sponsorship by an relative resident in Australia; Skill Migration, requiring skills or outstanding abilities that will contribute to Australia's economy; Skilled-Australian Linked Migration (previously known as Concessional Family), which combines skills and family sponsorship; Business Skills Migration, which encourages entrepreneurs to develop business in Australia; and migration under the Humanitarian Programme. Generally, a successful applicant for migration to Australia must meet the personal and occupational requirements of the category for which he or she is applying, be able to settle in Australia without undue cost or difficulty to the Australian community, and be of good health and character. In addition, successful applicants will need enough money to travel to and settle in Australia.

FAMILY STREAM MIGRATION
Approximately fifty per cent of the migrants entering Australia each year do so under the Family Stream of the Migration Programme. In 1997-98, this amounted to some 32 000 successful applications for entry, all of whom were sponsored by a close family member or fiancé(e) with the right of permanent residence in Australia. Family Stream migrants are selected on the basis of their family relationship with their sponsor in Australia, and there is no test for skills or language ability as there is for Skilled Stream migrants; they are still required, however, to meet the requirements of health and character which are applied to all migrants.

Family Stream applicants can be sponsored for migration (permanent residence) in one of the following visa categories:

Spouse: Issued to a husband, wife or de facto partner of the Australian sponsor. Since May 1997, it has been required that a de facto or interdependent partner of an Australian citizen or permanent resident must be able to demonstrate one year of co-habitation with the sponsor. The co-habitation requirement also applies to gay and lesbian partners of Australian sponsors, who should apply for an interdependency visa, but who otherwise are assessed in the same way as those applying for a spouse visa. In compelling cases, such as where a child of the relationship exists, the co-habitation requirement may be waived.

Fiancé(e)s overseas: Fiancé(e)s overseas must apply for a 'prospective marriage' visa which is valid for nine months from the date of issue. They must travel to Australia, marry their sponsor, and apply to remain permanently during that period. It is a requirement that the parties to a prospective marriage have met and be known to each other in person. If all requirements are met, applicants will be granted a two-year extended eligibility visa, followed by a permanent visa if the relationship is still continuing at the end of two years.

Interdependency: Interdependency visas are for people who have an interdependent relationship with an Australian citizen or permanent resident which demonstrates a genuine, continuing and mutual commitment to a shared life together. The application process is the same as for the spouse visa.

Dependent child: Parents are able to sponsor for migration their natural child or, in certain cases, their adopted dependent child. The granting of a dependent child visa must not prejudice the rights and interests of any person who has custody or guardianship of, or access to, the child.

Other relatives are covered under *Preferential Family and Family Subclass Visas*. There are four components:

Orphan Relative: This visa permits the migration of orphans (as defined in the Migration Regulations), who are under 18 years old, unmarried and a relative of the sponsor.

Special Need Relative: A 'special need relative' is one who is granted entry to Australia for the purposes of providing substantial and continuing care to a relative living in Australia who has been affected by death, disability, prolonged illness, or other serious circumstance. The need for such assistance must be permanent or long-term, and must not be available from other relatives in Australia or from Australian health and welfare services.

Aged Dependent Relative: Applicants for this visa must be single, old enough to be granted an age pension under the *Social Security Act 1991* (that is, over the age of 65 for men and 61 for women), and have been dependent on the sponsor for at least three years prior to applying. The sponsor must have lived in Australia for at least two years before lodging the sponsorship application.

Last Remaining Relative: This visa allows for entry of the last remaining brother, sister or non-dependent child outside Australia. You or your spouse must not have a parent, sibling or non-dependent child or step-relative (within the same degree of relationship) living outside Australia, and again your sponsor must have lived in Australia for at least two years prior to the sponsorship being lodged.

Any Family Stream applicant who is assessed by DIMA as at risk of becoming a charge on the Australian social welfare budget is required to obtain an assurance of support. This is a legal commitment by the sponsor to repay to the Commonwealth of Australia any social security benefits paid to those covered by the assurance within the first two years after migration to Australia. There is a limit on the number of sponsorships any sponsor may make and on the timeframe in which they may be made.

SKILLED STREAM MIGRATION

The skilled stream of Australia's migration programme is especially designed to target migrants who have skills or outstanding abilities which will contribute to the Australian economy. Current government policy is committed to increasing migration in the skilled stream, and seeks to address specific skill shortages in the Australian labour market, as well as to enhance the size and skill-level of the Australian labour force. In 1997-98 approximately 21 per cent of skilled migrants came from the UK.

There are five main categories of skilled migration:

Independent: Independent migrants are people selected on the basis of their education, skills and work experience, who are likely to contribute to the Australian economy. They are not sponsored by an employer or relative in Australia. This group is the largest sector of the skilled migration programme. In November 1997, a new component of the Independent migrant category was announced, known as the State/Territory Nominated Independent Scheme (STNI). This scheme enables State and Territory Governments to sponsor an additional 200 skilled migrants and their families per year, on the condition that the selected migrants live and work in nominated regional areas. Regions and skills are identified through a skill-matching scheme, providing a resource for potential employers who are considering nominating overseas workers to fill their requirements.

Employer nominated: Employers may nominate personnel from overseas for migration under the Employer Nomination Scheme. This option is available only when the position cannot be filled from the Australian labour market. They may also sponsor skilled workers under a Labour Agreement, which is negotiated to allow the recruitment of an agreed number of personnel subject to various conditions. Labour Agreements provide for the permanent entry of workers with skills in demand in certain industries.

Distinguished talent: This category permits distinguished individuals with special or unique talents to enter Australia, and is generally reserved for outstanding sportspeople, musicians, artists and designers who are internationally recognised in their field. It is open to very few applicants.

Skilled-Australian linked: Previously known as Concessional Family migration, this category has been moved from the Family Stream to the Skilled Stream. It is designed to improve the labour market impact of concessional family migrants, and to emphasise an increased skills focus. Migrants in this category are selected on this basis of skills, age, English language ability and family relationship. They must be sponsored by a relative already living in Australia.

Business skills migration: The Business Skills programme is designed to encourage successful entrepreneurs and other business people to settle in Australia and develop new businesses of benefit to the Australian economy. The current government has a strong commitment to increasing the entry of high quality business migrants, with numbers of visas granted almost doubling every year since 1994. You may be eligible for a Business Skills visa if you have net business assets of at least $300,000 with management responsibilities; if you are a senior executive employed in top-tier management of a company with an annual turnover of at least $50 million; or if you have a history of successful investment activity and agree to make an investment of at least $750,000 into a State or Territory government security for a period of three years. The expectation is that a business migrant will establish a new business or become an owner or part-owner of an existing business, and participate in the management of that business. The progress of business migrants is monitored after arrival in Australia, and where no significant steps are taken towards these goals within three years, the visa may be revoked.

The Points Test

The Australian Immigration Department operates a 'points system' for international immigration applications under the Skilled Migration programme. Applicants must meet certain criteria, based on their skills, experience, age and language ability. Points are awarded for each criterion, and applicants must gain sufficient points to reach the Pass Mark. The Pass Mark currently stands at 115 points, but changes frequently. In the Skilled-Australian linked category points are also awarded for an applicant's relationship to the Australian sponsor, with higher marks being awarded if the sponsor is an Australian citizen. Applicants who score close to the Pass Mark are held in a reserve Pool for up to 12 months following assessment. This cut-off point, known as the Pool Mark, is currently 110 points. There are a number of consultancies, advertised in *Overseas Job Express* or *Australian Outlook*, which provide assistance in preparing for the points test by advising applicants on how to maximise the number of points they can accrue.

Generally, the baseline requirements for success in the points test are that you must be a male under 65 years old or a female under 60 years of age at the time your application is lodged. You must reach either the pool or pass mark in force at the time of assessment of your application (which may not necessarily be the same as the marks at the time your application was lodged), and you must be proficient in English if your occupation is listed as one of the Occupations Requiring English (which means you must be fluent in both spoken and written English). The list of Occupations Requiring English has recently been significantly extended, so that now almost 80 per cent of all occupations are included.

Points for skill are awarded on the basis of your usual occupation, which is determined by the migration officer. Normally, you will have worked in this occupation continuously for at least six months in the last two years. If you have held more than one job which fits this description, you will be assessed against both of your usual occupations, and will be allocated the one which provides you with the best score. The Australian authorities will also assess your qualifications and experience, and the resulting 'skill level' of your occupation will affect how many points you can score. If your usual occupation requires a degree or trade certificate in Australia, you will earn 70 points, whilst a diploma or associate diploma will earn 55 points. Your points score will also depend on the amount of post-qualification work experience gained immediately before lodging your application.

The younger you are, the more points you will earn on the Age assessment, ranging from 30 points at age 18 to 0 points at age 50. If you are a Skilled-Australian linked applicant, you will earn an additional 15 points if you are sponsored by your adult child, 10 points when sponsored by a sibling, and 5 points for sponsorship by a nephew or niece. If your sponsor has been an Australian citizen for five years or more, you will be awarded a further 10 points. Other points may be awarded if your sponsor lives in a regional area of Australia, so that applicants are encouraged to settle outside major metropolitan areas.

You can obtain a self-assessment table for the Points Test from the High Commission in order to estimate your points score, or download it from the Internet at www.immi.gov.au/forms/958i-c.htm.

The costs of applying to migrate to Australia are as follows:

Application for Migration to Australia Forms Package	$10
Application for Migration Visa Charge (1st instalment)	$1055
Application for Business Migration(1st instalment)	$3040
Application for Migration (2nd instalment)	$2235
Application for Business Migration (2nd instalment)	$4470
Additional Charge for dependent spouse (or other dependent adult)	$2235
Employer Nominated Sponsorship	$4470
Application for Temporary Residence Visa (most categories)	$145
Application for Working Holiday Maker Visa	$145
Application for Student Visa	$285
Application for Prospective MarriageVisa	$1055
Application for Long-Stay Visitor's Visa (more than 3 months)	$35

Note that the second instalment of charges for permanent residency is payable only after the application has been accepted. Religious workers are fee-exempt in the Employer Nominated category. These costs are quoted in Australian dollars and will vary according to the exchange rate. The Australian High Commission will be able to advise of the current cost in local currency. Applicants for permanent residency should also allow for the cost of a medical examination by an approved practitioner, which will include screening for tuberculosis (chest X-ray), HIV and hepatitis.

Visa processing times vary according to the type of visa, and according to current demand. As a general guide, a spouse visa will take around 6 months, while family and skill stream migration visas can take up to 16 months. DIMA has recently decided that priority is to be given to applications sponsored by Australian citizens; those sponsored by non-citizens will now go to the back of the queue, and it is expected that waiting time on such applications will become even longer. Vistor's visas can be issued the same day, or instantly, if applying for an ETA.

Becoming an Australian Citizen

Many migrants, once they have completed all the requirements of permanent residency and feel settled in their new home, decide to demonstrate their commitment to Australia by becoming a citizen. Approximately 50 per cent of migrants take up citizenship within five years of arrival, and of the hundred thousand or so who do so each year, 25 per cent come from the UK. In recent years the Australian government has strongly encouraged immigrants to take up citizenship, and now offers various incentives for them to do so. One such incentive is currently in place in the migration programme, where those wishing to sponsor other family members to come to Australia will have their applications moved to the front of the line if they have become an Australian citizen. Many public sector jobs, especially in areas of national security, are now also open only to Australian citizens. Immigrants who become citizens have all the same responsibilities and privileges as Australian-born citizens: they are entitled to an Australian passport and may enter and leave the country without visa restrictions, they may register their children as Australian citizens, and they may apply for public office or to enlist in the defence forces. A booklet, *What it Means to be an Australian Citizen* is available from the Department of Immigration and Multicultural Affairs.

As a migrant, you will become eligible for Australian citizenship when you have lived in Australia as a permanent resident for a total of two out of the previous five years. You must be over the age of 18 to apply, though children may be included on their parents application, and must expect to live permanently in Australia or maintain a close and continuing link with it. There is a fee of $120 to apply for the grant of citizenship, which is reduced to $20 for those on certain pensions and other social security benefits.

Useful Addresses

British Passport Offices: Clive House, 70 Petty France, London SW1H 9HD, tel 0171-279 3434. There are also offices in Belfast, Glasgow, Liverpool, Newport and Peterborough.

Australian High Commission: Australia House, Strand, London WC2B 4LA, tel 0171-379 4334; fax (DIMA) 0171-465 8218. Open: Mon-Fri 9am-1pm. Telephone service open 2pm-4pm. Recorded information service (24 hours) 0891-600 333.

Australian Consulate: Chatsworth House, Lever Street, Manchester M1 2QL, tel 0161-228 1344; fax 0161-236 4074. Open: Mon-Fri 10am-1pm. Telephone service open 8.30am-1pm (temporary residence), 2pm-4pm (migration).

Australian Embassy: 2nd floor, Fitzwilton House, Wilton Terrace, Dublin 2, Ireland, tel +353 1 676 1517; fax (DIMA) +353 1 661 3576. Open: Mon-Fri 9.30am-12pm, 1.30pm-3pm.

New Zealand and Australian Migration Bureau (Registered migration agent no. 81678; approved member of the New Zealand Association for Migration and Investment),United Kingdom and Ireland: 70 Upper Richmond Road, Putney, London SW15 2RP, tel 0181-874 2844; fax 0181-874 1178; email migration-bureau@dial.pipex.com.

Germany, Austria, Switzerland: 26th Floor, Messeturm, Box 23, D-60308 Frankfurt, Germany, tel +49 069 9754 4648; fax +49 069 9754 4900; email info@NZAMB.nl.

Benelux, Russia, Middle East, Africa, Oranje Nassaulaan 25, 1075 AJ Amsterdam, the Netherlands, tel +31 020 671 7017; fax +31 020 676 0065; email

info@NZAMB.nl.
Asia-Pacific Region and the Americas, PO Box 5077, Wellington, New Zealand,
tel +64 04 472 9365; fax +64 04 499 1288; email odg.ebw@xtra.co.nz.

Information from the Department of Immigration and Multicultural Affairs is
available on-line at www.immi.gov.au. Details of Australian missions in the UK
are available at www.immi.gov.au/wwi/index_u.htm.

The Gay and Lesbian Immigration Task Force have a website at
www.glitf.org.au which provides up-to-date information on this particular area of
immigration law, as well as links to their electronic newsletter.

Setting Up Home

How do the Australians live?

The demography of Australia is changing rapidly, in line with trends in other industrialised nations. The traditional family unit no longer dominates Australian society, so that the couple with its fabled 2.1 children now comprises only 34 per cent of the population (down 10 per cent in the last ten years). One parent families account for another 10 per cent, and couples without children, 40 per cent. The 'greying' of the population is well-documented, as Australia's baby-boomers move into late middle age and their own children abstain longer and longer from establishing families of their own. The northern NSW/Queensland coastline is the premier 'grey spot' of Australia, with dozens of retirement communities, while areas with high proportions of children are generally located outside major towns and cities, especially in outback Queensland and the Northern Territory.

Australia has the highest level of home-ownership in the world, with over 75 per cent of Australian homes either mortgaged or owner-occupied. Most Australians live in single-storey houses with a garden at both the front and the back of the house. Gardens are usually designed to take advantage of the weather and will generally have at least one shaded patio to create an external living area. Most will have a semi-detached lockable garage, or at the very least, a 'car-port' (covered hard-standing). A basic family home is expected to comprise three bedrooms, an open-plan living and dining area, fitted kitchen, at least one bathroom, and a separate laundry (including a large sink, known as a trough, and fitted plumbing for a washing machine). Every home without exception (indeed, by law) will have a laundry, and it is unheard of to install a washing machine in a kitchen. Four-bedroom houses are also very common, but there are very few, if any, recently-built two bedroom houses. Most houses are likely to have a family room (informal living area) in addition to the usual 2 reception rooms, and will generally have 2 bathrooms, one of which is usually en suite. The focus of the bathroom is always the shower, which is *never* located over the bath. Australian showers come on hot and strong from the mains, and electric showers and booster pumps are not required; bathrooms are always tiled, thus a carpeted bathroom is a source of extreme amusement to Australians visiting Britain. Kitchens always include a cooker (known as a stove) and fitted cupboards, which in modern houses will include a large pantry cupboard. Carpets, curtains and light fittings are always included in the price unless stated otherwise.

A very large number of homes in Australia have a swimming pool and these must be secured with childproof fences and gates. Local councils inspect swimming pools annually to ensure that they comply with legal requirements in terms of safety and security, and regulations are strictly enforced: fences must be unclimbable and over 1.5m in height, and pool gates must be locked and on a self-closing spring. Pool cleaning equipment (vacuum, hoses, and leaf rake) should be included amongst the house fixtures and fittings. Most home pools are chlorinated, which means that you will need to add chemicals daily, however, increasingly, people are choosing either to install salt-water pools or to convert existing pools to salt-water technology. If you are lucky enough to have a salt-water pool, you will only need to add salt once a year, and then leave the converter to do the rest. Salt-water pools also maintain a higher water temperature than chlorinated pools.

Australian houses are usually built either of double brick or of brick veneer (an external brick 'skin' over a timber-framed dwelling). Building regulations in Western Australia require double brick construction, however, in the eastern states, where the topography is more inclined towards earth movement, brick veneer is more structurally sound. Roofs are generally tiled with terracotta or, in cheaper construction, (indistinguishable) coloured cement tiles, but colourbonded steel sheeting is currently fashionable, mimicking the traditional Australian tin-roof. Most Australian homes are fitted with insulation in the roof space and, sometimes, the walls. This insulation, made from fibreglass or wool fibre compacted to the size of a hay bale, helps to keep the house cool in summer and warm in winter. All homes are fitted with fly-screens over the doors and windows, so that doors and windows can be left open without admitting insects.

Buying a Home or Land

Properties and vacant land are advertised for sale in the Real Estate supplements of all capital city newspapers. Most local papers, including weekly freesheets, also carry extensive advertisements, and are a good place to start if you have decided on a particular area. Government or 'Crown' land is also occasionally advertised for sale, especially in outer suburban areas undergoing new development. If you are interested in building a new home at an economical cost (that is, *not* by subcontracting your own architect and builder), you should look at the newspaper section headed 'Display Homes' or 'Project Homes'. A project home is an off-the-peg architectural design offered by a builder and built especially for you, either on your own land, or on land supplied by the builder and offered as part of a package. Once you have selected a suitable design, you are free to customise it to a certain extent, choosing internal finishes, bricks, tiles, and landscaping. Many people choose to have the ceiling heights raised in project homes (they are usually designed to the legal minimum of eight courses of brickwork), and this will add around $3,000 per course to the cost of the design. Project homes are an extremely popular choice in Australia, and rather than simply buying a new home in a development, most people prefer this more individual option. A project home package for a home comprising 4 bedrooms, 2 bathrooms, and 2 or 3 reception rooms, including plans, building and land, in an outer suburban area of Perth can cost as little as $80,000. If you choose to supply your own land, your new home can be built for around $50,000. Examples of builders' project homes, known as 'display homes', can be viewed at various 'display villages', the locations of which are advertised alongside the relevant floorplans.

A guide to the sort of price you can expect to pay for an average family home around Australia is given below. For the price listed, you are likely to get a 3 bedroom, 2 bathroom residence on about a third of an acre of land in a low/mid-range suburban area.

Current Median Property Values by Capital City ($'000)

	Sydney	Melbourne	Brisbane	Adelaide	Perth	Hobart	Canberra
House	215.8	140.5	151.9	122.0	152.6	121.3	164.6
Townhouse/terrace/duplex	198.9	132.0	121.3	116.0	77.1	141.3	
Flat	198.7	103.3	120.4	87.6	96.9	94.4	126.3

(Source: Australian Bureau of Statistics, 1998)

If you are moving to the ACT, you should note that there is no freehold land available in Canberra. Instead, the Commonwealth Government grants 99-year leases on blocks of land for residential purposes, and these are released for sale to keep pace with demand. All residential land is sold at public auction, and unsold sites are available after auction at the Land Sales Office. Reserve prices are set at 80% of the assessed market value. Leaseholders are obliged to commence construction within twelve months and to complete construction in 24 months. All land released for sale under this system is within 30km of the city centre, and all sites are fully serviced, with social amenities added as the suburb develops.

Rent or Buy?

Housing in Australia is currently at its most affordable level for many years; interest rates are low, banking is highly competitive, and prices are relatively stable. Financial experts agree that buying your own home is the best step that you can take towards financial security, offering both the peace of mind of a secure roof over your head as well as significant tax benefits on your investment. It is currently very easy to obtain mortgage finance, and with low interest rates, paying off a property is likely to cost you less than renting one of an equivalent standard. Initial establishment costs can be high, however (see below), and it is likely to take several years before you can offset these against any gain on your investment. Residential property prices are affected by a number of variables, including migration, interest rates, government policy, consumer confidence, and general economic conditions. There is an observable cycle in the property market, and if you arrive at the peak of a particular cycle, you may be well advised to rent and invest your money elsewhere until a downturn occurs. The Real Estate Institute of Australia monitors property cycles, and publishes bulletins and statistics which can help you assess where the market currently stands. Market analysts currently forecast an 11 per cent per annum increase in property values in all Australian capitals, except Hobart, which should remain static, and Sydney, where demand is expected to fuel a property boom.

Finance

The home loan market in Australia has been highly competitive in recent years with a number of new players entering the fray and a myriad of options available. Having negotiated the maze, however, borrowers can currently enjoy exceptional value for money in their choice of investment. Non-bank lenders are now offering more flexible features, including the option to redraw on extra payments, and loans are being offered at competitive rates by established banks, credit unions, building societies, and new-style mortgage originators. Lenders will consider loans of up to 90 per cent of the property value, and mortgage eligibility is calculated on a formula based on the income level of the applicant, or of the applicant and partner in combination (usually 3 times one salary or 2.5 times both salaries). There is an increasing number of lenders offering no-deposit home loan packages to encourage potential buyers into the market, including builders who will supply no-deposit finance for buyers to purchase their project homes. Usually such offers will have hidden (or not-so-hidden costs) such as higher interest rates.

Application or establishment fees are charged by both banks and other lenders to cover the cost of setting up a loan agreement, including legal and valuation fees, and disbursements such as mortgage registration and stamp duty. The amount of these initial fees varies widely between lenders: some simply pass on their costs, others absorb them (a no-fees mortgage), while some of the bigger players, who have less to fear from competition, may charge as much as $800.

Lending terms and conditions can vary considerably between lenders, but in mid-1998 the interest rate stands at around 6 per cent per annum for standard variable home loans. The maximum term for a standard home loan is 25 years, with a few lenders offering 30 year terms, depending on the age of the applicant. Fixed loans are popular as they provide security against interest rate rises, and such loans are now more flexible than they have been with lenders offering the facility of extra repayments without penalty.

Australia's four largest banks are the Commonwealth (recently privatised), the ANZ, Westpac, and the National Australia Bank. All offer mortgage products and applications for a home loan can be lodged at any branch. Increasingly, suburban branches operate as little more than shop-fronts, with management and lending decisions taken at head office, so you need not necessarily approach your own branch for information. The Commonwealth Bank and the ANZ both have excellent websites which describe their range of products, and by entering your details online, you can receive an instant assessment of your eligibility for a mortgage. You can access the Commonwealth on www.commonwealth.com.au and the ANZ on www.anz.com.au.

Non-bank lenders are playing an increasingly important role in the mortgage market and are known as mortgage originators or mortgage managers. Such lenders, who include insurance companies and credit unions, act as intermediaries between borrowers and larger institutions. These big institutions are the real lenders behind mortgage originator loans, and are usually organisations like the Primary Industry Bank of Australia (PIBA) who do not wish to participate in the market directly. Other funds are obtained from securitisers, who raise funds on the financial markets and then redistribute them to originators. Industry standards require that independent trustees oversee originators and the loan monies that they collect to protect the interests of the borrower. Aussie Home Loans (AHL) is the most aggressive of the mortgage originators and advertises extensively on radio and in newspapers. Other major originators include FAI First Mortgage, Macquarie Residential Mortgages, Mortgage Masters, and Priority One.

In such a complex environment, borrowers are increasingly seeking the services of mortgage brokers, who are able to source the most suitable and cheapest loan for your needs. A good broker will be able to find you the best loan, explain it in detail, help complete the loan documents, and guide the application through to acceptance. Brokers make their money on commission from the lender, and there are no fees charged to the borrower. Almost half the home loans in Western Australia are now written by brokers and the trend is steadily increasing in the eastern states. Mortgage brokers advertise widely in the press and yellow pages, and some of the franchise real estate chains, such as Ray White and LJ Hooker also offer broking services.

Useful Addresses

Australian and New Zealand Banking Group, Minerva House, Montague Close, London SE1, tel 0171-378 2121.

The Commonwealth Bank of Australia, Financial & Migrant Information Service, 85 Queen Victoria Street, London, EC4, tel 0171-710 3999.

Westpac Banking Corporation, 63 St Mary's Annexe, London, EC3, tel 0171-621 7000.

Purchasing & Conveyancing Procedures

Every state in Australia has its own laws pertaining to real estate transactions, and its own licensing laws for real estate agents. In general, you should expect your real estate agent to hold certification from the appropriate state government authority, and preferably, that they or their agency should be a member of the Real Estate Institute of Australia (or state-affiliated branch). If your agent is a member of the REIA or its affiliates, such as REIWA (the Real Estate Institute of Western Australia), you will be protected in the case of any malpractice. Estate agents who are the Principals (proprietors) of an agency must be certified at a higher level, and any agent intending to conduct a sale by auction must hold a separate license to do so.

There are five types of fees for which you must budget when purchasing a property in Australia:

Solicitors/Settlement Agents professional fees. These are fees charged by a solicitor or settlement agent for conducting the legal business of the purchase on your behalf.

Search fees and outlays. These fees cover the cost of the searches undertaken to ensure that the property is free from encumbrances.

Stamp Duty. Stamp duty is a state government tax on the purchase price of the property. It is calculated as a percentage of the value of the transaction, and is affected by the area of land purchased and whether the purchasers intend to reside in the property. Concessions apply in some states (for example, Queensland) to first time buyers who will reside in the property. Stamp duty varies considerably from state to state, but is usually between one and three per cent of the value: on a family house valued at $200,000, you can expect to pay from $1,500 in Brisbane to $6,000 in Sydney.

Registration Fees. Fees are charged by the state department of land management or natural resources to effect the registration of transfer of ownership and related mortgage documents.

Lender fees. It is common practice for lenders to charge administration fees for setting up a mortgage. As the home loan market becomes increasingly competitive, however, such fees (which can be as high as $800) have become more negotiatable, and can be avoided completely if you shop around carefully.

The process of exchanging contracts to complete a property transaction is known in Australia as 'settlement'. Settlement is a far easier process in Australia than in the UK and the concept of the 'chain' does not exist. Once a vendor agrees to an offer on a property, a contract is signed stipulating a date for settlement, which will usually be 30 days from the date of offer. During this period, the purchaser arranges finance and completes all the legal formalities; settlement MUST take place on the nominated date, and if it cannot, the party at fault becomes liable for the payment of penalty interest. The conveyancing market has been deregulated in recent years and is no longer the exclusive province of solicitors. Most people now turn to specialist 'settlement agents' instead, who are trained in conveyancing and property law, but who are not lawyers. Settlement agent's fees are almost always much lower than those charged by solicitors for an identical service, and are generally in the region of $400-$800, depending on the value of the property and the state in which you reside. In South Australia the legal legwork on most property transactions is handled by a land broker. It is possible to do your own conveyancing, but it is not recommended: the risk of steep penalty interest payments in the case of delay through error or lack of expertise can outweigh the saving of a few hundred dollars many times over.

If you have not been granted permanent residency in Australia, any property purchase will require the prior approval of the Foreign Investment Review Board. Generally speaking, the Board will *not* approve the purchase of residential real estate by non-residents; however, each case is considered on its merits, and if you are a temporary resident or overseas investor hoping to buy in Australia, you should seek advice from a solicitor specialising in Australian property law. You can write to *Foreign Investment Review Board*, c/o the Treasury, Parkes Place, Parkes ACT 2600.

Real Estate Agencies

Most people buy and sell their property with the services of a local real estate agent, and fewer than ten per cent of all properties are marketed by their owner. Agents act on behalf of the vendor and not the purchaser, and their responsibilities include advertising and contract negotiation to obtain the best possible price for their client (who is, you should always bear in mind when you are buying, *not* you). Homes for sale will be advertised in the local press, and the larger, state-wide newspapers will generally publish a property section at the weekend (probably on Saturday). In addition, most will have extensive photo displays in their office window. The distribution of detailed description sheets giving measurements of each room, location of power points, and other features, is not an Australian practice, although top-of-the-range homes are often marketed through a glossy, descriptive brochure. Instead, when you approach an agent regarding a property, you can expect to be told only the price (or, increasingly, an acceptable price range), the number and types of rooms, and any other facilities, for example, swimming pool, reticulation, or air-conditioning. If the property is still of interest, the agent will arrange to accompany you on a private inspection, or you may be asked to attend the next 'Home Open'. The Home Open is a standard property marketing tool in Australia and involves opening the property to all-comers at a specified, advertised time, usually for an hour or two every weekend. During this time, the agent is in attendance and the owners are absent. Prospective purchasers, who are most likely to have seen the property advertised in that morning's paper, are free to walk around the house and garden and examine its suitability in privacy. The agent will take your name and address, and usually will chat a little to determine your bona fides. The Home Open is generally considered to be a convenient and low-key way of finding a property, and if you are house-hunting it is an easy way of lining up four or five likely places to see in one morning.

There are three different methods of listing a property with an estate agent, and you will often see one of the following terms somewhere in an advertisement:
Sole/exclusive Agency. This means that the property is being offered by one agent only, and can only be viewed by contacting the specified office. Advertisements for sole agency properties will carry the name of the particular agent (for example, Mike Jones of Smith White Realty) who has obtained the listing. All contact and requests for information must be directed to the named agent.
Open Listing. Under an 'open listing', any number of agencies can offer the property to buyers. This method is common in some states (Queensland) and unusual in others, or in some cases (Western Australia), common for more down-market properties or areas, and unusual at the middle and upper end of the market. It is not generally considered to be an effective way to sell, as there is no one agent with a keen incentive to make the sale.
Multilisting. Multilisting is very similiar to the American Multiple Listing Service (MLS), and means that a property is listed by a number of specified agencies. Multilisting is the least common method of marketing a property.

If you are looking for a property to buy, you can approach an agent to act on your behalf in the search. The agent will then obtain lists of all the properties for sale in your price range and desired area, and will arrange for you to view them. There is no fee to the purchaser for this service, and it can be a good way for a newcomer to find a suitable property, as the agent will have detailed local knowledge about shops, schools, and amenities, which you may lack. Your agent makes his or her money, once you decide on a property, by negotiating a *conjunctional sale*: the vendor's agent splits the sale commission 50/50 with the introducing agent, and everyone goes away happy. Conjunctional sales apply to properties marketed under sole agency as well as by other methods, and there are very few agents who will refuse to conjunct.

Buying at Auction

Many Australian properties at every level of the market are sold by auction. Auctions, and attitudes to sale by auction, vary from state to state: they are currently popular in Victoria, especially in Melbourne, and are used a great deal in Sydney, particularly for more expensive properties. Some franchise groups push vendors to sell by auction, but they are not universally popular: some agents consider them to be most suitable for distress sales (in which case, they can result in bargains), while others use them only in a competitive, rising market (in which case, you can end up paying too much). Vendors who sell by auction are responsible for the advertising costs of the agent.

Buying at auction can be an intimidating experience, and it is advisable to attend a few as a kind of 'dry run', to get the feel for what you will be up against. In Western Australia, auctions are conducted in the front garden of the property for sale, so it is easy to wander up and listen, whilst in other states, they are usually held in auction rooms. Success at auction depends on doing your homework: first, know your financial limits by visiting your bank manager beforehand, and *never* bid above that limit, no matter how persuasive the auctioneer's patter. Secondly, know the market, so that you have a clear idea of the true worth of the property; shop around, comparing prices of similar houses. Once you have identified the house you want, spend several weeks before the auction date visiting other auctions in the area to evaluate the level of bidding. Thirdly, make prior enquiries about the contract, establishing what the property includes, and making sure it is free from any important defects. Examine the building report and pest certificates, and ascertain the level of deposit which will be required in cash on the fall of the hammer (it is likely to be ten per cent).

On auction day, you should check the contracts again, to ensure that no changes have been made. Arrive early, and have a last look around if possible. At this point you should introduce yourself to the auctioneer and let them know that you are interested in buying. Sit in easy view of the auctioneer, preferably near the front or at the sides, where you can observe competing bidders. The auctioneer will then commence the patter and ask if there are any questions: bidders who play tough like to take this opportunity to unsettle the opposition by fielding queries about six-lane highways or high-rise tower blocks. Try and ignore such strategies and bid with confidence; bid low and bid often is the approach recommended by experienced agents. When bidding is slow, a common tactic of the auctioneer is to pull out 'phantom bids' or bids on behalf of the vendor, but if you suspect this, you are within your rights to stop the auction and demand to know against whom you are bidding. Properties are always auctioned with an undisclosed reserve price, and if it is eventually passed in, you will be able to try and negotiate privately after the auction.

Finally, some agents advise that if you really want the house, you could try making an offer in advance: the vendor may be as nervous as you are, and only to glad to tie it up without going through with the whole ordeal.

Contracts

Most property sales are concluded through the exchange of a simple standard contract issued by the state Real Estate Institute. This contract will specify the sale price and deposit (notionally 10 per cent, but in practice, highly negotiable), the date of settlement, and the fixtures and fittings to be included in the sale. You should note that, unlike in the UK, it is *expected* that fixtures and fittings will be included in a sale, and, if you are selling, you will be in breach of your contract if you so much as remove a light bulb without specifying your intentions. Cookers and dishwashers are considered fixtures and must remain in the property. The contract will also require that all appliances are in good working order, and this includes external plant such as swimming pool filters, air-conditioning, and ducted vacuum systems. At the time of making an offer, certain conditions are usually appended to the standard contract, and the failure of either party to meet the stated conditions will invalidate the sale. Usually a contract is signed subject to two main conditions: firstly, that the purchaser provide proof of mortgage finance or cash resources within 48 hours; and secondly, that the vendor provide a current white ant certificate within one week. White ants are a type of termite which can cause havoc with a building's structural timbers; they are a serious concern and their control is monitored by law. A white ant inspection certificate ensures that your property is free from infestation, or, if white ants have been found, that they have been destroyed by chemical treatment. Evidence of previous, treated white ant infestation is not an impediment to the sale of a property. A white ant inspection certificate costs around $150 and this cost is born by the vendor. If these conditions, and any others particular to your property, are met, the contract becomes binding. Should you change your mind for any reason, you will forfeit your deposit, and similarly, should the vendor break the contract, your deposit will be refunded plus the same amount again as a penalty payment.

Useful Addresses
L.J. Hooker is one of Australia's largest real estate groups with offices throughout the country. Their customer service centre (freephone 1800 62 12 12) will be able to recommend an office in your intended area as well as provide local information. They also have an excellent website at www.ljhooker.com.au, which provides useful advice on all aspects of buying and selling, and on-line property information.
Foreign Investment Review Board, c/o the Treasury, Parkes Place, Parkes ACT 2600.

Useful Publications
Consyl Publishing Ltd., 3 Buckhurst Road, Buckhurst Road, Bexhill-on-Sea, East Sussex, TN40 1QF distributes the Australian magazines, *Real Estate Weekly* and *The Homebuyer*, which contain illustrated for-sale advertisements for property around Australia. These can be ordered by mail from the above address or by telephone on (012424) 223 161.

Renting Property

Australians have a strong home-owning ethos. Most people prefer not to rent if at all possible and those who do rent in general occupy their rented property for less than a year. Rented housing in Australia is very much less expensive than in Europe, and both tenant and landlord rights are well protected. Amongst other things, tenancies are always covered by leases and there is no indefinite security of tenure. Renting out a property is not a risky venture for a landlord, who can easily have unsuitable tenants evicted, and thus, people are very willing to place their investment properties and homes on the rental market. Recent changes in taxation law, however, have meant that it is no longer as financially advantageous to buy property for the purposes of renting it out, and as a result the amount of property available to rent has declined, with a concomitant rise in rentals. Nonetheless, the average weekly rental in Melbourne, which is generally considered an expensive city in terms of property prices, is $240, clearly far less than in most major European cities.

Rents are not subject to state control in Australia, but are set by the lease agreement signed by both tenant and landlord. Usually, such an agreement will set the rent for a six month period, with a reassessment at the end of the lease period. In some states residential rents may be controlled, but only on properties which were tenanted prior to changes in the law. The Federal Discrimination Act prohibits discrimination by landlords against prospective tenants, and it is illegal to refuse a tenant on the grounds of sex or marital status, pregnancy, or ethnic origin. If you suspect that a landlord or agent has made an illegal refusal of your application to rent his or her property, you should contact the nearest Consumer Affairs office who will be able to advise you further. In general, however, landlords are interested in having their property occupied by rent-paying tenants, and you are unlikely to have your application for tenancy turned down if you can provide good references and evidence of sufficient financial means.

Properties for rent are advertised in the 'To Let' section of the property pages in city and state newspapers, and in weekly, free community newspapers. Real estate agents also usually have a specialist property management division which will also have listings of available properties, and you can approach agents directly in the areas in which you hope to find accommodation.

Tenancy Agreements

Very short term rented accommodation can be difficult to find in Australia as most property owners will only accept tenants prepared to sign a tenancy agreement valid for six months. It is occasionally possible to find an owner who is prepared to make a short term lease available, and in such cases the lease may later be extended by private agreement, allowing you to remain on a weekly or monthly basis after the expiry of the lease. Although this can be convenient for travellers, it does not give much security to longer term visitors, and you will need be willing to move at short notice should the owner decide to make other arrangements. In general, a first lease is given for six months and can be extended, provided that you and the owner both agree to any change of conditions, including a rent rise (most landlords do *not* automatically raise the rent every six months). Properties are almost invariably let unfurnished, but will include a cooker and, often, a fridge. Lease agreements in Australia usually conform to a standard format, and the contract can be purchased for a couple of dollars at any newsagent. They are simple to understand and offer fair and equal protection to both landlord and tenant. The underlying assumption in Australian rent law, however, is that the property does belong to the landlord, who has greater rights in terms of protecting and enjoying the benefits of his or her investment. There is, therefore, no concept of the 'sitting tenant' or of 'squatting', and unruly, destructive or non-paying tenants can be swiftly and effectively evicted.

Letting agents or property owners generally require tenants to pay a bond or deposit of four weeks rental, in addition to a month's rent in advance. The bond can sometimes be as much as six weeks rent, and owners may occasionally ask for up to two months rent in advance. You should, therefore, allow several thousand dollars to establish yourself in a rented property. The bond can be entirely or partly forfeited if the tenant defaults on payment or conditions of the lease. If you leave the premises and any furniture and fittings in a good condition, allowing for reasonable wear and tear, your landlord will refund your bond at the end of your tenancy. Most landlords will provide an inventory of the property, particularly if it is let furnished, and this will detail the condition of the house at the start of the lease (it might list, for example, existing scuff marks or cigarette burns). You should read and assess this inventory before you sign your lease, as signing will imply your agreement with its contents. The property will be inspected at the end of your lease, and may be inspected at any time during the period of the tenancy, providing the owner or agent gives 48 hours notice of their intention to enter. They must, however, by law, have good cause to effect entry, for example, if neighbours report obvious signs of neglect; and you have the right to be present during any inspection. End-of-lease inspections are usually very thorough indeed: expect to have extractor fan covers removed and inspected for dirt and grease, pictures moved, and carpets lifted. You will need to seek permission under the terms of a standard lease to effect any change to the fabric of the property, even if it is just to put up a picture hook.

The owner of a rented property is responsible for all council and water rates, as well as strata and management fees, but the tenant pays for all utility costs such as electricity, gas and telephone.

Rental Costs

In Australia there is very little 'social housing' of the type provided by councils and district authorities in the UK and Europe. Traditionally, the 'Great Australian Dream' has meant that even in the lowest socio-economic groups there has been a high expectation of home ownership, and concomitantly, that to be housed by the 'State Housing Commission' has been an object of shame. In addition, rent laws, as outlined above, have kept the private rental sector competitive and stable, so that few people have needed to fall back on the state to provide them with accommodation. Most commonly, state housing is available to socially marginalised groups, such as Aborigines and refugees. The criterion for eligibility is that the applicant must demonstrate an inability to secure decent accommodation in the private sector at a rent which is within their capacity to pay; however, given that rent assistance for private tenants, whether unemployed or on a low income, is available from the Department of Social Security, there are very few people to whom this might apply.

In the private sector, there is almost always a good variety of properties available to rent, although it is usually easier to find flats (known as 'units') than houses. A rough guide to current weekly rental values for unfurnished property is given below:

Sydney
A good selection of houses and units is currently available in most areas.

Type	modest	average	good
House			
3 bed	285	350	500+
4 bed	390	450	650+
Flat			
1 bed	150	195	250+
2 bed	240	280	300+
3 bed	320	370	400+

Melbourne

Properties are currently plentiful and rent levels for houses have fallen in the last twelve months, so that houses are only marginally more expensive than flats to rent.

Type	modest	average	good
House			
3 bed	240	290	320+
4 bed	310	360	450+
Flat			
1 bed	135	160	190+
2 bed	165	185	220+
3 bed	200	240	280+

Brisbane

Rental properties are in high demand and the selection of both flats and houses is currently limited.

Type	modest	average	good
House			
3 bed	200	240	300+
4 bed	260	310	370+
Flat			
1 bed	100	130	150+
2 bed	140	165	180+
3 bed	170	200	230+

Adelaide

A good selection of well-priced houses and flats is currently available for rental.

Type	modest	average	good
House			
3 bed	160	195	230+
4 bed	220	260	290+
Flat			
1 bed	85	100	115+
2 bed	120	135	160+
3 bed	180	195	220+

Perth

A good range of accommodation is available in most areas, particularly in the lower rental bracket.

Type	modest	average	good
House			
3 bed	160	195	230+
4 bed	225	260	295+
Flat			
1 bed	95	115	145+
2 bed	110	135	160+
3 bed	150	180	210+

Hobart

In Hobart, rental accommodation is usually very limited, and both flats and houses are scarce.

Type	modest	average	good
House			
3 bed	150	180	200+
4 bed	190	220	240+
Flat			
1 bed	80	95	110+
2 bed	90	110	130+
3 bed	105	130	150+

Canberra
There is a plentiful supply of reasonably-priced rental accommodation in Canberra.

Type	modest	average	good
House			
3 bed	210	260	300+
4 bed	290	320	360+
Flat			
1 bed	135	155	190+
2 bed	170	200	230+
3 bed	200	240	270+

Property Glossary

House: In Australia, a house is usually of the 'bungalow' type, that is, it is likely to be single-storied, unless stated otherwise.

Unit: Term in common use to describe a flat or apartment. A unit can be located either in a high- or low-rise development.

Town House:A compact house of two or more stories in a small development; it will usually share one or more party walls with neighbouring townhouses.

Villa. A compact bungalow-style house in a small, unified development, usually with one or more party walls and shared driveway.

Duplex/Triplex. Property development in which two or three compact, single-story houses in a unified architectural style are built on a large suburban block.

Terrace. A terraced house, with party walls on both sides. This type of housing is only found in old, inner-city areas, but is often sought after for its 'character and charm'.

Freehold. Most Australian houses and land are held on a freehold title.

Strata Title. Flats, townhouses, villas, duplexes and triplexes are usually held on a strata title. Under this system (which is being considered as a replacement for the leasehold system in the UK), a property owner owns absolutely the space enclosed by the exterior walls of the property, as well as a pro-rata percentage share of all the communal space of the development in its entirety. Strata fees are payable quarterly to a 'body corporate', which is a democratically-constituted management authority, and covers the maintenance of the fabric of the structure and communal garden areas.

Relocation

Relocation Companies

Although there are many relocation service companies offering assistance with intra-European and transatlantic moves, the antipodean sector of the market is poorly served. Relocators can assist corporate and domestic migrants with establishing the basis for life in a new home abroad, including finding accommodation, schools, and employment; however, those which operate between the UK and Australia concentrate almost entirely on the corporate market. The cost of using such services can be prohibitive for the individual, and in many cases removal companies may be more helpful for people undertaking a domestic move. Many of the larger removal companies offer more than a shipping service, and may be able to advise and assist in many other aspects of your relocation. There are a number of relocation companies in Australia, and these will usually be better able to act on your behalf in organising the essentials for your arrival.

Useful Addresses

Carroll, Dardis & Associates, PO Box 468, Claremont WA 6010, tel: 08-9383
2677 or fax: 08-9383 2677 (same number). Offers a meet and greet service at
the airport upon arrival, introductions to reputable real estate agents, bank
managers, accountants, solicitors, insurance brokers, motor car dealers, as well
as information on education and health care in Western Australia.

Expat International offer expatriate consultancy to corporations worldwide, visa
documentation, international and interstate relocations, and cultural awareness
courses. They are affiliated with the Migration Institute of Australia and the
Employee Relocation Council (USA) and have offices worldwide: check the
white pages telephone directory of your capital city, or contact them in
Australia at Level 4, 126 Wellington Parade, East Melbourne VIC 3002, tel:
03-9419 9351 or fax: 03-9416 0786.

Relocation Information Services, 160 London Road, Croydon, Surrey CR0 2TD,
tel: 0181-681 3692 or fax: 0181-686 4061.

Relocations International, POB 6112, Wellesley Street, Auckland, New Zealand;
tel +64-9-378 9888; fax +64-9-376 1882. Provides assistance in finding
accommodation as schooling, as well as social networking in Australia and
New Zealand.

Assistance from Religious Organisations

The Anglican Church Overseas Settlement Department
Although strictly non-commercial, the Anglican Church has an *Overseas
Settlement Secretary* whose job is to ensure that you are put in touch with your
local Anglican Church in Australia and given a warm welcome into the country.
Many people find that the common bond of faith is an excellent opening to new
friendships, and that their co-parishioners are a useful source of assistance in
settling in to a new environment. For further details, write to the Overseas
Settlement Secretary, Board for Social Responsibility, Church House, Great Smith
Street, Westminster, London SW1P 3NZ.

Other Denominations
Members of other denominations or religions should contact the organisational
headquarters of their religious group in their present country in order to obtain a
list of religious contacts in Australia. The National Council of Churches in
Australia offers *Refugee and Migrant Services* and further information can be
obtained from their office at 379 Kent Street, Sydney NSW 2001, tel: 02-9229
2215.

Insurance and Wills

Home Insurance

An increasingly competitive insurance market in Australia has meant that in recent
years both the number of policies available to the consumer, and their variety, is
widening all the time. Buying the right insurance for your particular needs can be
confusing, and many Australians now use brokers to help them negotiate the maze
of options. Noel Pettersen, executive director of the National Insurance Brokers
Association, advises that selective purchasing in the key to proper coverage, rather
than purchasing new insurance every time a new need arises. Buildings and

contents policies are very long and involved, and when shopping around you should ensure that you obtain a copy of any contract you are seriously considering and assess it before you sign. The most important section is found under 'Exclusions', that is, what is *not* covered. This list can be long, and should be thoroughly checked against your own requirements. In particular, note which *fixtures* are covered: hot water systems, air conditioners, carports, pergolas, fences, and outside blinds may or may not be included. Bushfires, landslides and riot damage may also be excluded, and should be weighed up against your likely need. Anyone living in a well-timbered bushland suburb *must* ensure that they have bushfire cover. Most policies cover damage by fire and explosion, but not flood; once again, assess this according to your proximity to water sources or the climate and topography. Note, however, that some policies may include bushfire or flood damage cover, but the small print may specifically exclude homes situated in high-risk areas. You should also consider whether the sum insured includes cover for demolition costs, clean-up, temporary accommodation, and architect's fees, in the case of major damage to the fabric of your home.

Home insurance premiums, like car insurance, vary according to assessable risk factors. The insurers will take into account factors such as the age of the house, the type of construction (brick, brick veneer, or weatherboard), the value of the house, its size and location. Home insurance is usually payable on a yearly or half-yearly basis (although for a small credit charge, some companies will even allow monthly payments); a typical 4 bedroom, 2 bathroom Australian family home in a suburban location is likely to cost around $400 per year to insure. Excess levels vary markedly from company to company, and generally by electing a higher excess level of, say, $500, the premium can be significantly reduced. The Insurance Council of Australia considers under-insurance to be the biggest trap in the insurance industry, and estimates that at least 40 per cent of homes are under-insured.

Under-insurance is the biggest cause of dispute between insurance companies and their clients, and you must be aware that if you are under-insured by a certain amount, any claim you make will be reduced by a pro-rata percentage by the insurance assessor. This could have serious consequences in the case of the destruction of a family home, and may mean that you are unable to rebuild in spite of being insured. You should make sure that your level of insurance keeps pace with inflation in the building industry.

Contents Insurance

Home contents insurance provides cover for personal effects kept in and around the home. Most contents insurance is of the 'new for old' replacement type; there are very few indemnity policies (which pay out only the current second-hand value of the insured items) available. Replacement policies should be read closely for restrictions. The best policies will replace new for old unconditionally, however, others will impose an age limit on items so covered (generally, 10 to 12 years), and some exclude soft furnishings. To discourage fraudulent claims, many insurers offer a voucher system for replacement in the case of theft or destruction; instead of sending a cheque for the sum involved, you will receive a voucher for the amount which must be 'spent' at an appropriate shop (for example, an electrical retailer, if your television has been stolen). Such a policy can be quite irksome, as you, the customer, are not given any choice of retailers, and thus may be limited in your choice of replacement item.

The level of premium payable varies quite widely from company to company, and depends to a large extend on the amount of cover which you require. Good home security will attract lower premiums, and before you start shopping around you can take a few simple steps by fitting deadlocks to external doors, keyed locks to windows, and becoming part of your Neighbourhood Watch Scheme. A replacement policy on contents valued at $30,000 is likely to cost around $350 per annum, however, if you take out a contents policy in conjunction with buildings insurance through the same company, you will generally receive a discount of between five and ten per cent on both policies.

Life Insurance

Personal, or life, insurance, is also available through all major insurance companies, as well as through many smaller specialist insurers. There is an ever-increasing number of different types of life insurance policies available, and most people turn to a financial advisor to choose a suitable one for their own particular needs and disposable income. Combined savings/insurance policies are popular, providing for both life cover and medium term investment. Basic life insurance policies, in general, attract lower premiums, but are less financially advantageous during the lifetime of the policyholder. Most insurers will offer free (though not necessarily unbiased) consultation services. In addition, you should note that if you are employed and therefore paying into a superannuation fund, you are likely to have automatic life insurance (death benefits) of at least $45,000, which will be paid to your nominated beneficiary in the event of your accidental or natural death.

If you already hold life/personal insurance before you enter Australia, you must consult your insurers regarding your relocation. You should also discuss your policy with a tax accountant experienced in overseas investments, as any capital growth and income derived from your policy is likely to be taxed at the maximum rate in Australia. It is often possible to have your policy and funds transferred to an Australian company without incurring any costs or sacrificing any bonuses, and this may be financially advantageous in the long term.

Wills

If you die without having made a will, your estate will be distributed to your next of kin according to the various statutes of the state which provide for intestacy. These statutes vary from state to state, and distribution of the estate will vary according to the number and relationship of any immediate kin; in cases where there is no traceable family, the estate usually passes to the State Treasury. Clearly, it is preferable to make a will, especially if you have a de facto partner: the state of Victoria, for example, does not recognise the automatic right of inheritance of de facto spouses. Commonwealth estate duties and State death duties have been abolished in recent decades, and under the present law no such taxes are payable on any deceased estate, regardless of its size.

Proper estate planning can be complex, especially where large assets are involved, and in many cases can be complicated by the usefulness of family trusts. Professional assistance is highly recommended in order to maximise an estate's freedom from capital gains tax for the beneficiaries. A will must also fulfil certain formal and legal requirements in order to be valid and thus it is advisable to seek professional legal advice. Solicitors' costs for this service are likely to be around $150 per hour, however, some solicitors now offer will-making 'kits' which guide clients through the process for a much reduced fee. Recently, however, the Australian Consumers' Association evaluated a number of such will kits and deemed only one, the 'Legal Kits of Victoria Will Kit' satisfactory in its coverage of all essential matters, including family provision and capital gains tax. Lawyers are permitted to advertise in Australia, and testamentary services are frequently advertised in newspapers.

Most Australian states have, in recent years, relaxed many will-making formalities in an attempt to protect the true intentions of testators, but there are still important obligations which must be followed to ensure the validity of your will. A will must be in writing and must be signed by the testator in the presence of two witnesses. If a witness is a beneficiary, or married to a beneficiary of that will, the gift to that beneficiary will fail (although the whole will may not necessarily fail). It is of the utmost importance that beneficiaries are not requested to witness the will. Wills may be revoked by the testator at any time after execution, by destruction, by a later will, or by marriage; divorce , however, does not automatically revoke a will.

A will made overseas which is valid according to the law of the country where it was made, will be accepted for probate in Australia (a probate is an order or grant by the Supreme Court in favour of the executor authorising him/her to collect the assets of the deceased and deal with those assets according to the terms of the will), even though that will may not be valid according to the law of the particular state in which the deceased lived. A testator who has already made a valid will overseas can deal with assets acquired in Australia by means of a separate ancillary will.

Useful information on will making and other financial planning matters can be found on the 'My Money' website at www.mymoney.com.au.

Utilities

Electricity, gas and water supplies are controlled regionally by state authorities, and costs vary to some extent between states, and between urban and rural areas. Remote outback areas may attract particularly high charges, especially for water.

Electricity and Gas

Most new homes in Australia are connected to both gas and electricity supplies. Australia's plentiful supplies of Natural Gas mean that this energy source is relatively cheap, and savings are passed on to domestic consumers; most people thus choose to use gas in preference to electricity whereever possible. Many older homes, however, are not connected to the gas supply, and although this can easily be arranged by contacting the local state gas authority, it is likely to cost several hundred dollars for the service to be installed. Some remote areas do not have a natural gas supply, and in these regions, LPG is commonly used, obtained in bottled form, usually from the local garage.

Electricity is the most important source of domestic energy, but is considerably more expensive than gas. In an effort to make electricity more competitive, state authorities such as Western Power (in Western Australia) have introduced 'SmartPower'. SmartPower is a demand management system which relates the price paid for electricity to the cost of producing it, which is greater at times of peak demand. In order to take advantage of this system, a SmartPower Meter must be installed (at a cost, currently, of $199). The SmartMeter records the amount of electricity used in your home during different charging periods, enabling you to monitor your appliance usage and thus shift the times you run your appliances (washing machines and swimming pool filters, for example) to lower your electricity costs. In general, a family with a swimming pool will recoup the cost of the SmartMeter within half a year, and will make ongoing savings of at least 30 per cent on their previous power bills.

The voltage in Australia is 240/250V and the current is alternating at 50 Hz. The power points take three-pin plugs which have two diagonally slanting pins above one straight pin. Appliances brought from the UK will work throughout Australia, after changing the plugs, but those from the USA will not.

Solar power

Australia is a world leader in solar technology, and Australian homes first began using solar power back in 1953. Today, many homes in areas with enough sunshine (most areas!) use solar power to heat their hot water. A solar hot water heater provides around 95 per cent of hot water energy needs (for washing and home heating) free from the sun, resulting in enormous savings on traditional energy costs. The capital cost of a solar hot water heater is high, but once installed, they are maintenance-free and have a very long lifetime, so that the initial costs are soon outweighed by the benefits. A solar hot water system looks like a largish, flat, black rectangle, with a cylinder at the top; it is installed on the roof, usually on the western side of the house where it will receive the most sun, and is aesthetically unobtrusive. Solarhart, Australia's largest supplier of solar hot water systems, has an informative website at www.solarhart.com.au.

Domestic Climate Control

Australian homes are very seldom centrally heated, except in those few areas where the climate is sufficiently cold to require it. Instead, most homes are heated on a fairly ad hoc basis, usually by a combination of portable electric fan heaters or radiators, reverse-cycle air-conditioning, and slow combustion stoves. Pot-belly stoves or other solid fuel enclosed fires are becoming increasingly popular as a means of heating the main living areas of the home, and can even be installed so that they heat the water supply as well. Coal fires are banned by law, and coal-substitute fires are extremely unusual; open fires and slow combustion stoves are wood-fuelled, most commonly by mallee roots, which can be bought by the tonne. A tonne of mallee roots (very dense knots of gnarled wood, which do not need chopping) will cost around $100, and will heat an average family home for an entire winter. Wood suppliers (who are often farmers clearing their fields) advertise in the classifieds columns of local newspapers.

Home cooling rather than heating is the focus of most Australian climate control, and almost every home will have some method of lowering the internal temperature. Electric ceiling fans are popular and very effective, as well as being cheap to run and to install. There are several different types of airconditioning in common use: the evaporative type is the cheapest and is generally portable, but requires an open window to work effectively; reverse cycle is more effective, and can also be used to heat the room in winter. The unit for reverse-cycle airconditioning is installed in an external wall. Homes in the upper end of the market will often have ducted airconditioning, which is run from a central plant in the roof or garage, distributing cold air through vents to every room. Air-conditioning is essential in the northern regions of Australia, both in the home and the car, and all offices and shops throughout Australia are air-conditioned.

Keeping cool on the cheap

Australian architects are very aware of the need to design for the climate, and new houses will, for example, have few or very small windows on the hot, western side. Large windows and patio doors will always be shaded by a pergola, often covered with UV resistant plastic. Solar films, which allow in light but not heat,

can be applied to windows, and are a cost effective way of keeping homes cool. Climate management in Australia is second-nature to locals, but methods may surprise those brought up in a cooler climate. The British response to the sun is to throw open all the windows and enjoy: in Australia, this would be considered eccentric, if not completely mad. If you want to keep your home cooling costs down, you should do as the locals do:
– at sunrise, get up and close every single window in the house. Pull down all blinds, close all curtains; if there are awnings or shutters on outside windows, pull them into place. Close any vent that allows the entry of external air.
– When entering and leaving your home during the day, make sure that any door is open for as brief a time as possible. The aim at all times should be to prevent the hot external air from coming inside.
– When the exterior temperature drops below the interior temperature (usually at sunset), it is time to open up. Throw open everything that has been closed: windows and doors will have lockable screens which will allow you to do this in safety. Leave everything open all night, to allow the house to cool down before the next day's onslaught.

On really extreme days, try 'hosing down' (but not if there are water restrictions in operation). This method involves soaking the exterior walls and patio areas with water from the garden hose, and should be done after dark to avoid instant evaporation.

Water

Water is a scarce and valuable commodity in Australia, and is treated with respect by most people. All urban areas are well served by high quality, clean water supplies from reservoirs, but extreme summer conditions and drought can mean the frequent imposition of water restrictions on non-essential water use. Public education campaigns encourage water-saving measures, such as shorter showers and water recycling (washing-up water on the garden, for example). Garden watering is generally done after dusk to avoid evaporation.

Water is supplied to homes and businesses by state authorities who build and maintain reservoirs, and ensure the safety and management of the water supply. Water rates are imposed to fund these services and are paid annually or quarterly by consumers. In addition, most authorities levy an 'excess water' charge, which is a per-litre charge for all water in excess of a certain (low) minimum covered by the water rates. The excess water charge, which can amount to hundreds of dollars per year for a family (especially if you have a pool, which will need daily topping-up), provides a keen incentive to economise on water use. Homeowners will pay both rates and excess water, while people who are renting will usually pay only the excess water charge, which is passed on by the landlord. Currently, the excess water charge levied by Sydney Water is 90 cents per kilolitre (1,000 litres). Water rates for 1998/98 are $88 per quarter. The high cost of water in Australia means that most authorities offer various payment options: a single, prompt, annual rates payment attracts a discount of 5 per cent; a biannual payment may be made without further charge; or a quarterly payment may be made, with a small credit charge. Seniors are entitled to a 25 per cent rebate on their water and sewage rates charges, subject to certain payment conditions outlined in literature available from local water authorities. Families suffering financial hardship can apply to make payments under pre-payment budget schemes.

Excess water charges mean that it is expensive to keep domestic gardens green during the summer months using mains water. Many Australian homes, therefore, have irrigation/sprinkler systems, known as 'reticulation', which water the garden automatically from a private artesian bore. Homeowners frequently pay to have a bore sunk in their garden, sometimes to a depth of up to 150 metres, to tap into the water-table. The cost of the bore can be very high (around $4,000) and is determined by its depth and the geographical structure of the land, however, in the long term, a bore enables enormous savings on water bills. Bore water can *only* be used for gardening, as it is unsuitable for drinking and its high mineral content means that it will stain swimming pool surfaces. During periods of water restriction, bore owners are the only people who are able to water their gardens sufficiently to maintain them. All mains garden watering must be done before dawn or after dusk to reduce wastage due to evaporation (and, in fact, even homes with bore reticulation usually follow this method to avoid scorching leaves and grass). Most newer Australian gardens have moved away from the traditional British garden towards gardens in which native Australian plants predominate. Native plants have adapted to dry conditions over the millennia and require very little water to stay alive; their cultivation also encourages native birdlife. Wood chips and extensive patio areas are also popular, reducing the area of garden devoted to lawn, which is expensive and time consuming to maintain in Australia.

In rural areas, domestic rain-water tanks are frequently used to collect precipitation for drinking, washing, and gardening. If your home or holiday cottage has a rain water tank, make sure that it has a cover to prevent rodents and native marsupials drowning in it and contaminating the water.

Australian mains water is completely safe, and the taste is generally good. In most areas the supply is fluoridated to promote dental health. Unlike the water supply in most British areas, Australian water is 'soft', that is, it does not contain limescale. This means that soaps lather easily, tap fittings and appliances do not require the same maintenance, and dishwashers do not need the addition of salt . During the summer months, however, garden hoses and domestic swimming pools can be the site of the bacteria which cause amoebic meningitis, and it is extremely important to maintain chemical levels in pools, and to let the water run for a while before allowing children to play with or drink from garden hoses.

Residential Rates & Other Charges

Council rates are levied annually and are the responsibility of the property owner. They are a tax on property and not on the individual. Tenants do not have to meet any council rates charges, which include a Refuse Charge for the collection of domestic rubbish, and charges for amenities provided by the council. Council rates are determined by the location and size of the property, and are calculated on its gross rental value. Rates will be higher if you buy a house in a high demand area with excellent services and amenities. On an average, middle-class Australian family home, you can expect charges of approximately the following:

Refuse charge	$170
General rates	$600
Instalment surcharge	$30
Total charge	$800

Rates and charges are payable to the local or shire council and can be paid in two instalments, in which case an instalment surcharge applies. A discount is sometimes given for prompt payment, but more often prompt payers are rewarded by entry into a council draw which will offer a substantial prize, such as an international holiday or free rates for a year. Details of the council raffle will be published in the local newspaper in addition to being supplied with the rates notice.

Telecommunications

Until the late 1980s, Australia's telecommunications were controlled by a state monopoly, Telecom Australia. Since then, the market has gradually been deregulated, allowing at first just a single competitor, Optus. In 1997, however, full deregulation was achieved, and there now are a host of options in the telecommunications market, resulting in vastly reduced costs and, in general, a much more competitive service. Telecom still dominates the local and domestic market, although Optus has a significant share of the interstate and international long-distance market. In NSW, local calls are now also being offered by Optus, and this service will soon be extended to other states. International telecommunications links are provided by the Overseas Telecommunication Commission (OTC). Since deregulation, ISDN suppliers have multiplied exponentially, and it is now possible to call abroad very cheaply by subscribing to one of these services, such as Global One Access or OneTel. Services and special offers are advertised in daily newspapers, and after subscribing, you simply prefix a special call-code to the number you want to dial. You will receive a separate bill from your supplier, and the service can be run concurrently with your Telecom or Optus account. Call rates to the UK are currently around 30 cents per minute and are falling almost daily – for comparison, in 1993, it cost $1.60 per minute to call England.

All Australian homes are fitted with a telephone line, and a second line with a different number can be installed for $150. Telephone bills are issued quarterly by each of the suppliers whose services you use. Telecom and Optus bills include local metered calls, STD (interstate/long distance national) calls, and ISD (international) calls, as well as service fees, equipment and any other charges. Service charges are around $40 per quarter, and customers can choose either to own their own telephone handsets (in which case there are no equipment charges), or to rent handsets from Telecom or Optus for around $5 per quarter per phone. Fax machines operate via the standard phone line, and their use is charged in the same way as a phone call. Mobile phone services are run by various providers, such as Pacstar, and offer much the same range of contract options as available in the UK and USA; once again, they are billed separately from the main phone number.

Probably the most significant difference between the British and Australian telephone systems is that local calls are charged at a *flat rate* of 25 cents from a domestic phone (on a payphone, 40 cents), regardless of the length of the call. Whether you are on the phone for three seconds or three hours, the cost of the call is always the same, and you never need to worry about running up your phone bill or calling during economy periods if you are phoning within the suburban boundaries of your city or town. Flat rate local calling is of particular significance in the electronic communications sector and is one reason why Australia leads the world in domestic internet access: for the cost of a 25 cent call to your internet service provider, you can surf the net for as long as you wish without incurring any further calling charges. Long distance national and international calls are, however, charged according to the distance and the length of the call, as well as by time zone: Day rate (9am-6pm) is the most expensive, Economy rate (7am-9am, 6pm-9pm) is somewhat cheaper, and Night rate (9pm-7am and all weekend) the most economical for national calls.

The codes for dialling Australia directly from the UK are:

Adelaide	00-61 8
Brisbane	00-61 7
Canberra	00-61 6
Darwin	00-61 8
Hobart	00-61 3
Perth	00-61 8
Melbourne	00-61 3
Sydney	00-61 2

This code should prefix the local number, which will be 8 digits long in most capital cities, and 6 digits long in more rural areas. Telephone numbers were made longer by a one digit prefix in May 1998, and numbers found in older phone directories and guides will no longer be current. International directory assistance (from the UK, call 155) can advise on these changes should you have any out-of-date contact numbers. To dial overseas from Australia, prefix the number you require firstly with your international call supplier over-ride number, then add the international dialling code 0011. International faxes are sent using the code 0015.

Removals

Most people making a long-term or permanent move abroad will want to arrange to take some or all of their personal effects with them. The costs involved in doing so can be high, but a carefully planned move will save you money by minimising setting-up expenses on arrival. Household items vary widely in replacement value from country to country, so a little research will pay off in deciding what to take and what to leave behind. In making your calculations you should consider the second-hand sale value of your effects in your home country against the both the cost of shipping and insurance, and the cost of replacement. Car boot sales are an excellent way to dispose of the accumulated junk that you will inevitably uncover when you start going through your cupboards with a major international move in mind, but don't underestimate the sentimental value of items: there are some things that will simply have to go with you, no matter how worthless or unlikely.

Household Goods

There are many removal companies specialising in international shipping. The large national firms advertise in the regional Yellow Pages telephone directories, along with smaller local firms, and any reputable firm will be able to outline their costs (charged per cubic meter) over the telephone. The quality of the service provided is an important consideration when undertaking an international move and you should make sure that the remover offers 'export-quality packing' and deals with every aspect of the customs and shipping process. Once you have established a short-list of removers, you should request a formal quote (which will be free of charge). An estimator will visit your home and examine the contents of every room to assess the cubic meterage to be packed and shipped. Antiques and other items of special value may be assessed at a different rate. Most removers also broker their own insurance packages, which are generally charged at around three per cent of the value of the consignment, and although this can amount to a considerable sum on an average family's effects, it is an indispensable expense. Your valued possessions will spend around three months going from store to ship to customs warehouse before finally being unpacked in your new home, and it is very rare for a consignment to arrive completely undamaged.

Professional removers are remarkably efficient and can pack an average family house in one or two days. For a move to Australia, they will use export-quality packing, which is much more time-consuming than packing for a local removal. The removalists will wrap all furniture items in paper blankets, dismantling them where possible, and will also individually wrap every item of kitchenware and any other small items. Everything else will be packed in specially designed heavy-duty cardboard cartons (such as book boxes, linen boxes and picture boxes). International shipping is costed by volume not weight, and a good remover will pack lightweight items, such as linen, inside empty furniture (for example, chests-of-drawers) to reduce volume. You should bear this in mind when considering what to take: it may mean that if you plan to take certain furniture items, you will in effect be able to take linen or children's stuffed toys for 'free'. It is possible to self-pack for an international move, but the small cost saving it permits is cancelled out by the higher insurance premiums you must then pay.

Extensive list-making will probably play a large part in your daily life when organising a move on this scale, and it is important to consider carefully which items to take with you to Australia. The British Association of Removers (address below) provides a useful list which may help in planning. As a general rule, it is much cheaper and easier to ship furniture than to replace it with new items at your destination, with some exceptions. Beds do not travel well, as a mattress which is packed vertically for three months will generally arrive with sagging springs; pianos do not benefit from the sudden climate change, may warp in the moist sea air, and frequently cannot be properly retuned; and vinyl seating is inappropriate for hot-weather countries. All Australian homes, whether rented or bought, come with a cooker installed (which is never taken with you when you move) and it is therefore redundant to ship your own. You would also be well advised to buy a new refrigerator on arrival, as Australian fridges are much larger and have extra fan assistance to cope with the climate, as well as a new television and video. British televisions can be converted to work in Australia, but it is expensive and often less than successful. Fax machines and telephones cannot be imported unless they conform to the Australian telecommunications standards. Most newer Australian homes also have built-in wardrobes, and so you may also decide to leave these behind, especially as their large volume makes freestanding wardrobes expensive to ship.

Taking your Car

Most removal companies also offer the option of shipping your motor vehicle and will supply all the necessary information including lists of customs and port charges, as well as providing a quote for shipping a private motor car from the UK to Australia. The services provided by the shipper should include full preparation for containerisation, for example, covering the interior with floor mats and seat covers, and inserting silica dessicant bags or pillows to help avoid the possibility of condensation damage in the car. The car will be packed into a 'sole use' twenty foot ISO Reefer Container and secured in accordance with manufacturers' recommendations at the removers' warehouse. The quote should include return haulage of the container to the UK export loading berth, all UK port and handling charges, all export and customs documentation, provision of Bills of Loading to a nominated address on arrival, and all freight charges through to the destination port. Insurance is calculated at around 1.5% of the car's value, and Australian unpacking and quarantine inspection charges are payable on arrival. Shipping to Australia takes between four and eight weeks, depending on the final destination.

In addition to meeting the costs involved in transporting your vehicle to Australia, you will also be liable on arrival for the cost of ensuring that your vehicle meets Australian safety standards under the Motor Vehicle Standards Act of 1989. This process, known as 'compliance', can be very expensive, and your car will not be able to receive temporary registration (and thus be driven) until it has been completed. The total amount of money involved in shipping a car to Australia, including freight, taxes, insurance, compliance, and reregistration, means that unless your vehicle is very special, rare or luxurious, it is rarely worthwhile. For those who decide to proceed, further information is given below in the section on Australian Customs.

Pets

Moving your pets to Australia is as complicated and expensive a process as moving yourself and your family. Australian quarantine rules are extremely strict in order to protect the disease-free status of Australian livestock afforded by the country's geographical isolation. Most commonly, new arrivals choose to import their family pets, generally cats or dogs, and for this an Import Permit must be obtained from the Principal Veterinary Officer (Quarantine) in the State or Territory into which you plan to bring your animal. Stringent health and certification requirements must be met, which include vaccinating the animal against an extensive list of diseases as well as testing for the absence of certain viruses 21 days prior to export. All cats and dogs must be treated for internal parasites 14 days before export and must pass a clinical examination 48 hours before shipment. Each animal must be accompanied by a certificate of inspection issued by an Official Veterinarian. The types of containers in which animals may be exported are also strictly specified by Australian law and an animal will not be permitted to enter the country if it arrives in a non-approved container. Both dogs and cats are required to undergo a period of quarantine on arrival in Australia at one of three centres (in Victoria, New South Wales, and Western Australia). If you are moving to another state, you will incur additional costs in freighting your animal to your new home after it completes its period of quarantine. Dogs and cats from approved rabies-free countries (which include the UK) which meet all the vaccination and certification requirements for import are currently quarantined for a period of 30 days.

Costs for importing pets are high: shipping a cat to Australia can range from £300 to £350, whilst shipping a dog the size of a labrador may cost as much as

£1,000. The cost of the extensive veterinary treatment and testing required for import needs to be taken into account, and you must also allow for the quarantine costs payable in advance in Australia. A pet quarantined for the standard period of 30 days will add at least another $1000 to your moving costs.

Useful Addresses

British Association of Removers, 3 Churchill Court, 58 Station Road, North Harrow, Middlesex; tel 0181-861 3331.

Crown Worldwide Movers (operating in the UK as *Scotpac*), Unit 9 Netherwood Estate, Radcliffe Road, Atherstone, CV9 1JA; tel 01827-714631.

Allied Pickfords, Heritage House, 345 Southbury Road, Enfield, Middlesex, EN1 1UP; freephone 0800 289229.

Karman Shipping Services (Motor Vehicle Shipping Specialists), 44 Chestnut Hill, Leighton Buzzard, Bedforshire LU7 7TR; tel 01525-851545; fax 01525-850996.

Ministry of Agriculture, Animal Export, Hook Rise South, Tolworth, Surbiton, Surrey KT6 7NF; tel 0181-330 4411. Information and application forms for Ministry of Agriculture export certificate; also lists of Official Veterinarians.

Ladyhaye Livestock Shipping, Hare Lane, Blindley Heath, Lingfield, Surrey RH7 6JB; tel 01342-832161.

Worldwide Animal Travel, 43 London Road, Brentwood, Essex CM14 4NN; tel 01277-231611; fax 01277-262726.

The Australian Quarantine Information Service: has detailed information on its website at www.dpie.gov.au/aqis/homepage/aqishome.html

Australian Customs Regulations

Australian Customs Service regulations are extremely stringent in order to protect Australian flora and fauna from the many diseases affecting plants and animals, such as rabies, foot-and-mouth disease, and BSE, found elsewhere in the world. Any wood or wooden artifacts, including furniture, must be declared to Customs on arrival in the country, so that they can first be quarantined and fumigated. This provision extends to items such as straw hats and wooden kitchen utensils. Garden equipment, lawnmowers, and outdoor furniture will be specially inspected, fumigated and cleaned (at your expense). Products made from protected wildlife species, non-approved cordless phones, live animals, and weapons and firearms (which are either prohibited or require a permit and safety testing) are also prohibited imports. You must also declare all goods of animal and plant origin, including all fresh, frozen or tinned food, fruit, vegetables and flowers. Penalties of up to $50,000 may be levied on people who contravene customs regulations, so it is important to take some care when filling out your customs declarations forms before shipping your personal effects, and when arriving in the country. International flights are fumigated before passengers are allowed to disembark to ensure that no diseases enter the country on your person, your clothing or luggage. Although the spray used can be slightly irritating (it is recommended that you cover your nose and mouth although the chemicals have been declared perfectly safe), it is an important part of the process of making sure Australia stays disease-free.

Like most countries in the world today, illicit drugs, including marijuana, are strictly prohibited and Australian Customs are very efficient in policing the entry of drugs into Australia. Flights arriving from Asia are often very slow to clear customs as officials will be especially rigorous in checking passengers travelling from or through this region. Under *no* circumstances should you agree to carry illicit drugs or any other package for anyone else, as you will bear the responsibility for any prohibited substance found in your possession.

Personal effects shipped into Australia for your own use, and owned and used by you previously, do not attract duties or other taxes on arrival in port. This exemption includes motor vehicles which have been owned and used by you for the previous two years, however, all other privately imported cars (including second-hand cars) will be subject to the same taxes at the same rate as commercially imported vehicles. Tourists and temporary residents may bring a motor vehicle or motor cycle into Australia for a period of up to 12 months without paying duty provided that it is re-exported from Australia at the end of that period. For this concession to apply, you will need a *Carnet de Passages en Douanes* issued by an overseas organisations which has a reciprocal arrangement with the Australian Automobile Association, as well as a cash or bank security equal to the amount of duty and sales tax otherwise payable.

The current duty-free allowance for travellers includes one litre of alcohol, 250 cigarettes and up to $400 of duty-free goods. It is your responsibility to declare anything else that may be liable for sales tax or duty. Duty-free shops at Australian airports are, in general, cheaper than those in the UK, and there are shops prior to Customs in the arrivals hall of most international airports, which means it may be better not to 'buy before you fly'.

The Australian Customs Service provides full information on all aspects of its operation on its website at www.customs.gov.au

Buying a Car in Australia

Australian cars are right-hand-drive, as in Britain, and since 1989 the importation of left-hand-drive vehicles has been prohibited. Although there remains a small number of left-hand-drive cars imported before 1989, in general, these cars are not well-suited to Australian driving conditions, and parts and servicing are expensive. For the UK immigrant, driving conditions and road regulations will be reassuringly familiar, although you will notice that cars tend to be larger than in Europe. Cheaper petrol, wider roads and easier parking all contribute to a preference for more spacious and powerful family vehicles. Australia has a well-established motor industry with Ford and General Motors Holden building a large proportion of cars on the road. Japanese cars also have a much stronger presence than in Europe, and Mitsubishi, Toyota and Nissan all produce cars in Australia to Japanese levels of quality control. The practice of 'rebadging' means that many models will be familiar in their appearance to visitors and new arrivals, although they are likely to have different names. European cars of any model are very expensive in Australia because of high importation costs, which now includes a prohibitive 'luxury tax'. This tax applies not only to obviously up-market luxury vehicles, such as Mercedes, but also to common or garden Peugeots, Fiats and Golfs; as a result there is a certain prestige value in driving such vehicles, although in many cases home-grown versions are superior in finish and performance. The luxury tax also applies to imported parts which can make servicing a car of European origin very expensive. As a general rule, you should expect to pay considerably more for a vehicle in Australia than you would in the UK, especially if you are considering a second-hand car.

The registration and taxing of vehicles is the responsibility of State Departments of Transport, and whilst some states (for example, NSW) have a system equivalent to the British MOT, others do not. As a result of this, and because of the high cost of new cars, there tend to be many more older cars on the road than you will find in the UK. It is important, especially if you buy an older vehicle, that you keep your car's registration (equivalent to a tax disk) current, as, once lapsed, renewal cannot be effected until the car has undergone an extremely thorough safety check at the police vehicle registration centre. Once headed for the inspection pits because of expired registration, it is usually difficult and expensive to get the car back on the road. Police also have the power to stop any vehicle in an obvious state of disrepair, and will frequently issue a 'Yellow Sticker' which identifies the car as unroadworthy. The car must not be driven until it has been repaired and inspected by the vehicle licensing authority. Emissions control is also taken very seriously and other drivers may, and often do, report vehicles with dirty exhaust emissions: the driver will receive a letter requiring that the problem be remedied, and this may be followed up by an inspection.

Most newer Australian cars have automatic transmission in preference to manual, and many have airconditioning and tinted windows to reduce problems of heat and glare. Sunroofs are unusual, as extreme temperature conditions make them impractical – Australians aim to keep heat out, not bask in it. All modern cars run on unleaded petrol, and for older cars, 4-Star (known as 'Super') is still sold. Many larger cars, particularly of the popular off-road variety, run on diesel, which is significantly cheaper than petrol.

New Cars

Buying a new car in Australia is little different from doing so in the UK or elsewhere. Manufacturers market their vehicles through licensed dealers who advertise in the daily press and in the local Yellow Pages. The new car market is currently very competitive and it is important to shop around widely. There is always room for negotiation on price or on bonus extras such as airconditioning, stereo, and additional safety features. Traditionally, new car prices are discounted significantly at the end of the Australian financial year which falls in late June, when dealers particularly aim to attract the business and fleet buying markets. Car models which are about to be superseded are also often very much reduced in price to enable dealers to clear their stock and can be excellent buys; look out, too, for ex-demonstration vehicles which may have no more than a few hundred kilometres on the clock. The daily newspapers in each capital city generally allocate one day of the week to a motoring section or motoring advertising (on Wednesday and Saturday in *The West Australian*, for example), and scouring these pages will generally reveal the best buys and allow you to compare dealer prices. A number of car buyers' guides and magazines are widely available in newsagents, providing detailed technical information and assessments of every car currently on the market. Note that there are a number of abbreviations in common use in car advertisements, including abs (anti-lock braking system), ac (air conditioning), at (automatic transmission), cc (cruise control), cl (central locking), ps (power steering), pw (power windows), srs (supplementary restraint system), and mags (alloy wheels).

Two out of every five new cars bought in Australia are registered in company names and if you expect to use your car for business purposes, most dealers will have specially tailored schemes to maximise the tax benefits for your company. Popular manufacturers like Ford, Holden, Toyota and Mitsubishi also provide business versions of their mainstream models. Leasing, rather than buying, is frequently advantageous to the business car user and offers both tax efficiency and ease of replacement. Other schemes offer a guaranteed replacement value (if the car is bought with dealer finance and serviced by them throughout the period of the contract), allowing an upgrade to a new model after a designated number of years.

Used Cars

As in Britain, new cars tend to depreciate dramatically in value once in use, and given their high price in Australia, many people prefer to buy a used car. These are available from both specialist second-hand dealers and through the used car division of licensed new car dealers, as well as by private sale. Cars offered for sale privately are usually advertised in the classifieds section of the main state and local newspapers, and in auto classifieds magazines such as *Car Mart*. Many dealers of new cars also sell used cars obtained by them through part-exchange (known in Australia as a 'trade-in'); such cars are likely to be more expensive than an equivalent vehicle sold privately, but will usually have the advantage of a dealer's warranty. By law, used cars offered for sale above a certain benchmark price (which varies from state to state) may not be offered for sale by a dealer without the provision of a warranty, the minimum terms of which are also laid down by the state government.

Travellers and temporary residents may find it more convenient to purchase a vehicle under a guaranteed buy-back arrangement. A number of firms specialise in selling cars by this method , ensuring that the vehicle is legal and roadworthy at the time of purchase and guaranteeing to repurchase it at the end of the stay.

Car theft is prevalent in many cities in Australia, so if you choose to buy a car privately you should ensure that the vehicle is neither stolen nor otherwise financially encumbered. If you buy a car on which the vendor still owes money, the vehicle can be repossessed if they default on any payment. Remember that the loan company has first call on its security, and you could lose a considerable amount of money. Vehicle registrations may be checked free of charge against the government registers of encumbered vehicles, listed below:

VIC: Vicroads, Vehicles Security Register, cnr Princess & Drummond Streets, Carlton VIC 3053, tel 13 1171.

QLD: QLD Motor Vehicles Security Register, 7th floor, 126 Margaret Street, Brisbane QLD 4000, or PO Box 38, Brisbane QLD 4001, tel 07-3227 7111.

SA: Vehicle Security Register, 60 Wakefield Street, Adelaide SA 5000, or PO Box 616, Adelaide SA 5001, tel 08-8232 0800.

NSW: Register of Encumbered Vehicles, level 2, 47 Scott Street, Liverpool NSW 2170. Tel 1800 424 988.

WA: Register of Encumbered Vehicles, 6th floor, 251 Hay Street, East Perth WA 6004, or PO Box 6355, East Perth WA 6004, tel 1800 198 333.

In the Northern Territory, enquiries should be directed to the NSW register.

When buying a used car, it is usual to pay to have an authorised, qualified mechanic from one of the automobile associations make a thorough mechanical examination. The cost of such an examination will be less than $100, but could save thousands by warning you off a potential lemon. It is not necessary to be a member of the automobile association to use such a service, although members will receive a discounted rate. Federal regulations govern safety standards including seat belts, emissions, tyres, and engine noise, and state governments may have additional legislation. A vehicle which fails to conform to safety standards will not be registered until modifications have been made.

Once you have found and purchased your new used car, you will need to fill out a form to transfer ownership into your name. These forms are available from the local vehicle licensing centre, and it is usually the vendor's responsibility to supply them at the time of purchase, signing the appropriate sections. The value of the vehicle must be declared on the form, and from this a transfer tax or stamp duty is calculated. The amount of stamp duty varies widely according to the value of the vehicle, ranging from tens to hundreds of dollars, and must be paid within 30 days to effect the transfer of ownership.

Motor Insurance

Third Party Insurance is compulsory in Australia and the cost of this insurance is included in the vehicle registration charge paid to the State or Territory government. Third Party Insurance covers the driver for injuries to any other person caused in the course of driving, however, insurance against third party property damage must be taken out separately, and is the responsibility of the car owner. Around 80 per cent of Australian car owners choose to take out extra private insurance.

In Australia, unlike Britain, it is the vehicle rather than the driver which is covered by any insurance. Thus, anyone who has your permission to do so may drive your car (providing they have a full Australian or equivalent licence and the car is privately owned) and will be fully covered by your existing insurance. Motor vehicle insurance tends to be slightly cheaper in Australia than in the UK, but is subject to the same kinds of variables. Factors affecting insurance costs include the make and model of the car, the location of your residence, and the age and experience of the usual driver. Sports cars and high performance cars attract higher premiums, as do 'modified' vehicles; and drivers resident in non-metropolitan areas are likely to pay less for their insurance, although this varies widely and may mean significant differences in quotes if you shop around. Young drivers under the age of 25 will invariably be charged more, however, most companies now offer scaled premiums for those over 25, as well as discounted policies for the over-55s. Drivers who borrow to finance the purchase of their vehicle will usually also pay more in premiums. Insurers are increasingly offering policy-holders a choice of excess, ranging from $50 to $500: a lower excess will generally mean a higher premium, although this can be offset by your no-claims record. Drivers with an motor vehicle insurance history gained overseas are usually able to 'import' their no-claims bonus, up to its full value. It is important to bring a letter from your previous insurer confirming your no-claims status so that it can be immediately applied to your new policy.

A new development in Australian car insurance has been the introduction of 'agreed-value' sum-insured options. In the past, most policies paid on the basis of the 'market value' of your car at the time of the claim, however, the new type of policy enables you to agree a fixed value for the term of your policy. An agreed value policy is generally a little more expensive, but may be worthwhile especially for older vehicles. Some policies also offer added extras such as travel and medical insurance. The cost of car hire and accommodation in case of accident may also be useful, as may be the use of a courtesy car while repairs are made. Some policies offer brand-new replacement vehicles for damaged cars less than one year old.

Third Party Property Insurance

Third Party Property Insurance (TPPI) would covers the cost of any damage done by your vehicle in the course of an accident, but does *not* cover the damage done to your own car. TPPI is a very economical insurance option, rarely exceeding $200, and is popular with owners of old cars with little resale value.

Comprehensive Insurance

Comprehensive cover costs considerably more than TTPI and ranges between $275-$600, with discounts of up to 65 per cent available to holders of a full no-claims bonus. Insurance companies assess their premiums by the following criteria

age: of both you and your car (if you are less 25 years old, you will pay more).

residence: do you live in a high risk area?

experience: how long have you been driving?

accident record: do you have one?

sex: in certain age groups females have fewer accident claims than males.

value: of the car.

make and model: some models pose a higher risk of theft or are more expensive to repair.

business or private use: insurance premiums are higher for business vehicles.

finance: unfinanced vehicles are cheaper to insure.

trailer/caravan: you are likely to need a separate policy for these vehicles to cover against damage cause by side-swiping.

The cost of comprehensive motor vehicle insurance varies widely according to these and other factors. The best policy is to shop around through the Yellow Pages, or by using an insurance broker. Forty per cent of policies are now placed through brokers, who have immediate access to a huge range of policies and are thus able to obtain the cheapest one for your needs with a minimum of difficulty. A broker is legally bound to operate in the interests of the policy buyer and not of the companies whose policies he represents. Nonetheless, it is important to ensure that a broker is reputable, and so you should check that the firm is registered with the NIBA (National Insurance Brokers Association). Brokers are paid either by commission from insurance companies, or by fees charged to the consumer for their advice; most brokers, however, will not charge a fee when arranging simple domestic and motor vehicle insurance. If a broker does charge a fee it must be fully declared at the beginning of the transaction.

Insurance companies, automobile associations offering insurance, and insurance brokers can all be found in the Yellow Pages. In addition, one major company, FAI, now allows customers to take out insurance over the internet at its website. Transactions may be undertaken 24 hours a day with the whole quote-confirmation-payment process conducted online in a secure environment. FAI currently offers a 10 per cent discount to customers using this service. Australia's biggest and most reputable insurance companies include AMP, MMI, FAI, Legal and General, SGIO, GIO, and RAC.

Useful Contacts

FAI Insurance, www.fai.com.au, tel 13 1000.

MMI Insurance, tel 13 2664.

Legal & General Insurance, tel 1800 812 159.

SGIO Insurance, tel 13 3233.

GIO Insurance, tel 13 1010.

National Insurance Brokers Association of Australia, tel 1800 252 558.

Daily Life

One of the great attractions of Australia for many immigrants and other new arrivals is its quality of life. Cosmopolitan cities border a landscape of sometimes awe-inspiring beauty, and most people enjoy circumstances in which work and play combine to provide the sort of relaxed and comfortable lifestyle available only to the very wealthy in Europe. Public facilities of all types are generally good, and standards in health care and education are very high relative to other industrialised nations. Housing is also generally more spacious and affordable than in the UK and other European countries (although more expensive than in the USA), and most homes have gardens and outdoor living areas designed to take advantage of the climate and opportunities for family and other entertaining. Australia is one of the world's most urbanised societies, and nearly 90 per cent of the population live in coastal cities consisting of sprawling suburbs with a high-rise city centre or CBD (central business district). All of Australia's state capitals are built on or very near the water – even the inland city of Canberra was designed around a giant artificial lake, allowing residents to partake in the water-based activities which are part of the Australian lifestyle. In the shadow of the city's skyscrapers, labyrinths of interconnecting courtyards and arcades offer shopping, cafés, and restaurants, and the country has in recent years become world-famous for its restaurant culture and cuisine. Leisure is important to Australians, and the weekend has become a sacred institution devoted to pottering in the garden, preparing the family barbecue, or sports. Parks and ovals are overtaken by children playing cricket, football, or riding their bicycles; some families head for the bush, others for the beach, and national parks are busy with picnickers. Recent changes to trading regulations mean that shops which previously closed at 1pm on Saturday are now open all day, but there is still significant resistance to Sunday trading. Nonetheless, larger shops will generally open for at least a part of Sunday and more and more working people are using the weekend to catch up on their shopping. In summer, though, the beach rules: called the 'great leveller', the beach is accessible to all ages and social classes and is the cornerstone of Australian life.

Education

Australian education is internationally regarded as being of a high standard, particularly in its tertiary institutions. An Australian honours degree holds a higher status than a UK honours degree in the UK university system, and holders of such degrees on scholarships to premier universities, such as Oxford and Cambridge, are exempted from one year of study at postgraduate level. International surveys of K-12 educational standards recognise Australian literacy and numeracy levels as being higher than in the UK across the board, and Australia also scores up at the top of the list, with Germany and Japan, in terms of science education. Early education practice is significantly different and many experts attribute later academic success to the different emphasis in teaching methods of young children.

Education is the responsibility of state governments, and is compulsory between the ages of five and 15. Upper secondary schooling begins after year 10 and continues on to age 17 or 18; these extra years are mandatory for students considering further education and school retention rates are very high, averaging around 70 per cent. Around 70 per cent of Australian children attend free, government-funded schools, which are mostly co-educational and non-religious; there are no free church-run, government-assisted schools, as in Britain. A parallel fee-paying sector also exists, and most such schools are run by various religious institutions. Children who need to attend boarding school in their secondary school years because of rural isolation will usually attend schools of this type, and their boarding costs are subsidised by the government. In the primary years, children in the outback are educated by the 'School of the Air' which provides distance learning by radio and correspondence.

Australian Outlook publishes a booklet called *Choosing a School for your Child* for emmigrants to New South Wales, Victoria and Queensland, details of which are given below. These publications give useful information regarding the kinds of schools available in these states, and answer many of the questions which arise when choosing a new school in an unfamiliar country.

Australia's academic year follows the calendar year, running from January to December, so that the long summer holidays of around six or seven weeks coincide with the Christmas period.

The Structure of the Education System

The educational system is much more uniform in Australia than it is in the UK, and both the private and state sectors operate on the same patterns and curricula. Primary education in Australia takes six or seven years, depending on the state, and secondary education either five or six years correspondingly. Wherever you live in Australia, the combined length of primary and secondary education is twelve years, and the school years are numbered Years 1 to 12. Western Australia, Queensland, South Australia and the Northern Territory offer seven years of primary school and five years of secondary school. New South Wales, Victoria and the Australian Capital Territory offer six years each of primary and secondary education, and Tasmania offers either six or seven years of primary and either six or five years of secondary, depending on the location of the school and the age of the student.

Preschool. Preschooling is available for children aged four and five years old, and provides educational programmes in which young children are encouraged to develop their abilities, skills and knowledge of the world. Preschool centres operate in association with local primary schools, and, where possible, are located in the same grounds. In Western Australia and some of the eastern states, there is an early learning continuum which covers children aged 3 to 8 years (K-3). The principles of this system recognise the distinctive learning patterns of young children, the nature of children's growth and development, and the value of home and community in learning. Children are encouraged to learn through play, experimentation, and interaction with other children and adults, learning to explore, manipulate objects, materials and technologies. Early reading is neither required nor pushed, and most children enter school in the year they turn six without any reading skills. Current research suggests that this is in fact more effective in encouraging later literacy than enforced early reading in the nursery years, and Australian results bear this out. Instead, preschools focus heavily on creativity and thinking skills which can be applied later to more academic purposes. Children attend preschool mornings only in their first year, and from 9am to 3pm in their second year.

Primary School Education. Children enter primary school in the year they turn six, and there is no concept of 'rising fives' or term-by-term age-group entry. There is very little multi-age teaching in primary classrooms, except where numbers and resources require combined classes (in some rural areas, and in suburbs with falling rolls). Classes in state schools have a maximum of 30 students and many are smaller, depending on area. State primary schools are almost invariably co-educational, however, many private schools offer single-sex education at this level. Each state sets its own curriculum, but all have common elements, emphasising English language, mathematics, social studies, health education, and physical education. Many primary schools offer foreign languages from year three, but in Australia there is a much greater focus on languages of the region, for example, Mandarin Chinese, Japanese, and Indonesian. It is less common for children to study French or German, and Latin is very much the exception. Philosophy and thinking skills are now taught in most schools from year five, and there is a strong emphasis on creative work from the earliest years. Oral communication skills are developed early, and children as young as five will be expected to speak to the class regularly on topics of interest. Sports are an important part of the school day, and in summer all children will have daily swimming lessons. School assemblies provide an opportunity for classes to make drama presentations and are largely the responsibility of the students. Parents are encouraged to attend these weekly occasions. The school day usually runs from 8.50am to 3.15pm, but this will vary slightly from state to state.

Secondary Education. After finishing either year six or seven, depending on the state, children progress on to secondary school, which is known as 'high school'. In the state sector these are usually of the comprehensive variety, although some states still run a streamed, grammar school system, and others offer special programmes to children gifted in certain fields. These specialist programmes in music, theatre studies, art or sport offer scholarships to talented students from all over the state or territory, and entry is highly competitive. High school students enjoy modern surroundings and facilities, and are taught a variety of subjects which includes the core studies of English, maths, science and social studies (history and geography), as well as art, home economics, and languages. In many high schools, students in the first year must take the whole range of subjects available despite personal preferences in order to try and help them develop wider interests or recognise previously undiscerned talents. This means that, regardless of gender, all students will have to study cooking, sewing, woodwork, metalwork, art, music, drama and sport, as required by the school. As students progress through the high school system, they are allowed to specialise in subjects of their choice, until they reach the final two years of school, in which subject choices are determined by future career preferences.

Special needs children. Special schools are provided for physically and mentally disabled children, and, within the state system, children with learning disabilities are provided with special tuition inside the regular primary or high school structure. Individualised programmes are delivered by specialist teachers or a team of special educators. Provision is made for children with dyslexia and dyspraxia in most schools.

Gifted and talented children. State education departments recognise the needs of gifted and talented children, and provide special programmes for them. All schools are responsible for the ongoing identification of gifted and talented children, and monitor their progress carefully. Such children are offered a 'differentiated curriculum', the guiding principles of which are: a stimulating and interactive environment, an acceptance of individual differences and potential, a willingness to provide appropriate teaching methods and materials to match those differences, and flexibility. Teachers must, by law, provide for gifted and talented children at all times.

Technology in schools. The various state education systems place a high priority on educating students to take advantage of new technologies. In Western Australia alone, $20 million over a three year period has been allocated for this teaching priority. Schools are well equipped with information technology facilities and offer teaching in this field to even the youngest students. Most schools are also on the internet and provide every class or student with an email address. In many private schools, all students are provided with their own laptop.

Vocational education. There has been significant change in post-compulsory schooling in recent years, with an increasing emphasis on work-based learning. Work experience has been an important part of school programmes for many years, and this has now been expanded into Structured Work-based Learning Programmes which combine school and industry-based learning. A number of initiatives have been introduced including INSTEP (Innovative Skills Training and Education Programme), Vocational Programmes, Fast Track Programmes, and several others. Approval and certification arrangements provide a means of recognising students' achievements in work-based programmes.

Distance education. Australia's vast size means that many students in rural areas are hundreds of miles from the nearest school. Every state, therefore, runs an active distance education programme, which caters not only for students who are unable to attend school by reason of their location, but also for ill or otherwise isolated children. State governments provide professional staff, resources, and support, as well as radio broadcasts and internet services, to children of all ages.

Post-compulsory Education. The compulsory years of secondary education finish at the end of year 10. Secondary Education Authorities in each state issue certificates of achievement, based on coursework and exams, and roughly equivalent to GCSEs, to students leaving school at this stage. Students who leave after year 10 tend to be less academically inclined and will generally seek an apprenticeship or some other form of vocational training. Retention rates for years 11 and 12 are very high compared to the UK, with between 70 and 90 per cent of students staying on, depending on the state and prevailing economic conditions. Students who hope to enter tertiary education take public examinations at the end of year 12. These go by different names in each state (in WA, it is the TEE, or Tertiary Entrance Examination; in NSW and Victoria, the HSC, or Higher School Certificate). Students study between five and seven subjects at this level, and these grades are combined to form a tertiary entrance aggregate, which is the sole criterion for entry to university. An anomaly exists between the UK and Australian systems at this point, in so far as Australian universities require A-levels for entrance by British students, but UK universities will not recognise Australian year 12 examinations as equivalent. If your children are likely to be transferring from one system to another at this crucial stage, it may be advantageous to consider the International Baccalaureat as an alternative qualification, as this is accepted by both university systems.

The Academic Year. Most schools begin their academic year at either the end of January or the beginning of February, and the year ends before Christmas in December. The year is divided into four ten-week terms, with holidays of approximately two weeks interspersing the middle terms. There are no mid-term breaks or 'half-terms'. Public and religious holidays are observed, and students and teachers are given the day off along with the rest of the workforce.

Uniforms. State school education is free from kindergarten to year 12. Parents do have to pay the costs of books and uniforms for state schools, but these are kept at a very low level. Uniform may or may not be compulsory, and is generally favoured by both pupils and parents. Schools try to keep it simple: in summer, shorts and a polo shirt for boys, or a cotton dress for girls; in winter, a tracksuit in school colours with a crest on the sweat shirt is most common. Hats, usually of the legionnaire type, are compulsory in terms one, two and four, and this policy is strictly enforced. The motto learnt by all small children is 'no hat, no play', and anyone who comes to school without a hat will be kept indoors. Uniform shops are run by most school Parents and Friends Associations, and you should expect to pay around $50 for a complete uniform. Trainers are usually worn with winter uniform, and sandals with summer uniform. Flip-flops (known in Australia as thongs) are forbidden. Secondary school students tend to prefer the Australian Akubra-style hats (wide-brimmed and made of felt) or straw hats. Factor 15+ sunscreen is provided free to all primary school students, and you should make sure your child goes to school with some on. It will be reapplied during the day by teachers.

Independent and Private Education. Independent, or private, schools account for a little over 25% of Australia's 9,865 schools and are becoming an increasingly popular choice, despite the often considerable expenses involved. Private school fees usually begin at around $4,000 per year per child, but may go up to as much as $13,000. Independent schools are usually associated with the various Christian denominations, especially the Catholic Church and the Church of England. There are also a number of schools in each state associated with the Baptist Church and non-denominational churches, as well as Jewish and Islamic Schools. Australian Bureau of Statistics surveys have shown a recent increase of around one per cent in the numbers of children enrolled in independent rather than state schools, concurrent the with closure of a significant number of state schools deemed to be suffering from 'falling rolls'. Many parents believe that their children will receive an enhanced education at private school, as the teacher-student ratio is usually lower. Class sizes in Australian schools average 30 students, but may be higher or lower than this, depending on the state budget and resources. Upper-school classes also tend to be much smaller, and in private schools the upper school class sizes are often as low as 15-20 students, while in state schools the size is more often around 18-25. There are, however, some outstanding state schools which consistently achieve standards of excellence in academic, sporting and creative fields. Information about special programmes is available from the local Education Authority, via the Department of Education in your state or territory, and rankings of academic excellence are published annually in the press.

Extra Curricular Activities. Australian students generally participate in a number of extra curricular school activities, which typically include camps, excursions, environmental groups, and sports. Most schools have a concert band or orchestra, a choir, a dance troupe and dramatic society which rehearse and perform throughout the year. Government schools provide free music tuition to certain children who have been recognised as talented after testing in years 3,4, and 6.

Once selected, children receive tuition and an instrument through to year 12, as well as specialist ensemble opportunities.

Entry of new arrivals. If you have children currently enrolled in the UK or European education system, you should bring with you recent school reports, including a reference from their teacher or Head Teacher. Samples of their work will also help the school assess the appropriate grade for your child. Ordinarily, children are placed in a year commensurate with the age of their peer group. Children who are significantly in advance of or behind the level of work being done by other children of the same age, however, may be placed according to their ability. It is rare for a child to be placed with children more than a year older or younger. The difference in the commencement of the academic year can create problems in choosing the right level, and children from English schools will generally be placed at the lower year level to allow them to catch up, as British education is perceived as being 'behind', especially at the primary school level.

Parents & Citizens Committees in Schools. Parents can expect to be more involved in their children's education than they may have been previously. Every Australian school has its own Parents' & Citizens' Committee (P&C), sometimes known as Parents' and Friends', which consists of parents, teachers and student representatives. These committees raise funds for school excursions or tours, school equipment, and assist in the administration of some aspects of school life, such as the canteen. The Australian school canteen is quite different to the British school canteen, as hot lunches are rarely supplied. Australians do not eat a large meal in the middle of the day, and hot weather does not bring on a craving for toad-in-the-hole and chips. Instead, school canteens are more like subsidised sandwich shops, and sell sandwiches, rolls, salads, pies, some sweet items, and drinks. Many P&C committees have designed healthy, economical and tasty lunch menus which have seen chips and crisps banned in favour of less fattening alternatives. P&C committees also decide on issues such as school uniform, homework policies and behaviour management policies.

Student Councils. Most schools no longer operate a prefect system in which certain children are appointed to school office by the teachers or head. Instead, in primary schools, all year sevens are given special responsibilities, and heads of sporting houses are elected by the student body. In secondary school, there will usually be a school council, consisting of representatives elected by each year group at the end of the previous year, who meet and advise school staff of student needs and problems, and who carry designated responsibilities. In general, schools try and operate an open and democratic process in the appointment of student officers, who in turn take their responsibilities seriously.

Further Education

UNIVERSITIES

The university academic year follows the calendar year, and teaching usually takes place between March and November. The university year is 'semesterised', and both semesters are divided into two halves by a one-week 'study break' (or should that be beach break?). Enrolments usually take place in December of the year prior to commencement, but application must be made through the student's school to the state tertiary 'clearing house' by the August before final public examinations are undertaken. Australia's tertiary education sector has been undergoing a process of overhaul during the last decade, mainly for budgetary reasons. The most significant change is mirrored in UK universities, with institutions which were established as technical colleges or colleges of further education acquiring university status. This has created a divided system, with a group of six universities – the universities of Sydney, Melbourne, Adelaide, Western Australia, Queensland and Tasmania – acquiring a kind of 'Ivy League' status; a prestigious second level of long established polytechnic-type universities, such as the University of NSW, Curtin and RMIT; thirdly, a group of respectable but lesser institutions, which in the UK might be known as 'red-brick' universities, such as Murdoch University and the University of New England; and lastly, the ex-technical colleges, like Edith Cowan University. There is a constant scrabble amongst the various institutions for research funding, and rankings are very important. Although officially all on a par, there is no doubt that public perception, the perception of employers, and the perception of overseas institutions in considering students for postgraduate research, is that there are clear differences in the levels of academic excellence attained by these institutions; competition for entry to the top two levels is always intense. Australian universities offer a wide choice of subjects and qualifications. Currently, for a population of 17 million, there are about 51 universities, which, according to Mr Kim Beazley, a recent Minister for Education, is as many as the country's economy can support. The vast majority of tertiary institutions are funded by a combination of state and federal grants, at a cost to the government of approximately $40,000 per student for a four year degree. This is second only to the USA's spending of approximately $US13,639 per annum per student. Unlike America, however, in spite of recent changes in the funding system, Australian tertiary education remains financially accessible to all.

Fees and other costs: Until 1989, tertiary education was absolutely free for all students regardless of means. By 1990, however, budgetary constraints had forced a rethink on this sacred cow of education policy, and the system was changed so that students became liable for fees under the Higher Education Contributions Scheme (HECS). Under HECS, students who are either Australian citizens, New Zealand citizens, or Australian permanent residents must pay a *part* of the cost of their further education, with the Commonwealth meeting the balance. Merit-based 'equity scholarships' are available to students in every state, which exempt them from meeting this contribution. The HECS contribution is a nominal sum, the precise amount of which varies according to a very complex formula derived from the type and combination of units a student studies. Subjects like medicine and engineering attract more HECS than humanities courses. The HECS contribution can be met in one of two ways: either by payment up-front at the start of each semester, which attracts a 25 per cent discount; or by 'deferral', in which case the government pays the contribution on behalf of the student. If a student chooses the deferral option, the debt must eventually be repaid once the student is in full time employment. Graduates begin repaying their loans when their income reaches $20,701 (1998 figures), and payments are deducted in the form of a tax levy of between three and five per cent. Compulsory repayments increase as the income increases, and the debt is usually painlessly paid off within a few years. Students who opt to complete an additional honours year on top of pass degree may be eligible for HECS exemption for that year, which is known as a HECS scholarship. There is no interest charged on HECS debts, but the debt is indexed annually to bring it in line with the cost of living. The adjustment is made on the first of June each year and applies to the portion of debt which remains unpaid.

In addition to tuition fees, students must meet the costs of their own text books, which may be between $500 and $1,000 per year depending on the course, however, most institutions have good secondhand bookshops where texts may be purchased more cheaply. Students are also charged fees to join their student organisations, known as unions, associations or guilds. These organisations provide and are involved in the administration of a large number of benefits and facilities, including sporting facilities, discounts, the issuing of student identification cards, insurance cover, photocopying, bookshops, catering, social functions such as balls, and student newspapers. Membership costs range from $65-$300 per annum. Until recently, membership of a university's student union was compulsory (except for conscientious objectors, who could choose to have their dues paid to a charity instead); however, in 1995, government legislation, aimed at weakening a united student voice in the light of controversial changes in the higher education sector, made it illegal to require compulsory membership. As a result, student unions now battle to attract new members, and are able to provide fewer benefits to students because of their diminished income.

Choosing a University: Selecting a university can be difficult, and most capital cities have a number of different institutions from which to choose. Every institution and department publishes a prospectus, and university libraries will usually hold a number of these from a range of universities across the country; and careful consideration of these will give a good idea of what is on offer. Most universities have an officer who deals with enquiries from prospective students, and schools will always offer careful guidance on appropriate institutions and courses. The *Good Universities Guide* published annually by *Australian Outlook* can help you make a more informed choice. The guide is available from the Readers Department, (Australian Outlook, 3 Buckhurst Road, Bexhill-on-Sea, East Sussex TN40 1QF) and covers all 51 universities in Australia, giving a brief summary of each, including breadth of course offerings, depth, flexibility of admissions policiy, mature-age opportunities, student-staff ratios, gender balance, research track record, affluence, graduate salaries, employment prospects, library quality, popularity with fee paying students and tuition fees. Details of various courses run by the different institutions, the entry marks required for each course, and entry procedures for the various courses are also given as well as a rating of Australia's top ten universities and details of comparative graduate employment rates and starting salaries. Although similar publications exist in Australia, this book has been specifically written for the British market. Annual rankings of the nation's universities are published in *The Australian*, as well as most city newspapers. Year after year, the top performing institutions include the Universities of Melbourne, Sydney, Western Australia, and NSW, Monash and Macquarie Universities, RMIT, and ANU, the Australian National University, in Canberra.

Student Funding and Loans: Australian university students usually survive financially on scholarships, part-time jobs, their parents (about 50% of all university students still live with their parents throughout their academic careers), the Youth Allowance, or a combination of all of these. Until July 1998, eligible students were funded by a national educational grant system known as Austudy. Only about 33% of students received Austudy, which was designed as an income support scheme rather than a full living allowance. Many students were not eligible for any Austudy allowance whatsoever on the basis of their parents' income, and relatively few were eligible for the full Austudy allowance. Austudy for students aged between 18 and 24 years has now been replaced by the Youth Allowance, a single payment made to all eligible young people and replacing not only Austudy but also the dole and other social security benefits. The Allowance is still subject to parental means test, but offers some advantages to students over the old system, insofar as they are now also eligible for rent assistance up to the value of $75 per fortnight. An interest-free loan of $500 is also available.

A pared-down version of Austudy remains in force for students over the age of 24. Eligibility for Austudy, and the amount which a mature or independent student can receive under the scheme depends upon enrolment in an approved full-time course (almost all university courses are approved), and on the applicant's income and assets, and, if applicable, those of his or her spouse. If you receive Austudy, you are also allowed to earn an income of up to $6,000 per annum without affecting your allowance. If you earn above this amount, your Austudy payments will be reduced proportionately. The Austudy supplement provides further funding through a government-sponsored personal loan, available through the Commonwealth Bank. Note that while Austudy is a *grant*, the Austudy Supplement is a *loan*, and although it can help students in need, many choose not to take it up as repayment conditions are onerous.

TAFEs

Tertiary education is also available at Technical and Further Education Centres (TAFEs) which offer vocationally orientated qualifications. There are approximately 230 TAFE institutions in Australia, but many of these have additional campuses and training centres (for example, in South Australia whilst there are only 19 TAFE institutions, there are 120 ancillary teaching centres). Every state and territory has a large number of TAFE colleges and centres, in both capital cities and major regional areas. More than 1,000,000 students are enrolled in a TAFE course, though many of these are part-time students. Many school leavers who want to upgrade their skills or adults who wish to retrain or re-enter the workforce, study at TAFEs either on a full-time or part-time basis. TAFEs specialise in trade training and pre-apprenticeships in a diverse range of trades, including building, vehicle, metal, electrical and automotive trades, electronics, plumbing, printing, catering, gardening, dairy farming, hairdressing, textiles, jewellery and watch-making, secretarial and business studies. Both evening and day classes are usually available for most courses. School Certificate and Higher School Certificate subjects are also available for mature students who may be aiming for university entrance. TAFEs also offer literacy and numeracy classes, as well as English as a Foreign Language for migrants and other new arrivals. There are also a number of short-term part-time courses available in subjects like Bar Service, Typing, Commercial Floristry and Woolclassing. In a recent survey conducted by the National Centre for Vocational Education, nearly 87% of TAFE students rated their lecturer's knowledge of course content and teaching skills, and their general level of satisfaction, very highly.

The cost of attending a TAFE is significantly lower than university. Fee-exemptions are given to students in receipt of Youth Allowance or Austudy, and there are concession rates for low-income earners. TAFE students do not pay HECS. Usually TAFE colleges will allow you to pay fees in instalments.

Overseas Students at Australian Universities

Australian universities rely increasingly on overseas students for a proportion of their funding. South-east Asian students make up a significant proportion of enrolments, and are concentrated in faculties offering business, commerce and economics, with some entering medicine and law. Currently, there are more than 70,000 overseas students studying in Australia. Around half of these are studying at a secondary level, attending short intensive English language courses (ELICOS) in public or private institutions, enrolled on TAFE courses, or preparing for university on special bridging courses. The remainder are attending university courses. The number of overseas students attending Australian universities has grown by 50% in the last five years, and some universities now hold graduation ceremonies in Singapore and Kuala Lumpur to cater for their south-east Asian alumni. The Australian government requires all institutions which accept overseas students to register with state authorities to assure continuing high standards of management and education.

If you wish to enter Australia to study, you will need to apply for a Student Visa, and this cannot be issued until you can provide evidence that you have been accepted for a course of study and have paid at least one half of the first year's annual fee for your course. It is important to note that you cannot change from Visitor status to Student status while you are in Australia, and that application for a Student Visa can only be made in your own country of residence. In order to retain your visa, you must have a satisfactory record of attendance at your institution, and achieve satisfactory academic results. Upon completion of your course, you must leave Australia before your Student Visa expires, and the Australian Government offers no leniency in this repect.

Overseas students do not receive the privileges of government-funded education as offered to Australian citizens and permanent residents. Universities vary considerably in the fees that they charge overseas students, and costs are determined by the demand for the course, the location of the institution, and its level of prestige. The government sets a minimum fee structure for each course, but institutions are free to charge above this level, and frequently do. Fees vary considerably between disciplines and are subject to regular revision (always upward!): as a general rule, you should expect a humanities degree to cost in the region of $14,000 per annum, a science degree to cost around $18,000, and professional courses like medicine and engineering, anything up to $40,000 a year.

Most universities have student accommodation associated with the campus, and overseas students will receive help in finding housing and settling in generally Establishment costs have been estimated by the University of Western Australia as being around $900, and annual living costs for a single student at around $10,000. Australian universities are committed to equity policies, and seek to provide an environment of equal opportunity, free from discrimination, for all students and staff. They will make special arrangements for students with disabilities, and usually provide good childcare facilities for students with children.

Overseas Students Societies: Most universities have student-run societies which cater for overseas students from specific countries and regions. These associations organise camps, social functions, speakers and orientation programmes, and will also offer assistance if you contact them before you arrive at the institution. Your university will supply you with contact names for appropriate on-campus student organisations. Universities in Australia are completely free from religious discrimination, and those with large overseas student populations, like the University of Western Australia, provide worship facilities for most major religious groups.

Useful Addresses

Choosing a School (NSW, QLD or VIC) magazines are available from the Subscription Department, Australian Outlook, 3 Buckhurst Road, Bexhill-on-Sea, East Sussex TN40 1QF.

State Tertiary Admissions Centres:

NSW & ACT. Universities Admissions Centre (UAC), 3 Rawson Street, Auburn, NSW 2144, tel: (02)-9330 7200.

QLD. Queensland Tertiary Admissions Centre, PO Box 1331, Milton QLD 4064, tel: (07)-3368 1166.

SA. South Australian Tertiary Admissions Centre (SATAC), PO Box 2, Rundle Mall, Adelaide SA 5000, tel: (08)-8223 5233.

VIC. Victorian Tertiary Admissions Centre (VTAC), Suite B, 40 Park Street, South Melbourne VIC 3205, tel: (03)-9690 7977.

TAS & NT. Students must apply directly to the admissions offices of the relevant institutions. Contact the institutions for closing date for applications.

WA. Tertiary Institutions Service Centre (TISC), 39 Fairway, Nedlands WA 6009, tel: (08)-9389 1466.

TAFE:

VIC. Vocational Orientation Centre, 131 Latrobe Street, Melbourne VIC 3000, tel: (03)-9663 5800.

NSW. TAFE Information Centre, 47 York Street, Sydney NSW 2000, tel: (02)-9212 4400.

SA. TAFE Information Centre, 31 Flinders Street, Adelaide SA 5000, tel: (08)-8226 3409.

QLD/WA. There are no central information centres, but information can be obtained directly from your nearest college. College contact numbers are found in the government section at the beginning of the telephone directory.

NT. Institute of TAFE, NT University, Darwin NT, tel: (08)-8946 6465.

Youth Allowance and Austudy: Telephone freecall 13 2316 for information.

International Schools

International Baccalaureate Schools are not common in Australia, although most capitals have at least one. A regional list of schools offering the IB is given below:

NSW

S.C.E.C.G.S Redlands, 272 Military Road, Cremorne, New South Wales 2090; tel (02) 9909 3133; fax (02) 9909 3228.

VIC

Lauriston Girls' School., 38 Huntingtower Road, Armadale, Victoria 3143; tel (03) 9822 9021; fax (03) 9822 7950.

Wesley College, Melbourne, 577 St. Kilda Road, Prahran, Victoria 3181; tel (03) 9510 8694; fax (03) 9510 9739.

Presbyterian Ladies' College, Burwood Highway, Burwood, Victoria 3125; tel (03) 9808 5811; fax (03) 9808 5998.

Mount Waverley Secondary College, PO Box 346, Mount Waverley, Victoria 3149; tel (03) 9603 6811; fax (03) 9887 9308.

St. Leonard's College, POB 62, Brighton East, Victoria 3187; tel (03) 9592 2266; fax (03) 9592 3439.

Tintern Anglican Girls' Grammar School, 90 Alexandra Road, Ringwood East, Victoria 3135; tel (03) 9879 4466; fax (03) 9870 6002.

SA

Glenunga International High School, L'Estrange Street, Gelnunga, South Australia 5064; tel (08) 8379 5629; fax (08) 8338 2518.

Mercedes College, 540 Fullarton Road, Springfield, South Australia 5062; tel (08) 8379 6844; fax (08) 8379 9540.
Pembroke School ,18 Holden Street, Kensington Park, South Australia 5063; tel (08) 8332 6111; fax (08) 8364 1525.

WA
Kingsley Montessori School:,18 Montessori Place, Kingsley, Western Australia 6026; tel (08) 9409 9151; fax (08) 9409 9158
Wesley College, Perth, POB 149, South Perth, Western Australia 6151; tel 61 9 367 5777; fax (08) 9474 1051.

Media and Communications

The Australian media provide much the same type of services as in the UK. Australia's film, television and radio output is highly regarded internationally and much of it is distributed overseas (including children's television and art films, along with 'Neighbours' and 'Mad Max'). Each state has a range of local and regional newspapers, as well as access to the national press. Editorial content is considered to be mostly fair and unbiased, although media monopolies are under constant surveillance to maintain standards and to prevent the exercise of undue political influence. Australians are news-hungry, and newspaper and magazine readership per capita is one of the highest in the world. Most news providers offer a good balance of domestic and international news. In the communications sector, the monopoly of the state-owned Australian Telecom has now given way to a more open market with several providers competing to supply both domestic and business users. The government agency, Australia Post, provides mail and ancillary services to the whole country. Australia has one of the highest proportions of personal computer ownership in the world and the percentage of users connected to the internet is second only to Finland (where doubtless web-browsing passes the time on those long, cold nights). As a result, Australian communications are heavily geared to the electronic environment – noticeably more so than in the UK – and most government agencies, schools, television channels, newspapers, and community services have websites on which they post constantly updated information. Even the telephone directories are online and at the touch of a button you can access and search Telstra's telephone databases for both business and residential numbers.

Newspapers

Australian newspapers are largely state, or indeed, capital city-based. There is one national daily newspaper, *The Australian*, owned by Rupert Murdoch's *News Corp*, and sometimes referred to as 'Murdoch's Australian charity'. This broadsheet newspaper is of a calibre equivalent to, say, *The Times* or *The Guardian*, but like most broadsheet newspapers in the UK, it fights a continuing battle for profitability. *The Australian*'s weekend sister publication, *The Weekend Australian*, is similar in style and, as with broadsheet weekend papers in the UK, comes groaning with additional arts, lifestyle, sports and business sections. The *Australian Financial Review* is the local equivalent of *The Financial Times*, and comes in the same recognisable pink hue. Apart from the omnipresent Rupert Murdoch, the other big player in Australia's newpaper industry is Fairfax Holdings. This group publishes respected major titles including *The Sydney Morning Herald*, *The Age* (both broadsheets, from Sydney and Melbourne respectively), *The Sun-Herald*, and

Business Review Weekly. Currently, Sydney has six major daily newspapers, Melbourne and Brisbane each have three, and other capitals and major regional centres have at least two. In addition, almost every area has a local community newspaper (usually weekly, and often of very high quality).

British expatriates can keep up with news from home which may not make the international press by subscribing to the *International Express*, sold throughout Australia and New Zealand. This newspaper is the international sister paper of the *Express* and *Express on Sunday*, and has the same tabloid format and human interest focus. It is printed in Sydney and Perth, and is available in Australia from local newsagents or by subscription from Johnsons International Media Services Ltd, 43 Millharbour, London E14 9TR; tel 0171-538 8288; fax 0171-537 3594, or in Australia through NDD; tel (02) 9353 9911; fax (02) 9669 2305. The *Guardian Weekly* is also widely available and offers a selection of higher-brow articles and features in English derived from the previous week's *Guardian*, *Washington Post* and *Le Monde*. Subscriptions are available from The General Manager (The Guardian Weekly, 164 Deansgate, Manchester M60 2RR).

Addresses of the major Australian newspapers are given below:

NSW
Sydney Morning Herald, 235 Jones Street, Broadway, Sydney NSW 2000, tel: 02-9282 2833.
The Australian Financial Review 235 Jones Street, Broadway NSW 2007, tel: 02-9282 2833.

The Australian, 46 Cooper Street, Surry Hills NSW 2010, tel: 02-9288 3000.
The Telegraph Mirror, 2 Holt Street, Surry Hills NSW 2010, tel: 02-9288 3000.
VIC
The Melbourne Age, 235 Edward Street, Melbourne VIC 3000, tel: 03-9221 2266.
The Age, 250 Spencer Street, Melbourne VIC 3000, tel: 03-9600 4211.
The Herald, 44 Flinders Street, Melbourne VIC 3000, tel: 03-652 1111.
The Weekly Times, 44 Flinders Street, Melbourne VIC 3000, tel: 03-9652 1111.
WA
The West Australian, Forrest Centre, 219 St George's Terrace, Perth WA 6000, tel: 08-9482 3111.
Sunday Times Forrest Centre, 219 St George's Terrace, Perth WA 6000, tel: 08-9482 3111.
QLD
The Courier Mail, Campbell Street, Bowen Hills QLD 4006, tel: 07-3252 6011.

Other Australian Newspapers
Australian Chinese Newspapers Pty Ltd, 1st Floor, 357 Sussex Street, Sydney NSW 2000, tel: 02-9261 3033.
Australian Consolidated Press Ltd, 54 Park Street, Sydney NSW 2000, tel: 02-9282 8000. The ACP produces Australian magazines such as *Women's Weekly*, *Street Machine* etc. and has a London office, the ACP Bureau, 112 Westbourne Park Road, London W2 5PL, tel: 0171-221 3913.

Magazines

The Australian Woman's Weekly is the most popular Australian women's magazine (and is also available in good British newsagents). Don't be misled by the name: this is a *monthly* magazine. When this long-standing publication underwent a makeover, including name change, a couple of decades ago, they decided against 'The Australian Woman's Monthly' as a title – for obvious reasons! The quality of this magazine is unmatched by any equivalent publication in the UK, and has appeal across the board. It is particularly famous for its outstanding cooking sections, and Australian Consolidated Press publish a continually updated range of cookbooks developed by the magazine staff. It is said that you can never go wrong with a *Woman's Weekly* recipe. The cover price of the *Woman's Weekly* is $2.60. Australian editions of *Woman's Day*, *New Idea*, *Vogue*, *Cosmopolitan* and *Family Circle* are available in all newsagents and most supermarkets, and there are innumerable special interest publications, such as *Australian Gourmet Traveller* and *House and Garden*, which are also of very high quality. The *Business Review Weekly* is probably the most important financial magazine, roughly equivalent to the *Economist* (which is available in good newsagents), and the main domestic current affairs magazine is *The Bulletin*, which in recent years has incorporated the American publication, *Newsweek*. *The Bulletin* is an old and prestigious publication, particularly well regarded for its efforts to foster new writing, especially poetry. Most international magazines with any significant level of circulation, such as *Time* and *National Geographic* are widely available, although their cover price may reflect import costs where special Australian editions are not printed.

Books and Bookshops

Books in Australia used to be expensive but are now much equivalent in price to their UK counterparts. All major British publishers distribute in Australia, although if you are looking for something unusual you may have to order. Scholarly publications and new hardcover releases tend to be much more expensive in Australia than the UK. There is also a significant Australian publishing industry, and much highly regarded fiction is currently being written there, meeting with international success (see, for example, the work of Peter Carey, who won the Booker Prize for *Oscar and Lucinda*, and that of Tim Winton, amongst many others). Large bookshops are found in all Australian cities, including a number of chains, such as Dymocks or Angus and Robertsons; there are also many smaller independent booksellers. The 'book café' has recently arrived in Australia and proved a popular innovation. Book cafés, as the name suggests, incorporate a small, high quality café in amongst the books, where people can meet for coffee, or just enjoy a break while they browse.

Book clubs and reading groups are hugely popular, and most cities will have hundreds of these small, informal groups which meet monthly for friendship and literary discussion: book cafés provide both a venue for meetings, as well as a selection of new texts for the next get-together.

Some specialist bookstores are listed below:

All Arts Bookshop: 160 Oxford Street, Woollahra, NSW; tel (02) 9328 6744. Collectors' reference books on antiques, Australian, Asian and tribal art. Phone and mail order.

Angus & Robertson Bookworld: 625 Hay St. Mall, Perth 6000; tel (08) 9325 5622. Australia wide and New Zealand.

Boffins Bookshop: 806 Hay St, Perth 6000; tel (08) 9321 5755; fax (08) 9321 5744. Technical and specialist books. Computer access to over one million USA, UK, NZ and Australian books in print. Local and overseas special orders.

Dymocks Booksellers: 705-707 Hay Street Mall, Perth 6000; tel (08) 9321 3949; fax 481 1964. Interstate franchise with comprehensive range of general, technical and education books. Computer access to over 100,000 titles. Will obtain any book in print.

Television

Many British television watchers are probably as familiar with Australian television productions as Australians themselves. Series such as *Burke's Backyard*, *Neighbours*, *Home and Away*, *A Country Practice* and the *Flying Doctors* are all regularly broadcast in the UK, and indeed, the popular soaps *Neighbours* and *Home and Away* have a much higher profile in Britain than in their country of origin, so that visiting Australians are often bemused by fervent requests for updates on the latest from down-under. Other famous TV exports include Clive James and Dame Edna Everage, and any child will tell you about *Bananas in Pyjamas* or *The Ferals*.

There are four main channels which broadcast nationwide. The Australian Broadcasting Commission (ABC) operates Channel Two, and is equivalent to the BBC. The ABC is funded by the federal government and provides commercial-free television and radio throughout the country. Advertisements for forthcoming features are screened only at the end of programmes. The three other channels, Seven, Nine and Ten, are commercially owned and operated networks which broadcast around Australia; like commercial television in the UK they are funded by advertising, although the frequency of broadcast advertisements is higher than on British television.

Although the channels are operated by national networks, they tend to have a focus in both advertising and news output, which is specific to every state. In very remote areas, it may only be possible to receive Channel Two and perhaps one other commercial channel specifically aimed at country viewers such as, in Western Australia, GWN (Golden West Network)

The Special Broadcasting Service (SBS) provides multi-lingual and multicultural broadcasting across the country. SBS is an optional channel for which you will require a special receiver or antennae. The SBS antennae can usually be installed for around $150, but these days most houses will already have one fitted. SBS broadcasts on channel eight. It is specifically designed for viewers of other ethnic origins, and regularly broadcasts foreign language films. Many people consider that the SBS news is the best available on Australian television, with a high international news content and in-depth analysis. SBS also broadcasts minority and international domestic sports coverage, and is a good way to keep up with your favourite teams back home. Weather forecasts on Australian television in general are more detailed and meteorologically sophisticated than those on British channels.

The best British and American television productions all come to Australian television, and you will not have to miss out on *Friends*, the *X-Files*, or any other favourites. Australian television is ratings-dominated, and during ratings periods the television programming is outstanding, with the best films and series from around the world competing for your attention and the advertising dollar. At other less crucial times, programming may be more mundane but tends, in general, to be better than UK television. The government requires a certain percentage of Australian-produced output (which may *not* be cheap-to-make games shows and the like), so that there is always a good flow of new and interesting local productions.

Cable and satellite television are available in Australia, with cable far more widespead than satellite. The channels available are exactly the same as in the UK: Nickelodeon, the Disney Channel, MTV, CNN, UK Gold, the Movie Channel, and so on. Cable networks are operated by Foxtel (another Murdoch venture), and Galaxy. Subscription rates are around $40 per month. There are three satellite stations, which once again broadcast much the same international fare as the cable channels. The majority of Australians do not yet subscribe to pay channels. Most do, however, own a video, and video shops are found in every high street. Videos are cheap to hire and many stores offer rental packages of, for example, seven weekly movies for $10, or two weekly movies free with a new release overnight rental. A new release video will cost approximately $7 to hire for 24 hours, and older movies can be rented for up to a week from as little as $2.

Television programmes are advertised daily in local newspapers, and a weekly liftout programme guide, usually in magazine format, is available in the weekend papers. There is no equivalent to the *TV Times* and *Radio Times*, as television stations do not hold the copyright of their programme schedules, making them freely available for reproduction in other media.

Probably the most important difference between Australian and British television is that there is no television licensing system. Naturally, you must pay for your own television sets and antennae, but you may have as many televisions in your home or business as you like and you do not have to pay for the privilege of watching them. The Australian Broadcasting Commission is funded from taxation revenue and no further charge is made for broadcasting services.

Radio

Like the BBC, the Australian Broadcasting Commission also owns and runs four radio networks which can be received Australia-wide. They are renowned for their excellent news coverage. Radio National is the ABC's general current affairs and talk station, and is middle to high-brow in its orientation. It produces programmes such as *The Science Show*, *The Law Report*, and *The Book Programme*, as well as daily drama, book readings, interviews, and etc. It also has a classical music station, and supports an orchestra in each state. The Australian airwaves have been deregulated for decades and across Australia there are 108 commercial stations on the AM band, 51 commercial FM stations, and 100 community radio stations, run by universities, ethnic groups; there are even Aboriginal radio stations which service the outback regions. Radio stations are often advertised on car bumper stickers, on television, or in the newspapers, so it easy to find and tune in to something to your taste.

Film Industry

The Australian film industry has been thriving for the last twenty years, and is one of Australia's major cultural exports. The Australian Film Commission assists in the growth of this industry by aiding project development through script and preproduction assistance, grant giving, and international promotion. The government is keen to support a vigorous and diverse cultural environment, and this is reflected in Australian films, which find a big audience both at home and abroad. Recent hits have included 'Muriel's Wedding' and 'Strictly Ballroom'. All the big international releases find their way to Australian cinemas, generally about six months before they hit the screens in Britain. Film going is a popular pastime, and tickets cost about $10. In some cities, certain week nights are 'concession nights', with all tickets costing under $6, and this has greatly boosted mid-week sales. In the summer months, the Festival of Perth has an outdoor cinema at the Somerville Auditorium in Crawley, which shows art-house movies. It is one of the great pleasures of life in Perth to take a picnic to the Somerville at dusk and sit in a deck chair under the pine trees by the banks of the Swan River, sharing a bottle of wine and watching a movie.

Post

The Australia Post is owned and run by the Australian Government, and in general provides excellent services. Post offices are open from 9am to 5pm Monday to Friday. Letters between Australia and the UK and the USA take between four-seven days to arrive, and parcels take between seven and ten days. The cost of postage for an average letter to Britain is $1.20, and an aerogramme costs 65 cents. Sea mail and Surface Air Lifted mail services are also available at a significantly cheaper cost, but are, naturally, much slower services. Most people send parcels SAL or Sea mail, particularly Christmas parcels, and Australia Post issues a list of send-by dates for guaranteed pre-Christmas delivery all over the world. To send parcels back to the UK in time for Christmas, the send-by date is usually at the beginning of October. Australia Post also offers a cheaper rate for Christmas cards, which should be in unsealed envelopes marked 'card only', and there is a different send-by date for international cards, usually four weeks before Christmas. There is no division between first and second class services for local letters, but only one standard service and cost. Local letters cost 45 cents and it usually takes one working day to deliver letters posted within the same metropolitan area, or two working days if the letter is from outside the metropolitan region or from interstate. Mail is usually delivered once a day from Monday to Friday in metropolitan regions, but in remote or rural regions the mail may only be delivered once a week and can also often be delayed by adverse conditions such as flooding, torrential rain or even snow. There is no Saturday delivery. Mail boxes are located at the front of properties, and mail is never delivered through a slot in the front door. In the case of blocks of flats, there is usually a structure containing one letter box for every flat, at the front entrance to the property. In some urban areas, it can be wise to lock your mailbox with a small padlock if it is in a communal block, as your mail is not otherwise secure.

Australia Post deals with around 4 billion letters per year and seeks to maintain a uniform standard letter service at a uniform price. It has a 'community service obligation' to fulfil this mandate. As well as letter services, Australia Post offers a telephone bill paying service. It has a website at www.auspost.com.au where you can assess your postage costs, locate postcode numbers, find out about services and special offers, and check the location of your nearest office or agency.

If you intend to travel extensively through Australia during your stay, it is possible to have letters and parcels sent to you at any office of Australia Post. Providing it is clearly addressed with your name and the words *Poste Restante*, followed by the name and address of the post office, the letter/parcel will be held for up to a month during which time you may, upon producing proof of your identification, collect it. If the letter or parcel is not claimed within a month, it will be returned to the sender. For travellers, there are also private mail holding and forwarding services available which can be useful if you have no permanent address. These services work on a membership basis, so that after paying a joining fee you are then able to call the service from anywhere in Australia to check if there is any mail or messages for you. The service will then forward your mail or messages to your present address.

Useful Addresses

A privately owned travellers' mail service is operated by the *Travellers' Contact Point*, 8th floor, 428 George Street, Sydney NSW 2000, tel: (02) 221 8744.

The main Australian post offices (known as GPOs) are at:
SA   14 King William Street, Adelaide SA 5000.
QLD   Shute Harbour Road, Airlie Beach QLD 4012.
       261 Queen Street, Brisbane QLD 4000.
       13 Grafton Street, Cairns 4870.
       25 Caville Avenue, Surfers Paradise QLD 4217.
       22 Flinders Street, Townsville QLD 4810.
NT   33 Hartley Street, Alice Springs NT 0870.
       48 Cavenagh Street, Darwin NT 0800.
ACT   Alinga Street, Canberra ACT 2601.
TAS   Elizabeth Street, Hobart TAS 7000.
       68 Cameron Road, Launceston TAS 7250.
VIC   Cnr Bourke & Elizabeth Streets, Melbourne VIC 3000.
WA   3 Forest Place, Perth WA 6000.
NSW   Martin Place, Sydney NSW 2000.

Telephones

The Australian telecommunications sector has been deregulated in recent years and the monopoly of Australian Telecom has given way to a new spirit of competition. The national government-owned provider has been 'rebranded' as Telstra, and its major competitor is Optus. To have a telephone line connected to your new residence, you should contact either of these two providers, who will supply you with your new phone number. If you connect with Optus, you can still receive and make calls to Telstra numbers, and vice versa. New customers are not usually required to pay a deposit (unless they have a bad credit rating), and fully-itemised bills are sent quarterly. There is a constant battle to provide the cheapest international calling rates, and if you expect to make a lot of overseas calls, it is worth watching the newspapers for special offers, such as Telstra's 'talk for as long as you like to the UK' deal for only $20. In addition, there are an ever-increasing number of international call providers, who offer exceptionally low rates, and these also advertise extensively in newspapers. If you see a special deal with, say, Telstra, and you are an Optus customer, you can still take advantage of it by prefixing your call with a special dialling code (which will be clearly stated in the advertisement). You will then receive a separate bill from the service you have been using at the end of the quarter.

Local calls in Australia are not charged on a timed basis – a single connection charge of around 25 cents on a domestic phone allows you to talk all day if you want to; similarly, 'phone calls' made for the purpose of connecting to the internet are also charged on a connection-only basis, making web-time much more economical in Australia than in many other countries where you are charged for time spent on-line.

Telstra's most popular value-added products (and Optus offers very similar inducements), are call forwarding, call waiting, faxstream (multi-receipient fax sending), international homelink, which allows you to automatically charge calls made overseas to your home number, and message bank, an answering service. The PhoneAway card is a prepaid international and domestic telephone card.

Public Telephones

Public telephones in Australia are very similar to those found in Europe. Local calls cost 40 cents, and STD and international calls are charged according to the rate (determined by the time of day at which you call), distance covered and the length of the call. The telephones accept 10 cent, 20 cent, 50 cent and $1 coins. Many telephones have the facility to accept major credit cards or automatic teller cards for the bigger Australian national banks. Phone cards are also available from newsagents and vending machines in denominations of $2, $5, $10 and $20. STD public telephones are available throughout metropolitan suburbs, outside post offices and in shopping centres. Red telephones are for local use only and are also found in shopping centres, pubs and outside delis. These different types of phone will soon be superceded by one standard type of Public Payphone, which is currently being installed around the country. These phones will accept all Australian coins, as well as Telstra's new Smart Card. They will allow users to switch from coin to card in mid-phone call if necessary, and have an easy-to-read display providing instructions in four languages. They also feature an adjustable volume level and hearing aid coupler in the handset. The booths are accessible by wheelchair.

If you are a British resident in Australia, it may be useful for you to apply to British Telecom for a BT Chargecard. This card is free and means that all calls you make from Australia are charged to your own British account. Contact BT on 0800-800 893 for an application form and further details.

To call the UK from Australia, you will need to dial 0011-44 and then the number, deleting the first 0 from the area code. To send faxes from Australia, the process is the same, except that the international prefix is 0015 followed by the country code, area code (minus the 0) and the number; thus to send a fax to Oxford, the code necessary would be 0015-44 1865 + number. To call Australia from the UK, dial 00-61 followed by the area code (deleting the initial 0) and then the number. The procedure for sending a fax to Australia is exactly the same as telephoning. The area codes for major Australian cities are given in the previous section, *Setting Up Home, Utilities.*

The emergency number throughout Australia is 000.

Cars and Motoring

The wide roads in Australia and the low risk of hazards such as fog and snow make driving in Australian conditions reasonably easy. City traffic, as all over the world, is subject to the problems of congestion and tortuous one-way systems, but the suburban and country roads are usually excellent. In more remote areas the roads are often primitive dirt or gravel surfaces best suited to rugged four-wheel drive vehicles. In any case these are the only vehicles suited to the tough outback conditions. Even in comparatively populated rural areas, apart from main roads and highways, most roads will be gravel. Generally, it is a good idea to keep your speed down on these roads as your car does not respond as quickly as it does on bitumen, and is likely to slide around. On city and suburban roads, highways and freeways, driving is straightforward, and with many of the major interstate and intercity highways hugging the coast, you can often enjoy some outstanding scenery along the way.

Fuel; Fuel costs vary from one area to another, and even within the metropolitan area, prices may vary considerably from suburb to suburb. Petrol tends to be more expensive in rural and remote areas due to freight costs. Petrol is comparatively cheap in Australia, and in 1998 prices hovered around the 75 cents per litre mark (making it approximately half the price of petrol in Britain). Four star petrol is known as 'super' in Australia, and is usually only between one and three cents per litre more expensive than unleaded petrol, as the government has chosen not to introduce a tax incentive on unleaded fuel. Diesel is readily available at petrol stations at a similar price to unleaded petrol, and two-stroke petrol is available for lawn-mowers, boat engines etc. Most garages also sell LPG (liquefied petroleum gas) for taxis and for topping up the boat and barbie.

Driving Regulations

As in Britain, Australian cars drive on the left. There are, however, significant differences in speed-limits, overtaking and other rules which are worth noting.
Speed Limits: Speed is restricted to 60km/h in built-up areas (defined as those with kerbs and street lighting) and to 100 or 110km/h on freeways or in country areas.
Overtaking: It is legal to overtake in the left (or inside) lane of a dual carriageway/freeway (this is known as undertaking). On a three or more lane freeway (motorway), it is legal to overtake in any lane. The extreme right lane is not established exclusively as a fast-lane, but it is courteous to keep to the left. It is not, however, obligatory to do so, so the British custom of driving up behind a car in the right lane, sitting on its tail and flashing your lights until it moves over to let you pass, is completely inappropriate. This kind of driving is likely to be interpreted as aggressive and may be met by an angry response from Australian drivers.
Road Etiquette: It is imperative that you give way to your right when entering a freeway or dual carriageway from a slip road. It would be considered bad driving

to come onto a freeway and expect cars in the left lane to move over to the right in order to let you enter the flow of traffic. Courteous drivers may do this, but it is not common practice, and drivers who do not change lanes to let you onto the freeway or dual carriageway are not considered rude.

The practice of flashing your lights also carries a different meaning in Australia. In Britain you may flash your lights to indicate to another car that it may enter your lane, that you wish to overtake them, or to warn another driver that their headlights are not on. In Australia, you may also flash your headlights to indicate to another driver that their headlights are not on, but most commonly drivers will flash their lights in order to warn oncoming drivers that there is a police speed trap ahead. It is, in some states, illegal to warn other cars that they are approaching a speed trap, but the tradition of Australian anti-authoritariansim lives on and most drivers derive satisfaction from helping others avoid a speeding fine.

Highway Code: You can check the rules of the road by obtaining a copy of the Highway Code from your local police station or traffic licensing centre. The Highway Code varies in its details from state to state, often on minor points, but there are a number of differences on such crucial points as priority at intersections. If you wish to drive interstate, it would also be helpful to obtain the Highway Code relevant to your destination as each State/Territory writes its own road laws. It is compulsory to wear seat-belts, both in the front and back, and the practices of both hitch-hiking and picking up hitch-hikers is actively discouraged, and in Victoria, illegal.

Licence Penalty Points: For minor driving offences, most States have a system of penalty points. Every driver has 12 points, and a certain number of points is deducted according to the gravity of the traffic offence. Details of the points allocated to a particular offence are outlined in the Highway Code. If a driver loses all 12 points within a certain period of time, the driver loses his/her licence for a minimum of three months; this, however, can be much longer if there is serious damage to property or persons involved. Serious traffic offences may be punishable by a jail term.

Drinking & Driving: Penalties for drinking and driving in Australia are very heavy, and may result in a criminal record. One Australian commentator has described the obsessive drives by the State and Territory governments to eradicate drink-driving as surpassed only by the similar fanatical endeavours of the Scandinavian governments. Random Breath Testing (RBT) is now legal and means that a driver can be pulled over at any time by the police, who will ask you to blow into a breathalyser in order to check the alcohol level of the blood. RBT vehicles are popularly known as Booze Buses, and are found at all times of the day and night, on both major and suburban roads. The permitted blood alcohol level in Australia is much lower than in the UK, and is currently 0.02 per cent. You will reach 0.02 per cent after only one glass of wine or beer. Australian drivers take the risk of being caught extremely seriously. Do not drink and drive in Australia. You are almost certain to get caught, may get a criminal record, will definitely get a very large fine, and will definitely lose your licence for at least three months. These days, very few people, even the young and foolish, take the risk. The positive side of this draconian policy is that statistics now show that the RBT system is successful and the number of alcohol-related road deaths has fallen considerably.

Breakdowns and Accidents

Automobile Association: There are a number of accident and breakdown services in Australia, but the biggest is the RAC (Royal Automobile Club). All companies offer varying levels of cover, but home-start is part of basic cover rather than an optional extra. Policies change and prices fluctuate, so you will need to contact the companies directly to obtain current details. On the whole, accident and breakdown cover is much cheaper than in Europe, and it is the car, not the driver, which is covered. In general, you can expect to pay around $50 for a year's breakdown cover. If you need a breakdown service and you are not a member, you can join at the roadside, however, a premium is charged for this service. The bigger companies also offer national and international accident and/or breakdown cover free, or at a minimal rate, and will cover the cost of towing a car from remote areas, or, in the event of a fatality, the cost of flying a body home. The standard of cover is excellent and membership is well worth the fee, particularly if your car is over five years old. Up to 75% of Australian motorists are members of an automobile association, twice the European rate of membership. As on European motorways, there are telephones every kilometre on Australian freeways for the purpose of calling for roadside assistance. Automobile associations also offer other benefits such as tourist information, including hotel guides and maps, as well as the facility to have one of their qualified mechanics check over a used car a member may wish to buy.

Accidents: If you are involved in a motor vehicle accident in Australia, whether as a passenger, pedestrian or driver, it is essential that you record the details of the other parties involved, including their full names, addresses, phone numbers, driver's licence numbers, the name of the insurance company of the other party, the names, addresses and phone numbers of any witnesses, and a list of damage to the vehicles involved. This inventory should be made at the scene of the accident, if possible. If the total cost of damage caused by the accident exceeds $1,000 you must call the police, and in this case, it is helpful to record the name of any attending officers. If you sustain any physical injury, no matter how minor, you should attend your GP and describe how your injuries were caused, and their extent, in detail. Medical records will often affect any amount awarded as compensation in any personal injury claim.

Driving in the outback: If you intend to drive in the outback, or undertake long distance trips, the Australian Tourist Commission can provide information detailing city to city links, motoring clubs, information on vehicle rental and accommodation, as well as essential rules for outback motoring. Drivers are advised to notify friends or relatives of expected times of arrival, and to confirm these upon arrival, to check intended routes carefully, to refuel at every opportunity and to keep an additional week's supply of food, water and fuel in case of a breakdown in remote areas. Many people have died of exposure and dehydration after breaking down in the outback. You are advised *always* to remain with your car if it breaks down in the outback, as the vehicle will provide shelter from the sun and serves as an obvious point of reference for rescue teams. The Royal Flying Doctor Service of Australia (RFDS) offers a service for outback travellers which includes advice on touring and emergency procedures, as well as hire of transceiver sets with emergency call buttons. It is advisable to contact the RFDS for information before embarking on a trip into the outback.

Useful Addresses

Royal Flying Doctor Service of Australia Federal Office, Level 5, 15 Young Street, Sydney NSW 2000, tel: 02-9241 2411. Contact this office for a list of RFDS bases Australia-wide.

Australian Automobile Association, 216 Northbourne Avenue, Braddon, ACT 2612, tel: 02-6247 7311.

Royal Automobile Association of South Australia Inc., 41 Hindmarsh Square, Adelaide SA 5000, tel: 08-8202 4600.

Royal Automobile Club of Queensland (RACQ), 300 St Paul's Terrace, Fortitude Valley QLD 4006, tel: 13 1905.

Automobile Association of the Northern Territory (AANT), MLC Building, 78-81 Smith Street, Darwin NT 0800, tel: 08-889.

Royal Automobile Club of Victoria (RACV), 550 Princes Highway, Noble Park VIC 3174, tel: 13 1955.

Royal Automobile Club of Tasmania (RACT), Cnr Patrick & Murray Streets, Hobart TAS 7001, tel: 13 2722.

Royal Automobile Club of Western Australia Inc., 228 Adelaide Terrace, Perth WA 6000, tel: 08-9421 4444.

National Roads and Motorists' Association (NRMA), 151 Clarence Street, Sydney NSW 2000, tel: 13 2131.

Driving Licences

Each of the states and territories has a separate authority responsible for the issuing of driving licences. The minimum age for holding a licence is either 17 or 18 years, depending on the State or Territory. A Learner's Permit may be obtained by a potential new driver three months before they reach driving age (i.e., at either 16 years and 9 months or 17 years and 9 months of age), after first passing a written test on the Highway Code. A learner driver may only be accompanied or instructed by someone who has a clean driving licence and who has been driving for at least seven years. Learners are not permitted to drive on freeways or in the dark, and must always display 'L' plates attached to the car. Although in practice most learners get at least some driving experience in the presence of a suitably qualified member of the family or friend, it is nonetheless compulsory to have lessons with a qualified instructor before attempting the driving test. Once a learner feels confident with the basic driving skills, the driving instructor will make an appointment for the driving test with a police examiner. On passing the test, which is usually at the second attempt (unless you are very lucky or proficient), drivers are granted a 'probationary' licence and are required to display 'P' plates on the car every time they drive, for the first year as a licence holder. Probationary drivers are subject to restrictions on speed and blood alcohol limits, and face severe penalties if caught exceeding these limits. After one year, the probationary driver is considered to be sufficiently experienced to be awarded a full driving licence. Driving licences must be renewed annually and a fee is payable for each renewal.

If you arrive in Australia with a driving licence issued overseas, different regulations apply. If you are considered to be a visiting driver (i.e., you are temporarily in Australia and usually reside outside Australia), you may drive any vehicle, including a locally registered one, provided you hold a current British driving licence or International Driving Permit (issued in your home country) for the class of vehicle to be driven. In Britain, an International Driving Permit can be obtained from the AA, even if you are not a member.

Obtaining an Australian Driving Licence: If you intend to become a permanent resident of Australia, you must obtain a driving licence issued by the relevant state or territory authority. Although you may be given a certain period of grace, which varies from state to state but is usually three months, you are required to obtain a driving licence as soon as you take up permanent residence. New settlers holding a current valid British driving licence must take a written test based upon knowledge of the State/Territory Motor Traffic Handbook (also known as the *Highway Code*) as well as a practical driving test. In addition, it is necessary in most states to undergo an eyesight test. A driver's licence issued in one particular Australian State or Territory is valid Australia-wide.

Car Registration

Registration fees are payable according to the type of vehicle and the expected wear and tear that vehicle will inflict on the State's or Territory's roads over the course of a year. In most states or territories, temporary residents and visitors are exempt from registration fees as long as the registration of the vehicle continues to be valid in the country of origin. A vehicle imported from abroad must be inspected by the nearest registration authority to ensure it is roadworthy immediately after its arrival in Australia. In addition, you will need to provide the following documents: a *Carnet de Passage* or other evidence that security has been lodged with Australian Customs, evidence that it is covered by Third Party Insurance in Australia, a current registration certificate from the country or origin, and a valid driver's licence from country of origin. Registration payments include Third Party Injury Insurance, and the costs vary between States. The combined cost of registration and TPI of a popular 6-cylinder family sedan ranges from $400-$600. Fees differ depending on whether the vehicle is intended for business or commercial use (for which standard fees apply) or solely for family or personal purposes (for which family vehicle fees apply). A family vehicle will receive a discount of around $50 on the annual registration fee.

To register your vehicle, contact your local traffic authority (listed below). In New South Wales you must get an endorsed Compulsory Third Party Certificate (The Green Slip) from an insurance company in order to be able to register your vehicle. Payment of the combined vehicle registration and TTPI can be made at any metropolitan Post Office or at the office of the relevant authority, although payment procedures are subject to change and you should check with the proper registration authority. In Western Australia payment of vehicle registration can only be done by post, at metropolitan Post Office branches, or at designated vehicle licensing centres, and not at the Police Department.

Useful Addresses

NSW – *Roads Traffic Authority*: PO Box K198, Haymarket NSW 2000, tel: (02) 9662-5000.

VIC – *Victorian Roads, Vehicle Safety Services*: 60 Denmark Street, Kew VIC 3101, tel: (03) 9854-2658.

QLD – *Queensland Transport, Registration Division*: GPO Box 2451 QLD 4001, tel: (07) 3253-4700.

WA – *Police Department, Traffic Licensing Centre*: 22 Mount Street, Perth WA 6001, tel: (08) 9222-6229.

SA – *Registrar of Motor Vehicles*: Katena Street, Regency Park SA 5000, tel: (08) 8348-9500.

TAS – *Registrar of Motor Vehicles*: 1 Collins St, Hobart TAS 7001, tel: (03) 6233 5201.

NT – *Motor Vehicle Registry*: Department of Transport and Works, PO Box 530, Darwin NT 5794, tel: (08) 9897-664.

ACT – *Registrar of Motor Vehicles*: Department of Territories, PO Box 582, Dickson ACT 2602, tel: (02) 6207-7000.

Transport

Although Australia is a vast country, transport networks are very good and it is relatively easy to explore it by air, rail and coach. Around 810,000 km of roads and 40,000 km of rail networks span the continent, and several major airlines offer a choice to travellers. Qantas was one of the world's first commercial airlines and has an unrivalled safety record; its main competitor is Ansett Australia, originally a domestic airline only, but now offering flights to south-east Asia as well. Scheduled domestic flights carry more than 18 million passengers a year. Trains operate in all states except Tasmania, and there are interstate lines travelling deep into the outback and along the lush coastline of the eastern seaboard. National Rail, jointly owned by the federal government and the governments of NSW and Victoria, provides a nation-wide service. In addition, Australia has about 70 ports of commercial significance, used mainly for trade, although cruise ships are enjoying a renewed popularity and regularly call at the ports of Sydney and Fremantle.

Air

Domestic travel in Australia is very expensive, due in part to the huge distances which separate major cities, but also because of price-fixing between the two major airlines. Tourists will find it is often cheaper to book internal flights from Britain through their travel agent than arrange them in Australia, although clearly this option is not available to anyone who has already taken up residence in Australia. Many international airlines offer free or discounted internal flights with their tickets, and there are also a number of air passes available which offer more economical travel within Australia. If you fly to Australia with Qantas, you are eligible to purchase discount passes for domestic flights on Ansett. Ansett has various deals for travellers. At the time of writing, these include:

Visit Australia Pass: £88 in Australia, or £115 if purchased in the UK, containing a minimum of two and maximum of ten flight coupons.

Special See Australia Pass. 40 per cent of the full fare on domestic flights. Additional coupons may be purchased on arrival in Australia. In London, tel: 0171-434 4071.

Youth and Fun Package. Fly from Perth or Darwin to Broome; includes five nights' accommodation.

South Pacific Pass. Discount fares for travel within Australia, New Zealand and the South West Pacific. A minimum of two sectors must be purchased prior to leaving the UK. Travel within Australia cost £90, and between Australia, NZ and Fiji, £115.

Offers such as these are constantly changing, but over a period of five years there have consistently been specials available for overseas visitors. Check with your travel agent for the latest information.

Rail

Australia has an extensive rail network, although it is impossible to travel the whole country by train. The remote outback of both the Northern Territory and Western Australia is not served by railway lines at all (the intense heat can cause track to buckle), and Tasmania, being both small and seabound, has never developed a rail system. The eastern coast of Australia,however, is well served by trains, and between Perth and Sydney runs one of the great railway lines of the world, *The Indian Pacific* which operates weekly. Four and a half thousand miles,

65 hours and two time zones after leaving the Sydney sunrise over the Pacific Ocean, you can enjoy the Perth sunset over the Indian Ocean. Other legendary train journeys include The Ghan (from Port Augusta to Alice Springs), the Prospector (from Perth to Kalgoorlie), and the Overland (from Melbourne to Adelaide). Interstate rail travel is expensive, and most travellers will choose to undertake it for the experience rather than the convenience.

There are currently two passes available for rail travel within Australia, which can be booked before departure. The Austrailpass allows you unlimited stops on most trains on the Rail Australia Network over a specified time period (determined by price). First and economy class passes are available, and an economy pass will cost between £219, for 14 days, to £342, for 30 days. Alternatively, the Flexipass provides four passes for travel for eight, 15, 22, or 29 days within a six month period, and costs between £185 and £470.

As some long distance rail services operate on a weekly basis, you are well advised to book ahead, particularly if you have a limited travelling time or are travelling in peak season. Tickets may be booked up to six months in advance. Single tickets are valid for two months and return tickets must be used within six months of using the outbound section of the ticket.

Bookings can be made in the UK through local travel agents, or directly through Rail Australia's appointed agent, Leisurail (PO Box 113, Peterborough, PE3 8HY, tel: 01733-335599 or fax: 01733-505451). Leisurail have a free brochure available on request.

Bus

Travelling by coach around Australia, while time consuming, is actually one of the best ways to see the country, as well as one of the cheapest. Nearly 80 per cent of independent travellers use coach services to get around Australia. There are a number of independent bus companies, and daily services operate to almost anywhere in the country from every major city. Prices are competitive and the standards are very high. Long-distance coaches are usually fitted with video and stereo facilities, and the bus drivers often consider themselves to be part of the entertainment, maintaining humour levels when they flag in the middle of a long trip. Every bus is fitted with air-conditioning, a toilet and drinking water fountains, and there are frequent stops at road houses for food, drinks, toilets and even showers. All coaches are strictly non-smoking.

Bus Companies

Greyhound Pioneer and McCaffertys are the two largest coach companies and both provide services to over 900 destinations throughout Australia. Both of these companies have booking agents in the UK who can be contacted for further details and fares. For Greyhound Pioneer, contact Greyhound International, tel: 01342-317 317, and for McCaffertys and Greyhound Pioneer, contact Visit Australia (21 Norman Road, St Leonards-on-Sea, East Sussex, TN37 6NH; tel: 01424-722 152 or fax: 01424-722 304).

Bus & Combined Bus/Rail Passes

There is a range of bus passes available for travellers in Australia and information can be obtained from travel agents in Australia, or in the UK if you intend to travel with Greyhound Pioneer or McCaffertys. The Greyhound Pioneer *Aussie Pass* allows you unrestricted travel over a given time period, for example, for 7 days travel within a 1 month period, at a cost of approximately £200, or for 21 days travel within a 2 month period, for approximately £500. The *Explorer Pass* allows the traveller unlimited stopovers within a given time en route to a specified destination. Depending on how much travel you intend to do, with a bus pass you can make substantial savings; a round-Australia trip, stopping at Perth, Adelaide, Melbourne, Sydney, Brisbane, Cairns, Darwin and returning to Perth, will cost approximately £650. McCaffertys passes include *Coast and Centre*, *Territory Adventurer*, *Top End Safari*, *Follow the Sun*, and *Outback Wanderer*.

In addition to the travel options given above, there are also a number of combined rail and road passes. New South Wales has a *NSW Discovery Pass* available for economy travel on all Countrylink rail and coach services (excluding national companies and the Indian Pacific train). Stopovers are unlimited and the pass is valid for one calendar month. The current cost of the pass is $249 (approx £120). YHA members receive a $25 discount. The *East Coast Discovery Pass* can be used for travel between Sydney and Cairns on the Countrylink XPT (train) and Queensland Rail, and offers unlimited economy travel between Sydney and Cairns. This pass currently costs £95.

Urban Transport

Most Australian cities are well served by public transport. Within the city centre, there are frequent and economical buses, and trains also service the central business district. In Melbourne, the city transport system also includes trams, which have become a feature and attraction of the city, and which are now considered to point the way forward in public transport planning strategies. Trams on a certain city route are free. Sydney has an underground rail system, and in Adelaide commuters use the O-Bahn. In Perth, the city council provides free bus services within a restricted area of the city. These buses are called 'City Clippers' and the routes are colour-coded. You can catch a clipper at any point along its circular route and stay on as long as you like, without paying a cent. In both Perth and Melbourne, these free transport services are provided to encourage city workers to leave their cars at home thus reducing city traffic congestion, however, many tourists and shoppers also take advantage of the excellent services. In common with many European city transport systems (but unlike the UK), in many Australian cities public transport tickets are valid for a certain length of time rather than for a single or return journey. If, for example, you buy a ticket (which is priced according to how many zones you need to cover), that ticket will be valid for a specific length of time, and will remain valid regardless of how many times you get on and off any buses or trains within that time period, and within the specified zones. Zones are set in concentric circles, so it is possible to travel into the city centre and then out to the other side of the city without purchasing extra zones. In addition, in Perth it is possible to use bus and train tickets interchangeably, so you can catch the bus into Perth and then use the same ticket to catch a train to another destination within the zonal distance, or vice versa. You usually pay the driver as you board for your ticket, and at stations there are automatic ticket vending machines. Australian cities are very sprawling and there are often long distances between various areas, and in consequence the public transport is perhaps not as frequent or as well established as in European cities. There is, however, considerable new investment in rail services, especially in Perth, which is constantly increasing its track miles. Most Australians drive their cars to work, although there is an increasing number of 'Park & Ride' schemes by which you drive to a convenient bus/rail depot, transferring to public transport into the city centre.

Banks and Finance

Banking in Australia is straightforward and the tellers (cashiers) are generally courteous and helpful. All banks are open the same hours nation-wide: from 9.30am to 4.00pm Monday to Thursday, and from 9.30pm to 5.00pm on Fridays. Building societies may open on Saturday mornings from 9.00am-noon, but regional and remote branches may have more restricted opening hours. Australian banking has all the usual electronic facilities that a UK customer will expect, plus a few extras. ATM machine cards can be used in all supermarkets, accessed by a tillside keypad and your usual PIN number; your shopping bill can be deducted immediately from your account, and there is nothing to sign. The four largest national banks are Westpac, the National Australia Bank, the Commonwealth Bank of Australia, and the ANZ (which is also has branches in New Zealand). Many building societies have gone through the same demutualisation process as those in the UK and now operate as banks: some of the larger ex-building societies now offer nation-wide services, including the St. George (Sydney-based), Town and Country (Perth-based), and Challenge (Melbourne-based).

Bank Accounts

If you are going to Australia for more than six months, or to work, it is worth opening a bank account either before you leave your home country, or immediately upon arrival in Australia. It is much easier to open an account with an Australian bank when you are actually in Australia, but accounts can also be arranged through bank offices in the UK. The Commonwealth, ANZ and Westpac all have branches in London which offer services particularly geared to new arrivals and migrants. Their advisors are extremely helpful, and will guide you in the best accounts to meet your requirements, as well as providing general advice about services. The Commonwealth Bank, for example, will establish a bank account for you with a convenient branch in Australia and transfer your funds prior to your departure so that when you arrive in Australia you have immediate and full access to their range of banking facilities (including automatic telling machines throughout the country). The Commonwealth Bank can only establish an account for you prior to your arrival if you intend to work in Australia, if you are migrating, or if you are a resident returning home after an extended period abroad. To qualify for their services in the UK branch you will need to be able to show them evidence that you have been given the relevant visa. Contact the Commonwealth Bank of Australia (details listed below) for further details or to speak with one of their consultants, 9am-5pm Monday to Friday.

The One Hundred Points System

Banking in Australia is much more open and available than in the UK, and there are very few people who will feel excluded from having an account, even with a bad credit record. References or proof of income are not required, however, proper identification is crucial and all banks must by law operate the '100 points system' of identification. Under this system you must conclusively demonstrate your identity and place of residence by providing various forms of identification, which are scored by the level of their official authority. A passport, for example, will provide you with 80 points, which you might back up with a Medicare card (20 points), a birth certificate (60 points), or a driver's licence (50 points). When you go to the bank to open an account, be sure to take a selection of appropriate documents with you, as you will be sent away empty-handed if you cannot comply with this government requirement.

International & Internal Money Transfers

If you wish to send an international money transfer from Britain to Australia, it will cost you a flat fee of approximately £15, and the transfer may only be sent through a bank, using the 'Swift' service. British Royal Mail money orders are not accepted by Australia Post. In Australia, international money transfers are made either by bank draft, which costs approximately $18, or electronically, at a cost of approximately $30. Within the country, travellers without a cheque (current) account may send money within the country by bank cheque (costing approximately $5, although the charge varies from bank to bank), or by Australia Post money order, the cost of which varies according to the amount sent. Postal orders are generally the cheaper option, and cost around $2.50.

Other Banking Services

Credit Cards
All Australian banks offer a credit card facility, and all the usual international credit cards, including Mastercard, Visa, Diners Club and American Express, are available via your local bank branch. If you intend to stay in Australia for less than 12 months, you may prefer to apply for a credit card in your home country before you leave and then establish a standing order to pay off your monthly credit card bill. It is a good idea to deposit any savings in a high interest account whilst you are away, allowing the interest from this account to cover the approximate charge of 2% on cash advances made against your credit card in Australia.

Direct Debits
Australian banks offer direct debit facilities, known as standing orders, for the payment of regular bills, and many also offer a telephone banking facility which enables you to authorise payment transactions by telephone.

Cheque Accounts
The cheque book facility only applies to specific accounts, and it is important to check whether the account you are considering offers this service. There is no cheque card system in Australia, so there is also no limit as to the amount of the cheque you are able to write. In order, however, to write a cheque, you will need to have your driver's licence, or other acceptable form of identification showing your full name and address, with you, and this information will be noted on the reverse of the cheque. Not all shops will accept cheques as payment is not guaranteed, so with smaller shops, ask first if they are prepared to accept one. Almost every shop now prefers the cashless transaction, and even the smallest corner deli will accept your ATM card. Very few Australian bank accounts offer free cheques, with most charging between 20 cents and $1.00 for every cheque issued against the account. As a result, Australians use cheques far more sparingly than the British, and use cash or credit cards a lot more. Cheques take five working days to clear, but foreign cheques may take up to four weeks and you will probably be charged a commission on the exchange of cheques made out in a foreign currency.

Investment Advice: Many expatriates tend to seek advice on money related matters such as employee benefits, retirement income funding, personal investments and savings. Companies specialising in providing worldwide financial services include *Brewin Dolphin Securities* of 5 Giltspur Street, London EC1A 9BD (tel 0171-248 4400; e-mail rlindsay-stewart@brewin.co.uk) and *The International Benefits Practice (Aon Consulting)*, Minet House, 66 Prescot Street, London E1 8HG (tel 0171-680 5508; fax 0171-702 1072).

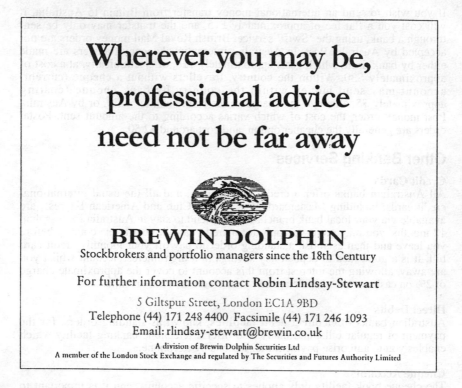
Money

Australia has had a decimal currency for the last 35 years, after abandoning the archaic pounds, shillings and pence system in 1965. The basic unit of currency is the Australian dollar, which is worth 100 cents. In 1993, 'coppers', or one and two cent pieces, were withdrawn from circulation, having become virtually worthless and more of a nuisance than an item of value. Their withdrawal has provided a certain complicating factor in Australian shopping, which will confuse the new arrival. Although coppers are no longer available to be given as small change, goods for sale are still marked up in terms of single cents (for example, $2.98). Your shopping will be rung up in these hypothetical numbers and the final total will be rounded off – always, by law, in favour of the customer. Thus, if your supermarket till total comes to $47.68, it will be rounded down to $47.65, and not the other way. Items paid for by cheque or cashcard, however, will cost the precise amount as stated, and will not be rounded off. This system sounds complicated but has been quickly accepted by Australians, and few people are nostalgic for the bad old days of a wallet full of dirty little coins. Australian coinage consists of the silver-coloured, cupronickel five, ten, 20 and 50 cent pieces, and of gold-coloured

$1 and $2 coins, which replaced notes of the same value in 1994. The 5 cent coin is very similar in size to an old sixpence, the 20 cent coin is easily confused with a UK 10 pence, and the 50 cent coin has the same hexagonal shape as its UK equivalent (but is larger than the recently released new version of this coin). The $1 coin is about the same size as the 20 cent piece, and has irregular milling which allows it to be easily distinguished by blind people. The $2 coin is smaller and thicker, and is much like a UK £1 in dimension. Australian notes are in denominations of $5, $10, $20, $50 and $100. In recent years, the Australian currency has been gradually redesigned to make it both counterfeit-proof and longer lasting. New $5, $10, $20, $50 and $100 notes have now been released, and are made of a kind of plastic which mimics paper but cannot be torn. It is considered virtually indestructible. The new plastic notes bear a forgery-proof transparent seal in the corner (i.e., you can see right through the note), and a hologram in the centre of the seal. All notes and coins bear the head of Queen Elizabeth II on the reverse side. Old paper notes have been quickly withdrawn from circulation and destroyed. Paper money is still legal tender, but will be returned to the mint for destruction on receipt.

The Australian mint also coins gold bullion and coin, known as Australian Nuggets. Each coin has a set purchase price (from $15-$100), but the actual value is determined by the daily-fluctuating price of gold, and the demand for the coins. The Australian Nugget can be bought Australia-wide at banks as individual coins or as full sets. They are popular as souvenirs for wealthier visitors.

Visitors are permitted to bring an unlimited amount of foreign currency into Australia, but there are strictly enforced regulations limiting the amount of money with which you can leave the country. Currently, it is difficult to leave Australia with more than the equivalent of $5,000. Should you be lucky enough to clean up at that illegal Australian coin game, 'Two-up', you would have to leave your winnings behind or, if you've been really lucky, otherwise invest it in Australian business or property. If you intend to take more than $5,000 out of Australia, you need to contact the *Cash Transaction Report Agency*. Banks are also legally obliged to report deposits of more than $10,000 in cash made into Australian bank accounts, primarily to safeguard against money laundering activities.

Useful Addresses
Australian & New Zealand Banking Group (ANZ), 55 Gracechurch Street, London EC3, tel: 0171-378 2121.
Commonwealth Bank of Australia, International freecall number 0800 89 2084.
Westpac Banking Corporation, 63 St. Mary's Annex, London EC3 tel: 0171-621 7000.

Taxation

Income Tax

Income Tax in Australia can be quite a complicated business unless like most Australian employees you pay tax through the Pay As You Earn (PAYE) system. If you are self-employed or own your own business and are thus not PAYE taxed, the process of assessing whether you are due to pay extra tax or even receive a rebate is almost impossible to fathom single-handedly. The completion and lodgement of a tax return is the responsibility of the individual, and Tax Packs containing forms and an information magazine, produced by the Australian Taxation Office, are available free from newsagents and Taxation Offices Australia-wide. The Tax Pack is reviewed annually, in an effort to make completing a tax return less difficult, but even so, the Tax Pack is a formidable publication which currently includes four income tax return forms (for individuals rather than businesses), detailed information and instructions. Both the format and the terminology are quite daunting and for this reason, fewer and fewer Australians are choosing to complete their own taxation returns and are turning to chartered accountants or licenced tax agents to complete the forms for them.

The Australian financial year begins on 1 July and ends on 30 June, and tax returns must usually be lodged by the end of October. Even if you think you are not liable to pay any tax, you are generally required to lodge a tax return in Australia if you are normally resident there, or if you are a non-resident who has derived an income in Australia. It is obligatory to lodge a tax return at the end of the financial year if any of the following are applicable:

1. You had tax deducted from your pay or other income (including Australian Government pensions, allowances or benefits);
2. You had tax deducted from interest, dividends or unit trust distributions (applicable only to residents);
3. You had tax deducted under the Prescribed Payments Scheme (an alternative to the PAYE system);
4. Your taxable income for the previous year was more than $5,400 (residents) or $1 or more for non-residents;
5. You incurred a net taxable loss, or are entitled to a deduction for a prior year loss;
6. You were a beneficiary in a trust estate that conducted business in Australia (including farming or mining);
7. You conducted business in Australia (including farming or mining);
8. You paid provisional tax on your previous year's assessment;
9. You were under 18 years of age as at 30 June and your total income from all sources, both within Australia and overseas, was more than $416;
10. You were issued with an assessment under the *Child Support (Assessment) Act 1989*.

Although taxation rules and regulations are subject to continual re-assessment and change, clearly most Australian adults will fall somewhere within these categories and are therefore required to complete and lodge an annual taxation return. It is important to note that despite the necessity of completing a taxation return, most pensions and state allowances are tax-free and should not be included in your taxation return.

Completing A Tax Return

In order to complete a tax return, you need to attach official statements detailing the amount of tax you have paid over the year. These statements are known as group certificates and are issued automatically by employers at the end of the financial year. If you do not receive a group certificate from your employer you must request one.

If either you or you employer have lost your group certificate, or it has gone missing in the post, you are usually able to get a copy from your employer. If your employer is unable to provide you with a copy, then he/she can give you a letter showing all the details of the original documents. In the unlikely event that you are not able to obtain a letter from your employer, you can fill in a Statutory

Declaration of lost or missing group certificates (available from your local Tax Office). If any information on your group certificate or tax stamps sheet is wrong, your employer must provide a letter showing your correct income and tax details.

Self-Assessment

If you choose to complete your own tax return, the tax office will work out your refund or tax bill based on the information you have provided. The tax office assumes the information you have provided is true and correct but you should note that after they have calculated your rebate or bill and informed you of their calculations in your Notice of Assessment, their computers continue to check for missing or incorrect information. Your tax return may also be subject to an audit and, should the original assessment be judged incorrect, the tax office will change it and send you an amended assessment. In addition to extra tax, you may be liable for a penalty if you fail to show reasonable care in the preparation of your return. Knowing this, it is understandable why many Australians simply don't want to take the risk and pay a professional to shoulder the responsibility.

Professional Assistance

If you would like assistance filling out your own taxation return, you will be able to find chartered accountants or other professional taxation assistance services in the Yellow Pages phone book. It is advisable to phone around as the cost of the service can vary greatly. The tax office recommends that if you get someone (other than them) to help you complete your return, you ensure that that person is a registered tax agent. Some agents offer a free initial assessment and discounts to pensioners. Tax return fees charged by a registered tax agent are tax deductible against your *next* annual tax return. In addition, tax help is available for seniors, people from non-English speaking backgrounds, the disabled or those on low incomes who cannot afford assistance with completing their tax returns. Tax Help Centres are run by community volunteers, and you should contact your local tax office for details of your nearest one.

There is also a Translating and Interpreting Service (TIS) available to specifically help non-English speaking people with their tax returns. The TIS offers joint meetings with interpreters and tax officers, and you simply call the TIS to make an appointment. The TIS phone numbers are found in the community information pages of your phone book.

The postal addresses and phone numbers of the various state and regional Tax Offices are listed at the back of the Tax Pack or in the government section of the telephone book.

e-tax

During October 1998, the Australian Taxation Office (ATO) trialled a new electronic tax preparation and lodgement software package, *e-tax '98*, which is based on the hard-copy *TaxPack*. *e-tax* will be available to the public from 1999. The ATO has developed high levels of security to ensure that personal income tax information is secure. When you complete the return, you will sign it electronically using the in-built public key technology, and the *e-tax* software will encrypt your tax return file for transmission over the Internet using a secure link.

The Australian Taxation Office has a very comprehensive and informative website at www.ato.gov.au.

Claiming back tax on expenses

If you are audited, you will usually receive written notification at the beginning of the audit, and you should follow the instructions contained in the letter. If audited, you will have to substantiate your work expenses claims, e.g. motor vehicle, other travel, clothing, tertiary studies, tools of trade, reference books and other expenses. It is, therefore, necessary to keep records of any work-related expenses in order to avoid additional tax and a possible penalty.

If you are an employee and the total of your claims is $300 or less, you must keep a record of how you worked out each of your claims. If the total of your claims is more than $300, the records you must keep are receipts, invoices or similar documentary evidence supported by or on behalf of the supplier of the goods or services. Cheque stubs are not considered acceptable as evidence. The receipt, invoice or documentary evidence must be in English or the language of the country where the expense was incurred, have the date on which the expense was incurred, name the person who, or business, which supplied the goods or services, show the amount of the expense in the currency in which the expense was incurred, give details of the nature of the goods or services, and show the date the document was made out.

A diary may be used to prove your claims for expenses which amount to no more than $10 each and which add up to no more than $200, or for which it was unreasonable to expect to get a receipt. The diary should contain all the details that would be required on a receipt or invoice. In addition, you must sign each entry in the diary.

The information outlined above should be kept for a period of three years and six months after lodging your tax return, in the case of salary and wage earners, or for seven years after lodging your tax return if you are self-employed and the claims are for car and travel-related expenses. Records of other business-related expenses incurred by self-employed persons should be retained for five years after lodging their tax return. If you appeal against an assessment, you must retain your records until the dispute has been finalised if that period exceeds the given record retention period.

You can claim for the cost of using your car for work or business purposes, for example, travelling directly from one place of work to another, or from one job to another. You cannot, however, generally claim for the cost of travelling from home to work.

Table of Income Tax

There is currently a tax threshold of $5,400 in Australia which is applicable to those stopping full-time education for the first time, those becoming residents of Australia, or those who stopped being residents of Australia. This threshold means that the first $5,400 earned is tax free.

There are many different tables of assessment of tax, which depend on personal circumstances and which are subject to annual change. The Tax Pack (see above) gives details about these assessment tables. The most commonly used Tables are described below:

Table A is applicable if you were a resident of Australia for the full financial year, you did not stop full time education for the first time, and you are entitled to the full $5,400 tax-free threshold.

Table A

Taxable Income	Tax
$1-$5,400	Nil
$5,400-$20,700	Nil+20 cents for each $1 over $5,400

$20,701-$38,000	$3,060+34 cents for each $1 over$20,700
$38,001-$50,000	$8,492+45 cents for each $1 over $38,000
$50,001 and over	$14,102+47 cents for each $1 over $50,000

Table B is applicable if you became a resident of Australia during the financial year. If this is the case, you are entitled to a pro rata amount of the $5,400 tax threshold. For the tax year you calculate this amount by adding up the number of months from when you became a resident of Australia (including the months in which you became a resident) to the 30 June. This amount is then divided by twelve to give you the proportion of the year spent in Australia and then multiplied by $5,400 to give you your tax-free threshold. If, for example, you have only been resident in Australia for two months, your tax threshold is assessed as 2/12 x $5,400 = $900, but if you have been resident for eleven months, your tax threshold is 11/12 x $5,400 = $4,950. This reduced tax threshold is known as R in the table of assessment given below.

Table B
For a taxable income of $20,700 or less:

Taxable Income	Tax
$1-R minus $1	Nil
R-$20,700	Nil + 29 cents for each $1 over R

For a taxable income of more than $20,700 S = ($20,700 -R) x 20%:

Taxable Income	Tax
$20,701-$38,000	S+ $6,003+ 34 cents for each $1 over $38,000
$38,001 and over	S + $11,885 + 43 cents for each $1 over $38,000

Your assessment can take up to eight weeks after lodging your tax return. If you are required to pay tax, you will be given thirty days notice. Tax can be paid by cheque or postal money orders made payable to the Deputy Commissioner of Taxation, in cash or cheque at any Post Office (you must take your Notice of Assessment with you), by mail (cheque or postal order only), at Tax Offices (take your Notice of Assessment), or by direct debit/refund. This last service is available from tax agents who lodge tax returns electronically.

If you cannot pay your tax by the due date, you may be given extra time to pay depending on your circumstances. You will have to provide details of your financial position including assets, liabilities, income and expenditure, and the steps you have taken to obtain funds to pay your debt. If granted additional time, you will be charged interest calculated on a daily basis. This rate is currently 16.7%.

Rebates

There are numerous rebates which may be available to you, and it is certainly worth being aware of them even if you are not currently eligible. A brief summary of some of the available rebates is given below:
Sole Parent: If you have the sole care of a child or student, you may be able to claim the sole parent rebate, even if you are not the parent. You can claim a maximum sole parent rebate of $1,116 for the whole financial year if you did not have a spouse (married or de facto), you had sole care of a dependent child or student whose separate net income for the financial year was less than $1,786, and you are not claiming a rebate for either a housekeeper or childminder for any part of the financial year.
Zone Rebate: People living in specified remote areas of Australia can claim a zone rebate. These areas are divided into two zones, Zone A and Zone B, and within

each zone there are 'special zones' which attract higher levels of relief. A special zone is categorised as a place where the nearest town or centre with a population of at least 2,500 is more than 250 km away. In Zone A, the maximum rebate available is $338 and in Zone B, $57. In the 'special zones' of both Zone A and Zone B, the rebate is $1,173.

Medical Expenses: You can claim a rebate of 20% of net medical expenses incurred over $1,000. There is no maximum amount which you can claim and the rebate is calculated on a percentage basis only.

Overseas Dependants: If your dependant is overseas, you may be eligible to claim a rebate if they are temporarily away from Australia or are waiting to migrate to Australia. Your dependant must migrate within five years from when you first entered Australia in order to take up residence, and you may be asked to provide evidence in order to substantiate your claim.

Other Taxes

Financial Institutions Duty and Debits Tax

Duties and taxes collected on certain types of bank, building society or other financial institution accounts are called Financial Institutions Duty (FID) and Debits Tax. These are automatically debited from your account by the financial institution which holds your account and will be shown on your statements or in your passbook. If you do not see any sign of FID or Debits Tax deductions on either your statement or passbook, this usually means that your account is not one which is taxable and so no charges have been made. If you can show that the deductions were made against your assessable income, you may be able to claim these as tax deductions in your tax return. This is a fairly complex area, so it is worth consulting a Tax Officer in order to ascertain whether your account is the type which can be taxed and whether you can claim these as tax deductions. Some financial institutions also charge administration fees, and if you are able to show that your account is used solely for investment purposes, it is possible to claim the administration charges as a tax deduction; however initial fees for the establishment of your account are not generally allowable tax deductions. In addition, if your bank account is necessary for your business, you are able to claim any governmental or institutional charges or fees on that account as tax deductions.

Provisional Tax

Provisional tax applies to those who earn more than $999 per year in non-salary or wage income from investments, business, primary production (i.e., farming or mining), distribution from a trust or any other source which is not covered by the PAYE system. Provisional tax basically pays the current year's tax, in much the same way as salary and wage earners do under the PAYE system. Currently, you do not have to pay provisional tax if your taxable income is below the relevant level shown below:

Single	$19,492
Married/de facto	$29,988 (combined income)
Married or de facto and separated due to illness	$37,346 (combined income)

It is important to note that provisional tax must be paid in advance and is based on the earnings of the previous year. If this amount falls short of the amount of tax owed as assessed by the Tax Office at the end of the financial year, the amount owing must be paid within 30 days from the date on which your Notice of Assessment was issued, or on 1 February of the following financial year, whichever is first. Provisional tax must be paid by self-employed people and is generally paid in quarterly instalments. If, however, you are able to substantiate your claim that more than 75% of your income is received in the last six months of the financial year, the Tax Office may adjust its demands for payment of taxes to bi-annual payments rather than quarterly.

Capital Gains Tax

Australia has had a Capital Gains Tax since 1985. You will be liable for this tax if you sell or otherwise dispose of any assets or receive any other capital amounts in a financial year. Examples of capital amounts include a forfeited deposit, premium received for granting a lease, or a capital gain distributed to a beneficiary of a trust. This includes any 'gifts' received, particularly those deemed as 'business' gifts, and the recipient is taxed on the gift at its fair market value.

Assets subject to Capital Gains Tax include:

1. Listed personal-use assets that you owned for personal use and enjoyment and which cost more than $100 to buy, e.g. a rare publication, artwork, jewellery, stamps, coins or an antique.

2. Non-listed personal-use assets (other than land or a building) that you owned for personal use and enjoyment and which you disposed of for more than $5,000 each.

3. Other assets include shares or units in unit trusts, options or rights to acquire shares or units and real estate (including your holiday home).

Capital Gains Tax is only applicable in the case of a deceased estate if the component assets are sold by an executor or disposed of for money by a beneficiary. There are no Death Duties in effect in Australia.

Other exemptions from Capital Gains Tax include:

1. The taxpayer's main residence and 'reasonable' land around it, although there is no exemption for houses owned by a family trust or private company and lived in by a trust beneficiary or shareholder.

2. Superannuation or life insurance policies.

3. Sale of motor vehicles and other personal-use assets with a disposable value below the amounts given above.

4. Compensation payments for stolen or destroyed property.

5. Expenses involved in improving or selling a property are taken into account against the amount of profit made in the sale. Usually, annual expenses such as repairs and interest payments on the asset are excluded from the calculation of the asset's value and any tax which may be owing.

Fringe Benefits Tax

The Fringe Benefits Tax was introduced in July 1986 by the government in an effort to control the amount of non-cash (and therefore non-taxable) benefits offered by employers as part of a job package. Companies cannot claim expenses such as business lunches and entertainment costs on behalf of the company, and any fringe benefits are considered an assessable part of an individual's or company's taxable income. Taxable fringe benefits include company cars, free or low-interest loans, free or subsidised accommodation or board, goods and services sold at a reduced rate or provided free, and expenses paid on behalf of an employee.

Cars are probably the most common fringe benefit, and Fringe Benefits Tax is normally paid by an employer when a car is owned or leased by a company and made available to an employee (or family member) for private use. Fringe Benefits Tax on cars does not normally apply to self-employed people or to a partnership if the vehicle is used wholly and exclusively for business. It does not apply to cars owned or leased by an employee, even when the cost of operating the car for business use is claimed as an expense against the taxable income. When Fringe

Benefits Tax is chargeable, it applies to all passenger cars, wagons, minibuses, panel vans and utilities designed to carry less than one tonne or a bus with fewer than nine seats. There are many variations and exemptions to the Fringe Benefits Tax and probably the safest way of working out whether you are liable or not is to get a professional to do it for you.

Higher Education Contributions Scheme

HECS regulations are described in detail in the Higher Education section of this book. The rate of HECS tax varies from 3% to 5% of your taxable income. In addition, since 1994, the Australian government has instructed employers to deduct additional taxation instalments to cover any possible Higher Education Contributions Assessment Debt in future years. These deductions will only be made if you earn more than $508 per week. For further details on HECS and taxation, you should request a copy of the booklet *HECS; Your Questions Answered*, available from your educational institution or any Tax Office.

Death Duties

Currently, there are no Death Duties in Australia, although Capital Gains Tax is widely considered to be death duty by another name and widely resented as such. There are, however, number of ways in which capital gains tax (CGT) on an inherited home can be avoided: principally, a beneficiary can sell inherited property within two years from the date of death without incurring CGT liability. Similarly, a beneficiary who lives in the home as his or her sole and principal place of residence after the death and until it is sold will not have to pay CGT. If you are making a will, you should seek tax advice on the most effective method of disposal.

Health Insurance and Hospitals

A report by the Australian Institute of Health and Welfare reveals that Australians born in the 1990s can now expect to live 15 years longer than those born in the 1920s; boys born in 1992 can expect to live to an age of 74.5 while girls will live to an age of 80.4. The Report found that Australia's mortality rate is currently 7.1 per 1,000 people per year, although Aboriginal people continued to have a mortality rate far higher than the national average. Interestingly, the report also compared the mortality rates of migrants and Australian-born residents and found that most migrant groups had death rates significantly lower than the Australian average. Greeks, Italians, Central and South Americans, Vietnamese and Yugoslavs had the lowest rate. In addition, among Australians aged 25-64, the death rate was 15% higher for men living in rural regions, and 9% higher for women in rural areas.

The report also notes an increase in the rate of multiple births with improving technology in the field of artificial conception, such as IVF treatment, and that dental health has improved dramatically over recent years such that few people under 35 years of age have lost all their teeth. Despite the large number of people on hospital waiting lists, the report also indicated that recent trends showed a continued decline in basic and supplementary private hospital insurance, and government measures have recently been put in place to offset this decline, by offering incentives to insure privately.

The report also shows that the nation's health is dogged by a rising suicide rate, with more Australians dying by their own hands than in traffic accidents. For the most part, victims are males between 15 and 24 years old, but women of the same age are also at risk. The survey indicates strong links between suicide and the socially disadvantaged and the unemployed, particularly in the Aboriginal population. In recent years, there have also been numerous Aboriginal deaths in custody, which were statistically disproportionate when compared to the average rate of suicides in prison. So alarming are the statistics, that the government has opened an inquiry into the rate of Aboriginal deaths in custody, and numerous investigative documentaries have been produced and broadcast in the media.

High cholesterol levels are a major contributor to health problems in Australia, and 49% of men and 39% of women were estimated to have cholesterol levels which put them at an increased risk of heart disease. Public health concern over this issue is reflected in the amount spent on drugs. The national drugs budget currently stands at over $2.5 billion, of which more than $90 million is spent annually on Simvastatin, which lowers blood cholesterol.

Cancer rates also appear to be on the increase, accounting for over 27% of Australian deaths, compared with 15% in 1965. Breast, lung and skin cancers are the most common killers. As a result of increased public awareness of these health risks, most Australian buildings, including restaurants, are now completely smoke-free. Australians are highly educated about the risk of skin cancer and the dangers of the sun, and now almost universally take thorough protective measures when outdoors.

The perception that Australians have apparently healthy lifestyles has also been challenged by the Australasian Society for the Study of Obesity which claims that by 1995 over half (55.2%) of Australian adults were overweight or obese.

There is unsurprisingly, a high demand on the nation's health services.

The Health Care System

Using the General Practitioner

The first point of contact in obtaining health care in Australia is the local GP, whom you are free to choose yourself. Whilst most people will have a preferred doctor, it is not necessary to register with a doctor, and you are able to go to a different practice at every visit, should you so wish. Depending on the doctor, you will either be billed for the consultation, for which you will be reimbursed by Medicare, the Australian national health system, or the doctor will 'bulk-bill' which means they will claim reimbursement directly from Medicare. Doctors who practise in low income areas generally bulk-bill in order to avoid asking their patients for payment, however this is largely a gesture of goodwill on behalf of the GP. Medicare covers consultation fees to approximately $25. If GP charges exceed this, the patient is liable for any amount in excess, which is known as the 'gap'.

Should you wish to have a second medical opinion, you simply make an appointment with another doctor. Generally, appointments are made over the telephone, and you can usually see your GP within two days of your call.

If a GP refers you to a consultant or specialist, you will be given a letter and required to make the necessary arrangements yourself. Even specialists seeing public patients consult in their own rooms, and there is no system of attendance at hospital out-patients clinics. There may be a waiting period before you are seen, although it is usually not long, and once again you will be billed and reimbursed through Medicare, to the value of 85 per cent of the consultant's fee. You may choose to see a consultant on a private basis, without referral, for which you will be unable to obtain a refund either from Medicare or from your private insurer.

There is an increasing number of clinics and medical centres opening in suburban areas. Most large practices will provide a Well-Woman Clinic, minor surgery, and other services. There may also be a pharmacy housed within the centre, from which you can purchase your prescriptions immediately.

Prescription charges are subsidised under the Pharmaceutical Benefits Scheme. Patients pay the full cost of medication up to the value of approximately $16, and the PBS meets the balance up to the list price; patients on benefits of any kind pay only $2.60. Contraception is not free in Australia, but is covered by the PBS.

Using Hospitals

Patients who require hospital attention or surgery can also choose to be treated either publicly or privately. If you opt for private treatment, you can choose both your attending consultant and the hospital, but will pay a considerable amount for this privilege. On the other hand, you can expect a great deal of luxury for your money, including 5 star food chosen from a daily menu, as well as immediate treatment. If you choose to be treated under Medicare, you do not have a choice of hospital or doctor (although you will have had some say in choosing your specialist during discussions with your GP in the early stages), and you may face a long wait for a bed; on the other hand, your treatment will be completely free. In the event of an emergency, all patients will be taken directly to a public hospital, and may be transferred if they wish once their condition has stabilised. Ambulance transport is not free, and many people choose to pay a small insurance premium annually to the St. John's Ambulance Brigade to cover themselves in case they or their family need to call on this service.

Health Insurance Contributions

Every Australian is covered by Medicare, which is financed through progressive income tax and an income-related Medicare levy. There is no additional charge equivalent to National Insurance in the UK. The Medicare levy is paid at a rate of 1.7 per cent of taxable income above an earning threshold of around $13,000, or $21,000 for couples, rising to 2.5 per cent of income for high earners; families with dependent children receive an additional earning allowance of $2,100 per child. People receiving state benefits fall below the earning threshold of the Medicare levy, and payments are made on their behalf by the government. If you choose to be privately insured, you are not exempt from the Medicare levy. A recent initiative, called the Private Health Insurance Incentive Scheme, however, offers a tax rebate of up to $450 for privately insured people, and is intended to reduce the strain on public facilities.

The Australian National Health System

Australia's national health system, Medicare, is outstandingly good as it has not suffered from the funding deficiencies of the NHS over the years (although nurses are generally considered to be badly underpaid); many Australians, however, do choose to have additional private medical cover. There has been a recent surge in so-called 'medical tourism', whereby people in need of major treatment, such as a hip replacement or heart surgery, visit Australia specifically to take advantage of the good facilities, medical expertise and reasonable costs. Medicare is funded by the federal government and hospitals and other facilities are built and run by the various state governments, who are also responsible by law for maintaining a uniform minimum standard of care. In order to be eligible for Medicare, you must first register by completing an application form obtained either from a Medicare regional office or from any post office. You need not necessarily have registered with Medicare before you receive any medical treatment, but will be required to do so before you can make any claim. After you have registered, you will be sent a Medicare card, which looks like a credit card, and this should be carried with you at all times. You will need to present this card on arriving at a hospital for treatment. Any children will be listed on the card of one or other parent. When you lodge a claim for a Medicare rebate, you will be required to quote your number or present your card; rebates are made in cash over the counter, and the process is straightforward. You can also lodge claims by post, which takes considerably longer, and forms are available in chemists, doctors surgeries, and post offices.

All immigrants are covered by Medicare, provided they pay the tax levy (included in general taxes), and temporary residents who stay in the country longer than six months may be covered by Medicare without having to pay the levy. Medicare covers in-patient and out-patient treatment at public hospitals, as well as hospital accommodation costs in public hospitals. Medicare refunds 85% of scheduled (government approved) fees, regardless of the kind of treatment or service received. The remaining 15% is called a 'gap' fee and is paid by the patient. The 'gap' is currently limited to a maximum of $28.10, and low-income earners and people on benefits are exempt, so that no-one is denied treatment by virtue of financial difficulty. If you need regular, expensive treatment, Medicare will cover all of the scheduled fees incurred over the rest of the year once the gap has reached a total of $150 for any financial year. Prescription drugs will only total a maximum of $10 for each of the first 25 items per year, after which any medication is received entirely free of charge.

It is important to note that Medicare does not cover the balance of doctor's charges, when these exceed the scheduled fee, or the 15% gap, if the doctor does not bulk-bill the government. You will not be covered for treatment and accommodation at a public hospital if you have been admitted as a private patient, or for treatment and accommodation at a private hospital. Medicare does not cover physiotherapy, chiropractic or dental treatment, although some orthodontic treatment is refundable, particularly if surgery is involved. Neither medical repatriation nor funeral costs are covered, and ambulance costs (including transport and treatment) cannot be refunded through Medicare.

Reciprocal Agreements

Visitors to Australia from the UK, New Zealand, Ireland, Malta, Italy, Finland, Sweden and the Netherlands are also covered by Medicare under reciprocal arrangements, and can receive treatment under Medicare for six months from the date of arrival in Australia. You are not, however, entitled to claim health benefits for a medical condition which existed before your arrival in Australia, including any illness caught on your journey to Australia, or for any on-going medication. Travellers from the countries listed above should enrol at a Medicare office, presenting a passport containing an appropriate visa, and proof that your are enrolled in the national healthcare scheme of your home country. If you are a short-term visitor and you do not come from a country which has reciprocal health agreements with Australia, it is advisable to take out private medical insurance, which is usually available through your travel agent and is likely to be included in any travel insurance policy.

Medicare Exclusions
There are two categories of new settler which are exempt from eligibility for Medicare. These are people entering Australia to retire, and those who have been

granted permanent residence in the family stream migration category, who are the parents of their sponsor and are more than 55 years old (men) or 50 years old (women). Retirees need to take out travel insurance and private medical insurance (either in their country of origin or in Australia), as they are liable for all expenses incurred in the case of medical and hospital treatment, including the cost of hospital accommodation. In the case of family stream migrants, any medical or hospital expenses incurred by the migrant parent (over the stipulated age limit) will be the responsibility of the sponsor, unless the migrant has private insurance. If only one of the sponsor's parents is over the age limit, then the sponsor is only responsible for the medical expenses incurred by that parent. In addition, if you enter Australia as a foreign diplomat or as a member of a foreign diplomat's family, you are not covered by Medicare. It is advisable to take out private medical insurance either before you leave your home country or take out a policy in Australia immediately upon your arrival.

Private Medical Insurance

Private health insurance is widespread in Australia, with around 70 per cent of the population choosing to take out additional cover. Private health cover is much cheaper in Australia than in Britain, and premiums are not indexed for age or sex. Most people enjoy the security of knowing that they have the right to choose both the hospital where they will be treated and the specialist who will treat them. In addition, private cover offers refunds for medical services not covered by Medicare, such as physiotherapy, prescription glasses and sunglasses, and dental work. Different levels of cover are available, from basic table (shared-room) through to a fully comprehensive, deluxe table. Costs vary from around one dollar a week, up to around five dollars per week for the ultimate in hospital care. Premiums are usually payable in monthly, quarterly or annual instalments and discounts are usually given for prompt payment or for payments made annually. Children and dependants are usually covered by their parents' private medical insurance.

The recent Private Health Insurance Incentives Scheme was developed to make private insurance a more attractive proposition, especially to the young and healthy. The incentive is worth a maximum of $125 a year for single people, $250 for couples, and $450 for families; top cover earns the maximum rebate, which reduces with lower levels of cover. Those eligible are individuals who earn up to $35,000 per year, or couples who earn up to $70,000. The incentive is claimed either via a reduction in health fund premiums, or as a tax rebate at the end of the financial year. Privately-insured pensioners are best advised to claim their entitlement up-front from the health fund, and not to resort to the tax system. To claim a tax rebate, you must first have a tax liability which is at least as large as the amount you wish to offset. More information about the scheme can be obtained from the Health Information Line (1800 676 296), from the Tax Office (13 2862), or directly from your health fund.

When choosing a health fund, points to consider should include whether there are any exemptions for previous known illness or for AIDS, what the waiting period is before you can make a claim, and what the benefit limits are for each service covered. Private health insurance companies advertise widely in the local newspapers and on radio and television, with some of the largest and best known being Medibank Private, the Hospital Benefits Fund (HBF), and the Medical Benefits Fund (MBF). Some smaller funds now offer rebates for alternative medical treatments, such as homeopathy and accupuncture, so if you use these services, it will be worth shopping around quite carefully.

It is also possible to arrange private medical insurance in advance. One of the best known UK companies is BUPA International; see below for contact details.

Useful Addresses
BUPA International, tel 01273-208181; fax 01273-866583; e-mail advice@bupaintl.com; Website www.bupa-intl.com
Department of Health and Social Security, Overseas Branch, Benton Park Road, Newcastle-Upon-Tyne NE98 1YX, tel: 0191-213 5000.
ATI Travel Insurance: 37 Kings Exchange, Tilesyard Road, London N7 9AH, tel: 0171-609 5000.
Columbus Travel Insurance:, 17 Devonshire Square, London EC2 4SQ, tel: 0171-375 0011.

Crime and Police

Australia has many of the crime problems associated with developed nations and urban life, but on the whole, residents and visitors report feeling relatively safe. In particular, compared with other western countries, Australia's homicide statistics are very low, and, in spite of popular opinion which seems to indicate an escalation, they remained static over the last decade. The Australian Bureau of Statistics recently found that the most frequently reported crime is unlawful entry with intent, with motor vehicle theft the next most common crime, followed by robbery and sexual assault. The defining feature of Australian crime is the rarity with which firearms are employed. Australia has very stringent gun laws (which have become even more so since the tragic Port Arthur massacre), and only 20 to 25 per cent of homicides in Australia involved a the use of a gun, compared to around 70 per cent in the USA.

Crime patterns differ throughout the states and territories: the Northern Territory, for example, has the highest per capita rate for homicide and sexual assaults, but the lowest for armed robberies. Western Australia has the highest number of motor vehicle thefts and burglaries, but its rate of murder and attempted murder are at or below the national average. New South Wales had the highest rate of armed robbery, which is attributed to the fact that it has the largest heroin-dependent population in Australia. Canberra had the highest rate of kidnapping, attributed to acrimonious marital disputes over custody of children, and South Australia has the highest incidence of robbery and blackmail. The International Crime Victims Survey has noted that urban dwellers in Australia are four times more likely to install security devices than their rural cousins, and 62 per cent more likely to feel the need for special locks on exterior doors and windows. These levels are exactly comparable to similar communities in other western industrial nations. Australian crime figures are, in general, much more closely in line with European ones than with US figures, and Australian rates of motor vehicle theft are very low compared with those in the UK.

Police forces are the responsibility of state governments, and are headed in each state by a Commissioner for Police. Regulations for each force vary, and some may carry guns on duty, depending on the state. In recent years, allegations of police corruption in WA, NSW and Queensland have resulted in purges and high public accountability. In general, the police enjoy a good public profile and maintain open communications with the community.

Local Government

Below the level of State government, administration of local areas is undertaken by an elected town or shire council. This body is responsible for the provision and maintenance of public facilities and amenities, such as leisure centres, libraries, and rubbish collections. Payments for all housing rates and even dog-licensing are made to the local government. Planning permission for new buildings, demolitions, and extensions are also the responsibility of the local government, and vocal public meetings are frequently held to hear public discussion over topical local issues such as town planning and new developments. The local government level is the only one at which voting is not compulsory and, in general, most Australians are somewhat apathetic and avoid close involvement in local government decisions. Addresses and telephone numbers of local governments are available under the 'Local Government' section at the front of state telephone directories.

Social Life

Australians are generally friendly and outgoing people; they, in fact, find the British extremely reserved and often find it difficult to establish relationships with them because of this cultural barrier. Most Australians will quickly invite you into their home, often on introduction, and a barbecue is the most likely first point of association for both neighbours and colleagues. Nothing, however, will repel this friendly approach more than polite formality. First names rule in Australia, from top to bottom, and people are likely to be insulted by any other form of address. So, how can you break the ice, meet the locals and both accept and be accepted by them? This section tries to give you a little insight into Australian social life and the kinds of people and attitudes you are most likely to meet.

Manners and Customs

On the whole, Australians are a lot more casual than their British or European cousins. You will find that people, while friendly and courteous, will be far more direct in asking questions or in telling you what they think. You are much less likely to experience the occasionally chilling British reserve, and are more likely to know exactly where you stand. When you meet an Australian for the first time at a social gathering you may find that you are asked a lot of questions which you may think 'forward' or even intrusive. This directness is the normal form of social discourse, and a similar directness of response will be expected. It is generally considered to be a time-saver, enabling friendships to develop to a deeper and more interesting level more quickly. Titles are rarely used, and most people regardless of their position will expect to be addressed in first name terms. It would be quite normal, for example, for an undergraduate student to be comfortable calling the Vice-Chancellor of their university, say, 'Fay' or 'Derek'; and the corollary of this is that it would be extremely insulting for a person of senior position to address someone of lower status as Mr or Mrs. Far from being respectful, it would be considered patronising. Australian women will expect others to use the title Ms on occasions when a title is required, and eyebrows will be raised if a woman chooses to indicate her marital status by the use of Miss or Mrs.

One Australian custom which cuts across social barriers is the use of 'mate' as a form of address. The concept of mateship is a peculiarly Australian phenomenon and has been much studied anthropologically. Mateship generally refers to a specifically male bond, and constitutes a somewhat macho, but nonetheless powerful, kind of friendship. Many Australian men consider their mates to be as important, or even more important, than their female partner; and this bond often lasts to the grave. To be described as someone's life-long mate is the highest of compliments. Conversely, however, Australians also often use the term 'mate' ironically, or as an aggressive indicator in potentially explosive situations. The tone of voice will clearly indicate the level of use. Australian men, regardless of ethnic origin, will almost invariably use this form of expression.

Australians have a great respect for people who get out there and try something new or difficult. They love to support the underdog, and newcomers who really 'give it a go' will readily win the admiration and friendship of their new acquaintances and colleagues.

There are a number of associations of migrant communities in Australia, and all major cities will have branches of the Chung-Wah Chinese Association, and Greek, Italian, Yugoslav, and Irish Clubs. The United Kingdom Settlers Association (146 Toorak Road, South Yarra, VIC 3141, tel 03-9866 1722) is specifically intended to provide assistance and a point of contact for new migrants from Britain. Other clubs may be found in the Yellow Pages of your telephone directly, or by contacting the Department of Multicultural Affairs in your state.

Sport

Sport is popularly considered to be the Australian national past-time, and is central to the social life of many Australians. Most Australian children are encouraged to play at least one sport from a very early age. Little Athletics, an athletics training programme for children from the age of five upwards, is held on Saturday mornings around the country, and is very popular. Regional and national competitions are attended by club scouts on the lookout for new talent. Similarly, cricket and football (Australian Rules) are enormously popular at every age and skill level, and most Australian boys play at some time or another for their local club. Cricket is becoming increasingly popular with girls, but usually not until secondary school age or even later. Sporting centres all over the country also offer volleyball, netball and five-a-side soccer, and single-sex or mixed teams often have their own leagues. Many young working Australians will play in one such team at least one night per week as a way of keeping fit and meeting their friends.

Australian Rules football is the most popular winter game, and is a predominantly male sport. Aussie Rules football is a national institution, and the AFL Grand Final is comparable to the FA Cup Final in the level of interest it excites around the country. Every state has its own team or teams which play in the national league, with the West Coast Eagles, the Sydney Swans, Carlton, Geelong, and Essendon amongst the big names. Aussie Rules is a fast and athletic game, with much handling of the ball and some impressive jumping and mid-air collisions. The game is played by two teams of 18 players who try to score goals against each other. The goal posts consist of four tall, evenly-spaced poles, the two outer ones slightly shorter than the inside ones, and there is a goal at each end of the oval. The oval-shaped football field is about three times the size of a soccer pitch. If a player touches the ball over the line between the two middle posts, he has scored a goal, the team gains six points, and the goal umpire (always dressed in a white coat) will gesture and energetically wave two white flags. If the player touches the ball over the line between a middle and an outer pole, he will have only scored a single point, and the goal umpire will gesture with one of his index fingers, waving just one of the flags. The game consists of four quarters, each quarter lasting 45 minutes. Running with the ball is allowed, as long as it is bounced every three seconds; failure to do this means being 'caught with the ball'. Bouncing the ball while on the run is in fact not easy as the ball is oval-shaped, like a rugby ball. Although some of the players at the interstate level have started to wear head protection and gloves (to give them a better grip on the ball), Aussie Rules players pride themselves on their toughness and fitness. The game is gruelling and extremely hard on the players. It is long and very physical, but can also be intense and exciting. The best way to see a game is to go to an important interstate match, and catch the enthusiasm of the crowd.

In the eastern states, rugby (both league and union) are also known as football, and Queenslanders in particular take the game very seriously. Western Australia, the Northern Territory and Tasmania do not share the enthusiasm of the other states for rugby, but the nation as a whole is proud of its top level international rugby team, the Wallabies. Football of the kind played in the UK is always known as soccer and has a small but enthusiastic following, particularly amongst European ethnic communities who often field their own teams in state soccer competitions.

Hockey is very popular with men, women and children, and Western Australia prides itself on its exceptional facilities at Curtin University, and on its track record of providing most of the players in the national team. The Australian Institute of Sport trains its specially selected hockey stars of the future at these facilities. The Australian men's and women's hockey teams are respected and feared worldwide and they both compete at the very top of the international circuit.

Basketball and tennis are widely played throughout the country, and Australia has produced many Wimbledon champions. Basketball is played at regional and interstate levels, and the national league is relatively new, but extremely well supported and avidly watched on television. Australian players like Luke Longley have gone on to positions in America's NBL teams, and there is considerable interchange between the two countries. Obtaining a ticket for an interstate match can prove to be very difficult as they are snapped up as soon as they become available. Baseball is an even newer sport to Australia, but there is also a national league which is becoming increasingly popular.

Netball and softball also enjoy almost universal participation amongst young girls. Around 90% of Australian schoolgirls play in non-school netball teams during winter, and there are also summer competitive leagues, playing on weekday evenings, which are very popular. Most schoolgirls play softball in the summer. The Australian school curriculum incorporates sport into the normal school day, and each school, whether private or state, usually participates in both an interschool swimming carnival and an interschool athletics carnival every year. In addition, there are interschool cricket, netball, football, and softball leagues with games scheduled during school time or immediately after school. Many private schools, however, hold their interschool sporting matches on Saturdays. In fact, Saturday mornings and afternoons are unofficially dedicated to sport around the country, and parents should resign themselves to the inevitabilitiy that for at least five years they will have to get out of bed early on a Saturday morning to deliver their offspring to the relevant sporting venue.

An important difference in Australian sport for children is the widespread use of 'modified rules' in almost every game. Under modified rules sports, even quite young children are able to compete in complete safety, whilst learning the basic skills of the sport. Primary schools will undertake careful coaching in every sport played, and there is a strong emphasis on skill development. Modified rules sports are known by names which differentiate them from their big brother sports: junior hockey is called minkey, junior baseball is teeball (currently wildly popular), junior Aussie rules is touch football, and junior tennis, short tennis.

Above all, though, water sports are the cornerstone of Australian social and sporting life. Water-skiing, windsurfing, surfing, boating and diving are all common leisure activities, as well as highly competitive sports. Many Australians own their own pleasure boat, whether a yacht, power boat, or launch. Swimming is an essential part of every school's sporting curriculum at both primary and secondary levels, and in summer students will swim in either the school or local pool at least two or three times a week, if not every day. Pupils are divided into classes according to their age and swimming ability, and are rigorously coached by qualified instructors. Students are expected to attain swimming qualifications to a high level, and from the age of 13 are coached towards attainment of life-saving qualifications. Most students will leave high school with the Royal Life Saving Society's Bronze Medallion and Instructors Certificate. Every public swimming pool is home to a competitive swimming club, and many young Australians join these at an early age, often eventually swimming at a state or even national level. Almost every Australian child is a safe swimmer by the age of six, and school classes are focused on the development of refined technique and stamina. If you are moving to Australia with children, it would be advisable to have swimming coaching before you leave, so that they are not left high and dry at school. Once in Australia, do not allow your children to swim 'widths' in public swimming pools: this is considered highly anti-social and derisory, and even three year olds will be expected to tackle the length or keep to the baby pool. The Australian swimming, diving and water-polo teams are amongst the world's best, and young teenage champions are now casting a hopeful eye towards Sydney 2000.

The Arts

Although Australians are famous for their love of sport, they are also enthusiastic supporters of the arts. Their expenditure on arts products ranks among the highest in developed countries, and research shows that they read more newspapers per head than any other nation. Australian cultural achievements are now well-known internationally, through the awards gained by its many arts exports. The movie *Strictly Ballroom* won the Prix de la Jeunesse at Cannes in 1992, and *The Piano*, the Palme d'Or in 1993. Thomas Keneally and Peter Carey have both won the Booker Prize for Literature in Britain, and the Australian Ballet was described by the New York Times as 'world class' on its recent tour. The Australian Youth Orchestra is widely regarded as one of the best in the world, and is the training ground for the country's finest musicians.

Government support has been an important factor in developing the arts, and funding currently totals more than $2.5 billion per annum. The 'Creative Nation' programme provides an on-going commitment to the development of Australia's cultural heritage. The Australian Broadcasting Commission supports orchestras in each capital city, and the Sydney and Melbourne orchestras are flagship ensembles which frequently tour internationally. There are two major organisations involved in ballet and opera on a national basis, the Australian Ballet, and the Australian Opera, and most states also have state opera and ballet companies of a high standard. Musica Viva, established 50 years ago to promote chamber music in Australia, now co-ordinates one of the largest ensemble music concert networks in the world. It also organises overseas tours for Australian chamber music groups and commissions works by Australian composers. Youth Music Australia, formed in 1948, has helped the careers of thousands of young musicians, and the Australian Chamber Orchestra is at the cutting edge of early music performance.

Aboriginal art, indigenous dance and music have recently begun to be introduced to national and international audiences. Companies like Bangarra and the Tjapukai Dance Theatre now take their performances around Australia and around the world. Aboriginal art, once confined to the ethnographic sections of local museums, now takes its place in contemporary art galleries internationally. Aboriginal writers, such as Sally Morgan and Jack Davis, and the late Kevin Gilbert and Oodgeroo Nunuccal, are well known throughout Australia. Sally Morgan's *My Place* is a moving account of the discovery of her Aboriginal heritage, and provides a keen insight into some regrettable episodes in Australia's history.

Many festivals and other large scale cultural events take place in Australia every year, and just a few of the most important of these are listed below:
Sydney Gay and Lesbian Mardi Gras
Moomba Festival (Melbourne)
Wangaratta Jazz Festival (Victoria)
The Festival of Perth
Artrage: The Festival of Perth Fringe
The Festival of Adelaide
Every state has excellent library services both at the local and state level, and the National Library of Australia provides research facilities for scholars from all around the country. It is also home to the national archives. There are good art galleries in every state, and a strong commitment to bringing international touring exhibitions to Australia.

Shops and Shopping

Shopping in Australia's metropolitan centres is generally excellent. In suburban areas, large shopping centres offer speciality shops for clothing and goods, as well as supermarkets. Bigger shopping centres often also have a 'food hall', offering a wide variety of economical meals from cuisines from around the world. Many also have cinemas complexes. Most older suburbs will have a 'high street' (although it will never be known by this name) very similar to an English high street, with smaller retailers, chain stores, and service outlets. Newer suburbs tend to be planned around a US-style shopping mall, and do not usually have the convenience of a 'corner shop', known in Australia as a 'deli'. In areas with large immigrant populations, delis often stock a wide range of exotic foods in addition to essential items. Shops are generally open from 9am-5pm, 5.30pm or 6pm Monday to Saturday, with 'late night trading' until 9pm one night a week (usually a Thursday or Friday). Shops are not usually open on a Sunday, as Sunday trading is still illegal except in designated 'tourist areas', although this legislation is currently under review. Delis and chemists are the only shops which are free from trading restrictions: delis are usually from open 8am-8pm and every city will have a number of chemists which are open 24 hours a day, 365 days a year. There is an increasing number of 24-hour shops in Australia, of the 7-Eleven type, and most cities have a handful of these scattered through the suburbs.

The quality of Australian produce and goods is generally good. Items bearing a green and gold triangular symbol have been manufactured in Australia, and these are generally more expensive than equivalent goods manufactured in south-east Asia, due to the higher cost of Australian labour. The high quality of Australian-made products is also reflected in their higher prices. In general, however, Japanese, Taiwanese, and Korean products, particularly electrical goods and vehicles, conform to Australia's strict quality standards and are usually very competitively priced. Australia is constantly seeking to improve its balance of trade by encouraging consumers to buy Australian, and in many cases appeals to loyalty and patriotism to counteract the imperative of the hip pocket.

Shopping in Australia can be an enjoyable experience, with a wide range of products available in modern, well-equipped shopping centres, as well as ample car parking. In rural and more remote areas, however, the situation can be very different. Choice is much more likely to be limited as shopping centres service much smaller populations, and prices may be significantly higher because of freight costs. Most country dwellers prefer to wait until a trip to the city before shopping for electrical goods or clothing.

Supermarkets
Supermarkets use the same barcoded shopping system as the UK, and your groceries will be electronically scanned at the till. One pleasant difference, however, is that in Australia if an incorrect price registers on the scanner – and you are on the ball enough to spot the mistake – the price of the item is voided from your receipt and by law you are given the item for free. Supermarkets thus have a keen incentive to keep their barcoding accurate.

Loyalty cards have not been introduced in Australian supermarkets (although some small boutiques and restaurants operate similar schemes), however, many of the larger supermarkets, such as Coles and Woolworths, print vouchers on the back of their itemised receipts offering free meal deals (on a buy one, get one free basis) at local restaurants and chains, and discounts on anything from carpet cleaning to photo processing.

Edge-of-town superstores are rare, and most people shop in either a large supermarket located in a shopping mall, or in one of the many smaller franchised supermarkets, such as Supa-Valu or Foodland, in the local high street. Supermarkets large and small advertise pages of weekly 'specials' in the local papers, and prices are very competitive.

The great majority of shops accept cheques and major credit cards with adequate proof of identification, and it is possible to use ATM cards at most supermarkets to pay by direct debit.

Bottle Shops
By law, alcohol may not be sold in Australian supermarkets. Alcoholic drinks can only be bought from licensed liquor stores, also known as 'bottle shops'. Drive-in bottle shops are very common, and provide the convenience of driving your car up to the shop, rolling down the car window and giving your order and money to the attendant in exchange for your cartons of beer or casks of wine. If availing yourself of a drive-in bottle shop, remember that in Australia you cannot drink and drive! Bottle shops are usually open from 10am -10pm, Monday to Saturday, and

until 8pm on Sunday. They generally stock an extensive range of quality wines, as well as the usual beer and spirits, and most will have a giant walk-in coolroom, where all white wines are kept chilled. You need *never* visit a bottle shop in summer and come home with a warm bottle of white wine; Australians visiting the UK are incredulous at the lack of refrigeration in off-licences. Larger alcohol-retailing chains, such as Vintage Cellars, hold regular wine tastings, wine discussion evenings for regular customers, and publish monthly newsletters analysing the latest releases and grape harvests. If you are having a party, most will accept the return of unopened bottles purchased from them in a bulk order (as long as labels and seals are not water-damaged from immersion in ice).

Clothes

Many European immigrants are of the opinion that the quality of clothing in Australian department stores is not as high as that found in equivalent stores in the EU. European clothes are usually made of better quality materials and to higher standards than the same kind of clothing in Australian stores, which is largely imported from South-east Asia. Having said this, the cost of clothing from a budget-priced Australian store such as K-Mart or Target (roughly equivalent to C&A), as well as from other mid-range chain boutiques such as Picnic, Oasis and Esprit, is, depending on the current exchange rate, as much as 50% less than clothing from UK stores of a comparable standard. Clothes from shops, such as Monsoon, which have branches in both the UK and Australia, are cheaper than their exact counterparts in England. European designer label fashions can be bought in all the capital cities, but at a price, and Australia has some very highly regarded designers of its own. You will find, however, that the dress code both at the office and at most social occasions is informal by European standards, especially in summer. Leather goods, especially shoes and bags, tend to be considerably more expensive in Australia, to the extent that it may be worth investing in a few good quality items before you leave the UK; for women, the same applies to Marks and Spencers lingerie, which is always gleefully acquired by the bagful by Australian tourists in England.

Food and Wine

Food

Australian food and eating habits have changed enormously in recent decades, to the extent that a bland, English-style, cuisine-less culture, has become one of the food meccas of the world. As recently as 20 years ago, Australian food was known only for its meat pies, slabs of steak, lamingtons, pavlovas, and pumpkin scones. In the post-war years, however, the gradual influx of waves of migrants from Italy, Greece, Yugoslavia, Turkey, Lebanon, India, Thailand, China, Malaysia, Indonesia and Vietnam, meant the enrichment of the longer-standing Anglo-Irish eating style. The sunny climate and outstanding fresh produce and seafood provided the perfect seedbed for the cuisines of the mediterranean and South-East Asia, so that now chefs are renowned for their 'fusion' food, mixing traditions from around the world.

Meat still plays an important part in the Australian diet, and the choice and quality is impressive by European standards, as well as being very inexpensive. Beef, lamb, pork and poultry of all cuts and types are available, as are more unusual options, such as kangaroo, emu, and crocodile. These latter items are speciality fare, but are beginning to be farmed for both the export and domestic markets. In recent years, 'bush tucker' has become popular, at least as a concept, and in each state there are a number of restaurants offering native aboriginal foods elevated from the campfire to the table. If you have a strong stomach, you may like to try witchetty grubs, usually served, tongue-in-cheek, poking out of a bush apple. Australia has a superb range of delicious seafood, including prawns, lobsters, crayfish, octopus, oysters, mussels, mudcrabs, and Balmain bugs (a small crustacean). A huge variety of fresh fish, most of which will be unfamiliar to European visitors, are available: try dhufish in Western Australia, for example. If you buy fish from a fish and chip shop, you are most likely to be served either shark or snapper: don't be put off by the idea of shark, as it is considered to be a good quality eating fish. The menu of the average fish and chip shop will also offer crab, prawns, squid (calamari), oysters or mussels, as well as a choice of homemade marinated pickles. Fruit and vegetables are all grown locally, and include many tropical varieties, such as lychees, avocados, and papayas.

Barbecues continue to be an integral part of Australian social life, but the cuisine has dramatically improved. These days any respectable barbecue will be laden with tiger prawns, marinated rump steak and chicken fillets, or perhaps a whole fish garnished with ginger and spring onions. Even without the spectacular beaches, Finlays Fresh Fish BBQ in Kalbarri, Western Australia, would make the six-hour drive north of Perth worthwhile. This shack in the sand will cook you up unbelievable prawns fresh out of the water, as well as fish and enormous steaks, barbecued for you by Mr Finlay himself. Finlay's mum takes your cash (about $8-$12 depending on what you are having) and prepares a range of salads and as many sauces for your meal, from which you help yourself. As you sit on the benches with a drink and watch the sun set in the vast sky, your prawns sizzle next to you on the barbecue.

Whether you have a barbie prepared by professionals like the Finlays, or one in your own back yard, or you grill-up on coin-operated gas barbecues provided by the local council, the food is likely to be great and the company congenial.

Restaurants

Australian food is distinguished by the outstanding quality and freshness of the produce. You can expect to eat at a cheap-and-cheerful restaurant for between $10-$15 for a two course evening meal and coffee, excluding wine. Portions are usually generous. In Perth, the wonderful Greco's, for example, will serve up enough superb Greek food to feed a family of four for a mere $20 in total: you will not find food of this quality and price anywhere in England. In cities with big multicultural populations (most of the capitals, and many larger regional towns), you will usually find family-run restaurants which offer great food at incredible prices: in Sydney, 'No Names' used to be famous for serving up giant plates of spaghetti with a hunk of ciabatta and olive oil for just $2, and in Perth, 'The Roma', run by the same Italian family for 30 years, still has queues outside on a Friday night for a plate of mama's pasta. You can eat at The Roma, and dozens of places like it, for $5 a head; the decor is very basic, but the service is good, and children are welcome. In Northbridge, there are very similar restaurants run by Vietnamese families, and serving up dozens of hot and spicy specialties. The variety of restaurants available in all major Australian cities is enormous, and is at least as varied as in London. Greek, Vietnamese, Mongolian, ethnic Chinese and Indian, Mexican, Lebanese, Portuguese, Italian, Russian, Thai and Polish are all available Australia-wide. Japanese food is very popular, and *ramen* shops and sushi bars are found in most suburban areas. Street markets, like shopping centres, will often have a food hall (if in Perth, try Subiaco Markets), where you can buy a good Japanese, Thai, or Italian meal for as little as $5. Australians are generally very accommodating towards families who bring their children to eat in restaurants, probably because of the influence of child-loving European and Chinese immigrants, and you will be treated with consideration and respect if you choose to introduce your offspring to fine dining at an early age.

At the top end of the market, there are innumerable first class restaurants, offering the finest food and wines. Modern Australian cuisine emphasises the quality of the ingredients rather than fanciful techniques, and there is a horror of 'over-worked' food. Service is discreet, and there will usually be a qualified sommelier to advise on appropriate wines (which will be predominantly Australian). Expect to pay up to $150 a head in the best restaurants, but it will be worth it, especially if, as many do, the restaurant comes with spectacular views over the river, harbour or ocean.

Café culture is firmly established, and unlike England, you can be sure of a really good cup of coffee in most establishments. The *Dome*, a national franchise of coffee provendors, takes its coffee very seriously indeed, and even casual staff spend a week in training, learning how to make cappucino, macchiato, and espresso as they are made in Italy. If your preferred cuppa is of the type known as a *latte* in England, you should ask for a 'flat white' (or with low-fat milk, a 'skinny flat white'). Any decent café will sell all its various coffees in decaffinated style as well.

Tipping is discretionary in Australia, however, if you should decide to tip your waiter, it is customary to leave between 10 and 15 per cent. Some restaurants include a service charge, but this is unusual.

Traditional Australian Food

Australians are particularly fond of fruit and vegetables, and an Australian fruit salad is likely to surpass anything you have previously eaten. Fruit salad is the traditional dessert to accompany a barbecue, and you may be asked to bring one if you are invited as a guest. Be imaginative and include all the various fresh and exotic fruits on display in your greengrocers. The pavlova is an Australian invention, also most often seen at barbecues. It was created for the ballerina, Anna Pavlova, on an Australian tour, and consists of a meringue base covered with whipped cream and seasonal fruits.

The lamington is another Australian institution, and consists of a cube of extremely light sponge which has been dipped in a special chocolate sauce and then rolled in coconut. School Parents' Associations invariably have 'Lamington Drives' as a way of fund raising: school members take orders from students, parents, friends and relatives for at least one dozen lamingtons each, and then a battalion of parents get together to prepare this delicacy. A box of a dozen lamingtons usually sells for about $4.00. Everybody loves lamingtons, and there are few more effective fund-raising endeavours.

Many Australians grow passionfruit vines in their gardens, and passionfruit icing is very popular for sponge cakes. If you are lucky enough to have a passionfruit vine, make sure that you give it plenty of water and you will be rewarded with the world's most heavenly fruit right through the summer months.

The most famous Australian take-away food is the meat pie. This is traditionally eaten at Aussie Rules Football matches, and by school children (or at least by those with undeveloped tastebuds); they are always served with tomato sauce. Commercially mass-produced meat pies are pretty horrible, and you really have to be drunk or desperate to eat one in these days of gastronomic variety. At a basic barbecue, perhaps one given by older Australians, expect beef sausages and a big slab of steak.

Wine

Viticulture is one of Australia's leading primary industries, and wine drinking has enjoyed enormous growth as wine production has become more sophisticated and eating habits have changed. Australia's climate and coastal fringe landscape is conducive to wine growing, and all states have extensive wine producing areas. The diverse climate, topography and soil types mean, however, that Australia is able to produce a wide range of wine styles, from delicate sparkling whites, to full bodied reds, and exceptionally rich fortified wines. There are currently 44 regions of significance to the wine industry, each of which produces distinctive wine varieties. Australia has around 60 different varietals, although most wine drinkers will be familiar with around only 20 names, including Chardonnay, Semillon, Sauvignon, and Shiraz. Lesser known types, such as Palomino and Pedro Ximenes, which do not appear on wine labels, are used for making sherry, and Pinot Meunier, is used in the production of sparkling wine. Every variety has a specific aroma and taste, known as the primary fruit characters, and many wines will use a blend of these different types. There are currently no less than 914 vineyards in Australia, and over 78,000 ha of land under vines. The top export markets for Australian wines are the UK and USA, and exports total around $1.1 billion annually; wine exports exceed wine imports by ten to one. The top five wine grape varieties currently under cultivation are Chardonnay, Shiraz, Cabernet Sauvignon, Semillon, and Reisling.

Regional Varieties
Some of the best known regional wine growing areas are described below:
Margaret River (WA). The wine industry in Western Australia was founded even before those of South Australia and Victoria, and for the next 135 years commercial viticulture was confined to the Swan Valley, around Perth. In the mid-1960s, the wine industry began to move south, with the first plantings at Margaret River and Mount Barker. Margaret River has grown to be one of Australia's finest and most vibrant wine producing regions, known for its Chardonnay, Sauvignon Blanc and Cabernet Sauvignon.

The climate of the Margaret River area is strongly maritime, more so than any other Australian wine region, and is the most mediterranean in style. Overall, the climate is similar to that of a Pomerol or St. Emilion in a dry vintage, which accounts for the quality of its Cabernet, Sauvignon, and Merlot varieties. Margaret River's reputation was founded on its Cabernet Sauvignon, and rests on it today. Virtually every winery produces one of these blends, and the style has evolved over the last few decades. The common threads of this wine are ripe grapes, which produce a sweet core, and a slightly earthy tannin. The Chardonnay variety was pioneered by the Leeuwin Estate, and is probably Australia's greatest example of the type. It tends towards a concentrated, complex, viscous and tangy taste, which does not cloy or become heavy. Permutations of Semillon and Sauvignon Blanc are combined to produce a regional speciality known as the Classic Dry White. This wine has a pleasantly herbal or grassy flavour.

There are many fine restaurants in the Margaret River region, a number of which are attached to vineyards: the most outstanding (and expensive) is without doubt the one on the Leeuwin Estate, which can only be described as the experience of a lifetime. Important regional events include the annual Leeuwin Concert, and the Porongorup Wine Festival.

Barossa Valley (SA). Vines arrived with the first settlers to South Australia and in the early days, suburban Adelaide was the site of extensive vineyards. The Barossa

Valley (including the Eden Valley), Clare Valley, and McLaren Vale were all established in the middle of the nineteenth century by German immigrants, and wine growing continues to play a central role in the state's economy. In 1996, South Australia produced half of all Australia's wine. The climate of the Barossa Valley is almost identical with that of Bordeaux, and is ideal for full bodied red wines, excellent fortified wine, and robust whites. Shiraz is the most important local variety, and the Barossa Valley is the home of Penfolds Grange, the greatest Shiraz wine made outside the Rhône Valley. Almost every Barossa winery will include a shiraz or shiraz blend amongst its offerings. The style is full bodied, rich in colour, with a touch of chocolate, and a hint of roasted flavour; the wines are long lived. Old vine Grenache and Mourvedre are currently in as much demand as old vine Shiraz, with intense competition between fortified and table wine makers for the available harvest. The Barossa Valley Reisling has a quintessentially Australian style, with strong passionfruit/tropical fruit/lime flavours, which build beautifully with bottle age. Semillon has had a renaissance in recent years, and is frequently given a toasting of American oak; it develops quickly into a robust, full-bodied wine.

Important local events include 'Barossa Under the Stars' (attracting performers such as Julio Iglesias), the Barossa Vintage Festival, and the Barossa Wine Show.

Clare Valley (SA). The Clare Valley has a continuous history of wine making which dates back almost 150 years. It is a high quality producer of long lived, intensely flavoured, and strongly structured table wine, which are all made in strictly limited quantities. The climate of the Clare Valley, in terms of its viticulture, is strongly dependent on its cool afternoon breezes which play an important role in slowing ripening on the vines. It is moderately continental, and irrigation is essential due to the winter-spring dominance of the rainfall.

Much of Australia's finest Riesling is grown in the Clare Valley: typically, it is an austere wine at first, with hints of passionfruit and lime, which quickly develops an touch of lightly browned toast. These wines are long lived and will improve in the bottle for up to 10 years. Cabernet Sauvignon is the other great wine of the region, and is always full-bodied, or even dense. Chardonnay, Semillon, Sauvignon Blanc and Grenache, either singly or in blends, contribute the other main wines of the region.

Important regional events include the Clare Valley Spring Festival, and the Clare Regional Wine Show.

Hunter Valley (NSW). The Hunter Valley, and particularly its upper region, was reborn in the 1960s and has become one of Australia's premier white wine areas. Typically, it produces soft, rich Chardonnays and quick maturing Semillons from its highly productive vineyards. Chardonnay is regarded as the outstanding wine of the region, with all wine makers producing examples of real merit. Rosemount Roxburgh is considered Australia's greatest example of the style, and is rich, complex, toasty and creamy, with a strong charred oak overlay. Hunter Valley Semillons are usually fleshy, soft, and likely to be oak-influenced, although in recent years there has been a strong move towards traditional, unwooded Semillon styles. These wines peak at around two to four years of age.

The Australian wine industry has an excellent website as www.wineaustralia.com.au which gives general information, the location of all vineyards, and events listings for the whole country. If you plan to sip your way around Australia, this is the place to start.

Brewing

According to Paul Hogan, speaking on behalf of Fosters, the 'amber nectar' is Australia's favourite drink, and many Australians would not dispute that claim. Every state has its own local beers, which are available nationally; the best known of these are Swan and Emu from WA, Tooheys and Fosters (NSW), Victorian Bitter, or VB, from Victoria, and Castlemaine XXXX from Queensland. You will also find that these days most Australians also drink international lagers, and Mexican beers like Sol and Corona are particularly popular. They are usually served with a slice of lime. Beer in pubs is always served ice-cold. Bitter beer or stout is not generally available on tap (draught) in pubs as Australia is an almost exclusively lager-drinking nation, and most Australians find the idea of 'warm beer' quite disgusting. You should, however, be able to find Guinness on tap in most pubs. Ciders such as Strongbow (dry, sweet or draught) or Woodpeckers are also available. Boutique beers are now an important part of the market: Redback and Matilda Bay are major players in this field, but are more expensive. Ice-brewed beers such as Hahn Ice are also trendy. Australia does not have a pub culture like Britain: people do not congregate at a local, and are more likely to drink in wine bars, pleasant beer gardens, or with friends at home. Pubs often have a 'sundowner', or happy hour, with cheaper drinks and sometimes entertainment, usually around the hours of summer sunset. The 'Sunday Session' is a similar occasion, held on a Sunday afternoon. For older Australians, the sundowner or the Sunday session is an important part of leisure and social life, however, younger people have developed different drinking habits and customs, and the pub industry is in a serious state of decline.

Public Holidays

The long weekend has become an Australian institution, and is taken very seriously as an opportunity to get in some quality leisure time. On Friday afternoons at the start of a long weekend there is inevitably heavy traffic as people head out of the city to various beach and bush locations, to be repeated on the following Monday evening as the traffic streams back. Every state legislates its own public holidays, however, there are also a number of country-wide holidays, which are usually occasions of national or religious significance. The following dates are public holidays throughout Australia:

New Year's Day, 1 January

Australia Day, 26 January. This is the day on which Australia celebrates the anniversary of the landing of the first fleet in at Port Philip in NSW, a date popularly considered to be Australia's birthday. All around the nation, local councils and authorities mount concerts and firework displays to help the celebrations get under way with a bang. Fireworks are considered a centrepiece of the occasion (especially as Guy Fawkes' Day is not commemorated and, after all, everyone needs an excuse to let off some rockets). In Perth, the 'Skyshow' is mounted from two barges moored in the Swan River. Hours before starting time, the river is lined with families and friends carrying their portable stereos, torches (to switch on and wave at the given signal), blankets and picnics. Two hours of music, lasers, fireworks and general goodwill follow, and a spirit of community dominates.

Good Friday

Easter Monday

ANZAC Day, 25 April. This national holiday commemorates the sacrifices of Australia's war heroes. Originally designed to recognise the soldiers of the

Australian and New Zealand Army Corps who died at Gallipoli during WWI in a defining moment in Australian history, it now includes all Australian military personnel and commemorates their participation in campaigns in both world wars, Vietnam, and Korea. Every major city and town hosts marches by old soldiers and, these days, their descendants, wearing uniforms and medals. There are dawn ceremonies at war memorials around the country, and the day is considered to be a solemn one. Many citizens line the streets to watch the marches. On the other hand, there is also a significant number of people who believe that ANZAC day has become irrelevant to Australia's younger generation, and who resent the glorification and sentimentalisation of war. Armistice Day (11 November) is not widely observed in Australia, and the tradition of poppy-wearing is now quite rare.

Queen's Official Birthday. This is a movable holiday which always falls on a Monday in June (except in WA). As Australia heads towards becoming a republic, we can expect this holiday to be replaced with something more appropriate.

Christmas Day 25 December.

Boxing Day 26 December.

Regional Holidays:

The dates of some of these holidays may be variable.

Labour Day	7 March	(WA/TAS)
Labour Day	14 March	(VIC)
Canberra Day	21 March	(ACT).
Bank Holiday	5 April	(TAS)
Labour/May Day	2 May	(QLD/NT)
Adelaide Cup Day	16 May	(SA)
Foundation Day	6 June	(WA)
Alice Springs Show Day	1 July	(NT)
Darwin Show Day	22 July	(NT)
Bank Holiday	1 August	(NSW/ACT)
Picnic Day	1 August	(NT)
Labour Day	3 October	(NSW/ACT)
Queen's Birthday	26 September	(WA)
Labour Day	11 October	(SA)
Recreation Day	7 November	(TAS)
Melbourne Cup Day	1 November	(VIC)

Time

Calculating the time difference between Australia and Europe or the USA can be confusing, especially in the southern hemisphere summer, when some states institute daylight saving, while others don't. Queensland, the Northern Territory and Western Australia do *not* have daylight saving (it has been voted out in various referenda held in these states) and thus, their clocks do not move forward one hour between October and March. In addition, you need to remember that in the UK, the clocks are put forward an hour from Greenwich Mean Time between April and October. Below is a list of the time differences from GMT of the different states and territories:

Eastern Standard Time – 10 hours ahead of GMT: New South Wales, the Australian Capital Territory, Tasmania and Queensland.

Central Standard Time – 9.5 hours ahead of GMT: South Australia and the Northern Territory.

Western Standard Time – 8 hours ahead of GMT: Western Australia.

The time difference between WST and CST is 1.5 hours, between WST and EST is two hours, and between CST and EST is 30 minutes. An hour plus or minus should be added to account for daylight saving, according to the time of year.

Metrication

Australia fully adopted the European metric system in the late 1970s. The Australian approach to metrication differed from the half-hearted British one, in that after a short period of public education through the media, imperial measurements were dropped completely. Consumers were never given conversions on packets, for example 1lb/454g, or alternative Farenheit and Celsius weather reports, as in Britain, so people learnt new ways very quickly. Today, Australia is totally metricated: if you ask for a pound of mince at the butcher you will not be understood. All street signs and road maps note distances in kilometres, as do speedometers: a freeway sign which reads 'Next exit 3.5', must be interpreted as a metric distance. Weights are calculated in grams and kilograms, and temperatures are given in degrees Celsius. Distances and measurements are invariably expressed as a decimal rather than as a fraction. If you have children at school, they will be expected to be conversant with the metric system, and no instruction whatsoever will be given in calculating imperial measurement. The modern Australian child is unlikely to have any idea how many inches there are in a foot, or ounces in a pound; and, in fact, this probably applies to anyone under 35.

Retirement

Introduction

Australia has traditionally been the destination of young people, and most new arrivals have generally been either backpackers travelling on Holiday Working Visas or young immigrant families. Indeed, it is well known that applicants under 35 are far more likely to be granted residency in Australia, and the Points System of visa eligibility actively discriminates in favour of youth by docking points as the age of the applicant increases. In the past, the average age of the Australian population was relatively low in comparison with that of other developed countries, however, these days, in common with most industrialised nations, Australia is experiencing the 'greying' of its population. On the other hand, the elderly are perhaps not as noticeable in Australia as in Europe, as the climate encourages them to remain healthy and active much longer.

In recent years, as Australia has become more accessible in terms of cost and ease of travel, there has been a marked increase in the number of older people both visiting Australia and choosing to retire there. The Australian government has now introduced a visa and residence classification specifically for parents of new migrant settlers which allows any child who has gained permanent residency to sponsor their parents to enter the country on a long term basis (see *Residence and Entry Regulations* chapter for details). The warmer weather, cheaper housing and yearning for contact with children and grandchildren are all powerful factors influencing the decision to leave a lifetime's history behind to start a new life on the other side of the world.

Many older people moving to Australia feel that the journey itself is one of the most daunting considerations, as it is both expensive, and physically gruelling. Travel agents, however, can recommend ways of breaking your journey without adding too much to the expense, enabling you to recoup in stages and minimise jet lag. Alternatively, if you buy a cheap ticket, you are likely to find that it is cheap precisely because it is not a direct flight and will stop for up to four hours two or three times during the course of the journey. Many passengers take advantage of these stops to wander around the airport, helping to avoid stiffness, cramping and swollen ankles. Airlines can provide wheelchairs and support staff (who will, for example, help you collect your luggage) providing prior notice is given; you should also tell your travel agent or airline of any special medical conditions or dietary requirements at the time of booking your ticket. It is useful to know that if you order special meals for your flight, you are likely to be served first which, in a plane carrying around 300 passengers, can make a big difference to your personal comfort. In addition to practical tips and advice, this chapter provides information specifically for those wishing to retire to Australia, including the names and addresses of government support agencies.

The Decision to Leave the UK

Many retired people experience the 'empty-nest syndrome' most keenly when their offspring have moved not just out of home, but thousands of miles away to Australia. Although the warmer weather, hours of sunshine and lower cost of living are factors appealing in their own right, the deciding factor is likely to be the pull of the heart strings. The fact that many older Europeans who move to Australia have never previously visited suggests that it is the people, rather than the place, which are the main attraction. Although it takes enormous energy and motivation to move to any country when retired, it requires a significant extra input to pack up and transport yourself beyond the comforting familiarity of Europe. The images most Europeans have of Australia have been carefully packaged by marketing experts to encourage tourism, and as a consequence they are generally aimed at the young and mobile independent traveller. In order to make sure that Australia really is the place in which you wish to spend the rest of your days, it is highly advisable to take an extended holiday of up to six months in order to gain a more accurate impression of what life in Australia as a retiree might be like. A long stay in Australia to allow you to familiarise yourself with its people and way of life may, to a certain extent, prevent you from eventually suffering the inevitable homesickness too intensely.

There are distinct advantages to be gained by retiring to Australia. Firstly, you will not need to master a foreign language, as you would if choosing to retire somewhere in Europe. Additionally, the weather in most inhabited parts of Australia is superb, with warm temperatures and glorious sunshine, and the coastal location of most Australian cities means that residents enjoy the benefits of fresh sea air. Senior Citizens are also well looked after, and receive many special benefits and discounts for various facilities and services including public transport, holidays, bills, restaurants, and hairdressing. Currently, the very favourable pound to dollar exchange rate, combined with the lower costs of living and property in Australia, mean that moving to Australia from most European countries after retirement, particularly to join children who have already migrated, can also be very financially advantageous.

People over the age of 60 in Australia are always known as 'Seniors'. The terms 'old age pensioner', OAP, and 'pensioner' were removed from the official vocabulary years ago, as being derogatory. Seniors are generally accorded a level of respect commensurate with their lifetime of experience.

Residence and Entry Regulations

The Residence and Entry requirements for retired people who wish to move to Australia are described in full in Chapter Two. Briefly, there are two ways in which it is possible to retire to Australia. The first method is only applicable if you do not have family already living in Australia. In this case, if you are at least 55 years of age and have no dependants other than your spouse, you may be able to enter Australia to retire providing you meet financial, health and character requirements. The Australian Government will only allow retired people who have no other connections with Australia to enter the country if they can support themselves and have the financial means to make Australian investments. In other words, you will be expected to contribute to, and not drain, Australian resources: you will need at least $A500,000 capital, or a combination of at least $A150,000 plus further income of at least $A35,000 per annum.

If you do have family in Australia, you may be eligible to enter as a retiree under the family stream migration programme, which enables parents to join children already living in Australia. This is by far the more common way to enter the country to retire. Full details of this scheme are given in Chapter Two. Basically, Category 103, Family Stream Migration, entitles the parent of any child, who must have been a permanent resident of Australia for a minimum of two years, to be granted residency in their own right. The potentially prohibitive financial requirements applying to non-family stream retirees do not apply in this case; however, your child must guarantee to sponsor you financially for two years after your arrival in the country.

Obtaining a Residence Permit

If you enter Australia on a Retirement visa, you will never be granted permanent residency. You will enter the country on a six month multiple entry visa which you then need to transfer to a four-year retirement visa. This visa is issued on a renewable basis, so your status as resident is more tenuous, perhaps, than for other categories of residency: applications for visa renewal can be refused if your circumstances have changed significantly or if you no longer meet the financial, health or character requirements.

If you enter the country on a Class 103 family stream migration visa, you will automatically be granted permanent residency after you have been resident in Australia for two years.

You should note that Australia really takes a very strict line on visas and immigration, and the authorities will not hesitate to deport people who do not comply with regulations, regardless of considerations of age or compassionate circumstances. Recently, for example, a British couple, who celebrated their retirement with a visit to Australia, were deported after staying on illegally for 16 years. The couple, who had worked and paid taxes in Australia during this period, were given no leeway, and were required to leave the country immediately and permanently. They were discovered after making a pension claim.

Possible Retirement Areas

Almost every major city in Australia offers ideal retirement conditions, in terms of beautiful weather and reasonable housing costs. Darwin, Alice Springs and other cities and towns in Australia's interior or northern regions, however, often experience insufferably hot weather in summer, which many people (both old and young) find difficult. The southern coastal regions have quite cool winters, but nowhere will conditions be as severe as a typical British or French winter. Many older people love the Mediterranean weather of Perth, Adelaide and Sydney, while others prefer the cooler temperatures of Tasmania or the unpredictable and varied Melbourne weather. A large number of Australians like to retire to Queensland, particularly favouring Cairns and the Gold coast, with its abundant tropical sunshine and cheap housing; others find the humidity oppressive and prefer a more temperate climate. In NSW, the Central Coast, particularly around Gosford, is a major retirement area, with many facilities for the elderly; and in WA, the regional towns of Safety Bay, Mandurah, and Dunsborough have a special appeal for retirees.

Retirement Villages

All cities and major regional towns have special accommodation available for seniors, known as Retirement Villages. The decision to enter a retirement village usually means both a major financial commitment and lifestyle change, and should be regarded as an investment in lifestyle rather than a financial arrangement: usually, any amount payable on refund will be considerably less than that originally contributed. By law, villages must consist of units for completely independent residents, units with assistance, including some nursing care and meals, for less independent residents, and rooms with 24-hour nursing care available for the fully dependent residents. There are both government and privately owned and managed Retirement Villages, and many are run by church groups of different denominations.

Buying into a retirement village can be complex, and will involve a contract. Such contracts are usually lengthy and replete with legalese, and it is wise to obtain the advice of a solicitor or accountant with experience in this area. Not all legal professionals will be aware of important issues for ageing people, such as contracting incomes, and advocacy organisations, such as the Council on the Ageing (addresses for each state are given below), can provide expert advice. Questions which should be considered are:

are there any conditions attached to changes of ownership?

what are the annual charges?

what are the ongoing costs? Look especially for items such as water levies, swimming pool maintenance, audit fees, and management.

who has decision-making power? Are there resident panels or elected representatives?

are there deferred management fees?

is there an arbitration process available in case of disputes?

You should also note that it is not necessarily automatic that you will be moved from one tier of care to another as your circumstances change. Instead, you may be required to terminate the original agreement and buy in again. Buying a home in a retirement village is not an investment, and there is no guarantee of security: if the development has problems, there may be no protection for the money you have put in.

If you plan eventually to enter a retirement village, you should shop around before placing your name on a waiting list. Villages are generally modern, well-equipped and are professionally managed with a high quality of care. They are often built close to shopping centres, public transport and police stations, and have contact with the community through local schools and churches. In general, the Australian attitude to Seniors is to keep them active and independent as long as possible, and the Retirement Villages, purpose-built according to strict legal guidelines, reflect this. Further information about retirement villages and other types of seniors accommodation is available from the organisations listed under *useful addresses* below.

Note that if you enter the country on the Retirement visa and you wish to buy a house in Australia, you will need to write to the Foreign Investment Review Board, c/o the Treasury, Parkes Place, Parkes, ACT 2600. As you will never be considered a permanent resident, you will not be eligible for a place in a government Retirement Village, and you may also find it more difficult to find a place in a private one.

Retirement Village Glossary

Accommodation unit. The part of the retirement village in which a resident has exclusive right to reside. This can be either an independent living unit, a service apartment, or a hostel bed.

Body Corporate Manager. The manager of the body corporate (legally-constituted owners' association) of a freehold retirement village. The role of the retirement village manager is usually greater than that of the body corporate manager, especially where a range of services are provided.

Deferred Management Fee. A fee paid to the operators for their part in the operation of the scheme over the time a resident stays in the village. It is usually expressed as a percentage of the price of the unit, and increases over the years as a person stays in the village.

Ingoing Contribution. The price for the right to reside in a unit in a retirement village.

Nursing Homes. Most nursing homes are regulated by the Commonwealth Government under the Aged Care Act 1997.

Sinking Fund. A fund established to provide for irregular expenditure (for example, external painting or roof maintenance). Residents usually contribute to the sinking fund through service charges.

Statutory charge. A means of protecting residents' ingoing contributions by registering a security similar to a mortgage on the title to the retirement village land.

Types of ownership. Generally these are either leasehold (usually 99 years), freehold or strata title. Strata title gives you ownership of the living area and a share of any property held in common.

Pensions (from your country of origin)

Australia does not have any reciprocal pension agreements with the United Kingdom. This means that although you are fully entitled to your British pension if you live in Australia, the level of pension payments will be frozen from the date you leave Britain, and you will not receive any cost of living increases in pension payments made after this date. Currently, pensions are indexed to the cost of living and are adjusted annually, but when you become resident of another country you forfeit this adjustment. Although this may seem a nominal sum to forfeit, over the years it may become a significant amount of money and your pension may cease to be adequate. This must be weighed up against the lower cost of living in Australia and the fact that there is no council tax or VAT on electricity and gas. British expatriates in five of the largest Commonwealth countries including Australia, formed an organisation in September 1994 as part of a continuing battle to improve the financial position of those pensioners residing in the 137 countries where British State pensions are frozen. There are currently 159,235 people in such a position in Australia, however the rule is waived in 33 countries, including European ones, where 230,000 British expatriates receive the same annual increments as pensioners in Britain.

If you intend to become a permanent resident of Australia, the process of transferring your pension payments is surprisingly simple. All you need to do is go to your local British DSS office and inform them that you are leaving the country. They will then make arrangements upon your instructions to have your pension paid to you in Australia, or into a bank account in the UK if you prefer. For further information, you should contact the Overseas Branch of the Department of Social Security in Newcastle (tel: 019122 59459, or the International Operations Branch of the Australian Department of Social Security, GPO Box 273C, Hobart 7001, tel: +61 3 6200 333 or fax: +61 3 6204 600).

Taxation (from your country of origin)

It is not often that one receives good news from the tax office, and therefore it perhaps comes as something of a pleasant surprise to learn that if you leave Britain and you are currently paid a pension, you will not have to pay any British tax on that pension when you leave the country provided you have received approval from the Inland Revenue and the Australian Taxation Office (ATO). If you are not currently retired and therefore are not receiving a pension, it is advisable to have a Retirement Pension Forecast made by the Department of Social Security. This is a simple process which involves going to your local DSS office and picking up a BR19 form. Upon its completion and return, the DSS will be able to give you some idea of what kind of pension you can expect to receive when you retire. This kind of information may be extremely helpful if you are considering the financial implications of moving to Australia, and may also help you with your taxation returns in Australia.

Although you will not pay tax on income currently received from a state pension in the UK, British residents who settle in Australia can now face taxes of up to 47 per cent on any growth in their pension fund since leaving the UK even before they retire. This problem has developed from a ruling brought in by the Australian Taxation Office in 1994, which seeks to prevent tax avoidance through off-shore funds. With this legislation came major tax advantages with suitable pension restructuring. This legislation applies to any pension scheme whether UK or offshore. It also affects defined pension schemes as well as personal contracts. When former British residents now living in Australia tap into their pension funds, any growth since the date they left the UK is now taxed as income – at the potentially and likely higher marginal rate of 47 per cent. This applies to any pension scheme. They should also be aware that even if money is left in the UK fund, payments *will* be regarded as income by the Australian Taxation Office. Anyone moving or retiring to Australia who holds an existing UK pension fund must seek professional advice. You should also be aware that UK life policies, unit trusts, personal equity plans and the new Individual Savings Accounts do not necessarily carry the same tax advantages in Australia as in their country of origin, and that there will be tax implications depending on the particular product in which you have invested. Anyone in Australia in possession of these products is required by law to maintain comprehensive records of their overseas holdings, and penalties are in place for those failing to do so. Geraint Davies, MD of Montfort

International PLC (Home Farm, Shere Road, Guildford, Surrey GU5 9BL, tel 01483-202072; fax 01483-202073; email mintech@modus-group.co.uk) is an acknowledged expert in this field, with experience of both UK and Australian tax laws, and can advise prospective emigrants of their potential tax liabilities and suggest ways of minimising them.

Australian Pensions & Health Insurance

If you meet the requirements for a Retirement Visa and are granted entry into Australia, you will not be covered by Medicare (because you will not have contributed towards its costs through the Medicare levy, paid via income taxes), and you will have to make arrangements in your country of origin or take out private health insurance in Australia.

If you enter the country as a Class 103 migrant, your permanent residency entitles you to full Medicare cover once you have been in the country for two years. Your sponsor (i.e., your child) is expected to meet any medical expenses you may incur the first two years, although some of this may be refunded. It is important to check with Medicare and/or your private health insurer as to the conditions which are attached. After two years, you will be entitled to full benefits as at that point you will be granted the rights of any other permanent resident. Full details on the health care system and private medical insurance are given in the chapter, *Daily Life*.

The full rate of the basic pension for a couple is currently around $15,000 per annum, with a further $2,000 worth of benefits accruing to most pensioners in the form of concessions. If you care for dependent children or students, you may be eligible for extra pension payments, as you are if you live in a remote area (Tax Zone A, see 'Taxation' Chapter Four). If you rent privately, you may be able to claim rent assistance of 75% of the rent paid above $A50 per fortnight, up to a maximum of around $70. These figures are all approximate, and subject to change, as rates are frequently reassessed by the Department of Social Security.

Pension entitlements are calculated under two separate tests: the income test and the assets test. The test which calculates the lower pension rate is the one used. **The Income Test** rules that a full pension must be paid if gross income is no more than $A86 per fortnight for singles or $A152 per fortnight per couple. Pensioners may earn up to $A4,500 a year without jeopardising any pension. If you are eligible for the pension but your spouse is ineligible, you will be paid half the combined married rate.

The Assets Test takes into account financial assets, excluding the family home. The full state pension will be paid if the total net market value of your assessable assets is no more than $A125,750 (for a single home owner), or $A215,750 (for a single, non home owner), $A178,500 (for a home owner couple) and $A268,500 for a non home-owning couple. A couple's combined assets must be less than $A160,000 if they own their own home for them to qualify for the full pension. If you are on a pension and your spouse is not, you will be eligible for half the combined married rate of the pension. You should also note that there is a difference between pensions and allowances: for those on allowances, such as the Mature Age Allowance, Newstart, and Partner Allowances, the thresholds given above are all-or-nothing. Allowees will lose their entire entitlement as soon as assets rise above these levels. Age, Disability, and Carer pensions, however, are phased out gradually, at a rate of $3 for every $1,000 in assets above the thresholds. The family home and superannuation are exempt from the Assets Tests.
Rebates
Single pensioners are permitted to earn non-pension taxable income up to $100 per

fortnight, and couples, up to $176 per fortnight, on top of their pension. In addition, pensioners receive a tax rebate of $1,260 for singles, and $860 for each member of a couple. The rebate reduces to nil when taxable income is over $21,780 for singles, and $17,048 for each member of a couple.

Seniors Benefits

Most of the benefits to which pensioners are entitled in Australia are claimed by presenting various cards issued by the Department of Social Security and other agencies. These cards give concessions to low-income earners as well as to pensioners for a number of different services. *Pensioner Health Benefits* and *Transport Concession Cards* are issued to pensioners who qualify for fringe benefits (check with the Department of Social Security for the current qualifications as they are continually under review). This entitles you to certain transport and medical services as well as the use of local amenities at very reduced cost. Holders of a Retirement visa are generally ineligible for any Department of Social Security Cards, and even Class 103 migrants only become eligible for certain DSS cards after they have been resident in Australia for two years. Some concessions, however, do not depend on a particular DSS or other authorised card, but only on age, so if you are able to produce any identification which states your date of birth, you may also be able to claim certain concessions. It is always worth checking before you pay for anything as to whether you are eligible for a concession on the basis of age. It is estimated that Seniors who take advantage of all the concessions on offer will save around $2,000 per year. The most common transport, amenities and health concessions are listed below.

Transport Concessions

All states and territories offer concession travel to people over 60 years of age, regardless of whether or not they are in receipt of a pension. You should contact your local public transport authority for information. Private bus services also offer concessions to Seniors and you should contact the appropriate company for details. Pensioners receive two vouchers each year for long distance travel within their state which cost just $A10 when used. These are only valid for interstate bus and rail travel. When travelling interstate, you use the voucher to get to the border and then you are charged only half the fare from the border to the capital city destination. These are not valid for interstate country town destinations, but only for capital city destinations. A 50% discount is offered to holders of a Pensioners Health Benefits Card for the Abel Tasman ferry service between Melbourne and Devonport, Tasmania. A Sydney rover ticket, usually costing $20, is available to Seniors for just $1.

Amenities

Seniors are generally also able to claim a reduction of 50% (to a maximum of $A250) for council rates, as well as some other services. Enquiries should be made at your local council. A 50 per cent rebate on water and sewage rates is usually offered to qualifying pensioners, and your nearest water authority office will give you further information. If you are eligible for fringe benefits, you should contact your state or territory electricity and gas authorities for any concessions which may be applicable on your electricity and gas bills. You may also be eligible to take advantage of a free mail redirecting service from your local post office if you move house within Australia, and also of a $A13.20 concession on each quarterly phone bill. Vouchers for telephone concessions are automatically issued to all pensioners, but further details are available from your local Social Security office. Most local councils offer registration of seniors' dogs for a nominal fee of around

$A2.00. The National Pensioners Association offers the over-50s discounts on literally thousands of products. You can join this Association for $15 ($20 for couples), and if you don't save $50 in the first year, your membership fee will be reimbursed. Under the NPA scheme, thousands of national traders offer discounts on nearly everything, from insurance, security systems, car tyres, carpets, motel accommodation, through to funeral services.

Health Benefits

The Pension Concession Card and The Commonwealth Senior Health Card can help with doctors bills, cut price pharmaceuticals, and ambulance services. The 1998 budget has introduced new rulings which mean that for the first time wealthier seniors who are ineligible for a pension can receive the Commonwealth Seniors Health Card. This entitles the holder to free access to public hospitals for elective surgery and reduced medical bills. The income limit for eligibility has been nearly doubled, from $21,320 to $40,000 for singles, and from $35,620 to $67,000 for couples. You will never have to pay more than $3.20 for a prescription, and if you pay more than $166 in a year for any drugs, all further prescriptions are free. As a pensioner, you are fully entitled to Medicare benefits, but there are many different health services which are offered at reduced rates to holders of such cards. In addition, free dental treatment is offered at some hospitals and dental clinics to holders of a Pensioner Health Benefits Card, a Health Benefits Card or a Health Care Card. It is worth contacting your local hospital to obtain information on the free treatment to which you are entitled and those treatments for which you would only have to pay a concessional rate.

Assistance may also be given for the cost of spectacles from some state government health or community service departments. You should contact your local department for details but should also be aware that this assistance is determined by a strict means test.

Free hearing aids, maintenance, repairs and batteries are also available from hearing centres of the National Acoustics Laboratories if you hold a Pensioner Health Benefits Card or a Sickness Benefits Card. For assistance, you should contact your nearest National Acoustics Hearing Centre, listed under the Commonwealth Government departments section at the front of the white pages telephone directory.

There are a number of associations which have been established to address those health problems which particularly affect older rather than younger people. These organisations offer information, advice and assistance, and have branches in every state and territory, the addresses of which can be obtained from the national bodies listed below:

Useful Contacts

Australian Hearing, tel 13 1797.
Diabetes Australia, 218 Northbourne Avenue, Braddon, ACT 2612, tel: 02-6230 1155.
Arthritis Foundation of Australia, 52 Parramatta Road, Forest Lodge, NSW 2037, tel 02-9552 6085.
Stroke Recovery Association Inc., PO Box 673, Petersham 2049, tel: 02-9550 0594.
Continence Helpline, freecall 1800 330 066.

If you move to Australia as a Class 103 migrant, there is a possibility that at some time your sponsoring child will have either to care or obtain care for you as you get older. There is a national body of carers which provides support in the form of counselling and advice, organises respite care or temporary relief, gives advice about benefits and other support services which may be helpful, and also puts your carer in touch with other carers. For further information, contact the *Carers Association of Australia Inc.* (PO Box 76, Lyons ACT 2606, tel: 06-282 5730).

Wills and Legal Considerations

This has been discussed in more detail in Chapter Three, but the clear message is that if you move to Australia, you should really make another will as there are variations in the law which may significantly and adversely affect your estate. If you wish to have a will drawn up for you in Australia, it is relatively easy to find assistance as solicitors advertise in telephone directories and also on television and the printed media. The Public Trustee Office specialises in the drawing and storing of wills and it is reassuring to know that their funds are protected by an Act of Parliament. The Trustee's funds are guaranteed by the government and so the office of the Public Trustee can never die, go bankrupt or leave the state, ensuring the efficient and legal execution of the affairs of your estate. The Public Trustee Office's will drafting service is free, and this includes any subsequent alterations and storage in a fire-proof safe. For further information contact The Public Trustee, GPO Box 7, Sydney NSW 2001.

If you intend to pass on substantial assets in your will, you may wish to consider establishing a Testamentary Trust. For pensioners, this means that when assets pass to the surviving spouse, those which are included in the Trust will not count against the assets test, ensuring that any pension is protected. Where child beneficiaries are involved, a testamentary trust will significantly reduce tax liability. This is a highly technical area, however, and professional legal and financial planning advice is essential.

Prepaid Funerals
Although a subject most prefer not to think about, any discussion of wills and estates should include mention of funeral arrangements. Many seniors want to give their family the comfort of knowing that their funeral arrangements have already been made and paid for in advance. To serve this need, funeral directors now offer pre-paid funeral packages which involve making contributions today to offset future costs. If you enter into such an arrangement, you should ensure that the contract is covered under the Funeral Benefit Business Act, so that your contributions are paid into a trust fund. A contract should specify the amounts to be contributed, whether the amount will cover the full cost of the funeral, and any management, entry or surrender fees.

Funeral Bonds offer another alternative, and are a type of friendly society bond attracting tax and social security exemptions. The proceeds of funeral bonds must go towards the funeral expenses of the holder, but bonuses paid during the lifetime of the holder are tax free. The capital value of any funeral bond is exempt from the Assets Test up to $5,000.

Hobbies and Interests

Sporting Activities
In 1987 a report commissioned by the New South Wales Department of Health revealed that more than half of all physical decline in any age group aged over 65 can be attributed to boredom, inactivity and a fear that infirmity is inevitable. Since that report, there has been a widespread effort to promote continuing

physical and social activities amongst seniors in the community. In Australia, the favourable weather means that popular pursuits differ somewhat from those in the UK and Europe. Bingo, for example, is very much less popular in general, and many more seniors engage in outdoor activities. Bowls is especially popular, and in every suburb, seniors can be seen clad in white playing both competitive and friendly lawn bowls in the summer sun. You should contact your local shire or community centre for information on how to get involved in your local lawn bowls club. Golf and tennis are also widely played, and are not restricted to wealthy club members: most districts will have well-maintained public golf courses and tennis courts which can be used for a small daily fee. Most public swimming pools will have seniors sessions, as well as hydrotherapy classes and seniors aquarobics. The very hardy amongst the senior community can also usually be seen at dawn, enjoying a communal early morning swim at their local beach; many veterans swear by this method of keeping fit, and enjoy it winter and summer. There is also a variety of associations and clubs which cater specifically for their older, as well as younger, members, some of which are listed below:

State Cycling Organisations provide organised rides as well as advice on what kind of bike to buy and maintenance.
Bicycle NSW, Level 2, 209 Castlereagh Street, Sydney, 2000, tel 02-9283 5200..
Bicycle Institute of Queensland, PO Box 5753, West End 4101, tel 07-3844 1144
Bicycle Tasmania, 15 Tarana Road, Blackman's Bay, TAS 7052, tel 03-6229 3811..
Bicycle Victoria, 19 O'Connell Street, North Melbourne, VIC 3051, tel 03-9328
    3000.
Cyclists' Action Group (WA), 2 Barsden Street, Cottesloe 6011, tel: 08-9384 7409
    (after office hours).

Walking for Pleasure is an organisation which specialises in hiking and camping, and is a programme developed by the Department of Sport, Recreation and Racing in New South Wales. Walks are graded Very Easy (which means it is suitable for wheelchairs and prams), Easy, Medium, Medium/Hard and Hard. The benefit of this programme is that you actually get to meet and talk to other people from all walks of life and age groups while you are exercising.
Federation of Victorian Walking Clubs, 332 Bangule Road, View Bank, VIC 3084, tel 03-9455 1876.

Australian Yoga Masters' Association offers gentle, relaxing exercise often recommended for those in rehabilitation after strokes or surgery.
Yoga Masters' Association, 183 Pittdown Road, Kentshurst, NSW 2156, tel 02-9654 9030.

Cultural Activities
If you prefer to be challenged academically rather than physically, most universities and colleges offer part time courses for mature age students, and you should contact the relevant institution for details. There is also the *Australian College for Seniors* (ACFS) which offers education programmes specifically aimed at vintage students. It is not necessary to pass entrance exams or to have any qualifications, the only requirement is that you are aged over 50. The ACFS consists of more than 40 participating colleges, universities and adult education organisations throughout Australia and is run in co-operation with Elderhostel in the United States of America. It offers international learning tours such as a literary tour of England or a trip to Bangkok and Chiang Mai where the information is presented by speakers from leading universities of Thailand. Although some courses may be expensive

(ranging from $A500 for a local workshop to $A8,000 for an international study tour), it is possible to combine your pension, the concessional travel fares and a tax-free grant from the Commonwealth Government of $A200 to go on such learning holidays. Enquiries should be made through the University of Wollongong (Northfields Avenue, Wollongong NSW 2522, tel: 02-4221 3531, 02-4221 3484 or fax: 02-4226 2521). The University of the Third Age also runs courses through the University of Western Australia (tel: 08-9380 3838), who will be able to provide details on their constantly changing selection of courses. Local libraries are usually the best source of information on academic, cultural, and social activities for all age levels of the community.

Senior Citizens' Clubs and National Clubs

Senior Citizens' Clubs are very active throughout Australia and welcome new members. Most suburbs or districts will have an SCC, which will usually be affliated with the National Seniors Association. These clubs organise a wide range of activities for their members, including talks and visits to places of interests, as well as indoor activities such as regular bingo and chess afternoons, film screenings, and community exchanges. Interaction between Seniors Clubs and local primary schools is especially popular, with schools in particular valuing the input from older members of the community. Seniors with special expertise or knowledge of local history may be asked to talk to junior classes during the course of their studies in relevant fields.

The Older Women's Network (OWN) was established recently to counteract the marginalisation of older women, and is committed to speaking out against ageist and sexist stereotyping. This group, which has an excellent website at www.zip.com.au/ownnsw, publishes a newsletter and has its own theatre group, aboriginal studies group, and health group. It also runs a consumer advocacy service. Contact details are given under 'Useful Addresses' below.

If you would like to meet and socialise with other settlers from your country of origin, you should check your local telephone directory or with the Department of Multicultural Affairs for information on national clubs such as the Italian Club or the Chung Wah Association. There are also Irish, Scottish, English and Welsh Clubs in most capital cities throughout Australia (check your white pages telephone directory), as well as a United Kingdom Settlers Association in Victoria.

Religious Associations

Many churches and other religious groups also provide activities and coffee mornings during the week, as well as a welcoming service for people new to the area. Most churches advertise in their local newspaper, so you should check your local freesheet or the telephone directory for further details. In addition, members of the Church of England may wish to contact the Anglican Church's *Overseas Settlement Secretary*, Board for Social Responsibility, Church House, Great Smith Street, Westminster, London SW1P 3NZ, who will put you in touch with a parish community at your destination.

Seniors' Travel

Many seniors like to take advantage of their increased leisure time to see something of Australia, and there are a number of travel options specially designed for this category of traveller. As mentioned above, in the secion on Seniors Benefits, state governments provide heavily subsidised interstate coach and rail travel. Airlines frequently offer discounts, usually as part of a special promotion, and it is worth asking before you book whether there are any new schemes or offers being launched in the near future. A new service called 'Senior Citizens

Stopovers Australia' also provides an economical accommodation option for travellers. Under this scheme, seniors with a spare room in their home, or even a driveway suitable for a caravan, pay a small once-only membership fee of $20, after which they are placed on a contact list. This list is circulated to all members, who must be available to host overnight visitors, as well as enjoying the opportunity to stay with other members on their travels. This service is currently being established and is electronically-based. If you are interested in joining, contact the organisers, Paul and Anne Tomlinson via their website at www.wantree.com.au/annet.

Useful Addresses

Clubs

Australian American Association, 39 Lower Fort Street, Sydney NSW 2000, tel: 02-947 1092.

Australia Britain Society, National Office, 39 Martin Place, Sydney, NSW 2000, tel 02-9223 5244.

Australian Irish Society, 52 Killeaton Street, St Ives, NSW 2075, tel 02-9440 0695.

The United Kingdom Settlers' Association, 146 Toorak Road, South Yarra, VIC 3141, tel 03-9866 1722.

Older Women's Network, 87 Lower Fort Street, Millers Point, NSW 2000; tel: 02-9247 7046; fax: 02-9247 4202.

Councils on the Ageing (COTA)

The Australian Council on the Ageing is a national non-profit organisation designed to provide assistance and independent advice to seniors on issues such as accommodation, financial management or health. COTA is also a major lobby group for older Australians. It has a national branch and branches in each state, many of which have a freecall number for enquiries.

Council on the Ageing (Australia), Level 2, 3 Bowen Crescent, Melbourne 3004, tel: 03-9820 2655; fax: 03-9820 9886; e-mail: cota@cota.org.au

Australian Capital Territory, Hughes Community Centre, Wisdom Street, Hughes 2605, tel: 02-6282 3777; fax: 02-6285 3422; e-mail: cotact@netinfor.com.au

New South Wales, 6th floor, 93 York Street, Sydney 2000, tel: 02-9299 4100; fax: 02-9299 4414; freecall: 1800 449 102; Seniors Information Service: 13 12 44; e-mail: cotansw@ozemail.com.au

Northern Territory, 18 Bauhinia Street, Nightcliff 0810, tel: 08-8948 1511; fax: 08-8948 1665.

Queensland, Units 1-3, 82 Buckland Road, Nundah 4012, tel: 07-3256 6766; fax: 07-3256 6788; e-mail: cotaq@ecn.net.au

South Australia, 45 Flinders Street, Adelaide 5000, tel: 08-8232 0422; fax: 08-8232 0433; freecall: 1800 182 324; Membership services: 1800 677 249; e-mail: cotasa@cotasa.org.au

Tasmania, 2 St John's Avenue, Newtown 7008, tel: 03-6228 1897; fax: 03-6228 0481; e-mail: cotatas@bigpond.com

Victoria, Mezzanine Level, Block Court, 290 Collins Street, Melbourne, tel: 03-9654 4443; fax: 03-9654 4456; freecall: 1800 136 381; e-mail: cotavic@vicnet.net.au

Western Australia, 2nd floor, Wesley Centre, 93 William Street, Perth 6850; tel: 08-9321 2133; fax: 08-9321 2707; e-mail: exec@cotawa.asn.au

Independent Living Centres

Independent Living Centres provide information for those with disabilities or limited mobility who live independently. They also demonstrate and develop products designed to help such people live more easily and retain their independence. Products include bathroom and toilet aids, as well as aids to help with communication, eating, drinking, walking and sitting. Transport and lifting equipment is also available. Information on where to hire such products, as well as their cost and availability, is available from these centres. The quarterly journal *Independent Living*, published by the Independent Living Centres also provides information and updates. Visits to Independent Living Centres are by appointment only.

Australian Capital Territory: 24 Parkinson Street, Weston 2611, tel: 02-6205 1900.
New South Wales: 600 Victoria Road (PO Box 706), Ryde 2112, tel: 02-808 2233.
Queensland: Goring Street, Coorparoo, QLD 4151, tel 07-3397 1224.
South Australia: 80 Daws Road, Daw Park 5041, tel: 08-8276 3455.
Victoria: 705 Geelong Road, Brooklyn, VIC 3025, tel 03-9362 6111.
Western Australia: 3 Lemnos Street, Shenton Park 6008, tel: 08-9382 2011.

SECTION II

Working in Australia

Employment
Temporary Work
Permanent Work
Directory of Major Employers
Starting a Business

Employment

Overview

Australia is currently experiencing the highest level of job optimism since mid-1995, although it is expected that the Asian currency crisis will begin to affect growth soon. The most recent figures available from the Morgan and Banks Job Index show that Western Australia and NSW are both enjoying job growth of around 26 per cent, along with the country's lowest levels of unemployment. In other states, however, figures are less encouraging, with Queensland registering growth of only 9.8 per cent, and Victoria, the second worst figures at 17.6 per cent. Information technology and advertising were the employment sectors which showed the strongest growth, with sales, finance and accounting, and engineering also doing well. Net job losses were predicted in blue-collar areas, especially in manufacturing industries. Unemployment now stands at around 8 per cent, and is expected to drop to less than 7 per cent by 1999. Strong retail figures suggest that around 36,000 new jobs will be created in the retail sector during 1998, and the travel industry also estimates the creation of another 55,000 jobs over the next year, particularly in traineeships and apprenticeships.

There are currently nearly 50 skilled occupations which are experiencing labour shortages in Australia. These include chefs (Asian cuisine/International standard), registered nurse specialisations (A&E, psychiatric, ICU), accountants specialising in taxation and auditing, lawyers, ultrasonographers, engineers, school teachers, computer professionals (powerbuilder, AS400, and SAP), and occupational therapists. There is also a shortage of qualified childcare workers and co-ordinators. Tradespeople, especially those qualified as motor mechanics, electrical mechanics, vehicle painters, panel beaters, toolmakers (1st class), sheetmetal workers, boiler makers, welders, metal fitters, and refrigeration/air-conditioning mechanics, are also in demand in many areas of Australia. It is expected that this shortage of qualified tradespeople will worsen in coming years, as the numbers of apprenticeships available fall. A long-term decline in apprenticeships has seen places cut by half in the last six years, from 62,000 to 31,000. In some areas, skill shortages are so severe that the National Electrical Contractors Association has applied for special permission from the Commonwealth Government to bring in overseas-trained electricians to fill skilled jobs. Many companies are now using labour hire contractors to fill jobs which would previously have been done by apprentices, leading to rapid growth in the short-term contracting sector.

Skill shortages show the same pattern across all states, with a few exceptions. In NSW, cadastral surveyors, actuaries, and concreters are in demand; and in Victoria, dentists, enrolled nurses, and bricklayers. In Queenland, extractive metallurgists, locksmiths, and cabinetmakers are needed; in South Australia, communications tradespersons, and printing machinists; and in Western Australia, petroleum/drilling/chemical/civil/mechanical engineers and associate professionals are all required, as well as cooks in country areas.

The recent government report, *Australia's Workforce 2005: Jobs in the Future*, projects significant changes in the composition of the working population over the next decade, with long-term trends towards more part-time work, a middle-ageing of the workforce, and an increased proportion of female employees. Prospects for employment vary according to industry sector and the skill level of the occupation. The employment prospects of highly skilled occupations, such as managers, professionals, and para-professionals are expected to enjoy continued growth, especially in those occupations which meet domestic consumer needs. Other professional groups, such as engineers, which are employed in export or import-competing industries, will also experience strong growth, and their services are expected to be in increasing demand as these industries introduce new technologies. Production workers in manufacturing, including machine operators and labourers, will face declining or weak employment growth as industry strives to raise labour productivity to meet international competition. To offset decline in traditional industries, the government is strongly focused on the need for vocational education, skill building, and the multi-skilling of the workforce. It is seeking to build on emerging competitive strategies to take advantage of improved technologies, innovative marketing, better management, and organisational change, and more and more mature workers now accept the need to retrain or develop their skills.

Migrant unemployment currently stands at 6.9 per cent for migrants from English-speaking countries, and at 10.3 per cent for others. Recent arrivals generally have a higher unemployment rate than those who have lived in Australia for some time. The Department of Employment, Education, Training and Youth Affairs (DEETYA) publishes a quarterly magazine called the *Australian Jobs Review* which is intended to give migrants an overview of the prevailing labour market conditions. This publication is available on-line at www.deetya.gov.au/divisions/epad/ajr. DEETYA also publishes a monthly skilled vacancy survey available at www.deetya.gov.au/divisions/epad/svs.

Useful On-line Employment Information Sources
New South Wales Government www.nsw.gov.au. Includes information on doing business with the NSW government, Sydney 2000 Olympics, rural information, reports and papers, related links.
Australian Taxation Office www.ato.gov.au. Information on Australian tax laws.
Tasmania Online www.tas.gov.au. Includes information on investing in Tasmania, and migrating to Tasmania.
Queensland Government Online www.qld.gov.au. Includes information on business in Qld, and government departments and agencies.
Government of Victoria www.vic.gov.au. Includes information on state projects.
Melbourne City Council www.melbourne.vic.gov.au. Includes information on products and services of Melbourne City Council.
Department of Workplace Relations and Small Business www.dwrsb.gov.au. Workplace relations in Australia, small business, maritime transport, policy and legislation, government employment, and related sites.
Business Migrant Information and Referral Service, www.srd.nsw.gov.au. Information for potential investors and business migrants.
Australian Governments' Entry Point www.nla.gov.au/oz/gov/. Entry point to all Australian government websites.
The Australian Yellow Pages Telephone Directory www.yellowpages.com.au. National searchable database.

Residence and Work Regulations

In order to work in Australia, you must hold an appropriate temporary or permanent residency visa. The Australian immigration authorities are draconian in their treatment of illegal workers, and anyone caught working without a visa should expect to be deported immediately. In 1997/98, over 11,600 illegal workers were tracked down and detained, largely through a data-matching programme operated by the Department of Immigration and Multicultural Affairs. Data-matching links the computers of the Australian Taxation Office, the Department of Social Security, and the Health Insurance Commission (Medicare), making it almost impossible to get away with flouting immigration laws. DIMA is currently focusing its efforts to locate illegal workers in industries which employ large numbers of casual workers, especially the rural sector, where cash payments have traditionally made it easier to work outside the purview of the eagle eye of the tax office.

The eligibility criteria, requirements and procedures for obtaining residency in Australia, whether on a short or long term basis, are described in detail in Chapter 2, *Residence and Entry Regulations*; those visas which allow foreigners to work legally or to seek employment in Australia are described in brief below.

Working Holiday Maker Visa
Applicants for a Working Holiday Maker Visa must:
– be a citizen of Canada, Japan, the Republic of Korea, the Republic of Ireland, Malta, the Netherlands, or the United Kingdom;
– be between the ages of 18 and 25 (or, exceptionally, 30);
– intend to leave Australia after the expiry of their visa;
– be capable of finding temporary work as a means of supplementing holiday funds;
– have a return ticket and sufficient funds to cover living expenses in Australia;
– have no intention of working for more than three months for any single employer.
The purpose of the WHM visa is to allow young people the chance to tour extensively in Australia, with the option of working for up to three months in any one area. If you are granted this visa, you will only be able to consider employment of a temporary or casual nature.

Employer Nominations Schemes
This scheme allows employers to recruit highly skilled workers from overseas if they are unable to fill a vacancy in Australia. The Nominee must:
– be less than 45 years of age;
– have qualifications and experience that match the vacancy requirements;
– have vocational level English;
– have attained at least three years experience in the job since they qualified.
The Employer must:
– prove that they have exhausted all possible avenues to employ an Australian citizen for the position;
– demonstrate an excellent training record and commitment to training and up-grading skills of semi-skilled Australian workers.

Business Class Visas
There are many different types of business visas which permit professionals to work in Australia as temporary residents for short or long term. The conditions and requirements of these visas are detailed in chapter 2, and include not only business fields, but also educators, entertainers, and others. The three main classes of business visa are:
Temporary Business Entry: a short-term business visa that allows multiple entry to Australia for three months at a time, valid for five years or for the life of the passport;

Business (Long-Stay) visa: caters for people who intend to pursue business-related activities in Australia. This visa covers a variety of different circumstances, from foreign firms bringing employees out on overseas assignments to overseas business people wanting to establish off-shore operations in Australia. Educators, entertainers, and others are likely to be covered by this visa, which is valid for three months to four years;

Business Skills (Migrant) Class or *Business Skills (Resident) Class*: targets executives and investors who wish to establish themselves in Australia permanently.

Medical practitioners wishing to work in Australia should note that there is currently an embargo on working visas of any type for overseas-trained doctors.

Permanent Residents

Migrants entering Australia on permanent residency visas are not subject to any restrictions or regulations, other than those which govern the working practices of all Australians. There may, however, be specific conditions attached to the class of visa granted, particularly if you are entering under a regionally-sponsored migration scheme which may oblige you to work or settle in a remote area. The skilled stream of Australia's migration programme is designed to facilitate entry for people who have skills or outstanding abilities deemed to be valuable to Australia's economic advancement. If you have been accepted as a skill-stream migrant, you are, in effect, one step ahead in the job search process, insofar as you are likely to have been accepted on the basis that your particular experience and training are in demand. Current immigration policy addresses specific skills shortages in the Australian labour market, and this policy is applied to skilled-Australian linked migrants (sponsored by a family member already resident in the country), as well as to independent migrants (who are *not* sponsored by a relative or employer in Australia). For detailed information on permanent residency visa criteria and requirements see chapter 2, *Residence and Entry Regulations*.

Business Stream Migration

The Business Skills visa class of the Migration Programme is designed to encourage successful business people to settle permanently in Australia and develop new business opportunities. Business migration benefits the Australian economy by developing its international markets, creating employment, introducing new or improved technology, and by adding to commercial activity and competitiveness in general. Business migrants are expected to contribute to these benefits by establishing and conducting new business, by transferring capital, and by investment. The following criteria apply for different types of applicants and visa categories under the Business Skills programme:

Business owners are required to demonstrate that they have had a successful business career and that for two of the previous four fiscal years have had net business assets of at least $300,000. In addition, they must have been involved in and responsible for the overall management of a business in which they have at least a 10 per cent ownership share, and which has employed no fewer than five employees. Business owners must also pass a points test which assesses factors such as annual turnover, annual labour costs, total business assets, age, language ability, and net personal assets.

Senior executives must demonstrate that they have had a successful business career and that for two of the previous four years they have been employed in the top three levels of management in a business with an annual turnover of not less than

$50 million. They must also pass a points test which assesses factors such as age, English language ability, and net personal assets.

Investment-linked applicants must demonstrate a history of successful ownership and management in business and/or investment activities, as well as make an investment into a State or Territory government security of between $750,000 and $2 million for a period of three years. They must also demonstrate assets worth at least 50 per cent more than their proposed investment, and must pass a points test which assesses age and English language ability.

Established business in Australia applicants must demonstrate that they have managed a business in Australia in which they have at least 10 per cent ownership for 18 months prior to application. They must have assets in Australia worth $250,000, of which $100,000 must be invested in their business, and they must have been resident in Australia for a total of 9 out of the previous 12 months prior to application. As with other categories, applicants must pass a points test which takes into account such factors as turnover and exports, number of employees, net assets, age and English language ability. A sub-category of this visa class makes special concessions for applicants who have established businesses in regional areas outside NSW and the main urban centres of Melbourne, Perth, Brisbane, and south-east Queensland. Under the 'Regional Established Business' category, asset and turnover criteria are slightly more lenient.

Once a business migrant has arrived in Australia he or she must meet visa conditions and business obligations. The expectation is that they will establish a new business, or become an owner or part-owner of an existing business; and that they will take an active part in the management of that business. Having established a successful business initially as a temporary resident, a business skills migrant is expected to remain in Australia permanently to continue that business. The progress of business migrants is monitored after their arrival in Australia, and where no significant steps have been taking towards meeting these obligations within the first three years after arrival, the Minister for Immigration and Multicultural Affairs has the power to cancel the right of residence of the business immigrant and his or her family.

Skills and Qualifications

Successful applicants under the Skill Stream or the Skilled-Australian Linked Stream of the migration programme are required to have a prescribed level of professional experience and qualification. As explained more fully in chapter 2, these skills are assessed during the application process by means of the 'Points Test'. Points awarded for skill levels are based on your current occupation and the level of your qualifications, which must be of a standard recognised as industry-appropriate in Australia. Your current occupation is defined as the one which you are presently doing, or which you have performed over the last twelve months and which you regard as your usual occupation. Thus, if you have obtained qualifications in one field (say, a degree in modern languages) but are currently working in a field which does not *directly* utilise those qualifications, you will, in effect, be assessed as unqualified. This clause creates difficulties for many applicants who are working in areas such as information technology or office management, where in many cases skills have been acquired 'on-the-job' or through graduate programmes. Concessions are made for workplace training, however, and each case is assessed on its individual merits. Points are awarded for length of professional experience (usually three years is required) and for membership of professional or industrial associations. The table below shows the current value of the different qualification and skill levels under the Points Test. Trade certificates, diplomas, and degrees must be recognised as 'acceptable' (i.e., equivalent to an Australian qualification) in order to score any points.

Points Test: Employability and Qualifications Assessment

Qualification	*Points*
Trade certificate/degree/diploma with at least 3 years post-qualification work experience	70
Trade certificate/degree/diploma with 6-36 months post-qualification work experience	60
Diploma with at least 3 years post-qualification work experience	55
Diploma with 6-36 months post-qualification work experience	50
Trade certificate/degree/diploma (recognised overseas and assessed by Australian authorities as requiring only minor upgrading), with at least 3 years post-qualification work experience	30
Post secondary school qualifications	25
Trade certificate/degree/diploma but qualifications are held unacceptable	25
12 years of primary and secondary education	20
Less than 10 years of education	0

NOOSR Bridging Courses for the Overseas Trained
The National Office of Overseas Skills Recognition (P.O. Box 1407, Canberra City, ACT 2601, Australia) can provide advice on the acceptability of any qualification which you hold. They also offer bridging courses for overseas qualified professionals, whose qualifications have not yet been recognised in Australia, enabling applicants to meet the academic and professional requirements for registration or entry to regulated professions. Government-regulated professions include: dentistry, veterinary science, medicine, law, radiography, pharmacy, architecture, physiotherapy, and nursing. Accountancy, dietetics, social work, engineering and surveying are self-regulating. You will be eligible for support on a NOOSR course if you have permanent residency in Australia, have overseas professional qualifications at Bachelor's degree level or above, and you have obtained details of the training you require from the body which assessed your qualifications. Contact NOOSR for information and advice (tel 06-240 7644; free call 1800-020 086).

Sources of Jobs

On-line Resources

If you are job-hunting in Australia from overseas, by far the best, quickest, and most convenient resource is now the World Wide Web. There are dozens of Australian recruitment agencies on the Internet, all of which advertise frequently up-dated lists of positions, as well as providing registration and CV lodgment services. Two major Australian media groups, Newscorp and Fairfax, which between them publish the greater part of Australia's mainstream newspapers, also put their classified recruitment sections on-line, and these are up-dated daily. The websites of these two corporations together carry around 20,000 job advertisements per week. In addition, the Australian Job Network (the government job-finding organisation) has an excellent site searchable by location, job type, and interactive map. In most cases, jobs listed on the AJN site will detail conditions and pay, and although it may be difficult to apply for jobs listed here from overseas, it will give you a good idea of the kinds of work available in almost any field.

Useful Australia-specific Recruitment Websites
Australian Jobsearch (government site): jobsearch.deetya.gov.au
Employment.net.au: www.employment.net.au
Employment Opportunities Australia: www.employment.com.au
Fairfax Holdings: www.fairfax.com.au/jobs. This site lists daily advertisements carried in a range of national papers. It carries around 10,000 advertisements per day, and is searchable by job type and location.
The Australian: www.newsclassifieds.com.au. This Newscorp site carries the daily advertisements run in *The Australian* and a number of other major newspapers owned by the group.

Individual agencies can be quickly located using the search engine, Yahoo! and the search terms 'Australia' in conjunction with 'recruitment' or 'employment'.

Newspapers

UK Newspapers and Directories
The Directory of Jobs and Careers Abroad: published by Vacation Work (£11.95) has a section on Australia including contacts and other sources of employment information.
Overseas Jobs Express: a fortnightly publication which lists over 1,000 overseas jobs including professional, non-professional, seasonal, temporary, permanent, long and short term employment. A year's subscription costs around £28 and is available from OJE (A2, Premier House, Shoreham Airport, BN43).
TNT Planners: produce a quarterly information booklet which carries advertisements for numerous Australian recruitment agencies. The magazine is available from travel agents or from TNT Planners (14-15 Child's Place, London, SW5 9RX; tel 0171-373 3377). TNT have a useful website at www.tntmag.co.uk.

Australian Newspapers
Jobs are advertised in community, local, regional and national newspapers. Most major daily newspapers carry a large recruitment section on Saturdays, and many carry advertisements for specialist professional positions on certain days (for example, tertiary education sector jobs in *The Australian* on Wednesday). Professionals and executives are advised to consult *The Australian* in additional to their state newspapers, as most high-status jobs will be advertised in this paper, regardless of location. A list of state and national newspapers is given in chapter 4, *Media and Communications*.

Professional Associations and Specialist Publications

Most professions in Australia have a national association or governing body, which is also likely to have state chapters. In some cases, membership of an associaton is compulsory for practising members, and in such instances, membership fees are tax deductible. Most professional associations publish a journal which, in specialist fields, may be the best source of employment information. Specialist publications provide another important source, and will usually report on developments in their field, as well as advertising job vacancies. Conferences and development courses will also be advertised in such publications.

Working Holiday Assistance Schemes

BUNAC
The British Universities North America Club (Dept RS1, 16 Bowling Green Lane, London, EC1R 0BD, tel: 0171-251 3472), has a 'Work Australia' programme, which is designed to help students deal with all the organisational aspects of a working holiday. The service includes help with flights, insurance and a working visa, comprehensive orientation sessions in the UK and on arrival in Australia, a group stop-over in Bangkok en route, two free nights accommodation in Sydney, and various support services throughout your stay. For more information, contact the BUNAC representative at your university, or contact BUNAC direct at the number given above.

SWAP
The Student Work Abroad Programme (SWAP) also runs programmes in Australia for students on working holidays. SWAP is administered by Student Services Australia in conjunction with STA Travel (PO Box 399, Carlton South, VIC 3053, tel 03-9348 1777; fax 03-9347 8070). Canadian students should contact any office of Travel CUTS, which is part of the Canadian Federation of Students (243 College Street, Toronto, Ontario M5T 2YI).

Employment Wanted Advertisements

Placing an advertisement in a local or community newspaper can be a useful way of finding casual work, but is unlikely to land you secure long-term employment. Most people using 'Situations Wanted' classifieds are looking for occasional cash jobs, such as gardening, baby-sitting, or cleaning. If you are on a working holiday, this may be one of the best ways of picking up occasional work to suit your travel schedule, and will probably pay at least $10 per hour. For graduates, short-term tutoring, particularly around exam time, can be quite remunerative, and most local papers will have a separate column advertising services of this type.

The Australian Job Network

In May 1998, a new government initiative known as the Australian Job Network replaced the long-established job-finding service, the CES. The Job Network is a national affiliation of more than 300 private, community, and government organisations, working co-operatively to provide assistance to job seekers. The Department of Employment, Education, Training and Youth Affairs (DEETYA) – which itself is soon to be reorganised into the Department of Employment, Workplace Relations and Small Business – provides a very comprehensive website detailing available jobs, and with links to other employers, at http:// jobsearch.deetya.gov.au.

Employment Agencies

UK-based Australian Employment Agency
Bligh Appointments is the largest employer of working holiday makers in both Sydney and London, and can help students and others in the search for temporary

work before they even leave the UK. They specialise in secretarial, accounting and IT jobs, and offer good rates and an immediate start. Bligh have offices at 9th Floor, 428 George Street, Sydney NSW 2000, tel: 02-9235 3699, and in London at 1st Floor, Top Deck House, 135 Earls Court Road, London, SW5, tel: 0171-244 7277.

Personnel Consultancies
Personnel consultancies generally specialise in placing staff in sales, marketing, finance, accounting, IT, engineering, office administration, and hospitality. While many employment agencies also cover these areas, personnel consultants deal mainly with executive placements and upper and middle management. They advertise available jobs in major newspapers and usually offer a complete recruitment service. If you are seeking work of this kind, you can contact a personnel consultancy 'on spec' to discuss your qualifications and experience, and any potentially suitable vacancies. A list of personnel consultants and contact numbers can be found in the local Yellow Pages.

Employment Agencies
Employment agencies deal in both temporary and permanent work, usually in either the secretarial, clerical, accounting, and IT fields, or in hospitality or heavy industry. Most advertise in the Yellow Pages and are found in prominent locations in the CBD and other urban centres. The international firms Drake Personnel, Kelly Girl, Centacom and Adecco all have agencies in Australia. In addition to the large, generalist agencies, there are many smaller, specialist firms, particularly in fields such as nursing, legal temping, banking, and IT. If you are a registered nurse or teacher, it is vital that you take proof of registration and qualifications with you.

Useful Addresses
Adecco Sydney are the official staffing services supporter of the 2000 Olympic Games. They have a website at www.adecco.com.au, and can be contacted at their Sydney office on tel 02-9231 6622.

Au Pair around the World: tel/fax 07-5530 8999. Australia's leading au pair agency with offices Australia-wide.

Crowe HR supply legal temping services and paralegals; tel 02-9261 5100; email staff@crowe.com.au; website www.crowe.com.au.

Global Technical Recruitment; tel 02-9411 6866; fax 02-9411 6966 provide specialist engineering staff Australia-wide.

Select Appointments specialise in placing professional, motivated travellers. They have positions for receptionists, data entry operators, secretaries, accounts clerks, medical and legal secretaries, WPOs, and warehousing staff. Select have offices in Sydney, tel 02-9206 2311; Perth, tel 08-9321 3133; Brisbane, tel 07-3406 3900; Melbourne, tel 03-9297 4700; email select@select-appointments.com.au

Macquarie Nursing Service, tel 02-9871 5111; e-mail: wengra@bigpond.com.au Macquarie is the oldest established nursing agency in Sydney and places registered, enrolled, and assistant nurses in both metropolitan and country areas.

Michael Page Technology, Level 19, 1 York Street, Sydney, 2000; tel 02-9254 0350; fax 02-9254 0355; e-mail: mpageit@ozemail.com.au Temporary and contract work for analyst programmers, business and systems analysts, IT specialists.

Taylor and Associates: Head Office: PO Box 99122 Newmarket, Auckland, New Zealand; tel (09) 520 0765; fax (09) 520 0764; e-mail nzjobs@tayassc.co.nz UK Representative Office: PO Box 1401, Chester, Cheshire CH1 1FF; tel 01244-321414; fax 01244-342288. Professional migrant jobsearch consultants specialising in Australia and New Zealand.

Labour Hire Contractors

Labour hire contractors specialise in placing skilled manual workers and tradespeople, labourers, storepersons, process workers and factory staff. These agencies generally do not operate high street offices and are found in industrial areas. Most advertise in the Yellow Pages, and it is usually best to visit in person, taking any trade or City and Guild certificates you may have. Qualified tradespeople are well paid in Australia, and in states with booming construction industries there is usually a shortage. Bricklayers are particularly in demand and can expect to earn a high wage, whilst mine workers can earn more than $1,000 per week. Mining work is very labour-intensive and unskilled workers are often needed; modern mine sites operate equal opportunities policies, and most employ women in a wide range of capacities. There is a strong demand for skilled mechanics and *Travellers Contact Point* (tel: 02-9360 1500) are always seeking temporary and permanent staff in this field.

Chambers of Commerce

The Australian Chamber of Commerce and affiliated state Chambers of Commerce advise and provide information on employment in Australia. They also produce detailed regional summaries of employment and economic growth, and are particularly useful as a point of contact for small businesspeople. The Australian-British Chamber of Commerce aims to promote business growth and development within Australia, and to encourage reciprocal trade between the UK and Australia.

Useful Addresses
Australian British Chamber of Commerce, Level 3, Suite 302A, 14 Martin Place, Sydney, NSW 2000, tel: 02-9221 0355.
Australia and New Zealand Chamber of Commerce UK, 393 Strand, London, WC2R 0LT, tel 0171-379 0720; fax 0171-379 0721; Website: www.anzcc.org.uk
Australian Chamber of Manufacturers, 380 St Kilda Road, Melbourne VIC 3000, tel: 03-9698 4111.

Company Transfers and Job Exchanges

If you are currently working for a company which has offices or branches in Australia, opportunities may exist for either permanent or temporary transfer. Outside the multinationals, it may be possible to find work in Australia under an exchange scheme. Such schemes are common in the teaching profession, and you should contact your local education authority for further information. Many exchanges provide not only a job swap, but also all the domestic necessities – you may find yourself minding your colleague's pets for a year, but on the other hand, you'll probably also find yourself minding their pool!

Aspects of Employment

Salaries

Pay rates in Australia fall broadly into four bands: the lowest paid earn an average of $340 or less per week, mid-range salaries cluster firstly around $573 and then, in the upper-mid-range, around $751 per week, and finally, the highest paid employees can expect a weekly pay packet of over $1,000 per week. Rates of pay are differentiated between the public and private sector, and by gender and age. Men still tend to receive a higher weekly income than women in the same sector (although this can be accounted for by gender divides within industry, rather than direct discrimination, which is, of course, illegal). Younger people are likely to be paid less than their seniors. Employees earning at the top end of the salary bands are likely to fall into one of two key industries – finance and insurance, and mining – whilst those at the bottom end are generally found in the retail trade and in the hospitality industry. The table below illustrates the current full-time adult average weekly earning in Australia:

Full-time Adult Average Weekly Earnings (A$)

Industry	Male	Female
Mining	1,157	789
Manufacturing	687	561
Electricity, gas, water	831	683
Construction	725	601
Wholesale trade	696	588
Retail trade	578	497
Hospitality	544	507
Transport and storage	777	635
Communications	829	720
Finance and insurance	1,215	675
Property and business	808	601
Civil service and defence	767	680
Education	852	749
Health and community services	825	654
Cultural and recreational services	795	696
Other services	753	573

Source: The Australian

In the age range 20-24 (which covers most working holiday makers), computer professionals can expect to earn approximately $667 per week, accountants $587, sales and marketing professionals $605, registered nurses $519, secretaries $475, bar attendants $415, and waiters $396. The traditional working holiday stand-by, fruit picking, may be easy to find, but is poorly paid. Workers are paid not by the hour but by the quantity of produce harvested. In Mildura, the average harvest picker can expect to earn $80 a day.

The Australian Bureau of Statistics estimates an annual increase of 4 per cent per annum on the rates of pay. The Australian economy currently has a negative CPI (Consumer Price Index) and zero inflation, so that there are no economic factors expected to offset this estimated increase. Industries with a shortage of skilled labour are expected to experience a greater increase in pay rates, while salaries in those areas where there is an oversupply of labour may see wages decline.

Award Rates, or recommended minimum wages, are set by both the Commonwealth and State governments for various trades and industries. Many, if not most, employers pay above the Award Rate, but you should find out if there is an Award in place before entering into negotiations with an employer. The appropriate union will be able to advise you on Award Rates and Conditions.

Benefits and Perks

Only the most senior positions attract additional benefits in Australia since changes in taxation laws have made fringe benefits economically unattractive.

Cars, health insurance plans, entertainment expenses, and even frequent flyer points are now all taxed as income, so that any benefit is offset by a commensurate loss of salary. Benefits earned under incentive schemes are also taxable. Childcare and workplace crèches, however, are not included in the fringe benefit tax, and indeed, employees using external childcare can claim a rebate on their expenses via the local Medicare office.

All employers pay superannuation (private pension contributions) for their employees at a basic rate of 6 per cent of salary, and this will rise to 9 per cent by 2002. Many employers also offer an additional percentage or two, up to around 10 per cent, and this is now the most common form of employment incentive.

Most senior executives can still expect to receive a company car, but in general, benefits offered at any other level of employment are likely to be industry-linked. Thus, if you work for a major bank, you can expect to be eligible for subsidised borrowing, or in health insurance, for free or discounted health cover. Most Australian employees do not expect, or indeed want, any other fringe benefits which may cut into the cash in their pocket.

Superannuation

Superannuation is Australia's answer to the economic burden of state pensions in the context of an ageing population; in essence, it is a compulsory private pension planning scheme. All employees are required by law to pay a percentage of their salary into a superannuation fund designated by their employer, to which the employer also contributes an additional minimum percentage payment on the employee's behalf. If you move jobs, you are entitled to transfer your superannuation package to your new employer's chosen superannuation fund without incurring any penalty. The transfer of super from one fund to another is known as a 'roll-over'. Alternatively, if you wish to remain with your current fund, you can ask your employer to contribute to that fund instead, although they are not obliged to do so either by law or under any award. Contributions to 'super funds' are of two types: preserved and voluntary. Preserved contributions comprise the minimum compulsory contributions, described above, and these cannot be withdrawn or otherwise utilised until the age of 60 (even if you retire earlier). In addition, however, employees are entitled to make on-going voluntary contributions or occasional lump sum contributions to their fund, and this component is non-preserved, i.e., it can be withdrawn on leaving a job. Self-employed people are advised to take out a 'self-employed' superannuation policy available from banks and life insurance companies.

If you leave the country permanently, your superannuation will remain locked into a fund until you reach retirement age.

Working Hours, Overtime and Holidays

The Australian working week averages 35-40 hours over a five day week, with government positions taking the middle road at precisely 37.5 hours. In most jobs, you can expect to work an eight hour day with an hour for lunch, although some shift-work industries, such as nursing or hospitality, will usually require much greater flexibility. Flexi-time is common, and allows you to set your own working hours around a compulsory 'core time' (usually 10am to 4pm). Extra hours worked can be 'banked' against time off on full pay, which is in addition to statutory leave. Flexi-time is very popular, and is in place in almost all government jobs, tertiary education administration, and in many private companies. Minimum working pay and conditions are set by either the Commonwealth or State governments.

If you are required to work on a Sunday or public holiday, you should be paid at twice the normal rate. At any other time, overtime is paid at 1.5 times the normal rate. Employees are entitled to a statutory minimum of four weeks paid leave per annum. Holiday leave is sweetened with a bonus known as 'holiday loading', which means that your salary is increased by an extra 17.5% during the period you are on leave. Many industries and professions offer increasing leave entitlements linked to length of service, and may, in some cases, offer as much as eight weeks' holiday per year. Untaken leave can usually be carried over from year to year, and many people choose to bank up holidays in order to take extended travel breaks.

After between seven and ten years consecutive service with a single employer (ten years in government positions), an employee is entitled to 'long service leave' of up to six months on full pay or twelve months on half pay. Long service leave conditions vary considerably between employers, and in many cases additional incentives such as a travel allowance may be offered. There is no equivalent to long service leave in British employment legislation.

In addition to annual leave, all employees are granted a period of paid sick leave, the length of which will be specified in their contract. Most employers give between two weeks and three months paid sick leave. Any absence of more than 48 hours generally requires a medical certificate (the term 'sick note' is not used in Australia) from a GP in order to claim payment. Many employers also offer compassionate leave of several days per year, which can be used in times of personal emergency such as a bereavement. Compassionate leave and sick leave cannot be carried over from year to year.

Trade Unions

The trade union movement in Australia has become much weakened over the past decade, with fewer Australian employees joining unions than ever before. To offset loss of membership, many unions have amalgamated with others in related trades and professions, forming super-unions with increased negotiating power. The unions which have remained strongest are those representing industries in which there is continued unrest, particularly in teaching, nursing, policing, and wharfside occupations. 'Closed shops' are illegal, but the powerful BLF (Builders Labourers Federation) is occasionally known to operate union-only sites. Most workplaces have a union representative, and if you choose to join, dues can be automatically deducted from your salary. Union dues are a tax-deductible expense. The Australian Council of Trade Unions (ACTU Australian Workers' Union, Head Office, 245 Chalmers Road, Redfern NSW 2016, tel: 02-690 1022) is the national trade union organisation and can provide advice on the union most appropriate to your circumstances and occupation.

Employment Contracts

In Australia every employee is covered either by a contract or a 'workplace agreement'. Workplace agreements are signed by both employer and employee, and stipulate the agreed conditions of employment, including hours, leave arrangements, uniform or safety-wear requirements, and notice and termination procedures. Even casual workers must be covered by one of these contracts, which is then lodged with the State Commissioner for Workplace Agreements as a legally binding document. Workplace agreements have not entirely replaced employment contracts, though they are nearly identical in purpose and effect, however, it is usually only in more senior and permanent positions that employees are covered by a contract.

A contract should specify all leave entitlements (holiday, sick, parental, and compassionate leave), overtime conditions, benefits, superannuation contribution levels, hours (including flexi-time arrangements), long-service leave, uniform regulations, and health and safety observances. It should also clearly stipulate termination procedures, which will usually follow the form of a first and second verbal warning, written warning, and formal interview (which may be attended, at your request, by a union representative). If a contract is broken by either party, the injured party is able to sue the other party for breach of contract through an industrial tribunal. Temporary workers and travellers should particularly note that if you fail to give the contractually defined period of notice of resignation, your employer is legally entitled to withhold wages equivalent to that period.

Work Practices

Different industries have different codes of practice, and you should be made aware of these by your employer at your interview or when you commence work. Most industries which expose their employees to physical safety hazards require that appropriate safety gear be worn, and this will generally be supplied by the employer. Almost all workplaces, including many restaurants, are now smoke-free, and smokers are expected to take their 'smokoes' outside the building. Health and safety regulations are rigorously upheld in the workplace, and most offices and sites will appoint a member of staff as its 'H and S' representative. This representative will make sure that regulations are not breached by any management practice and that any new legislation is promptly enforced. Australian offices are generally far less authoritarian than British ones, especially in the corporate and public sectors. The dress code is likely to be more casual, and employer and employee are expected to be on first name terms, regardless of the extent of their difference in status.

Women in Work

Discrimination on the basis of gender is illegal in Australia and equal pay for women has been an accepted basic right for decades. Nonetheless, women in Australia, like their counterparts throughout western industrialised nations are still behind in the wages stakes, and their participation at the highest levels of management and industry is still low. With girls now easily outstripping boys in educational achievement, and with the gender balance tipping in favour of women in many university courses (women now outnumber men in medicine, for example), it is likely that this situation will change in coming years. Currently, a number of incentive schemes, such as WISE (Women in Science and Engineering), are in place to encourage women into male-dominated professions, and some public employers, particularly in the tertiary sector, operate positive discrimination policies to draw highly qualified women back into the workforce after childrearing.

Amongst young people, women now outnumber men in the workplace. At age 25 and above, 66 per cent of men are employed compared with 48 per cent of women; in the 16-25 age group, however, this ratio is now reversed, with female participation peaking at 66 per cent at age 25. Women, in general, seek more flexible employment opportunities and are more likely to be found in part-time or freelance work. They are also likely to seek shorter hours, with statistics showing that single mothers work around 12 hours per week fewer than men with similar family responsibilities. Women comprise around 76 per cent of the part-time workforce. In income terms, five per cent of women managers are in the lowest quartile of pay compared with one per cent of men, while there are 20 per cent more male managers in the highest income quartile than their female counterparts. At the lower end of the scale, 68 per cent of women labourers are in the lowest quartile of the pay scale, compared with 42 per cent of men. The industries with the greatest disparities between male and female earnings are the finance sector (average weekly earnings, male: $1,215; female, $675) and mining (male: $1,157; female, $789).

Maternity Benefits, Parental Leave and Employment Rights

Maternity Benefits
Australia, along with New Zealand and the United States, is one of the few industrialised nations in which the state does not pay maternity leave benefits. Government sector employees are entitled to three months paid leave, however, few women employed in the private sector receive paid maternity leave. All women are entitled to unpaid maternity leave of not more than 52 weeks, taken either during or after their pregnancy. On the expiry of the leave, the employee is entitled to return to her previous position or an equivalent, if that position no longer exists. All new mothers who are legal residents of Australia are entitled to receive the Maternity Allowance, a one-off lump sum payment of $750 made by the Department of Social Security. In cases of multiple birth, the Maternity Allowance payment is paid for each child born (including still-births). In addition, the DSS offers an incentive payment for immunisation called the Maternity Immunisation Allowance. This allowance is designed to combat falling levels of immunisation and provides parents with a lump sum of $200 on presentation of proof of full immunisation in their 18 month old child.

Paternity and Adoptive Leave
All Australian workers, and not just mothers, are entitled to parental leave, which in addition to maternity leave also comprises paternity and adoptive leave. Paternity leave may be taken in conjunction with the birth of a child to a spouse or defacto partner, whilst adoptive leave may be taken in conjunction with the adoption of a child under the age of five years. For both types of leave, ten weeks notice of intention must be given to the employer. Any employee who has completed at least 12 months continuous service, whether full or part time (but not casual), is eligible for parental leave, however, paternity leave cannot be taken simultaneously with maternity leave for the same child. Employees are entitled to take up to 52 weeks parental leave, which must be completed before the child's first birthday (or the first anniversary of an adoption). You cannot be dismissed for taking parental leave and your application for it cannot be legally refused by your employer. On your return to work, you are entitled to your old job back or, if it no longer exists, to one at an equivalent level, and your seniority and accumulated leave must be preserved in your absence.

Employment Rights
All employees have a basic right to a fair and reasonable working environment and conditions. Reasonable working conditions include the right to personal and physical safety, and thus, if you suffer injury at work due to your employer's negligence or unsatisfactory working conditions, you have the right to claim worker's compensation for any injury, discomfort, and loss of earnings you may incur as a result of that injury. Sexual harrassment is also considered to be a fundamental

denial of the right to a fair and reasonable working environment, and employers have been taken to court because they have allowed offensive or pornographic posters and pictures to be displayed in common staff areas. Most public employers and many larger corporate ones will have a sexual harrassment officer on their staff who will provide confidential advice and liaise in the case of complaints.

As an employee, you have the right to a fair dismissal, and each trade and industry has its own rules regarding acceptable practice. It is illegal to breach the contractually stated dismissal procedure, and if you believe that you have been treated unfairly, you can take your employer to an industrial tribunal for unfair or constructive dismissal.

Discrimination in the workplace (or, indeed, anywhere) on the grounds of ethnic origin, gender, religious or political beliefs, or nationality is against the law, and if you have reason to believe that you are experiencing discrimination of any kind, you should contact your local Department of Employment, Education, Training and Youth Affairs (DEETYA) office for advice on how to pursue a complaint.

Useful Addresses

Department of Workplace Relations and Small Business, Federal awards, tel 1900 937 450.

DEETYA: have an informative website at www.deetya.gov.au

ACTU: Your Employment Rights provides information on legislated employment rights at www.actu.asn.au.

Social Security and Unemployment Benefits

Australia has a full cradle to grave state welfare system which has, in recent years, been significantly streamlined. Social security benefits, including unemployment and family benefits, are not, however, available to temporary residents, and migrants are also ineligible to claim any kind of benefit until they have been resident in Australia for a full two years. The two year 'no-claim' period has been newly introduced by the government following public concern that migrants were taking advantage of Australia's social security system; previously, new settlers could start claiming benefits within 26 weeks of arrival. There are no reciprocal social security arrangements between the UK and Australia (except in respect of pensions, discussed below). The Department of Social Security provides detailed information on all its available benefits, including pay rates (which are regularly updated), current policy, and discussion papers, on its website at www.dss.gov.au. Within Australia, there is a DSS office in each capital city and in most major regional centres, where advisors will provide current information and discuss your eligibility for benefits.

Pensions

Australia is currently raising the retirement age for women to bring it in line with the male retirement age of 65 years. Currently, women can receive the pension from age 61.5, and this is being phased upwards in 6-monthly intervals, to bring it to the point where women born after 1 January 1949 will not be eligible for the pension until age 65. The pension is paid fortnightly at a maximum rate of $354.60 per fortnight for a single person and $295.80 each per fortnight for a married couple. To be eligible for an Australian pension, you must have been resident in

Australia for at least 10 years, of which five of those years must have been in a single extended period. It is important to note, however, that a reciprocal agreement exists between the Governments of Australia, New Zealand and the UK which allows new settlers to claim the pension without delay upon reaching pensionable age. Australian age pensions are subject to income and assets tests.

UK Pensions in Australia

If you currently receive a pension paid by the UK government, it will be frozen from the time you leave Britain, so that you will no longer be eligible for any pension rate increases awarded after your departure from Britain. You will, however, be entitled to full payment of your current pension once you arrive in Australia, and this can be arranged through the Department of Social Security in Britain prior to your departure.

If you are a UK migrant with permanent residency and reach pensionable age in Australia, you should make arrangements with the DSS in Britain in order to claim your UK pension entitlement, together with your Australian pension if you are eligible for the latter. As with retirees, your UK pension will be frozen at the rate current when you reach pensionable age and you will not receive any pension rate increases awarded in the UK.

Other retirement and pension issues are discussed more fully in Chapter Five, *Retirement*.

Short-Term Employment

There are many opportunities in Australia for short-term and casual employment. The Australian government has never felt it necessary to restrict drastically its working holiday maker scheme, even in times of economic downturn, as it is clear that travellers are prepared to take on the kind of temporary jobs that locals seeking a career or job security shun. Some industries, especially in the primary sector, rely on itinerant casual workers to fill their labour needs, and the adventurous traveller should find plenty of scope for some once-in-a-lifetime employment experiences.

Agriculture

Primary industry is the backbone of the Australian economy and there is a great variety of work available on farms and stations all year round. These opportunities are not just limited to working the land: mechanics, builders, tractor drivers, welders, domestics, cooks, and teachers are all needed. Horse riding skills or an HGV licence will improve your chances of finding work. If you have a farming background, preferably with experience in cereal crops, you will find it easy to get seasonal farm work, especially in heavy tractor soil tillage, drilling, single pass seeding, and combine harvesting. Pay varies between a flat rate of $90-$120 per day, or $9-$12 per hour before tax. You are likely to have to work between 50 and 80 hours per week, seven days a week, particularly during seeding.

Fruit farmers rely on backpacker labour at harvest time and this kind of work is ideal for travellers as it is of brief duration and offers the opportunity to 'follow the crops' from region to region. The summer months, from October to April, are the prime time for harvest work around Australia. The work can be hard, but once you become proficient you can expect to earn around $300 per week after tax.

Table of Harvest Work Opportunities

Month	Crop
Western Australia	
Jan-Mar	Grapes
Mar-May	Apples, pears
Mar-Jun	Crayfish
Mar-Jun	Oats, wheat, barley
Mar-Oct	Prawns, scallops
May-Sep	Squash, rockmelon
Apr-Nov	Melons
Jun-Dec	Peppers, tomatoes
Jul-Aug	Bananas
Jul-Dec	Wildflowers
Oct-Jan	Mangoes
Victoria	
Jan-Apr	Pears, peaches, apples, tomatoes, tobacco
Feb-Mar	Grapes
Sep-Nov	Asparagus
Oct-Dec	Strawberries
Nov-Feb	Cherries, berries
Nov-Dec	Tomato weeding
New South Wales	
Jan-Mar	Stone fruit, grapes, pears, prunes
Feb-Apr	Apples
Mar-Jun	Cotton picking
Sep-Dec	Asparagus
Sep-Apr	Oranges
Nov-Dec	Cherries
Nov-Apr	Oranges
Dec-Jan	Onions
Dec-Mar	Stone fruit
Dec-Apr	Blueberries
Queensland	
Feb-Mar	Pears, apples
Feb-Apr	Rockmelon, ginger
Mar-Dec	Wide range of vegetables
Apr-Jun	Citrus fruit
Apr-Nov	Beans
Apr-Dec	Tomatoes
May-Oct	Broccoli
May-Dec	Sugar cane
Jul-Sep	Ginger
Jul-Dec	Onions
Sep-Nov	Tobacco
Nov-Jan	Plums, cotton, peaches
South Australia	
Jan-Mar	Dried fruits

Feb-Apr	Apples, pears, grapes, peaches
Feb-Aug	Brussels sprouts
Jun-Sep	Pruning
Sep-Jan	Oranges (juicing and packing)
Oct-Feb	Strawberries
Dec-Feb	Apricots

Tasmania

Mar-May	Apples
Dec-Jan	Soft fruit
Feb-Apr	Grapes
Mar-Apr	Hops
Jan-Feb	Scallop splitting

Almost all harvest work is advertised through the Australian Job Network, and now that all these government employment agencies offices are electronically-linked, it is no longer necessary to go to the appropriate regional office to find out what work is available. Instead, you can visit the AJN in the city or town where you are currently located and, using the computer terminal and interactive map, find out what opportunities are available throughout Australia. Once you have found the kind of work you want, in an area that interests you, you will need to travel to that region to be interviewed by the local employment officer, however, the on-line service does make co-ordinating your work and travel much easier.

If you intend to do harvest work, you will need to be fit and healthy, and capable of working long hours in hot, dry, and dusty conditions. There is usually minimal accommodation available during the harvest, however, most orchards have on-site camping facilities if you have your own tent or caravan. Farms can be located as much as 100 km from the nearest town, so this kind of work is most practical if you have your own transport.

Aquaculture is a rapidly growing area of primary industry in Australia, and fishing work is available in many coastal areas. Crayfish, prawns, scallops, and abalone are all harvested according to very strict seasonal regulations, and work in these areas can be very highly paid. Many fishing trawlers, especially those with processing facilities, also take on workers, however, this kind of work often requires being at sea for extended periods and is not for the faint-hearted. The seas around the Australian coastline can be perilous.

Mining

Working in the mining industry in Australia can be both challenging and very financially rewarding. There is plenty of work available for unskilled labourers, and the best way to find such work is usually to visit the personnel offices of large mining companies at their city headquarters. If you strike lucky, you could find yourself on a plane within a few hours – finding mining work really is about being in the right place at the right time. There are mines and related mining activities all over Australia, from giant iron-ore projects in the north-west to small family-run gold and precious stone prospecting ventures in the south. Miners usually work a seven-day week, often from dawn to dusk, and sometimes for as many as six weeks straight. The pay is likely to be over $1,000 per week, and there is very little to spend it on on-site. If you work above the 26th parallel (the Tropic of Capricorn), you are entitled to extra pay, known as the 'tropical loading' or 'remote area allowance'. Most mining companies are now prepared to employ women on-site, and indeed many prefer to do so, as women are considered to respond less aggressively to the pressure-cooker atmosphere of isolated mine sites.

Nursing

There is a large demand for supply nurses in Australia, especially during the Australian autumn and winter months, from April to December. Specialists nurses, particularly A&E, ICU, and psychiatric, are always needed, and any qualified and experienced nurse is likely to have no difficulty in obtaining work from a nursing agency. To work as a nurse in Australia, even on a temporary basis, you will need to be registered with the Nurses' Registration Board of the state in which you hope to work, and many agencies will help you with this procedure. Bigger agencies will provide you with a pager so that you are not tied to the telephone – an important bonus for travellers who have better things to do.

TEFL

Australia has a flourishing TEFL market which caters mainly to south-east Asian students. There are large English language schools in every capital city all of which require casual, short, and long-term teachers for their various courses. To teach English as a Foreign Language in Australia you will need a recognised TEFL qualification and some prior teaching experience, and many back-packers now choose to take an appropriate course before they leave home in order to have this remunerative option during their travel. Casual TEFL teachers can expect to earn between $15 and $25 per hour. Perth, Sydney, and the Gold Coast have the largest and most active TEFL sectors.

Au Pairing

Au pair work is another backpacker standby, and there is considerable work available for those with experience and good references. Once confined almost entirely to remote rural families who needed the services of a child-minder cum governess, changing work patterns have led more and more urban families to employ full- or part-time nannies or au pairs. Australian families generally will *not* expect anyone employed as a childminder to undertake household duties other than those required for the immediate well-being of their children. Extra work, such as ironing, should be specified by the employer in advance and agreed to by you, and you can negotiate extra pay for these additional duties. Australian anti-discrimination laws do permit employers to specify the gender of a childminder; many families prefer to employ women to care for their children, and male applicants can be legally rejected. Some families, however, might actually prefer a male au pair, especially if the children are boys and like playing sports. There are numerous domestic and specialist au pair agencies supplying staff in this field.

Tourism and Hospitality

Australia's tourist industry is one of the country's largest employers, and there is a wide variety of jobs available. Hotels require childminders, porters, and kitchenhands, in addition to more qualified and experienced employees such as chefs, waiters, and bar staff. A silver service or bar attendant qualification acquired before you leave on your travels will equip you to find well paid work in every city.

Croupiers are required by casinos (there are one or two very large ones in most states, but no Las Vegas-style gambling mecca) and this kind of work is very highly paid; you will, however, require training and experience to be considered.

There is work available for instructor level PADI-qualified divers at the major dive spots around the coast, especially on the Great Barrier Reef and off Exmouth, in north-west WA. Divers should note that PADI is the most common certification system in Australia; BSAC-qualified divers will find it easier to find work if they convert their qualifications before travelling.

Travellers already very experienced in the Australian outback can find work as guides in some of the national parks, particularly Kakadu, and many coach companies also take on tour leaders and coach drivers with an appropriate licence and experience. Queensland offers the greatest opportunities in terms of resort work, however, most jobs are found by word of mouth: if you hope to work, say, on the Gold Coast, the most likely way of picking up work is to go there and ask around. The AJN, once again, is the best first port of call for work in the tourism and hospitality sector.

Office Work, Telemarketing and Sales

Office temps are particularly in demand during the Australian summer months and over major holiday periods such as Christmas and Easter. Most commonly, short-term work is available in secretarial, clerical, word-processing and data entry positions, all of which require some degree of skill and previous experience. The banking, finance, and stockbroking industries always require temps, especially during peak periods, such as the end of the financial year (30 June). Unskilled casual work is often also available at this time when large supermarkets and department stores do their annual stocktake. There are innumerable employment agencies supplying both general and specialist short-term staff, and these are listed in the Yellow Pages. The AJN is generally less fruitful as a source of this kind of work, although temporary government and public sector positions will be advertised there.

Telemarketing does not appeal to everyone, but can be financially rewarding if you are successful. Turnover is unusually high in this industry, and telemarketing firms have no hesitation in employing backpackers as it is rare for any staff, whether itinerant or not, to stay the pace for more than a few weeks. Telemarketing jobs are usually advertised in the employment classifieds of major city and local newspapers.

Travellers are advised to avoid sales jobs offering commission-only remuneration, and especially those which advertise 'travellers welcome'. In most cases, such jobs offer one-way transport to a remote location, from which you will be required to make enough sales to fund your own way back to civilisation.

Volunteering

Countless charitable organisations throughout Australia rely on volunteers to help run their many aid, development, and conservation programmes. Becoming involved in such enterprises offers the working holiday maker an opportunity to experience a different side of Australian life whilst gaining new skills and contributing to a worthwhile cause. If you are interested in volunteering in any capacity, contact the Charities' Commission in your state (listed under Government Organisations in the White Pages) who will be able to supply you with a list of all the charities registered with them. Visitors to Australia who are interested in the country's unique landscape are often particularly attracted to conservation work, and the *Australian Trust for Conservation Volunteers (ATCV)*,

(15 Lydiard Street, North Ballarat,VIC 3350, tel 03-5333 1483), can help with placements in this field. Volunteers are expected to raise at least $600 to contribute towards their food, lodging, and travel expenses.

Tax Notes for Travellers

Working holiday makers pay tax on their earnings like any other Australian employee, however, as you will only be working for a short period it is possible that your earnings will fall below the tax threshold and that you will, therefore, be eligible for a tax refund at the end of your visit. Everyone who works in Australia must have a 'tax file number', and you will need to apply for one as soon as you start work or, preferably, even sooner. The tax file number can take up to six weeks to be issued, and until you receive your number and are able to pass it on to your employer, you will be taxed at the maximum rate of 50 cents in the dollar. Application forms for a tax file number are available from all post offices. Non-residents with a tax file number pay tax at a rate of 29 cents in the dollar.

Before you leave Australia, you should lodge a tax return (also available from the Post Office inside the 'Tax Pack'). Every employer for whom you have worked should have supplied you with a 'group certificate' on leaving; you will need to keep these and attach them to your tax return as proof of your total earnings. The taxation office will assess your return, usually within a couple of weeks of lodgment, and a refund cheque (if applicable) will be forwarded to your nominated address, either in Australia or overseas.

Permanent Work

Agriculture and Food Processing

It is generally acknowledged that Australia's wealth was founded on the sheep's back, and today agriculture is still the backbone of the Australian economy. The traditional export products of wheat and wool, however, have long since ceded prominence to other sectors, including fisheries and viticulture, and exotic produce such as native bush meats and wildflowers.

The food processing industry is Australia's largest manufacturing sector, and is expected to experience continued growth of around 10 per cent per annum. It is projected that employment growth areas in this industry will shift away from factory processing and into sales, research, development and marketing. This trend reflects both a move away from convenience foods by consumers towards high quality fresh produce, as well as a competitive imported food market.

Automotive

Australia has a strong automotive industry with Ford, General Motors (Holden), Nissan, Mitsubishi, and Toyota all producing cars in Australian factories. Car sales are currently buoyant, reflecting the general economic upturn, and sales of locally produced cars are strong as luxury taxes make imported cars expensive. All automotive manufacturers are investing heavily in robot technology, so that the employment outlook for factory floor workers is poor, whilst that for people skilled in computer technology is good. Overall, there has been a decrease of around 3 per cent in manufacturing jobs in this sector in the 12 months to May 1998. The Department of Employment, Education, Training, and Youth Affairs

(DEETYA) assesses the short and long term employment prospects for automotive workers as average.

Executive Employment

Executive employment prospects are generally good, particularly with smaller companies. After a period of rationalisation during the recession, business has stabilised and most firms are experiencing reasonable growth. DEETYA assess the employment outlook for generalist managers and administrators as average in both the short and long term, whilst those with specialist skills have above average prospects. In the 12 months to May 1998, this occupation group experienced overall growth of 0.3 per cent, with around 1 per cent of managers and administrators unemployed.

Finance and Property

The property and business services industry experienced the highest growth of any sector in the year to May 1998, with a growth rate of nearly 9 per cent (or over 71,000 jobs).

Finance, on the other hand, saw a small decrease in the number of jobs available (down 0.5 per cent), although average weekly earnings remain very high in this sector, and are second only to mining at around $1,200 per week. DEETYA has assessed the short and long term employment prospects in finance as generally sound, and in property and business services as average.

Information Technology

Information technology is a major growth sector in the Australian economy and is projected to continue to expand through to 2005. Job prospects are strong for well-qualified and experienced professionals, and there is a particular need for people with Powerbuilder, AS400, and SAP skills. The government is keen to encourage the IT sector, particularly in areas where application of new technology will enhance Australia's competitiveness in the export market.

Medical

There is currently an embargo on the entry of medical practitioners into Australia for employment purposes. Overseas-qualified doctors already granted permission to work in Australia are required to pass stringent registration examinations before they are permitted to practice.

Both State Registered and State Enrolled Nurses are in demand throughout Australia, particularly those qualified in specialist fields such as accident and emergency, intensive care, and psychiatry. You will need to have your qualifications ratified by the Nurses Registration Board in the state in which you live and then register with this Board before you are able to apply for work.

Health therapists, such as physiotherapists, occupational therapists and speech therapists, also need to have their qualifications approved by Australian authorities before practising in Australia. In some cases, further study may be necessary before your registration can be accepted. There is currently an identified shortage of occupational therapists in Australia.

Petrochemicals

There has been massive investment in oil and gas exploration, particularly in the North West Shelf Natural Gas Project off the coast of Western Australia. Engineers of all types are in demand in this industry, and petrochemical engineering is identified by DEETYA as an area of particular employment shortage. Deep sea divers are also required. Growth in the professional and para-professional occupations of the petrochemical industry currently stands at around 5.4 per cent.

Retailing

As the Asian currency crisis bites into the Australian economy, retail optimism is falling, however, the current position is stable and the retail sector is riding high on exceptionally good Christmas trading figures for 1997. Employment prospects in both retail sales and management are good, and increased by nearly 4 per cent in the 12 months prior to May 1998. DEETYA assesses both the short and long term outlook for employment in retail management as sound and in retail sales as average.

Steel and Non-ferrous Metals

Australia is one of the world's largest exporters of iron ore, although its steel processing sector is much less developed. Mining is a major employment sector, and is the highest paid industry in the country, with average weekly earning in excess of $1,500 per week. Mining experienced a 4 per cent growth in employment in 1997/98 and DEETYA has assessed it short and long term employment prospects as sound in professional, skilled, and semi-skilled occupations. The Australian mining industry is one of the most highly productive in the world and is a significant investor in capital equipment. British equipment suppliers enjoy a large share of the underground black coal mining market.

Australia is also rich in other natural resources including manganese, uranium, diamonds, zirconite, mineral sands, lead, zinc, copper, gold, silver, alumina and bauxite. These mining industries operate on a large scale across the country and are all significant employers of skilled and unskilled labour.

Teaching

The demand for primary and secondary school teachers in Australia currently outstrips supply in all states. To teach in Australia, you will be required to be four-year-qualified, that is, you must hold either a bachelor's degree plus a one year Graduate Diploma of Education (equivalent to a PGCE), or a four-year Bachelor of Education. Teachers currently teaching in both the state and private education sector who are not qualified at this level are now required to upgrade their qualifications by means of external study and summer schools. Primary school teachers require a specialist degree in primary education while secondary school teachers normally teach in a subject area related to their degree major. Whereas once private schools were prepared to employ non teacher-trained graduates, this is now extremely rare and teachers arriving from overseas with experience but no qualification are unlikely to find work in either the state or private sector. Teaching, tutoring and lecturing posts in the tertiary sector are very oversubscribed and obtaining a position is highly competitive.

Education is the responsibility of the state government, and to obtain work as a teacher you will need to apply to the Ministry of Education in your state. Some states require new teachers on the permanent register to work for a period in a remote rural location before offering a choice of more convenient schools. If you are unable to do this, you may have to undertake work on a temporary or casual basis for some years before being offered permanency.

Regional Employment Guide

This section summarises the employment opportunities and economic strengths of each state and territory, and should be read in conjunction with the analysis contained in the *Regional Guide* in Chapter One.

Western Australia

Permanent

Western Australia is currently one of Australia's fastest growing economies, with high levels of business investments matched by the strongest employment figures in the country. Manufacturing and services are the state's fastest growing sectors, and the government has identified and is promoting a group of key strategic industries to reduce dependence on raw materials export. These strategic industries include building and construction, defence and aerospace, education and training services, health and medical services, information technology and telecommunications, marine industries, mining equipment and services, oil and gas equipment and services, processed foods and wine, and professional services. There is significant involvement in Asian markets by Western Australian industry, and state production is heavily export-focused. WA is Australia's leading exporter, with merchandise exports totalling A$19.3 billion in 1997. Iron ore ($3.1 billion) and gold ($2.9 billion) were the state's largest mineral exports, and wheat and alumina the largest items respectively of agricultural and processed raw material exports. In 1996/97 WA's principal 'elaborately transformed manufactures' (ETM) exports were titanium dioxide pigments (26 per cent) and ferries and pleasure craft (21.3 per cent). WA is the world's leading producer of high speed ferries.

WA has one of the world's largest and most technologically advanced mining sectors, and mineral and energy production, and exporting is forecast to experience continued growth in the next five years. Bulk commodity export is under some pressure, however, as a decreasing international scarcity of non-reproducible natural resources has made the market highly competitive. Reforms have been implemented within the industry to make it more competitive and these have included a decline in traditional award-type employment which has been replaced by staff-only operations. There is likely to be a sharp increase in contracting-out in the mining industry.

The state's natural resources include iron ore, gold, diamonds, alumina, nickel, mineral sands products, oil and natural gas. Western Australia also has the world's largest zirconia plant. ALCOA, Worsley Alumina, and Dampier Salt are the three major investors in mineral extraction and processing, and between them employ around 4,000 people. The gold industry is based inland around Kalgoorlie, 600km east of Perth, and this area is currently experiencing renewed rapid growth after a period of recession. Only the diamond industry is expected to experience any decline in the short-term, with implications for the economic strength of the Kimberley region. The oil and gas industry is also a major contributor to the state's economic base and is centred off-shore on the North West Shelf, which contains one of the world's largest deposits of natural gas. Oil and gas exploration is on-going in Western Australia, and further major finds are expected. Since 1994, numerous international companies associated with the petroleum industry, including Western Geophysical, Nopec, Drillex, WS Atkins, ESD Simulators, and Global Drilling, have all established South East Asian regional headquarters in Perth. Engineers, metallurgists, and other mineral extraction industry professionals are in demand in Western Australia, and employment prospects in both the short and long term are good.

There are nearly 3,000 different manufacturers in Western Australia, with an annual turnover of more than $10 billion. Food processing, base metal processing, wine production, and pharmaceuticals have experienced strong growth over the last five years, with continued expansion forecast. Agriculture is increasingly focused on niche markets, such as emu, kangaroo, ostrich, deer and genetically modified animals, and on value-added crops, such as specialised noodle wheat. The raw grains market (wheat, oats, and barley) has a positive medium term outlook. In forestry, there has been rapid expansion in eucalypt plantations in the south west of the state, and a new pulp and paper mill is expected to create large numbers of jobs in this region. The fisheries industry is experiencing rapid growth, hampered only by the restrictions of wild harvesting. Mariculture (sea-based) and aquaculture (land-based) fish production is therefore being encouraged, and these industries have a strong economic outlook.

The services sector of the Western Australian economy currently accounts for more than 70 per cent of the state's GDP. The financial sector has expanded rapidly since deregulation in the 1980s and there are now more than 20 banking groups represented in the state. WA exports consultancy services in mining, engineering, forestry, agriculture and conservation, and the state's highly regarded medical research and hospital facilities have made Perth a centre for Australia's 'medical tourism' industry. The service sector's biggest growth area is currently tourism and it is projected that over 200,000 new jobs will be created to service this industry in WA in the next five years.

Temporary

Harvest work is available throughout the year, mainly in the south-west of the state; casual work in the fishing industry around Carnarvon is available between March and October. General agricultural labouring can usually be found on cattle stations, and on sheep stations, particularly at shearing time. The hospitality industry always needs short-term employees, with work available year-round in Perth and during the tourist season in other major centres (May to September in Broome, and the summer months in other areas). Unskilled mine work is relatively easy to find in the north west and can be highly paid. In Perth, all the usual temporary employment opportunities, including office work, teaching and nursing, are readily available.

Northern Territory

Permanent

The Northern Territory has experienced real economic growth of 5% per annum every year for the past ten years, and in 1996/97 benefited from an increase of 83% in private capital expenditure in mining, capital investment, and tourism. More than 600 rooms were added to the Darwin tourist accommodation sector in 1997, however, the retail trade is currently experiencing a downturn, with figures dropping nearly seven per cent in the past year. Advertised job vacancies are increasing steadily in the Territory and are generally stronger in the dry season, from May to October.

The mining industry in the Northern Territory's biggest earner, contributing $1.6 billion annually to the state economy, more than four times the national average, and the sector is the state's major employer. There are 14 operating mines, and minerals, including alumina, manganese, gold, bauxite and uranium, dominate the territory's overseas exports. Zinc, lead and silver are mined at Woodcutters mine, McArthur River, and uranium is mined at Alligator River. Gold mines are located in the Adelaide River/Pine Creek region, the Tanami Desert and at Tennant Creek. Oil and gas production occurs onshore at Mereenie and Palm Valley in the Amadeus Basin, and offshore on the Jabiru and Challis fields in the Timor Sea. Natural gas production for export is being developed on the Petrel and Tern gas fields in the Bonaparte Gulf. Oil and gas account for approximately 35 per cent of the state's exports.

In the East Arnhem region of the Northern Territory, which comprises the eastern half of Arnhem Land and Groote Eylandt in the Gulf of Carpentaria, bauxite and manganese are produced in two of the world's largest mines of their type. Gove Joint Venture mines bauxite on the Gove Peninsula, exporting it as alumina and aluminium hydroxide. The mine, which is managed by Nabalco, employs more than 1,000 people, of whom more than 260 are independent contractors. The mine is expected to be operational until 2035. Manganese is mined by the BHP subsidiary, Groote Eylandt Mining Company (GEMCO), which produces more than ten per cent of the world's manganese output. Mining support businesses in the region turnover around $45 million per annum. Apart from the mining industry, the East Arnhem region supports mainly small business, in particular retail and property services.

Growth industries in the Northern Territory include building and construction, and prawn fishing. More unusually, another growing industry services the need of farming, mining, and conservation sectors to harvest the 30,000 head of wild buffalo and feral cattle which cause huge damage as they rampage across the fragile landscape. Tourism is one of the territory's most significant employment sectors, and is centred on Alice Springs, Darwin and Kakadu National Park.

Temporary
Most temporary jobs are provided by the tourist industry, especially during the tourist season from May to December (all year at Alice Springs). Remote resorts have a high staff turn-over and are frequently able to offer short-term employment. There is occasional station work available to those with good horse skills.

South Australia

Permanent
The South Australian government has identified a number of key industry sectors which it intends to promote vigorously into the next century. These industries, which currently represent the state's principal investment opportunities, include information technology and telecommunications, mining and mineral processing, water management, food and wine, engineering (especially foundries and tool making), defence and aerospace, automotives (both vehicle and component manufacture), and traded services, particularly health and tourism. All these industries already have a strong presence in the economy, and various government initiatives are in place to encourage further growth.

South Australia's information technology development programme, IT2000, aims to make the state an internationally recognised centre in the five specialist areas of software development, multimedia, spatial information, electronic services, and education and distance learning. Motorola, TechSouth, AWA Defence Industries, Telstra, and Tandem have already made major investments under the IT2000 programme, and the state hopes to attract other key investors. The global communications giant, Motorola, has established its Australian Software Development Centre in Adelaide, and the US-based Tandem Computers will build its Advanced Development Centre in Adelaide. By 2000, the ASDC will employ 400 research and development engineers, and will provide investment, technology transfer, research and development, and exports from Australia valued at over $A240 billion. Technology Park in Adelaide is home to more than 35 technology organisations including British Aerospace Australia, Computer Science Corporation, and Celsiustech. There are a further six research centres, including the Signal Processing Reseach Institute, which undertakes research in mobile and defence communications, and an independent Information Industries Development Centre is soon to be developed at Technology Park. Electronic Data Systems, Microsoft, and IBM have all committed investment funds to the project. The world's second biggest software company, Oracle, is also establishing a research centre in Adelaide in the field of spatial imaging. The cable television provider, Galaxy, has its national Customer Services Centre in Adelaide and is expected to employ over 1,000 people by the year 2000.

The motor vehicle sector is South Australia's large single industry, with Mitsubishi Motors Australia and General Motors Holden together employing over 9,000 people. Mitsubishi have recently invested $500 million at their Clovelly Park plant, which in 1996/97 produced 48,000 vehicles. The automotive components industry in SA provides over 20 per cent of the national production, and directly employs a further 6,000 people. South Australia's also attracts around 40 per cent of the nation's defence development budget, and research and development for the $5.3 billion Collins Class submarine project is currently underway in Adelaide.

The state is rich in natural resources, including coal, copper, gold, iron ore, lead, silver, uranium, crude oil, natural gas, dolomite and gypsum. The world's largest zinc smelter, owned by Pasminco and BHAS, is located at Port Pirie, and the Santos Moomba Field in Cooper Basin is Australia's largest producer of oil and gas.

South Australia is also Australia's leading wine producing state, and accounts for 65 per cent of the country's wine exports. There are over 180 small to medium sized businesses involved in wine production spread throughout the six wine growing regions. The major producers, Penfolds, Orlando Wyndham, BRL Hardy, and Mildara Blass, have a national and international presence. Aquaculture is also thriving and incentives are in place to encourage development in this industry. Blue fin tuna, abalone, and Pacific oysters are farmed and exported on a large scale, and the farming of freshwater crayfish and barramundi is currently being developed.

Temporary
Grape picking is available in the Barossa Valley and Adelaide Hills from February to April, as is other harvesting work throughout the rest of the year. Hospitality and office temporary work is available in Adelaide all year, and particularly during the summer months.

Tasmania

Permanent
Tasmania has been the butt of 'would the last person to leave Tasmania...' jokes for so long that it hardly needs saying that this is a state gripped by considerable

economic difficulties. Unemployment figures are the worst in the country, and youth unemployment is particularly severe. The state government is currently conducting a 'Resettlement Tasmania' campaign to woo back the lost sons and daughters of the Apple Isle, but most people are waiting for things to improve before taking their chances again in a state where all the traditional industries are under threat.

Tasmania is rich in mineral resources, especially iron, copper, lead, zinc, tin, and tungsten, and a recent geological data survey has revived interest in gold mining in the region. There are six major mining operations at Henty, Savage River, Beaconsfield, Hellyer, Mt Lyell, Pasminco Roseberry, and Renison. After a long period during which the mineral resources industry was starved of investment, the Tasmanian Government is now committed to developing the infrastructure and investment conditions necessary to encourage the growth of multiple-stage mineral processing in the state. This enhanced processing capacity is expected to inject a further $2,000 million into Tasmania's economy.

Tasmania has a highly diversified rural sector, of which the major components are the vegetable, dairy, sheep, and beef cattle industries. Continuing problems in the wool market have meant that the sheep industry, once the mainstay of Tasmanian agriculture, is now the poor relative of vegetable and dairy farming, and recently, beef has experienced a similar downturn. Tasmanian agriculture is strongly export-orientated, both to mainland Australia and internationally. The farm gate value of raw agricultural produce currently averages around $600 million per annum. Dairying is considered to have the best medium to long term prospects and is already the state's largest agricultural industry: in addition to 747 dairy farms, Tasmania has seven fresh milk processing plants, one UHT milk processing plant, seven manufacturing plants, ten farm cheese producers, and three cheese shredders. The industry employs 2,000 people at farm level and a further 1,600 people at factory and distribution level. Emerging rural industries include emus, poppies, lavender, and wine grapes, whilst apple farmers are experiencing renewed economic growth.

Sea fisheries are a rapidly growing industry and currently account for a gross value of more than $200 million per annum. The most valuable sector of the fisheries market is Atlantic salmon, which is mainly grown in the marine farms of the state's south east. Abalone and rock lobster account for half the total value of Tasmanian marine production, and the marine farming sector as a whole provided over 40 per cent. Tasmania's wild fisheries have now reached the limits of their sustainable exploitation, however, intensification and expansion is projected for in the area of cultured fisheries. Around 2,000 people are employed in marine industries in the state.

The largest sectors of Tasmania's manufacturing industry are food, beverage and tobacco, which together contribute 30 per cent of total turnover. Wood and wood products, textiles, clothing and footwear, paper and paper products, chemical and petroleum products, basic metal products, fabricated metal products and transport equipment industries also contribute to the state's economic base, however, there has been a marked decline in employment in these sectors in recent years. Retailing is experiencing slow to moderate growth. There is strong growth in the tourism sector, particularly in 'wilderness' and eco-tourism.

Temporary

Hospitality work is available in the Mount Field and Ben Lomond Ski Resorts during the ski season, from June to August. Fruit picking is available from December to April in the Huon Valley, Derwent Valley, Tasman Peninsula, and West Tamar. Scallop splitting work can be found in Bicheno in January and February.

Victoria

Permanent

Many international corporations, including Saab, Kodak, General Motors, Ford, Ericsson, Mercedes Benz, BMW, Toyota, Kia, Hewlett-Packard, Olivetti, NEC, Oracle, Kraft, Heinz and Simplot, have their Australian base in Victoria. A strong commitment by the government of Victoria to encourage international competitiveness in local business has lifted exports of 'elaborately transformed manufacturers' (ETMs) by 16 per cent to $6.3 billion in 1996/97. Export growth is currently strongest in chemicals, the automotive industry, information technology, and medical and scientific equipment, and job prospects are strong in these sectors.

Victoria's food processing industries account for around a third of the state's export earnings. Forty per cent of the nation's aluminium production occurs at the primary aluminium smelters at Portland and Point Henry. Almost half of Australia's $2 billion telecommunications industry is based in Victoria, and the state is home to around a third of the country's software development companies. Victoria is also the centre of Australia's textiles, clothing and footwear industries, and continued growth is expected in niche and designer sectors. Over half of Australia's automotive industry production occurs in Victoria, with Ford, General Motors and Toyota all manufacturing in the state, together with more than 500 components producers.

Traded services, such as the health and education sectors, are also becoming highly competitive in the export market and are actively seeking new business overseas. The education sector currently generates around $500 million in annual exports and is experiencing continued growth. The Australian Stock Exchange (ASX) is based in Melbourne and operates a national share market linked through an automated trading system. Melbourne stock brokers account for more than half of all capital raisings on the ASX. Futures markets in currencies and traded commodities can be accessed through a network of specialist brokers.

Melbourne has Australia's largest throughput cargo airport and largest container sea port. The Port of Melbourne handles 40 per cent of Australia's container trade. The two terminal operators at Swanson dock, Australian Stevedores and Conaust are committed to developing their facilities to operate at international best practice performance levels. Investment in the redevelopment of these terminals over the next 20 years will exceed $300 million.

Geelong is Australia's eleventh largest city and plays a major role in the country's wool production and textile industries. In addition to these traditional industries, the city is now developing its economic base in high-technology industries, education and research. Geelong is home to manufacturers of textiles, clothing, footwear, petroleum and coal products, chemicals, basic metal products and transport equipment. It is the centre of the Australian aerospace industry, at Avalon Airport, while major assembly and maintenance plants are operated by ASTA and Hawker de Havilland in Melbourne. Ford Motor Company, Shell Oil Company of Australia and the aluminium giant ALCOA are the largest among the many industries which have chosen to expand in this region.

Temporary

Harvest work is available around Mildura and Shepperton from January to April, and around Echuca and Lilyfield from September through to February. The Northern Victoria Fruit-growers' Association in Shepperton, Victoria, and the Victorian Peach and Apricot Growers' Association in Cobram, Victoria, are both able to offer jobs during the harvesting season. Hospitality work is available during the ski season in the Snowy Mountains. Temporary secretarial, office and administration work, as well as hospitality work (including gaming), is widely available in Melbourne.

New South Wales

Permanent

The strength of the New South Wales' economy lies in its diverse range of industries. The state is one of the world's leading service economies, and has a significant manufacturing and primary industry base. More than 80 international businesses have their Australian base in New South Wales, in fields including information technology, telecommunications, aerospace, medical equipment, pharmaceuticals, environmental industries, industrial textiles, shipping and railways, construction and mining equipment, metal and minerals processing, processed foods, paper and pulp, banking, tourism, advertising, film, and audio products. European, US, and Japanese companies are all represented.

New South Wales is Australia's premier agribusiness state, accounting for around one third of the national primary industry output, and many leading agribusiness companies have their headquarters in Sydney. NSW agribusiness industry includes farming, processing, transport, distribution, export, and supply. The industry's strengths have traditionally been in bulk commodities and minimally processed products such as wool, grains, meat and sugar; however, recent innovation and new product development has made the sector increasingly market focused. In particular sector growth is focused on the Asian food market, with heavy demand projected for western foods over the next five years.

The state has a well established chemical industry and is home to the country's largest petrochemical complex. Its mining and mineral processing industries generate an annual output of over A\$12 billion, of which coal production accounts for 80 per cent. The major minerals derived from the state's rich mineral resources are black coal, copper, gold, silver, lead, zinc, mineral sands, and gemstones. NSW is also the major minerals processing state with established steel and aluminium production, and new copper smelting capacity currently coming into operation. The government of NSW is now spending \$35 million to expand the geological database of the state in order to attract new mineral and petroleum exploration and development. The Lithgow Minerals Processing Park has been located in the central west of the state to encourage development in that area.

The electricity sector dominates NSW's energy industry and employs over 4,000 people. The government monopoly has recently been restructured to form three independent power generators, Pacific Power, Delta Electricity, and Macquarie Generation. The NSW gas sector is 95 per cent controlled by Australian Gas Limited (AGL), a publicly listed company with 2,100 employees. Environmental management is a growth industry in the state, and is currently the largest in Australia.

Sydney is one of the Asia-Pacific region's most dynamic financial centres and is the base for Australia's major financial institutions, accounting for around 65 per cent of the domestic market. The Sydney Futures Exchange traded the third highest volume of futures against all Asia Pacific futures exchanges in 1995, and Sydney is expected to become the regions second largest financial centre, after Tokyo, by 2000.

The state is also a leading information technology and telecommunications (IT&T) centre, and the base for almost half of Australia's IT&T industry. This sector is forecast to grow rapidly over the next five years. The state is a significant producer of digital material content for multimedia, and has a strong film and television production sector. Fox Studios in Sydney will soon become the largest film and television studios in the southern hemisphere, and will offer many opportunities in the digital post-production industry.

NSW is a major centre for aerospace, electronics and defence industries. These industries are among the fastest growing in the state with extremely strong investment growth expected over the next five years. The state is the base for over 30,000 defence personnel and Sydney Harbour is an important naval base and centre for marine repair activity. Airframe and systems support, sensors, processors, and defence aerospace training systems are all under development in NSW, as is world-leading C2I technology.

Cultural industries generate an estimated $4.3 billion in turnover for NSW, and education is a growing market, with over 50,000 international students studying at various educational institutions. Food processing comprises 8 per cent of the state's GDP and retail trade for 15 per cent of the economic output. Both these sectors are significant employers. NSW's largest service sector is tourism which currently injects $15 billion a year into the economy.

Temporary
The full range of temporary work opportunities is available in NSW, ranging from harvest and seasonal farm work in almost every region, to hospitality and office work, particularly in Sydney.

Australian Capital Territory

Permanent
Employment opportunities in the ACT are concentrated in Canberra. Most permanent work available is either service-based, reflecting the city's political function, or in the extensive public service which supports the government and federal ministries. The Commonwealth Government is the territory's biggest employer.

Temporary
There is little temporary employment available in Canberra, apart from occasional clerical and hospitality work.

Queensland

Permanent
Queensland currently has Australia's most thriving economy, and benefits from rich natural resources, diversified agriculture, and a vibrant tourist industry. The state government has recently allocated large sums towards maintaining Queensland's favourable economic position, including a $1.6 billion Infrastructure Rejuvenation Package to be implemented over the next three years. Total capital works expenditure for 1997/98 is estimated at $4.3 billion, with a further $4.8 billion to be spent over five years in developing the state's regional road networks, and another $690 million on Queensland Rail.

Infrastructure developments to which the government has made a commitment include the installation of a water management system and new weir in the Atherton Tablelands, a new cruise liner port in Brisbane, expansion of the Dalrymple Bay Coal Export Terminal, and a ten year development of the Port of Mackay. The Queensland Hospital Project will upgrade all the state's hospital facilities, and gas turbine power plants will be built at Yabulu and Mt Stuart. New wharf facilities are being built at Fisherman Islands to handle large container vessels.

Agriculture is the cornerstone of Queensland's economy, with grains, beef and wool dominating rural industry. Tropical and citrus fruits, dairy products, vegetables, cotton, and tobacco are also important, and the state has the world's highest yielding sugar cane industry. Queensland's fishing industry is second only to Western Australia's, with nearly 5,000 commercial fishing vessels currently in operation, mainly fishing prawns, crustaceans and fin fish for export to Asia, Europe and the USA. Recently established food processing plants include a high technology piggery and integrated pork processing facility (DanPork Australia), and an upgraded Golden Circle Canned Fruit and Vegetable Plant.

Mount Isa mine is one of the world's leading producers of lead and silver, and is ranked in the world's top ten for copper and zinc production. The state's high-grade coal and bauxite reserves are among the largest in the world, and magnesite, phosphate rock, and limestone are also mined. Queensland is the largest Australian producer and exporter of black coal. Large resources of magnesite, oil, shale, uranium, tin, mineral sands, clay and salt remain untapped, and continued development is projected. New mines are currently being developed at Cannington Base Metals Deposit (BHP), Century Base Metals Project (Century Zinc), Ely Mining Project (Alcan South Pacific), Ensham Coal Mine (Bligh/Idemitsu), and Enterprise Mine (MIM Holdings), amongst many others. Minerals mined in these projects include lead, zinc, bauxite, copper, gold, and predominantly, coal. In addition, a number of minerals processing plants are being brought online, such as the Sun Metals Corp Zinc Refinery in Townsville, and Dupont/Ticor Sodium Cyanide Plant, and the Boyne Island Aluminium Smelter. Coal seam methane gas is being recovered from productive coal along the western flank of the Bowen Basin, and a 27 km gas pipeline is now under construction to connect coal seam methane supplies with the PG&E gas pipeline.

Manufacturing industries in Queensland have developed to support the state's mineral processing and agricultural industries. The manufacturing sector is dominated by food, beverage, and tobacco processing, fabricated metal products, and chemicals, petroleum and coal products. The processed food industry employs around 37,000 people, and is Queensland's largest manufacturing sector. The state's service industries include the construction, wholesale and retail trades, communications, business and financial services, and tourism.

Queensland has Australia's most successful tourism market and this sector employs a significant proportion of the state's workforce. There are currently four major tourist resorts under development at Coomera Waters, Cowan Cove, Port Hinchinbrook, and East Hill, an integrated urban/resort project, covering 245 hectares.

Temporary
Fruit and vegetable picking is available throughout the state, particularly at Stanthorpe, Bowen and Warwick. Employment in the hospitality sector is widely available at resorts during the tourist season, especially on the Gold Coast, and work on prawn trawlers can be found at Cairns and Karumba. Mining and cattle station work is available in the Mount Isa region.

Directory of Major Employers

Below is a list of the top one hundred companies in Australia by market capitalisation (as at August 1998). It must be noted, however, that recent economic reports show that small companies are now the main creators of jobs in the private sector. Statistics show that it has, in fact, been companies with fewer than 50 staff which have continued to create thousands of jobs throughout the recession. Many of the larger companies are reducing instead of increasing their workforce; once a company has reached a minimum threshold level, it can avoid paying payroll tax, higher superannuation benefits and increased training levies. If you choose to look for employment with a smaller company, you should focus your search on those which produce high-value-added, high-technology products for export to Asia. Such companies have experienced growth in excess of 30% in recent years, despite the recession.

Many of the companies listed below have dozens or, in some cases, hundreds of subsidiaries with diverse operations unrelated to their principal activity. They have numerous Australian and international branches, and you should contact the company directly for details of their other offices.

Finance, Insurance and Property

Australia and New Zealand (ANZ) Banking Group Limited, 100 Queen Street, Melbourne, VIC 3000, tel 03-9273 5555. Banking services.

Commonwealth Bank of Australia, 1st Floor, 48 Martin Place, Sydney NSW 2000, tel: 02-9378 2000. Banking services; subsidiaries include electronics, shipping, investment and the Commonwealth Development Bank which services the small business and rural sectors.

GIO Australia Holdings Limited, 2 Martin Place, Sydney NSW 2000, tel: 02-9228 1000 or fax: 02-9235 3909. Insurance.

National Australia Bank Limited, 24th Floor, 500 Bourke Street, Melbourne VIC 3000, tel: 03-9641 3500 or fax: 03-9641 4916. Banking services.

QBE Insurance Group Limited 33 Ainslie Avenue, Canberra, ACT 2601, tel 02-6240 3434. Insurance.

St George Bank Limited, 4-16 Montgomery Street, Kogarah NSW 2217, tel: 1300 362 555. Banking services.

Westpac Banking Corporation, 60 Martin Place, Sydney NSW 2000, tel: 02-9226 2866. Banking services.

AMP Limited, 33 Alfred Street, Sydney, NSW 2000, tel 02-9257 5000. Insurance.

Lend Lease Corporation Limited, 46th Level, Australia Square, George Street, Sydney NSW 2000, tel: 02-9236 6111 or fax: 02-9252 2192. Finance and property development.

National Mutual Holdings Limited, Level 11, 44 Market Street, Sydney, NSW 2000, tel 02-9563 2786. Insurance and financial services.

Westfield Trust, Westfield Holdings Limited, Westfield America Trust, Westfield Towers, 100 William Street, Sydney, NSW 2000, tel 02-9358 7466. Property trusts.

Stockland Trust Group, 157 Liverpool Street, Sydney, NSW 2000, tel 02-9321 1500. Property trust.

Colonial, 330 Collins Street, Melbourne, VIC 3000, tel 03-9200 6111. Finance.

Macquarie Bank Limited, 20 Bond Street, Sydney, NSW 2000, tel 02-9237 3333. Banking services.

Australian Foundation Investment Co. Limited, Level 15, 101 Collins Street, Melbourne, VIC 3000, tel 03-9650 9911. Investment trust.

BankWest, 108 St George's Terrace, Perth, WA 6000, tel 13 1718. Banking services.

The Franked Income Fund, 175 Macquarie Street, Sydney, NSW 2000, tel 1800 800 343. Investment.

HIH Winterthur International Holdings Limited, AMP Centre, 50 Bridge Street, Sydney, NSW 2000, tel 02-9650 2000. Insurance.

Australian Consolidated Investments Limited, Level 441, 1 Macquarie Place, Sydney, NSW 2000, tel 02-9247 7000. Investment.

Reinsurance Australia, Level 41, 264 George Street, Sydney, NSW 2000, tel 02-9247 6565. Reinsurance.

Washington H. Soul Pattinson & Co. Limited, 160 Pitt Street Mall, Sydney, NSW 2000, tel 02-9232 7166. Equity investment.

Chemicals & Pharmaceuticals
Orica, 1 Nicholson Street, Melbourne, VIC 3000, tel 03-9665 7111. Chemicals, fertilisers, paint.

Food, Beverages, and Brewing
Foster's Brewing Group Limited, 77 Southbank Boulevarde, Southbank, VIC 3006, tel: 03-9633 2000. Brewing.

Lion Nathan Limited, Level 11, 1 Macquarie Place, Sydney, NSW 2000, tel 02-9320 2200. Brewing.

Coca-Cola Amatil Limited, 71 Macquarie Street, Sydney, NSW 2000, tel 02-9259 6666. Food.

Foodland Limited, 218 Bannister Road, Canning Vale, WA 6155, tel: 08-9311 6000. Food wholesaling.

George Weston Foods Limited, Level 20, 821 Pacific Highway, Chatswood, NSW 2067, tel 02-9415 1411; fax 02-9419 2907. Flour milling, baker.

Goodman Fielder Limited, Level 42, Grosvenor Place, 225 George Street, Sydney NSW 2000, tel: 02-9258 4000 or fax: 02-9251 5839. Milling, baking, processed foods.

National Foods Limited, 5 Queens Road, Melbourne, VIC 3000, tel 03-9234 4000. Food and consumer products.

Freight, Transport & Security
Brambles Industries Limited, Level 40, Gateway, 1 Macquarie Place, Sydney NSW 2000, tel: 02-9256 5222 or fax: 02-9256 5299. Transport and other services.

Mayne Nickless Limited, 17th Floor, 60 Albert Road, South Melbourne, VIC 3205, tel 03-9254 0800; fax 03-9254 0884. Transport and security.

Qantas Airways Limited, Qantas Centre, 203 Coward Street, Mascot, NSW 2020, tel 02-9691 3636. International transport.

Industrial Resources, Mining, and General Industrial
Broken Hill Proprietary Company Limited, BHP Tower, Bourke Plaza, 600 Bourke Street, Melbourne VIC 3000, tel: 03-9609 3333 or fax: 03-9609 3015. Oil, steel, mining.

BTR plc, 390 St Kilda Road, Melbourne, VIC 3000, tel 03-9222 5700. Diversified industrial.

Rio Tinto, 55 Collins Street, Melbourne, VIC 3000, tel 03-9283 3333. Diversified resources.

WMC Limited, Level 16, 60 City Road, Southbank, VIC 3006, tel 03-9685 6000; fax 03-9686 3569. Diversified mining.

Comalco Limited, 31st Floor, 55 Collins Street, Melbourne VIC 3000, tel: 03-9658 8300 or fax: 03-9658 3707. Bauxite.

Pacific Dunlop Limited, Level 41, 101 Collins Street, Melbourne VIC 3000, tel: 1800 333 257. Diversified industrial.

Wesfarmers Limited, 11/40 The Esplanade, Perth WA 6000, tel: 08-3927 4211 or fax: 08-9327 4216. Diversified industrial.

Southcorp Holdings Limited, 469 Latrobe Street, Melbourne, VIC 3000, tel 03-9679 2222; fax 03-9679 2288. Diversified industrial.

Normandy Mining Limited, 100 Hutt Street, Adelaide, SA 5000, tel 08-8303 1700. Diversified mining.

Howard Smith Limited, Level 22, 1 York Street, Sydney, NSW 2000, tel 02-9230 1777. Diversified industrial.

Pasminco Limited, 380 St Kilda Road, Melbourne, VIC 3000, tel 03-9288 0333. Base metals.

CSL Limited, 45 Poplar Road, Parkville, VIC 3052, tel 03-9389 1911; fax 0309389 1434. Miscellaneous industrials.

F.H. Faulding & Company Limited, 1/23 Lexia Place, Mulgrave, VIC 3170, tel 03-9560 2533. Miscellaneous industrials.

Email Limited, 33 Wedgwood Road, Hallam, VIC 3803, tel 03-9554 0800. Diversified industrial.

Futuris Corporation Limited, 12A Wandsworth Street, North Parramatta, NSW 2151, tel 02-9890 9518. Diversified industrial.

Orogen Minerals Limited, Level 10, 19 Pitt Street, Sydney, NSW 2000, tel 02-9251 6488. Diversified resources.

Australian National Industries Limited, Level 5, The Merlin Centre, 235 Pyrmont Street, Pyrmont NSW 2009, tel: 02-9577 6700 or fax: 02-9577 6888. Contracting (shipbuilding and repair services). Heavy engineering.

MIM Holdings Limited, Suite 2203/52 Martin Place, Sydney, NSW 2000, tel 02-9221 1966. Diversified mining.

Leisure

Tabcorp Holdings Limited, 5 Bowen Crescent, Melbourne, VIC 3000, tel 03-9868 2100. Casinos and gaming.

TAB Limited, 495 Harris Street, Ultimo, NSW 2007, tel 02-9211 0188. Casinos and gaming.

Village Roadshow Limited, 235 Pyrmont Street, Pyrmont, NSW 2009, tel 02-9552 8600. Leisure activities.

Manufacturing, Building & Construction

AMCOR Limited, Level 23, 40 City road, Southbank, VIC 3006, tel: 03-9694 9000 or fax: 03-9686 2924. Forest products.

Boral Limited, AMP Centre, Level 39, 50 Bridge Street, Sydney, NSW 2000, tel 02-9220 6300. Building materials.

CSR Limited, Level 24, 1 O'Connell Street, Sydney NSW 2000, tel: 02-9235 8000 or fax: 02-9235 8555. Building materials.

James Hardie Industries Limited, 65 York Street, Sydney NSW 2000, tel: 02-9290 5333 or fax: 02 9262 4394. Building materials.

Leighton Holdings Limited, Level 5, 472 Pacific Highway, St Leonards NSW 2065, tel: 02-9925 6666 or fax: 02-9925 6005. Building contractor.

Pioneer International Limited, Level 46, 1 Farrer Place, Sydney, NSW 2000, tel 02-9323 4000. Building materials.

Carter Holt Harvey Limited, Ailsa Street, Box Hill, VIC 3128, tel 03 9258 0555. Forest products.

Media & Communications

News Corporation Limited, 121 King William Street, Adelaide SA 5000, tel: 08-8206 2000. Diversified media.

Telstra Corporation, Corporate switchboard, tel 1300 368 387. Telecommunications.

John Fairfax Holdings Limited, Level 2, 379 Collins Street, Melbourne, VIC 3000, tel 03-9249 9999. Publishers.

Seven Network Limited, Level 14, 1 Pacific Highway, North Sydney, NSW 2060, tel 02-9967 7777. Television.

Western Australian Newspapers Holdings Limited, tel 1800 199 134. Publishers.
AAPT, 9 Lang Street, Sydney, NSW 2000, tel 02-9377 7000. Telecommunications.
Rural Press Limited, 12 Todman Avenue, Kensington, NSW 2033, tel 02-9313 8333. News media.
Hoyts Cinema Groups, 505 George Street, Sydney, NSW 2000, tel 029273 7373. Film industry.
Ten Network Holdings, 1 Saunders Street, Pyrmont, NSW, tel 02-9650 1010; fax 02-9650 1111. Television.

Petroleum, Gas, and Energy Resources

Woodside Petroleum Limited, 1 Adelaide Terrace, Perth, WA 6000, tel 08-9348 4000. Oil and gas producer.
Santos Limited, Level 29, 91 King William Street, Adelaide, SA 5000, tel 08-8218 5111. Oil and gas producer.
Oil Search Limited, 21st Floor, 1 O'Connell Street, Sydney, NSW 2000, tel 02-9251 8400. Oil and gas producer.
Caltex Australia Limited, Level 15, 44 Market Street, Sydney, NSW 2000, tel 02-9248 2999. Petroleum, coal.
Cairn Energy PLC, 191 New South Head Road, Edgecliff, NSW 2027, tel 02-9335 5500. Oil and gas producer.
QCT Resources Limited, Level 10, 307 Queen Street, Brisbane, QLD 4000, tel 07-3229 9600. Coal.
United Energy Limited, 43 Centreway, Mount Waverley, VIC 3149, tel 03-9222 9222. Electricity, gas.
Australian Gas Light Company, 6th Floor, 37 St George's Terrace, Perth, WA 6000, tel 08-9225 4420; fax 08-9225 4430. Natural gas exploration and distribution.

Retail

Coles Myer Limited, 800 Toorak Road, Tooronga VIC 3146, tel: 03-9829 3111.
Woolworths Limited, 540 George Street, Sydney, NSW 2000, tel 02-9323 1555.
Harvey Norman Holdings Limited, A1 Richmond Road, Flemington, NSW 2140, tel 02-9201 6111.

Tobacco Products

Rothmans Holdings Ltd Level 42, 100 Miller Street, North Sydney NSW 2060, tel: 02-9956 0666 or fax: 02-9956 7442.

Miscellaneous

Brierley Investments Limited, Gateway, 1 Macquarie Place, Sydney, NSW 2000, tel 02-9241 1599; fax 02-9247 6369. Entrepreneurial activities.

Starting a Business

Australia used to be considered the 'Lucky Country' or the 'Land of Opportunity' and businesses of all shapes and sizes blossomed across the country. Aspiring entrepreneurs have always been a part of the Australian social landscape, and small businesses such as plumbers, caterers, painters and decorators, landscapers, hairdressers and beauticians, and pottery studios have not only found space for themselves in the Australian market, but remained buoyant and generated fairly prosperous incomes.

With the recession of the 1980s, however, came a much more depressed business climate, and large and small businesses collapsed in dramatic profusion. Although the Australian economy has recovered well (only to be hit anew by the crisis in the Tiger economies) it has in general become far more difficult for new businesses to survive their first year. A recent survey conducted by the Family Business section of the Australian Business Development Office found that 30 per cent of family-owned businesses survive to the second generation, 15 per cent to the third generation and only 3 per cent beyond the third. Business growth is now being encouraged and protected by legislation, assistance, and an extensive network of government small business offices and advisors, to ensure that once off the ground, new enterprises stay airbourne, while tax incentives are now offered in the recognition that the earlier tangle of red-tape and taxation was enough in itself to discourage new business. In the Family Business Survey, 51 per cent of responders identified the level of taxes and costs as being major inhibitors of business growth, 36 per cent felt that lack of funding restricted their business's growth, while 32 per cent attributed this to economic conditions. Twenty per cent found that the lack of suitably qualified employees prevented their business from performing as well as it could or should, and 15 per cent found that the lack of skills among family members involved in the business was a significant factor in inhibiting the business.

The manufacturing and services industries are currently the most successful sectors of the market, largely due to the devaluation of the Australian dollar. The need to become more competitive internationally has forced small businesses to provide higher quality products and services at costs which can challenge international businesses. Economic analysts believe that this trend is likely to continue for some time, and the government is particularly keen to encourage an export-based economy, offering many incentives to businesses to export both products and services.

Business migration to Australia is currently at its highest level in years, with both top-flight executives and well-heeled investors heading south to take advantage of the relatively stable economic conditions, highly qualified labour market, and the various incentive programmes available to help build new enterprises.

This chapter aims to give practical advice about starting a new business, as well as suggestions as to those businesses which are likely to succeed in Australia: careful research and preparation will help prevent your business from becoming one of the failures. It also provides preliminary information regarding the taxation rules and regulations relevant to creating a new business and also the procedures for buying an existing business. The *Useful Addresses* section at the end of the chapter may be particularly helpful in providing contact names and addresses of advisors and authorities to help you get off the ground.

Establishing a New Business

If you have an idea for a new venture, you will need to do some careful market research and ask yourself some searching personal questions. Do you have the right background or qualifications to set up the sort of enterprise you are considering? Are you prepared to risk almost everything to achieve your goals? You will need to be completely familiar with your product or service, and have detailed technical knowledge of it. You must also ensure that there is a market for this product, and you should identify the size, geographical and socio-economic distribution of that market. Research is the key to success and you would be well advised to find out as much as possible about both your target population and your competition. This kind of information can be gained from government statistics (the Australian Bureau of Statistics is particularly helpful), universities and institutes of technology, small business agencies, advertisements, and telephone directories (both the yellow pages and the business directory). In addition, you should find out whether there is a trade association which deals with the product or service you are offering, as this is likely to be a good source of information, advice and assistance. The Australia and New Zealand Chamber of Commerce UK www.anzcc.org.uk is a primary source of information, and has an invaluable database, updated daily, of over 6,000 Australian and New Zealand businesses which provides a valuable research tool for anyone considering setting up a business in the region. This organisation (contact details below) also offers regular investment and business seminars, as well as a library of information on Australian and New Zealand business, taxation, and government regulations.

Intellectual Property Protection

Legally protecting your business image and the products which you have developed can be vital in maintaining your competitive advantage. Businesses built on innovation and design need to protect their intellectual property rights, which in commercial terms means your proprietary knowledge. There are several different types of intellectual property in Australia, and methods of protecting them:

Patents are for inventions which are recognised as new, novel, non-obvious, and useful. Inventions that serve an illegal purpose or which are unrelated to manufacturing processes are not patentable. A patent lasts for up to 20 years and gives its owner exclusive rights to exploit the invention or to authorise others to exploit it.

Trade marks are granted to protect words, symbols, pictures, sounds, smells, or a combination of these, distinguishing the goods and services of one trader from those of another.

Designs refer to the features of shape, configuration, pattern or ornamentation which can be judged by eye in finished articles. A new or original design may be registered for up to sixteen years. Registration gives the owner the exclusive rights to make, use and sell articles incorporating the registered design.

Circuit layout rights are granted for three-dimensional configuration of electronic circuits or layout designs.

Trade secrets protection covers know-how and other confidential information.

Copyrights are granted for original material in literary, artistic, dramatic or musical works, films, broadcasts, multimedia, and computer programmes.

Plant breeder's rights are also available and are granted for new varieties of plants. These are administered by the Plant Breeder's Rights Australia agency, under the Department of Primary Industries and Energy.

Intellectual property rights are administered in Australia by the government agency IP Australia, which is part of the Department of Industry, Science and Tourism. Formerly known as the APIO, IP Australia provides valid IP rights and related services, monitors the Australian IP system, and partakes in the development of international IP law. The agency also administers the Olympic Insignia Protection Act 1987. IP Australia has an informative website at www.ipaustralia.gov.au.

The Patent Co-operation Treaty (PCT) allows companies to file an international patent application, protecting the product in all participating PCT countries. There are 74 countries participating in the PCT, including the USA, Canada, Mexico, the UK, Austria, Belgium, Switzerland, Germany, Denmark, Spain, France, Greece, Ireland, Italy, the Netherlands, Norway and Sweden. There are also many other participating countries from eastern Europe, Africa and the Asian-Pacific region. The patent application consists of several forms and a detailed set of drawings, and the cost of submitting an application is dependent upon the complexity of the drawings. A schedule of fees is available from IP Australia and applications are submitted to this office. There are Patent Offices in every PCT country.

If your product is competing with others of a similar type, it may be advantageous to register a *trademark*. A trademark must be registered with the Patent Trade Marks and Designs Office in Australia, and once registered will be protected indefinitely provided that renewal fees are paid seven years after registration and every fourteen years thereafter. Processing time for trademark applications is currently around twenty months, and this time lag should be incorporated into your business plan. On acceptance, your trademark will be published in the *Official Journal*, after which objections may be filed within three months. If there is no opposition, registration occurs within twelve months. The total time taken to register your trademark, from date of application, can thus be as long as 32 months. If there are any objections raised about your application, you may have to amend your application and will experience further delays.

New products can also be assessed by the Standards Association of Australia which provides recognised specifications for a wide variety of items. If your product meets the strict standards of this organisation, you will be able to use the SAA mark and benefit from the associated product credibility.

Registering a Business

Establishing a new business means you must comply with numerous licensing laws and other regulations. You must register your business with the Australian Taxation Office and obtain a tax file number (TFN). Depending on your business structure, you may also need to register with the Australian Securities and Investments Commission and obtain an Australian Company Number (ACN). Business registration with the Australian Taxation Office and with the ASIC can now be completed electronically via the Australian Government Business Entry Point website at www.business.gov.au, and this site also provides electronic links to the Business Names Registration offices in each state and territory. Before you start a business, or if you are not sure which licences, permits or approvals your business needs, you should contact your local Business Licence Information Service (also via the above website), which will provide you with all the necessary application forms.

Forming a Company

Any new company may be registered either as a proprietary company or a public company. When a company is registered under the Corporations Law it is automatically registered as an Australian company and thus may conduct business as a company throughout Australia without needing to register in each individual state or territory jurisdiction. Most companies in Australia are registered as proprietary companies under the Corporations Law. Proprietary companies are generally cheaper and easier to register than a public company. A private company only needs to have a nominal share capital to commence operating. Directors and a company secretary must be appointed and as soon as is practically possible after incorporation, a public officer has to be appointed for taxation purposes. For proprietary companies, there must be at least two directors, one of whom must be an Australian resident. Public companies must have at least three directors, two of whom must be residents of Australia.

There are several steps in the process of registering a company:

Choosing a name

First, you must select a name, which may either be one of your choice, or the company ACN (Australian Company Number). Before you decide on a name, you should consult the alphabetical listing of company and business names available by checking the National Name Index at the ASIC Internet site. The ASIC will reject your name if it is identical or similar to any other company name. A company name must indicate the company's legal status, with a proprietary company including the word 'proprietary' or its abbreviation Pty in the name. The liability of a company's members must also be indicated, so that where liability is limited, the name must end with the word 'limited' or its abbreviation. The British form, PLC, is not used in Australia (where it is usually Pty Ltd).

Registering a company

Next, you will need to obtain the consent of proposed directors and a company secretary, and then formally appoint them via the application process. After your application has been received and successfully processed by ASIC, a certificate of registration will be posted to the registered office of your company, and only once you have received this can the directors officially commence operating as a company. Such operations include opening bank accounts, which cannot be done prior to the completion of registration. The law requires that the company's name be clearly displayed at the registered office and at each business address, and the Australian Company Number (ACN) must appear on the common seal, every public document issued, all documents required to be lodged with ASIC under Corporations Law, and on every eligible negotiable instrument issued.

Off the Shelf companies

The formation of a company from scratch takes between one to two weeks from application and will cost approximately $A1,000, not including professional fees (which are likely to be high). If you need to establish the company very quickly, agents and solicitors can also offer ready-made 'off-the-shelf' companies, which can be purchased more cheaply, as legal expenses are then kept to a minimum. Shelf companies are incorporated with names, which in most cases will be unsuitable, and amendments will then need to be made to the company's Memorandum and Articles of Association. A change of name usually takes approximately four weeks to be processed and approved, and the ASIC must issue a *Certificate of Incorporation on Change of Name*. The additional cost of changing the name of the company and the Memorandum and Articles is around $200. If you do choose to buy a shelf company, you should consult with your advisers to consider whether the Articles of Association need to be amended. You need to consider whether the existing constitution specifies: the rights of directors to decline to register a future share transfer; the requirements if a shareholder ceases to be a director or employee or dies; the chairperson's casting vote; the shareholder/director's voting rights; and who controls the company. Different levels of shareholding confer different rights and there may also be different classes of shares conferring different rights.

When you purchase a shelf company, you should receive a complete set of first board minutes and statutory books. If you do not receive these, it would be advisable to obtain them from the previous owners as they can often contain important information and you are expected to hold them.

Partnership/Sole Trader Legalities

If you are starting the business as a partnership or sole trader (see *Business Structures* below), there are no legal formalities involved other than the notifications required for tax purposes. In the absence of a partnership agreement, the partnership will be governed by the Partnership Act of the relevant state or territory, which will specify how a partnership should adminster its affairs. Most partnerships, however, prefer to draw up a tailor-made agreement to meet their own particular needs. Partnership agreements are usually drawn up by a solicitor and should include details of the arrangements for partners' capital, banking accounts, profit-sharing, salaries (if relevant), drawings, change or termination of partnership and voting rights. This agreement is particularly important if a dispute between partners arises, but business experts claim that the more important course of action is to avoid such potential disputes by choosing the right partner/s in the first place.

If you are planning on setting up a company, please note that this information is intended only as a guide. It is *essential* that you seek professional advice in the process of forming a company, and that you are fully aware of your obligations and commitments when registering a company.

Choosing an Area

If you choose to buy an existing business your area will generally be predetermined, but if you are starting your business from scratch, the decision of where to locate your business, including the type of premises you require, can be vitally important to its future. The needs of your business should determine its location. Various factors, such as whether you expect frequent deliveries from suppliers or visits from customers, and whether you need to attract passing trade can influence your decision as to the best location; you will also need to consider the likely needs of your staff, especially in terms of public transport and parking.

Renting Business Premises

The rents of commercial property vary greatly across Australia. Perth currently has a fairly substantial amount of vacant industrial and office space and so the rents offered (calculated in dollars per square metre) are low compared to similar properties in Sydney, Melbourne or Canberra. Similarly, the rates of leasing commercial property in Darwin, Adelaide, Brisbane and Hobart are markedly lower than that of comparable properties in the central business districts of Sydney, Melbourne and Canberra.

Whether leasing or purchasing, you need to make sure that the premises have adequate facilities such as security, access, essential services (including electricity, water, waste collection, energy efficiency, sound and thermal insulation), flexibility of design should you wish to expand at a later date, and that the dimensions in terms of height and floor space are sufficient. Furthermore, you need to ask your solicitor to check that your type of business will not breach any environmental laws if you conduct your business in those particular premises. The buildings must comply with fire and safety regulations, town planning and other regulations, and the Health Act and Shops and Factories Act (obtainable from the Government Printer or various technical publishers) applicable in your state or territory.

If you choose to lease premises, ensure that the lease is checked by a solicitor and, if possible, an accountant. The terms of the lease are always negotiable, and your solicitor or accountant will advise you on the negotiation of terms and conditions. You should attempt to negotiate a rent free period, a lower initial rental, reduced annual escalations, payment by the landlord for any improvements or refurbishments to the property, and payment by the landlord of any outgoings associated with the property. You should identify who is responsible for insurance, property taxes and maintenance, what your rights are to make alterations or renovations, and whether the lease permits sub-letting of the premises. Your negotiating power will depend on the state of the property market at the time; at present, this tends to be favourable to lessees.

The term of the lease can be important, as a long lease may reduce flexibility. A shorter lease with the option to renew can be preferable, depending on the current economic conditions and your choice of premises. When considering a lease, it is helpful to ask for a plan which clearly states the extent of the premises being let, and to make sure that the proposed use of your building does not breach any terms of the lease. Before you sign, you should also compare the rent, rates and service charges (usually given on a dollar per square metre basis), annual escalations and rent review clauses with those of other premises. You should also be aware that a verbal lease, which is binding on both parties, is recognised by law but should be avoided as such agreements are fraught with difficulties.

Your choice of premises will also have tax implications, as payments for the rent of business premises are tax deductible, but the rate of such deductions will vary according to the age of the building. Moveable furnishings and equipment within the buildings are subject to higher rates of depreciation for taxation purposes.

Raising Finance

You can have the best ideas, products and service in the world, but if you cannot manage to raise the finance to put your plans into practice, your dreams (not to mention potential profits) will remain unrealised. Before you approach any potential source of finance, you will need to fully prepared to explain your business concept and to answer any questions about your proposal. A thorough and careful business plan is the first key to success.

The Business Plan
A completed business plan is a summary and evaluation of your business idea. It is the written result of the planning process, and a blueprint for your business operations. Your ability to make it work depends on checking your progress against the plan and reviewing that plan as your business evolves. In the early stages of development, when you are seeking finance, your business plan may well

be the only tangible aspect of your intentions. The business plan which you present to a bank or other money lender should contain a fully considered financial plan, including a budget for at least the first 18 months. You should make sure that you include an allowance for unexpected and intangible expenses, as one of the most common reasons for business failure is the lack of planning for such contingencies, in particular taxes such as provisional tax (tax paid against estimated future earnings).

There are many publications available which will help in preparing your business plan, and assistance is also available from your nearest Small Business Development Corporation, industry associations, chambers of commerce, and from business advisors and accountants. A draft business plan is available on-line through the Australian Government Business Website at www.business.gov. au/event/502003.html.

The Commonwealth Bank of Australia also offers a guide in its *BetterBusiness Planner* available either as a software package or in hardcopy form. The software package includes a sample business plan, financial templates which automatically calculate budgets and cash flows, and follow-up software to keep track of your business plan's progress. You can obtain the *BetterBusiness Planner* from the Commonwealth Bank's Business Line, tel 13 1998 (8am-8pm, week days).

Financing a Business

One of your first steps in drawing up a business plan is to consider the different sources of finance available to you. The Commonwealth Bank of Australia strongly recommends that business owners should look much more carefully at maximising the business's ability to generate internal funds in order to avoid relying too much on external sources for the funding of its operations. Although a new business is hardly likely to be in the position to generate enough internal funds in order to become self-sufficient for up to three years, you should think very carefully about trying to borrow as little as possible from outside sources in the long term, and incorporate self-sufficiency into your long-term business proposal. Once you have done this, you need to look very carefully at all the different financial institutions and the options available to you in order to choose a lender, or a combination of lenders, that is most appropriate to the needs and goals of your company, and your repayment capacity. Lenders will also expect a significant level of personal capital investment in your business. One of the most common reasons for finance refusal is that applicants have not allowed for sufficient personal contribution; this is seen, at best, as a demonstration of lack of commitment.

As discussed in Chapter Four, *Daily Life*, there are many different financial institutions in Australia. Deregulation of banking has led to increased competition and, as a consequence, more innovative and sophisticated banking techniques have been introduced. In addition, opportunities to obtain loan funds have greatly increased and there are now many more options available in terms of structuring loan agreements. In an effort to encourage the growth and development of Australian industry and resources, a number of industrial banks have been established, including the government-owned Australian Industry Development Corporation (AIDC) which provides development finance, equity funding and financial advisory services. Other methods of raising finance can include accessing venture capital, which may provide funding for high risk projects, or floating a company on the stock exchange.

Types of Finance

Equity, long term loan finance and working capital finance are the three principal types of finance available for starting a new business in Australia. Equity is usually contributed by the owners of the business, and businesses with significant equity are more easily able to attract financial backing from other sources. If you are seeking finance for a major project, such as investment in plant and machinery for your business, long term loan finance likely to be the most appropriate option. In many cases the loan will be secured against the business or the equipment purchased. In addition, the financial institution will generally require personal guarantees from the business owners. There is usually a substantial difference between the amount of the loan and the value of the asset in order to allow for risk and for the costs involved should the business fail. There is a variety of options available in obtaining long-term business finance. Firstly, it is important to calculate how much of your own personal contribution can be used as share capital and how much can be used as loan capital (this proportioning of capital can affect your taxation, see *Taxation* below for further details). Cash subscription from your family and friends can also be used as long term finance, as can cash received from any other sponsor or from venture capital. Most often, however, long-term business capital is raised through a bank or finance company loan, or through leasing or hire purchase finance. It must be noted, however, that leasing or hire purchase finance generally have interest rates which are significantly higher than other sources.

In the present very competitive finance market, banks and other lenders are increasingly offering tailored loan packages, and the variety of types of finance is growing exponentially. Options are also changing almost every month, and the best advice is to start by approaching the major banks to discuss the available financing methods. Most larger bank branches now have specialist business advisors who will be only too happy to guide you – remember they are selling a product, too!

Government-Backed Finance

The Australian government, at both Federal and State levels, is very keen to promote new business, and to ensure that such businesses are successful. Government agencies exist in every state to provide various kinds of assistance, technical as well as financial. Financial assistance can include direct cash grants, subsidies and tax concessions, while technical assistance will include both professional and technical advice, and research and development seminars. There are many opportunities for small business to benefit from government-backed schemes, with substantial incentives available to all kinds of enterprises. Currently there are over 200 different financial assistance schemes run by the state and federal governments and by various industry agencies. *AusIndustry* (Hotline: 13 28 46; e-mail: ausindustry@dist.gov.au; Website: www.ausindustry.gov.au) is the best starting point for obtaining information on these schemes. Their database, *BizLink*, contains information on all Federal, State and Territory government support programmes, as well as programmes offered by industry associations and chambers of commerce around Australia. The AusIndustry Hotline can also put you in touch with sources of information in research and development, networking, management, strategic planning, benchmarking, diagnostic reviews, environmental management, marketing, export planning, and business licensing.

Rebates and subsidies are also offered to employers as an incentive to provide employment and to encourage them to provide training for their employees (or to allow employees to attend trade or development courses). Such schemes, which are usually aimed either at the youth or long-term unemployed workforce, are administered by the Australian Job Network, which can provide further information. Employment incentive schemes are a favourite vote-winner for governments and tend to be rejigged with each budget and change of government.

Most states and territories also provide financial assistance in the forms of loan funds or guarantees to businesses, however, this assistance is generally only provided as a final resort. Other assistance can include transportation and freight subsidies, and advice services in such areas as effective business operations, production processes, technological development and export market opportunities. State Government assistance is generally given to encourage the establishment of new businesses or the expansion of existing industries within the state or territory, and in order to receive such assistance businesses must demonstrate that they are viable, both in the short and long term, and that they can provide assessable benefits to the state. The government will be likely to favour business which will create new permanent jobs, provide new skills, increase the state's technology or production capacity, tap new markets outside the state, or offer diversification of the state's industrial base or range of products. For further details about State Government assistance, you should contact your state's Small Business Development Corporation or similar body, the Australian Job Network, or AusIndustry (see *Useful Addresses* below).

Importing/Exporting

Australia currently has a policy of gradually and systematically removing trade tariffs on imported products, however, in those industries still subject to protection 'bounties' are sometimes offered, which are direct cash payments to Australian manufacturers (operating within Australia) in lieu of, or supplementary to, assistance provided by means of tariff or customs duty. Bounties can assist manufacturers to compete more effectively with imported products. You should contact the Australian Customs Service in your capital city for further information.

If your business is involved in exporting goods from Australia, AUSTRADE (The Australian Trade Commission) will be able to provide marketing advice and assistance. The Grants for Industry Research and Development (GIRD) scheme is designed to help new companies that have not yet incurred any tax liability, or other companies that are not able to take advantage of tax concessions. The Federal Government offers tax incentives which are detailed below in the 'Investment Incentives' section.

Summary of Financing

Although a potential financier will want a thorough plan, they will not want a long report, so you should try to keep your proposal down to between ten and twelve pages. You must ensure that you describe your product, the premises from which you intend to operate, relevant information about members of the management team, your marketing strategy, competition, past performance (if any), financial projections and assumptions relating to them, the financial resources required and what changes will be necessary if your assumptions prove to be either pessimistic or optimistic, and your assessment of the risks involved in the project. A professional-looking presentation is important, as this is the document that will 'sell' your business to lenders. It is vitally important to obtain impartial professional advice when preparing a business plan, but you must also be fully involved: when you come face to face with the bank manager, you are the one who will have to answer all the questions.

Accountants

A good accountant is essential to the success of your business. You will find that the process of creating a new business or buying an existing one is so complex and involved, that you will not be able to complete it without expert assistance. Your accountant should be registered with one of the industry associations, and it is essential that you confirm this. You should also 'shop around' and obtain quotes in respect of hourly rates and estimated annual expenses. Your accountant will act as your financial and, on many occasions, as your legal adviser, and will often undertake duties which could also be done by a solicitor. If the advice you receive is false or misguided, it could mean the failure of your business and possibly even fines and legal costs. For this reason, you will want to make sure that the accountant you decide to use is reliable and reputable. Large accountancy firms are likely to be considerably more expensive, but may be more reliable and offer backup guidance; your accountant is really another business investment you will have to make, and you will want to reduce the element of risk. It is advisable to consult your accountant on every initial business decision you make, as a good accountant will always give you more impartial advice than you may receive from a real estate agent, bank business advisor, or business broker.

Useful Addresses

AusIndustry, tel Hotline 13 28 46; e-mail: ausindustry@dist.gov.au

Department of Industry, Science and Tourism
NSW: Level 17, Maritime Centre, 207 Kent Street, Sydney, NSW 2000; tel: 02-9256 0900; fax: 02-9252 3652.
VIC: 9th Floor, 161 Collins Street, Melbourne, Vic 3000; tel: 03-9268 7555; fax: 03-9268 7599.
QLD: 12th Floor, Santos House, 60 Edward Street, Brisbane, QLD 4000; tel: 07-3231 5111; fax: 07-3229 0017.
ACT and NT: 20 Allara Street, Canberra, ACT 2601; tel: 06-213 7379; fax: 06-213 7668.
WA: 8th Floor, Griffin Centre, 28 The Esplanade, Perth, WA 6000; tel: 08-9327 9500; fax: 08-9327 9520.
SA: 11th Floor, Terrace Towers, 178 North Terrace, Adelaide, SA 5000; tel: 08-8406 4700; fax: 08-8406 4717.
TAS: 4th Floor, AMP Building, 86 Collins Street, Hobart, Tas 7000; tel: 03-6234 1588; fax: 03-6234 1646.

Small Business Agencies
These provide advice and referral services for intending, starting and existing businesses in each state.
ACT: Business Link, PO Box 192, Deakin West, ACT 2600; tel: 02-6283 5200; e-mail: mailto:businesslink@actchamber.com.au
NSW: Small Business Advisory Services, State and Regional Development NSW, Level 35, Governor Macquarie Tower, 1 Farrer Place, Sydney, NSW 2000; tel Hotline 13 11 45; fax: 02-9228 3626.
NT: Business Services, Department of Asian Relations, Trade and Industry, Ground Floor, Development House, 76 The Esplanade, Darwin, NT 0800; tel: 08-8999 7997; fax: 08-8999 7924; Hotline: 1800 193 111.
QLD: Department of State Development, Level 21, 111 George Street, Brisbane,

QLD 4000; tel: 07-3221 1620; e-mail: info@dtsbi.qld.gov.au

SA: The Business Centre, 145 South Terrace, Adelaide, SA 5001; tel: 08-8233 4600; fax: 08-8231 1199.

TAS:Small Business Tasmania, Tasmania Development and Resources, Ground Floor, ANZ Centre, 22 Elizabeth Street, Hobart, TAS 7000; tel: 03-6233 5858; fax: 03-6233 5800.

VIC: Small Business Victoria, level 5, 55 Collins Street, Melbourne, Vic 3000; tel: 132215 (local call cost); fax: 03-9651 9725; email sbv@sbv.vic.gov.au.

WA: Small Business Development Corporation, 553 Hay Street, Perth, WA 6000; tel: 08-9220 0222; fax: 08-9325 3981; email info@sbdc.com.au

The Australian Copyright Council, 245 Chalmers Street, Redfern NSW 2016, tel: 02-9318 1788.

The Australia and New Zealand Chamber of Commerce UK, 393 Strand, London WC2R 0LT, tel 0171-379 0720; fax 0171-379 0721; e-mail: (www.anzcc.org.uk).

The Institute of Patent and Trade Mark Attorneys of Australia, 1 Little Collins Street, Melbourne, Vic 3000, tel 03-9650 2399 or 1800 804 536.

Inventors' Association of Australia, 40 Winmalee Road, Balwyn VIC 3103, tel: 03-9836 9927.

United Kingdom Patent Office, Cardiff Road, Newport, Gwent, NP9 1RH, or filings by hand may be made at 25 Southampton Buildings, London WC2A 1AY, tel: 01633-814586 (for international applications), 01633-812151 (for international preliminary examinations), 01633-814000 (operator service) or fax: 01633-814444.

Accountants

Most accountants advertise in the Yellow Pages of their state telephone directory. The Institute of Chartered Accountants, the Australian Society of Accountants in your capital city or the National Institute of Accountants can also provide lists of professionals associated with their organisation. A brief list of other contacts is given below.

Australian Accounting Group, 56 Neridah Road, Chatswood NSW 2067, tel: 02-9411 4866.

Ernst & Young, The Ernst & Young Building, 321 Kent Street, Sydney NSW 2000, tel: 02-9248 5555 or fax: 02-9262 6565.

Institute of Chartered Accountants in Australia, level 4, 37 York Street, Sydney NSW 2000, tel: 02-9290 1344; fax 02-9262 1512.

PJ St Clair & Co, Chartered Accountants, Level 8, 235 Macquarie Street, Sydney NSW 2000, tel: 02-9221 4088.

Banks

Trading Banks:

ANZ Banking Group Ltd, 100 Queen Street, Melbourne, VIC 3000, tel 03-9273 5555.

Commonwealth Bank of Australia, 108 Pitt Street, Sydney NSW 2000, tel: 02-9378 2000.

National Australia Bank Ltd, National Australia Bank House, 255 George Street, Sydney NSW 2000, tel: 02-9237 1111.

Westpac Banking Corporation, 60 Martin Place, Sydney NSW 2000, tel: 02-9226 3311.

See also the banking section of Chapter Four, *Daily Life* for the British branches of these banks.

Merchant Banks:
BNP Pacific (Australia) Ltd, 12 Castlereagh Street, Sydney NSW 2000, tel: 02-9235 1688.
BT (Bankers Trust) Investment Bank Australia Ltd, Level 15, 2 Chifley Square, Sydney, NSW 2000, tel 02-9259 3555.
Chase Manhattan Bank, AAP Centre, George Street, Sydney NSW 2000, tel: 02-9250 4111.
Macquarie Bank Ltd, 20 Bond Street, Sydney NSW 2000, tel: 02-9237 3333.
Standard Chartered Bank Australia Ltd, 345 George Street, Sydney NSW 2000, tel: 02-9232 6599.

Finance Companies:
Australian Guarantee Corporation (AGC), 130 Phillip Street, Sydney NSW 2000, tel: 02-9234 1122.
Avco Financial Services Ltd, Level 12, 255 George Street, Sydney NSW 2000, tel: 02-9324 7000.
Custom Credit Corporation Ltd, 136 Exhibition Street, Melbourne, VIC 3000, tel 180 037 018.
Esanda Finance Corporation Ltd, tel 13 2373.

Real Estate:
There are countless real estate agencies in every area of Australia. To locate those in the area of Australia to which you are moving, try a searching Telstra's on-line database at www.telstra.com.au.

Useful Publications
Books and Information Packs
Vacation Work Publications Other books in the *Live and Work* series may be useful if you are considering exporting; each book in the series contains a 'Starting a Business' section relevant to the particular country or area covered.
Australian Bureau of Statistics, Level 5, St Andrews House, Sydney Square, Sydney NSW 2000, tel: 02-9268 4111, 02-9268 4611 or fax: 02-9268 4668. The ABS publish yearbooks containing the results of every recent survey and research project, which are useful when undertaking initial market research.
Australian Financial Review Books, 81 George Street, Sydney NSW 2000, tel: 1800 251 949.
Doing Business in Australia is published by Ernst & Young as part of their *International Business* series and is available from their Australian office listed above under *Accountants*. Copies are also held by their international branches, and you should consult the telephone directory in your country's capital city for further information.
Commonwealth Government Bookshop sell books published by the Australian Government Publishing Service, 32 York Street, Sydney NSW 2000, tel: 02-9299 6737; fax 02-9262 1219.

Periodicals
Australian Business for Sale News is a magazine produced every two months which gives information and details about franchises, distributors, investments, dealerships and partnerships for sale. It is available from Australian Business for Sale News, 250 Riley Street, Surry Hills, NSW 2010, tel 02 9281 0542. Alternatively, the periodical is available in the UK as a volume from the Subscription Department, Australian Outlook, 3 Buckhurst Road, Bexhill-on-Sea, East Sussex, TN40 1QF.

Australian Economic Analysis Pty Ltd, 21 Holbrook Avenue, Kirribilli NSW 2061, tel: 02-959 4123.

Australian Financial Press, 802 Pacific Highway, Gordon, NSW 2072, tel 02-9499 4022.

The Australian Financial Review, 235 Jones Street, Broadway NSW 2007, tel: 02-9282 2833.

The Franchising Council of Australia has a website at 203.17.238.93/main.html.

Relocation Agencies and Business Services

In addition to assisting with housing, education and employment arrangements on your behalf, many of the relocation companies also specialise in finding appropriate business premises and in relocating complete companies, including plant and machinery. These services tend to be very expensive and are best suited to large, international companies. Most large UK relocators either have offices overseas or have reciprocal arrangements with certain firms in Australia, however, many UK relocators are established to provide services for those relocating to the UK from other countries. If you require the services of a business relocator it may be most appropriate to engage the assistance of a specialist Australian firm, of which some are listed below.

Useful Addresses
The following relocators specialise in the relocation of executives, company personnel and their families.

Allied Pickfords, 19-21 Rowood Road, Prospect NSW 2148, tel: 02-9636 6333 or 12 2554.

Australiawide Relocations Pty Ltd, 18/209 Toorak Road, Toorak VIC 3141, tel: 03-9826 0001 or fax: 03-9827 0762.

Australian Way Corporate Relocation, 9 Lower Almora Street, Balmoral, NSW 2088, tel 02 9969 0171.

Executive Relocations, 8 Howitt Street, South Yarra VIC 3141, tel: 03-9827 4668.

Expat International, 4/126 Wellington Parade, East Melbourne VIC 3002, tel: 03-9419 9351 or fax: 03-9416 0786. Expat International are affiliated with the Migration Institute of Australia and the Employee Relocation Council (USA).

Grace Removals, Executive and Commercial Relocations, Carter Street, Lidcombe NSW 2141, tel 13 1442.

Ideas for New Businesses

The various state governments have all identified strategic industries in which the greatest opportunities for investment lie, and these are outlined in the Regional Employment Guide (chapter 6). Most governments offer incentive packages to investors in these sectors. In overview, Australia's key development areas are currently mining and mineral exploration, information technology, niche-market agriculture, food processing, tourism, and traded services. New businesses which either compete directly in these sectors, or which provide related services, are the most likely to succeed. Retailing is less buoyant and import businesses are suffering because of the Asian currency crisis and relatively weak Australian dollar. Both federal and state governments are, however, strongly export-oriented, and any business which exports Australian goods and services is likely to be eligible for a variety of export subsidies and incentive schemes.

Olympic Business Opportunities

The Sydney 2000 Olympics will be the biggest international event ever staged in Australia and will place Australian goods and services in the global spotlight. Some 200 nations will be sending more than 10,000 athletes and 5,000 technical officials to the games; in addition, 15,000 representatives of the world's media are expected to attend. For many months before and after the Games, tens of thousands of overseas visitors will arrive to attend international conferences and exhibitions organised in Australia to capitalise on the event. No-one knows exactly how much extra business will be generated by the Olympics, but companies throughout Australia will all be touched by and will benefit from them.

By the time the Games open on 15 September 2000, around $3.2 billion will have been spent building the Sydney facilities, with around $1.2 billion having been provided by the private sector. Every conceivable product and service will be needed, and many are already being provided now: limited edition T-shirts are available in Sydney, whilst in Perth, hundreds of thousands of $5 Olympic coins are being minted. Whilst the majority of large contracts are likely to be won by major companies, these organisations will sub-contract smaller businesses to supply products, goods, and services. The main merchandising programme for the Olympics runs from 1 January to December 2000, and is expected to be worth around $1 billion. Only officially listed and licensed merchandise may carry the Sydney 2000 logo and other Olympic symbols, and legal action will be taken against their unauthorised use.

Currently, only 25 Australian firms have been licensed to use the Olympic insignia, and entrepreneurs who wish to acquire this right need to satisfy stringent selection criteria, and to provide a business and marketing plan. There is no charge for having your product or service evaluated for a licence. The Sydney Organising Committee for the Olympic Games (SOCOG) includes family companies in its list of suppliers, and is constantly looking for new ideas and concepts, particularly in the environmental area. SOCOG and the Team Millennium Olympic Partners (see below) offer opportunities for small business involvement through the supply of products, goods and services, including fitouts and servicing of Olympic venues.

Enquiries about contracting for fitout work should be directed in writing to: Project Specialist Facilities, SOCOG, GPO Box 2000, Sydney, NSW 2001. Licensing enquiries for both the Olympics and the Paralympics should be directed in writing to: Senior Manager, Licensing, SOCOG, GPO Box 2000, Sydney, NSW 2001.

The Team Millennium Olympic Partner (TMOP) are companies who are contributing more than $25 million in cash, goods, or services to run the Games, and they are all potential clients for small business. The TMOP companies include:

AMP	Ansett
BHP	Coca-Cola Amatil
Energy Australia	John Fairfax Holdings
Fuji Xerox Australia Pty Ltd	IBM Australia
John Hancock Mutual Life Insurance Co	Kodak (Australasia) Pty Ltd
McDonald's Australia Ltd	Newscorp Limited
Panasonic Australia Pty Ltd	SMH/Swatch
Telstra	The Time Inc. Magazine Co Pty Ltd
UPS Pty Ltd	Visa
Westfield Shopping Towns	Westpac Banking Corporation

The Olympic Business Information Services, OBIS, (tel 02-9242 6995; fax 02-9251 9301; e-mail:obis@mpx.com.au) has been established to keep businesses informed of existing and forthcoming opportunities in the planning, development and construction phases in Sydney. You can register your business with the OBIS database to receive updated information on tenders, contracts and proposals. The Sydney 2000 Olympics Commerce Centre (tel 02-9233 3600; fax 02-9233 5211; e-mail: infor@olympicscommercecentre.asn.au) provides a business enquiry service including referrals to the relevant Olympic authorities, a reference library of fact sheets, research results, and guides, and seminars on Olympic related business issues. The Industrial Supplies Office (tel 02-9819 7200) is also maintaining a database, known as the Olympic Register of Industry Capability, to help identify suppliers for the Olympic site. The major construction companies are all using the ISO register. There is no charge to register a company on this database.

Women in Business

The Australian Bureau of Statistics predicts that by the year 2000 more businesses in Australia will be owned by women than by men. Women are opening businesses at nearly twice the rate of men and have a higher success rate, particularly in the first five years. Women are considered to be more successful in business because they are willing to acquire formal business skills and to develop non-formal management skills such as networking and flexibility, which may give them a competitive advantage over men. In many states, women-centred business networks have been developed, and these are generally viewed as valuable resources by women in business. A survey by Yellow Pages Australia found that both men and women believe that women business owners are more persuasive, more prepared to ask for advice, better at dealing with customers, learn faster, are more hard-working, and are more pleasant to deal with. The trend in business ownership and operation by women is towards a far greater involvement in the services sector of the economy, with around 83 per cent of businesses operating in this sector owned by women. Most states have specific programmes to encourage the development of women in business, and details of schemes in each state can be found on-line at www.abol.net/abl/buswomen.

Buying an Existing Business

One of the options you may have when starting in business is to purchase an existing operation. Getting in to business in this way can be much less risky and more quickly profitable than starting your own business from scratch, but it is not entirely risk free and your success will depend heavily on how wisely you choose and evaluate the business you buy.

Buying a business will include the purchase of plant and equipment, stock in trade and, usually, a goodwill component. Goodwill is represented in part by location, existing customers, reputation, but also by other factors which can influence the profitability of the business or its income-producing capacity. The correct assessment and identification of the value of a business is crucial in the process of buying a going concern, and it is highly recommended that you obtain professional assistance in making this assessment. When you investigate a prospective business purchase you should make sure that you examine the following: financial statements, payables and receivables, employees, customers, location, facilities, competitors, registration, zoning, and image. Financial figures should be accompanied by an audit letter from a CPA firm, and you should make sure that business licences and other legal documents can be easily transferred and determine the costs involved in doing so. Customers are your most important asset, however, and you should make sure that they are as solid as the other tangible assets that you will be acquiring. Check if the current clientele has a special relationship with the present owner (are they long-time friends, neighbours, and relatives?). How long have these accounts been with the business, and what percentage of income do they represent? Will they leave when the business passes to new hands? Make sure, too, when you are buying a business that you understand the competitive environment in which it operates. Check whether local price wars are common, or whether any competitors have gone out of business recently. You can track down this information by contacting an industry association or by reading trade publications. Finally, look at how a business is perceived locally and in general. This 'goodwill' factor cannot necessarily be established from a balance sheet, and you will need to evaluate everything from the way it services customers, to how employees answer the phone. Talk to customers, suppliers, competitors, banks, and owners of other businesses in the area to learn more about a firm's reputation, and remember that it can be very difficult to change a negative perception.

Transferring Ownership

Transferring the ownership of a business requires a management plan to ensure a smooth transition of the business and its assets (including goodwill and the customer base) from one owner to the next. You will need to notify the Australian Taxation Office and, in the case of an incorporated business, the Australian Securities and Investments Commission of the transfer, and supply details of new directors and the transfer of trading name. You may also have to transfer ownership of any licences which are required to operate the business, for which you should contact your local *Business Licence Information Service*.

Franchising

Franchising is the fastest growing area of Australian business, with many new business owners attracted to the ready-made brand awareness and back-up available to franchisees. Each year, franchising contributes approximately $50 billion to the Australian economy, and with over 600 different types of franchise available, accounts for about 20 cents in every retail dollar spent.

The Franchising Council of Australia should be your first port of call if you are considering this type of business option. The FCA have a strict code of conduct which protects members from unscrupulous operators, and can also direct potential franchisees to accountants and lawyers who are member of the FCA and who understand the specialist field of franchising practice. The FCA publishes *The Franchisee's Guide* for intending franchisees, available from the FCA Franchise Library for $15. They also have a very comprehensive website at http:// 203.17.238.93/franchising/weighing.html.

The position of the franchise in the market in which it trades should be carefully assessed. You should not only look at the particular franchised business in relation to its own activites, but also make an assessment of the prospects for the industry overall.The franchise will either be dealing in goods, products, or services, and you should consider whether these are new or have distinct advantages over their competitors. Check that the franchised business has been thoroughly proven in practice, or whether it is exploiting a fad or current fashion which may be transient or short-lived. If the product is strongly associated with a celebrity name, remember that fame can fade as quickly as it came, and that your business may fade with it.

The basis of any franchise operation is the franchise agreement. This must be considered very carefully and it is advisable to consult your accountant or solicitor before signing anything. Before you enter into any franchise agreement, you need to consider whether you are technically able to deal with the product or service, as well as the extent of the competition. If the franchise involves evolving technology, you will also need to assess whether the franchisor also has the expertise and resources to be able to compete successfully in the market. If your product is manufactured overseas, or is composed of parts made elsewhere, you must identify delivery times and calculate the risk of delays and the potential for foreign currency losses. In addition, you will have to ascertain whether there are any import duties or regulations which have an impact on the price of the product. You should also be clear on how much assistance is given, and control exercised, by the franchisor, and you would be well advised to investigate the franchisor's financial credibility and stability. It can be beneficial to talk to other franchisees about the business and the franchisor's methods of operation. It is imperative that you understand what the duration of the franchise is, what costs and fees are involved, whether you have to pay any royalties to the franchisor (and if so, how much), and what the arrangments are for termination.

Franchising offers significant benefits to business owners, and can be considered as going into business with an experienced partner. A good franchisor will offer training and continuing assistance; and the franchisee will benefit from established brand recognition and a customer base. The franchisee will usually need less capital than they would if setting up business independently. Business risk is significantly reduced, however, you should not entertain the misapprehension that you will not be exposed to business risk because you are under the umbrella of a franchise.

Other Businesses

Most businesses for sale are advertised with real estate agents, business brokers, trading associations and in the national and local newspapers. A successful acquisition depends on a thorough study of the business or company from many different angles. Your accountant should check out the value of stock and the cash flow of the business. Profit should be calculated after the fair working salaries of proprietors or partners have been deducted. Your accountant should also advise you on the stamp duty and tax implications of the purchase of a particular business. The last three years' accounts of the company (audited if possible) should be examined, together with current management accounts and projections (if available), particularly in terms of the valuation of assets, contingent liabilities and the company's tax position. Finally, you need to ensure that you will be able to raise the finance required before committing yourself to the purchase, and this applies to the purchase of either a business or a company. Further details are given above in the section *Raising Finance*.

Business Structures

Companies

Most small businesses in Australia are embodied in some kind of legally recognised entity. Australian company law is mainly governed by the Corporations Law of individual states, which is basically the commonwealth legislation for the

Australian Capital Territory with minor variations pertinent to that particular state. The Corporations Law contains the rules, procedures, accounting and reporting requirements for companies. This is administered by the Australian Securities and Investments Commission (ASIC) and detailed information regarding Corporations Law can be obtained upon request (see address below).

Public and Proprietary Companies

A company is a legal body distinct from its individual members. Generally, investors combine their capital to form a company and share its profits. Usually, this is without the risk of loss beyond their original investment or guarantee amount. Companies can buy, sell and hold property, sue and be sued, and enter into contracts. They have what is known as 'perpetual existence', which means that unless there are exceptional circumstances (such as in the case of default on payments to their creditors), they cannot be involuntarily terminated. Of the various types of companies which operate in Australia, two types of corporations have limited liability (public and proprietary/private), and there are also no-liability companies and foreign companies. Public companies can invite public subscription of their shares and be listed on the stock exchange, whereas proprietary companies cannot. A proprietary company must have at least two, but no more than fifty, members. It is not allowed to invite public subscription of its shares. A no-liability company is usually only used by specific mining companies and oil and gas ventures, and a foreign company is considered to be one which originated overseas but conducts business in Australia.

The advantages of a limited (registered) company are: the liabilities of the company are the responsibility of the company so that shareholders are liable to lose only the share capital they subscribed although directors may be personally liable for any debts incurred when the company is unable to pay its debts; after tax, profits of the business can be retained within the company to provide funds for future expansion; in some cases greater superannuation benefits can be secured; tax on company profits is currently 39 per cent compared to the current maximum personal tax of 47 per cent (excluding the Medicare levy); it is easier to spread ownership of the company; and the company has an ongoing existence and does not need to be wound up in the event of death or permanent disability of any of the directors or shareholders.

The disadvantages of a limited company are: financial and certain other information must be filed on public records (although in the case of a proprietary company accounts need not be lodged and only certain declarations and statements are required to be made); loans can be made to directors of proprietary companies, however in the case of other companies, the shareholders in the general meeting have to approve such loans as part of a scheme for making loans to full-time employees and disclosure of such loans must be made in the company's accounts; there may be tax consequences of making loans to shareholders and/or directors; compliance with the extensive requirements of the Corporations Law can be time consuming and costly; lenders often seek personal guarantees from directors which tends to significantly reduce the value of limited liability; tax is payable when accumulated profits are withdrawn from the company as dividends or extra remuneration; auditors must be appointed unless all shareholders agree that this is not necessary; and losses in a company are not distributable to the shareholders and therefore cannot be offset against other income of the owners.

Partnership

As an alternative to the company structure, many small businesses choose to structure themselves as a partnership. A partnership is usually formed by two or more persons (individuals or companies) in order to conduct business for profit as co-owners. It is governed by the Partnership Act of the relevant state and the terms of the partnership agreement, which should be in writing. This partnership agreement means that each partner has the same rights, liabilities and powers as any other partner, unless the agreement specifically states otherwise. As a member of a partnership, each partner is jointly responsible for partnership debts. In Western Australia, Tasmania and Queensland, limited liability partnerships can be used. A limited liability partnership allows some partners who are not as involved in the management of the partnership to have a limited liability. The Australian Taxation Office requires that partnerships maintain 'appropriate' accounting records, but they are not legally required to be audited. Unlike a company, a partnership is not usually considered as a separate legal body from its partners. This means that the partnership's profits are taxable to the individual partners, regardless of the distribution of those profits. Even so, partnerships must also file an annual tax return separate from and in addition to that of each partner.

Joint Venture

Another form of business structure is the unincorporated joint venture. This occurs when an Australian entity joins with either an Australian or foreign entity to create a venture for their mutual benefit. Examples of such joint ventures are most often found in various mining and exploration projects. A contractual relationship exists between the joint venture participants and this form of business entity has recently become increasingly popular. Unincorporated joint ventures are often considered to be partnerships for tax purposes if the income is jointly derived, which means that each 'partner' is required to file partnership tax returns. It is possible, however, to set up an unincorporated joint venture so that participants share in the production rather than the income. This kind of joint venture is not considered to be a partnership by Australian law, so each venturer is required to state its share of the income and expenditure from the joint venture project in the venturer's tax return. Incorporated joint ventures are considered to be the same as ordinary companies, and are treated and taxed accordingly.

Sole Trader

It is possible to be a sole proprietor if you individually own an unincorporated business and you receive all the business profits and incur all of its liabilities. On the whole, if you are the sole proprietor, you will be actively involved in the management and conduct of the business. You can form sole proprietorship without official approval and you need not have your financial statements audited. You do, however, need to supply the tax authorities with proper accounting records.

A sole trader/partnership structure has the following main advantages: confidentiality is maintained since the public has no access to financial accounts; PAYE (income tax) and Medicare levy contributions do not need to be paid when proprietors or partners draw cash but is paid on a partner's share of the profits; losses from the business can be offset against other income; and it is relatively easy to transfer the business to another legal structure (e.g., limited companies) at a later stage. This structure does, however, have disadvantages which include the following: the owner is personally liable for the business, which means that if one partner fails to meet his share of the partnership debts, other partners will have to settle them; there is less flexibility in transferring ownership (for example to other family members); and in the event of death, permanent disablement or retirement of the sole trader/partner there may be difficulties in maintaining the business structure.

Trusts
Trusts are not normally used for a sizeable partnership or joint venture with Australian residents, but more for wholly owned projects or ventures. This is largely due to the fact that a trust is not considered to be a separate legal body to the beneficiary's property, and so it may not enter into contracts in its own right. As a result, creditors and bankers will not grant credit to the trust or allow it to open and use a bank account unless personal guarantees are obtained from the trust or beneficiaries. The advantages of a trading trust are: confidentiality is maintained since the public has no access to the trust's accounts, although certain information is disclosed in the trustee's accounts; income is distributed to beneficiaries who pay tax on their allocation of profits at their respective personal tax rates; trusts are not subject to income tax on their profits provided they are fully distributed to beneficiaries; a discretionary trust is usually preferred because it provides flexibility to the trustee to allocate income amongst various classes of beneficiaries under the trust; and to some extent, limited liability can be achieved through the establishment of a trust with a company acting as a trustee. The main disadvantages of a trust are: generally banks and financiers require assurances from solicitors that the trust has been properly constituted; in the case of corporate trustees, there is a necessity for compliance with the extensive requirements of the Corporations Law; and losses derived in a trust are not distributable and therefore cannot be offset against other income of a beneficiary (owner) of the trust.

There are also subsidiary businesses, branches and representative offices, but these are usually owned by existing foreign companies that wish to operate in Australia.

Duties of Directors & Company Office-Bearers

Every company, whether public or private, must appoint directors and a company secretary. These company officials have clearly defined duties under law. The directors of a company are not necessarily actively involved in the daily management of the business, but they are responsible for the actions of the management of the business. In accordance with the Corporations Law, a director must act with the utmost good faith towards the company and its members, and must not obtain any benefit for him/herself from the activities of the company, other than remuneration. A director is expected to exercise skills which reflect his or her qualifications and experience. Although a director is responsible for the keeping of the statutory records and the books of account, this duty is usually delegated to an appropriate professional, such as an accountant. The Corporations Law clearly specifies the kinds of books and records which must be kept and it is important that you seek professional advice in these matters. A director may accept a loan from the company providing that loan has been approved by the shareholders. It must be noted that such loans must be shown in the accounts in accordance with statutory requirements. A director has the power to appoint an alternative director who has the full powers and duties of a director. If the business becomes insolvent, the directors become personally liable for any debts contracted by the company during the period of insolvency.

Within one month of the first and every annual general meeting, companies must provide the ASIC with their directors' names, ages, addresses, company share-holding and details of other public company directorships. The appointment of additional or new directors, the company secretary, and an auditor (if required) should also be made at this time. Banking arrangements and the end of the company's financial year (normally 30th June) should also be determined. Shares should be allotted and transfers of subscribers' shares should be approved. Arrangements should also be made for keeping statutory books such as the Register of Members, Register of Directors and a Minute Book, and the company's registered office must be specified. A Public Officer must also be appointed for income tax purposes.

The company secretary is responsible for statutory duties and must be a resident of Australia. Public companies must have at least five members, while proprietary companies need only have two. Wholly owned subsidiaries, public or proprietary, have no minimum requirement. A proprietary company must have between two and fifty shareholders, whereas public companies must have a minimum of five shareholders and have no maximum limit. Shares may be sold for cash or otherwise issued, but details must be reported to the ASIC. For both public and proprietary companies, the minimum capital derived from shares is one share per subscriber. The minimum time required to establish a company is three to four days and ASIC fees must be paid during the process of registration.

Running a Business

Once you have had your business plans approved, secured financial backing, established the business as a legal entity, chosen and registered its name, and have obtained premises from which to operate your business, then it is time to consider the daily operations of your new livelihood. Here, the critical factors are staff and taxes. If you manage to get both of these areas right, it is likely that your business will run smoothly and be a success.

Taxation

Australian business taxation law is extremely complex and if you are starting a new business there are a certain number of things you will have to do and decisions you will have to make. Taxation issues are made even more complex if you have been employed in Australia prior to setting up your business. Furthermore, the structure you choose for your business may have significant tax consequences, so it is important to investigate taxation thoroughly when planning its structure. There is simply no avoiding the tax maze and it is vital that you get professional advice from the outset. Doing so is likely to mean considerable expense, but will save you costly mistakes in the long term.

Sole traders and partnerships are subject to very different taxes to either companies or trusts. Essentially, for a sole trader or partnership, any profit earned from the business is added to any other income that you have and you are taxed on the total. Your level of taxable income is determined by the financial statements you produce, however there are some adjustments that are made to the income shown on the statements in order to arrive at a taxable income. You may, for example, be allowed to claim special deductions such as those available for research and development costs. Tax concessions and grants are available to cover research and development costs, and for businesses seeking to develop new export markets. Some of the income you receive may not be subject to tax, such as the rebates paid to you under special youth employment schemes. Depreciation can be claimed on all of your plant equipment and other business fixed assets, and items valued at less than $300 or with an effective life of less than three years can be written off in the year of acquisition.

Companies are taxed differently because they are considered to be separate legal entities from their owners. A company is subject to income tax on its taxable income whereas the partners in a partnership are taxed on their share of partnership taxable income, even though a tax return must be lodged for the partnership. An important difference to note is that there is no variation according to income of the tax rate for companies as there is for individuals. Both resident and non-resident companies are subject to corporate income tax of 39 per cent.

The calculation of a company's or family trust's taxable income is roughly the same as that use to assess a partnership or sole trader, with some significant differences. Firstly, providing that it is at a reasonable level, the remuneration of the company's directors (or owners in the case of a family company) is a deductible expense in determining the company's taxable income. Secondly, there is a complicated system known as 'Dividend Imputation' which refers to the distribution of a company's dividend income. Dividend imputations distributed by Australian resident companies have a tax advantage attached to them if the dividends are paid from profits which have been taxed in the company's hands at the company rate. Basically, this means that the system allows shareholders a tax rebate to the extent of the difference between personal and corporate income tax rates. Any excess rebate may be offset against any other income tax of the shareholder, including capital gains, and these dividends which have been relieved of tax are known as 'franked'. If the company holds on to its dividend, it will generally be subject to credit under the 'Dividend Imputation' system. Your taxation adviser will be able to explain the system of tax payment as companies must pay instalments of tax by certain dates.

If you decide to take over an existing company, you should ask your accountant to help you draft taxation warranties and indemnities which should appear in the purchase agreement, as these will protect you from any unexpected tax liabilities that may arise as a result of the acquisition. The capital gains tax exempt status of assets owned by a company may be lost when ownership of the company is changed.

As the owner of a business, whether new or already in existence, you will be expected to pay Sales Tax, Fringe Benefits Tax, PAYE deductions and Prescribed Payments Tax. Sales Tax is a Federal Government tax which is intended to be paid only once on goods going into use in Australia. It usually applies to wholesalers on sales to retailers, but some manufacturers and importers may have to pay it. This tax is collected and administered by the Australian Taxation Office. It is calculated on the last wholesale price of the goods and generally applies only to new goods and not to services or second-hand goods, apart from imported second-hand goods which have not been previously used in Australia. Some goods, including clothing, food and medicines are always exempt from sales tax and others may be conditionally exempt from sales tax because of the status of the person who uses them (for example, a Government department) or the use to which the goods are put. Patents and copyright are not subject to sales tax, as is also the case with services, unless the cost of the service effectively forms part of the selling price of goods. If your company is liable to pay sales tax, you need to register with the Taxation Office in order to be allocated a Sales Tax Registration Number. In accordance with the law, this number can then be quoted to suppliers to acquire tax free goods. Your business will then be expected to make a self-assessment, and complete and lodge a monthly sales tax return, although if your business's annual sales tax liability is less than $50,000 quarterly sales tax returns need only be made. Small businesses with an annual sales tax liability less than $10,000 do not have to pay sales tax on the goods they sell. These rules may all change in the near future as the Liberal government was recently elected to its second term on a platform which includes the imposition of a VAT-like tax, known as the 'GST' (Goods and Services Tax).

If you employ staff, you are responsible for deducting taxation instalments (PAYE) from your employees' wages and paying it to the Commissioner of Taxation. In order to do this, you must register as a group employer with the Commissioner of Taxation and each employee must submit to you their personal particulars, including a tax file number, on an income tax instalment declaration form. PAYE must be deducted from wages, overtime pay, commissions, fees, bonuses, gratuities, lump sum payments and any other allowances.

The Australian tax year ends on 30 June, and for companies that also end their financial year on this date, tax returns must be filed by the following 15 March or, in certain circumstances, 15 December of the end of the following tax year. If an alternative financial period has been adopted by the company, its tax returns must be filed at the earliest by the fifteenth day of the sixth month following the year-end, with a maximum extension to the earlier of the fifteenth day of the ninth month or 15 June following the end of the alternative financial year. Tax returns of individuals, partnerships and trusts must generally be filed by 31 October each year and an extension may be granted if the return is to be filed by a registered tax agent. It is important to note that penalties of up to 200 per cent of tax underpayment may be imposed for filing an incorrect return, together with interest charges and penalties for the late filing of returns or payment of tax. These penalties are strictly enforced, and the sophisticated data-matching processes employed by the ATO make tax evasion nearly impossible and certainly foolish .

The Australian Taxation Office has a comprehensive website which offers assistance to small business owners, including a wide range of electronic pamphlets to download. You can access the ATO site at www.ato.gov.au. Many TAFE colleges also now offer short courses and evening courses in managing your taxation affairs as a small business owner.

Fair Trading

Fair trading concerns the ethical environment in which you interact with other business and customers. The Federal Government has recently announced a fair trading reform package for small business, which strengthens the Trade Practices Act. The new package protects small businesses against unconscionable conduct, and imposes a mandatory Code of Conduct for franchisors, to protect franchisees. It also offers support for alternative dispute resolution to provide businesses with quicker, less costly, and more efficient remedies; and has extended the banking Industry Ombudsman to small businesses. The Australian Competition and Consumer Commission (ACCC), on-line at www.accc.gov.au, and the Department of Workplace Relations www.dwrsb.gov.au can provide information on both your obligations as a trader and the laws which are designed to protect your business.

Useful Addresses

AUSTRADE (Australian Trade Commission), AIDC Tower, Maritime Centre, 201 Kent Street, Sydney NSW 2000, tel: 02-9390 2000.

Australian British Chamber of Commerce, Level 3, Suite 302A, 14 Martin Place, Sydney, NSW 2000, tel 02-9221 0355.

Australian Bureau of Statistics, 5th Floor, St Andrew's House, Sydney Square, Sydney NSW 2000, tel: 02-9268 4111, 02-9268 4611 or fax: 02-9268 4668.

Australian Business Economists, 309 Kent Street, Sydney NSW 2000, tel: 02-9299 2610.

Australian Business Research, 7/231 North Quay, Brisbane, QLD, tel 07-3236

3777.

Australian Chamber of Manufactures, 380 St Kilda Road, Melbourne VIC 3000, tel: 03-9689 4111.

Australian Customs Service, Head Office 447 Pitt Street, Sydney NSW 2000, tel: 02-9213 2000; Infocentre, tel 1300 363 263.

Australian Industrial Research, 64 Clarence Street, Sydney, NSW 2000, tel 02 9299 5244.

Australian Securities and Investment Commission (ASIC), Level 8, 55 Market Street, Sydney NSW 2000, tel: 02-9911 2500 for general enquiries, document lodgment and searches. Business Centre, Level 8, 55 Market Street, Sydney NSW 2000, tel: 02-9911 2570. Corporate Regulation & Investigations, Level 10, 135 King Street, Sydney NSW 2000, tel: 02-9911 2200.

Australian Stock Exchange Ltd, 20 Bond Street, Sydney NSW 2000, tel: 02-9227 0000.

Australian Trade Commission (AUSTRADE), Australia House, Strand, London WC2B 4LA, tel: 0171-438 8535.

Department of Immigration and Multicultural Affairs, Benjamin Offices, Chan Street, Belconnen ACT 2617, tel: 02-6265 1111.

Department of Industry, Science and Tourism, 20 Allara Street, Canberra City, ACT 6000, teel 02-6213 6000.

Department of Workplace Relations and Small Business, Garema Court, 148-180 City Walk, Canberra City, ACT 2600, tel 02-6243 7333.

Foreign Investment Review Board, c/o The Treasury, Parkes Place, Parkes ACT 2600, tel: 02-6263 3762.

IP Australia (Patent, Trade Marks and Designs Office), 47 Bowes Street, Phillip, ACT 2606, tel 02-6283 2211. Trade marks helpline, tel 02-6283 2999.

Reserve Bank of Australia, 65 Martin Place, Sydney NSW 2000, tel: 02-9234 9333.

Securities Exchanges Guarantee Corporation Ltd, 87 Pitt Street, Sydney NSW 2000, tel: 02-9227 0400.

Standards Association of Australia, 1 The Crescent, Homebush NSW 2140, tel: 02-9746 4700; www.standards.com.au.

Export

The Australian Institute of Export, 14 Gilda Avenue, Wahroonga, NSW 2076, tel: 02-9487 7459.

Business Brokers

Australiawide Realty Pty Ltd, 35 Homer Steet, Earlwood NSW 2206, tel: 02-9558 2537.

Century 21 Real Estate, Business Brokers, 80 Grafton Street, Coffs Harbour NSW 2450, or PO Box 1445, Coffs Harbour NSW 2450, tel: 02-6651 3322.

Chris Couper & Associates, Business Brokerage, 93 Surf Parade, Cnr Surf Parade and Victoria Avenue, Broadbeach QLD 4218, tel: 07-5592 0687.

Resort Brokers, 4/49 Station Road, Indooroopilly, QLD 4068, tel 07-3878 3999. Contact Ian R Crooks.

Talberg Pty Ltd, 115 Mary Street, Gympie, QLD, 4750, tel 07-5482 7708. Wilsons Business Brokers Pty Ltd, 59A Stewart Avenue, Hamilton South NSW 2303, tel 02-4962 3388, fax 02-4969 5682.

Taxation

Australian Financial Investment and Taxation Services, 25 Belmore Road, Randwick NSW 2031, tel: 02-9399 8333.

Australian Sales Tax Consultants Pty Ltd, Level 10, 1 Market Street, Sydney, NSW 2000, tel 02-9267 9344.

Australian Taxation Office, GPO Box 2669, Cameron Avenue, Belconnen, SCT 2601, tel 13 2861.

Australian Tax Planning Consultants, 122 Dutton Street, Yagoona NSW 2199, tel: 02-9707 1833.

Institute of Chartered Accountants in Australia, Level 14, 37 York Street, Sydney, NSW 2000, tel 02-9290 1344; fax 02 9262 1512.

Employment

The Australian Employers' Federation, 313 Sussex Street, Sydney NSW 2000, tel: 02-9264 2000.

Australian Industrial Relations Commission, 80 William Street, East Sydney NSW 2001. For state award enquiries tel: 02-9243 8900 or federal award enquiries tel: 02-9282 0888.

New Zealand

SECTION I

Living in New Zealand

General Introduction
Residence and Entry Regulations
Setting Up Home
Daily Life
Retirement

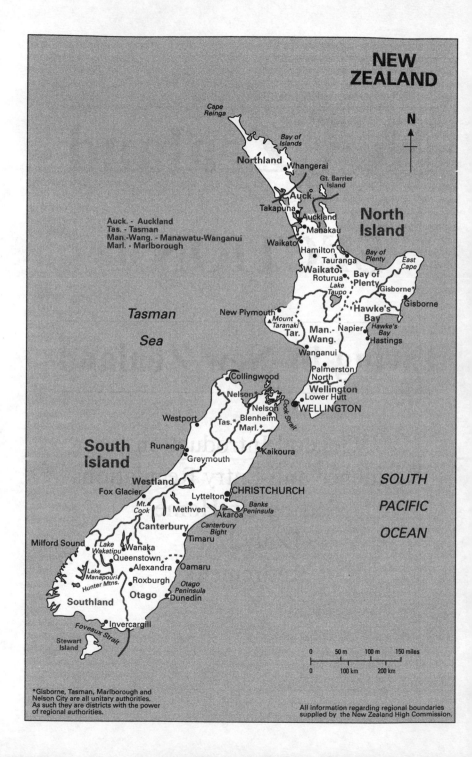

NEW ZEALAND

N

Cape Reinga

Bay of Islands

Northland

Whangerai

Gt. Barrier Island

Auck.

Takapuna

Auck. - Auckland
Tas. - Tasman
Man.-Wang. - Manawatu-Wanganui
Marl. - Marlborough

Auckland

North Island

Manakau

Waikato

Hamilton

Tauranga

Bay of Plenty

East Cape

Waikato

Roturua

Lake Taupo

Bay of Plenty

Gisborne

Tasman

New Plymouth

Mount Taranaki

Tar.

Man.- Wang.

Napier

Hawke's Bay

Gisborne

Hawke's Bay

Hastings

Sea

Wanganui

Palmerston North

Wellington

Lower Hutt

Collingwood

Nelson *

Westport

Tas. *

Nelson

Blenheim

Marl. *

Cook Strait

WELLINGTON

South Island

Runanga

Greymouth

Kaikoura

SOUTH

Westland

Fox Glacier

Lyttelton

Mt. Cook

Methven

CHRISTCHURCH

Banks Peninsula

PACIFIC

Akaroa

Canterbury Bight

OCEAN

Milford Sound

Lake Wakatipu

Wanaka

Canterbury

Timaru

Queenstown

Alexandra

Oamaru

Lake Manapouri

Roxburgh

Hunter Mtns.

Otago

Otago Peninsula

Southland

Dunedin

Invercargill

Foveaux Strait

Stewart Island

| 0 | 50 m | 100 m | 150 miles |

| 0 | 100 km | 200 km |

*Gisborne, Tasman, Marlborough and Nelson City are all unitary authorities. As such they are districts with the power of regional authorities.

All information regarding regional boundaries supplied by the New Zealand High Commission.

General Introduction

Destination New Zealand

New Zealand has a reputation for being similar to Britain but with a slower pace of life, fewer social problems and many more sheep. While there is some truth behind this impression (there are thirteen sheep for every human), New Zealand is not just a little England in the South Pacific. It is still true that the majority of New Zealanders are of British descent, but a significant and growing minority of New Zealanders are Polynesians, either descended from the original Maori inhabitants, or more recently, immigrants from Asia.

New Zealand political traditions derive from Britain, but constitutionally it has often been several steps ahead. New Zealand gave women the vote in 1893, 25 years before they were enfranchised in the UK. In 1938 it was one the first countries in the world to set up a comprehensive system of social security, from child care benefits through to pensions, and including a national health system that provided a model for the British NHS.

Since European settlement first began in the early 1800s, links with Britain have been close. The first generation of settlers grew up regarding England as 'home', and this attitude is still widespread. New Zealand foreign policy was basically an extension of British policy and 'where England' leads, we follow' as one New Zealand prime minister put it, led New Zealand into a number of wars as a British ally. When Britain joined the European Community in the early seventies, New Zealand found its own path in the world and its own identity as a Pacific country, rather than an outpost of Europe located in the Antipodes. There is a degree of residual colonial defensiveness in dealing with expatriate Britons but in most cases, it does not go much beyond a bit of teasing about pommy accents. In general visitors and immigrants get a warm welcome. New Zealanders deserve their reputation as some of the friendliest people in the world; when they invite you to come and stay it is genuinely meant.

Newcomers will find that while elements of the culture owe something to Europe (the national obsession with sports revolves around two British exports, cricket and rugby) New Zealand has its own distinctive character. Polynesian, particularly Maori culture is a growing influence. Auckland, the largest New Zealand city has the biggest Polynesian population in the world. There are new immigrant communities from various Asian countries as well as a long established Chinese community. The different groups make for an interesting and at times volatile cultural mix. New immigrants will find that it is important to respect the cultural traditions of different groups, particularly the Maori, as they were the first inhabitants of the islands. The Maori call themselves the *Tangata Whenua*, which means 'the people of the place'.

In many other respects New Zealand will seem quite familiar to Europeans and in particular, British immigrants. The main language is still English, the system of government, schools, health care are all similar. European style arts and culture can be found in the big cities. If you are looking for a country with fewer social problems than Europe, where the environment is cleaner and the pace of life is more relaxed, New Zealand could be the place for you.

Pros and Cons of moving to New Zealand

Despite having a comparatively low GDP per capita compared to other developed countries, New Zealanders enjoy a high standard of living. While it is true that income per head of the population compares unfavourably, the upside is that the pound goes a long way in New Zealand. Other attractions for immigrants are the non – quantifiable factors that make for quality of life: clean air, clean water, miles of unspoiled beaches, and some of the most spectacular scenery in the world. If your idea of the good life is a city where rush hour lasts for ten minutes and the nearest beach is no more than 30 minutes away, then you will enjoy the New Zealand lifestyle. About 400,000 Brits agree with you as this is the number of Britons registered with the British High Commission as living permanently in New Zealand.

New Zealanders enjoy a wide range of outdoor activities: climbing, hiking, swimming, surfing, canoeing or mountain biking in their spare time. Aucklanders own more yachts per head of population than any other city dwellers in the world. Two great attractions of the country are the parks and reserves and the sea. Even New Zealand's biggest cities are within 20 or 30 minutes of hills and forest largely free from human habitation and all the major cities apart from Hamilton are on the coast. With a lifestyle revolving around outdoor pursuits, the night life in smaller towns is not exactly lively. In the big cities the scene is more interesting. European style cafés and bars have proliferated in the last decade and there is always the traditional Kiwi pub – watering holes more noted for the cheapness of the beer than the social ambience. Licensing laws are liberal and some pubs and cafés in the big cities are open 24 hours.

Working practices are similar to the UK. The standard working week is five days, 37.5 hours, although many people increase their earnings by extra work and overtime. Professionals on salaries can expect to work quite long hours, particularly at the start of their careers. Wage workers used to enjoy a high level of employment protection: national pay rates and conditions were set down in awards, legal documents which bound employers. Most bargaining was done by unions at a national level. Employment protection has been considerably weakened over the last decade and in some areas of the labour market, particularly casual work in catering, horticulture and agriculture, pay rates and conditions can be very poor. The social security system, once relatively generous, has also been cut back. On the other hand personal tax rates on high incomes are lower than in many European countries; there is no capital gains tax, GST (the equivalent of VAT) is 12.5% and the highest income tax rate is 33%. Unemployment has dropped by nearly half in the last decade.

Rented accommodation is not hard to find, although it can be expensive in Auckland and Wellington. Rental agreements can either be on a renewable basis where the tenancy continues until either side gives notice, or for a fixed term, usually one year. Houses are usually let unfurnished, while apartments and townhouses may let furnished or unfurnished.

Pros:
>It's a good time to invest in the Economy
>Favourable exchange rate
>High quality of living
>Diverse ethnic mix
>Cheaper living costs
>Relaxed lifestyle
>Easy access to beautiful areas of countryside
>Friendly locals
>No language problem

Cons:
   Small economy
   Remote; it takes 26 hours to England
   Can be parochial and inward looking
   Unsettled climate in some parts
   Not much sophisticated night life
   Limited range of the Arts and culture familiar to Europeans

Economic and Political History

The original inhabitants of New Zealand were the Maori, a Polynesian race who arrived by canoe from the central Pacific around 840 AD. They lived a nomadic lifestyle initially dependent on hunting a large flightless bird called the moa, which is now extinct. More permanent settlements followed based on cultivating the kumara, a type of sweet potato and harvesting the seas. By the time the first Europeans arrived in the 18th and 19th centuries, the Maori had settled throughout the warmer North Island. They had developed a strongly tribal and family based society with a complex oral tradition. They were skilled craftspeople, particularly in woodcarving and weaving, and also in warfare. War between tribes was common, part of the competition for status and authority.

The first Europeans to sight New Zealand were members of a Dutch East Indies Company ship led by the explorer, Abel Tasman. They anchored off the coast of the North Island in 1642, at a place they called Murderer's Bay because four of their crew were killed by local Maori. Tasman gave the country the name Niieeuw Zeeland after Zeeland, an island in the Baltic sea. The Maori name for the country is 'Aotearoa', the land of the long white cloud. Other explorers followed Tasman's lead. James Cook arrived in 1769 and returned again twice in the 1770s. Members of his second expedition were the first Europeans to make landfall in New Zealand. As with Tasman's first contact with local tribes, there were misunderstandings at first, the Maori interpreting the arrival of the strangers as a hostile force. Ten of his men were killed and eaten in one incident. Other meetings were more favourable, local Maori for the most part being curious to meet the strangers and to trade.

Trade and commerce provided the impetus for the first semi-permanent European settlements. Whalers and sealers arrived in the 1790s. They set up bases along the coasts but generally did not make permanent homes in the new country. Next to arrive, in the early 1800s, were the missionaries, who established stations around the Bay of Islands, on the north east of the North Island. They began preaching the faith amongst the tribes as well as introducing European cultivation techniques, literacy and other useful skills. They were the first to write down the Maori language so that they could translate the scriptures into Maori. Other settlers with more worldly ambitions soon arrived. They were interested in exploiting natural resources such as timber and flax. Local Maori tribes began cultivating wheat and maize to trade with the new arrivals. New Zealand's export trade in agricultural produce began in the 1840s with the export of potatoes, wheat and pigs to Australia. The bulk of the produce was grown by Maori farmers. Contact between Europeans and local tribes was confined to the small areas around the settlements, the whaling bases around the coasts of the South Island and the lower North Island, the mission stations in north and the trading settlements at various points. For most of the first half of the 19th Century, the balance of power between the settlers and the tribes was still very much in favour of the Maori as the early settlements were dependent upon the goodwill of local tribes for their survival. However this was about to change. The Maori population was declining as a result of the spread of foreign diseases against which they had no immunity, and firearms which transformed the ritualised inter-tribal wars into massacres.

By 1840, a balance of firepower had led to a virtual halt in inter-tribal warfare, the cost in lives being too high. The legacy of the warring period was large scale loss of life, disruption of land tenure and social dislocation.

The decline in the Maori population alarmed the missionaries. They were also concerned about the rough, lawless lifestyle of the early settlements. Accordingly, back in Britain, the Church Missionary Society put pressure on the British Government to annex New Zealand as a Crown Colony, and to establish the rule of law. Thus in 1840, New Zealand was made a part of the Empire. A treaty was signed at Waitangi, a little settlement in the Bay of Islands between the new Lieutenant Governor, Captain William Hobson and representatives of local Maori tribes. Hobson then sent copies of the treaty around the country for other tribes to agree to, but some important tribes failed to sign. The terms and significance of the Treaty of Waitangi have been a source of controversy ever since. Under the English text, the tribes ceded sovereignty to the British Crown and gained the rights of British citizens. The Maori text, hastily translated by local missionary, Henry Williams, is considerably vaguer in its terms. In particular, Williams used the unfamiliar term 'kawanatanga' a transliteration of the English word governorship to express the concept of sovereignty. It is doubtful that the first signatories understood that they were handing over rule of the land to the newcomers.

During the late 1830s plans for widespread colonisation were developed under the auspices of Edward Gibbon Wakefield's New Zealand Company. Wakefield intended the settlements to mimic the pre-industrial class structure of England but the actual settlements bore little resemblance to his plans. Street plans formally laid out in Britain did not necessarily take into account the geographical vagaries of the mountainous land in New Zealand.

Prospective immigrants attracted by the promise of cheap land may not have been aware that the company and its agents did not always acquire the land legitimately from the tribes, especially as the pressure to provide more land increased. Maori land tenure is complex as land is not owned by individuals but by the tribe as a whole. Company agents were not particularly scrupulous about whose signatures they obtained on sale documents and as the increasing numbers of new settlers demanding land put pressure on them to provide it, their methods undoubtedly became more dubious.

New Zealand was directly governed by the British Crown between 1840 and 1852. After pressure from the settlers, self government was granted in 1852. As European settlers increased in numbers and demand for land grew, conflicts occurred with the Maori people over land tenure. The tribes disputed a number of deals undertaken by New Zealand company agents and resistance movements to further land sales developed.

The settler government ignored its responsibilities to protect the Maori rights under the Treaty. Skirmishes between the government and the tribes began in the 1860s and full scale war developed. It took nearly 15 years for the forces of the government, reinforced by troops from Britain to defeat Maori opposition. Even at the end of hostilities in the 1870s Maori tribes in the centre of North Island still held out against government control. The wars exacerbated the decimation of the Maori population and resulted in the confiscation of the land of the 'rebellious' and 'loyal' tribes alike. The loss of the land and the resulting social breakdown, probably contributed more than any other factor to the decline in the Maori population at the end of the 19th century.

Meanwhile European settler numbers were increasing spurred on by the discovery of gold in the South Island in the 1870s, and the invention of refrigerated shipping in the 1880s which made it viable to export meat and dairy products to Europe. The gold deposits were soon mined out but the agrarian economy founded in the late 19th century has remained the basis of New Zealand's economic prosperity. Economic security brought on social reform, at least for the European population. First the extension of the vote to women (1893), then a new system of industrial relations, based on minimum wage rates for every industry (1894) and one of the earliest pension schemes (1898). Maori were legally equally able to vote but property owning, which was based on European patterns of individual tenure, rather than Maori communal tenure effectively disbarred many of them until its abolition in the late 19th century.

New Zealand was involved in both World Wars as a British ally. The disastrous Great War campaign at Gallipoli in Turkey in 1915 proved to be one of the defining moments in forming a separate national identity. New Zealand lost more soldiers as proportion of its population than any other allied country: nearly one in three men between the ages of 20 and 40 were killed or wounded. The interwar years brought the election of the first Labour government which continued the tradition of pioneering social policy programmes started by the Liberals. The 1938 Social Security Act established a national health service and a universal social security system. Public education to secondary level was free to all. World War Two saw New Zealand participating again as a British ally, but in the post-war years it began to rely less on Britain for defence and to form closer relations, with Australia and the United States. Britain's entry into the Common Market in the 1970s confirmed the loosening of colonial ties. At the same time closer links were being developed with other countries in the Asia-Pacific region.

Economic restructuring resulting from the increasingly poor performance of the economy since the late 1970s and race relations have been the major policy issues over the last two decades. Economic change is discussed in the section below. The prevailing belief that relations between the races were harmonious was challenged by a number of Maori political movements in the last twenty years, ranging from radical groups calling for the restoration of Maori sovereignty to tribal leaders taking a more conciliatory stance. Two common concerns unite the diverse strands of Maori protest movements: a call upon the government to honour the terms of its original treaty with the Maori people and a concern with the inequality between Maori and European living standards. Income, life expectancy, health, and education standards differ markedly between the two groups. The Treaty became central to government policy towards the Maori and in 1985 the Waitangi Tribunal was given power to hear grievances relating to Maori land. The government's obligations towards the Maori as an equal partner under the Treaty were acknowledged. Maori became an official language in 1987 (English being the other) and knowledge of Maori culture is increasingly required by Government departments and stressed as equally important as cultural heritage. Tensions remain between the Maori and the Government over historical injustices, particularly the large scale acquisition of Maori land by Europeans in the 19th century through confiscation, extortion, blackmail and theft, and the Government's neglect of its duty to protect Maori rights under the Treaty.

Economy

Agriculture has always been the basis of New Zealand's economy. The temperate climate is ideal for growing grass suitable for rearing farm animals cheaply, but it took a century and a half of effort to cultivate the ten million hectares of arable land currently in production. Much of it was initially unsuitable for agriculture being heavily forested, while the mountainous terrain has provided a challenge to develop alternative cultivation techniques. Nearly two-thirds of farmland is too rugged to be fertilised and sown by tractor. Instead New Zealand farmers pioneered the use of light aircraft to spread fertiliser and seed.

New Zealand was able to exploit its agricultural potential with the development of refrigerated transportation in the 1880s. Meat and dairy products joined wool as the basis of exports to Europe. At the end of the 19th century, New Zealand was one of the richest countries in the world. As a former colony, it enjoyed close cultural and economic links with the UK. For most of the following century, 75% of New Zealand's exports went to the UK. Britain was also the major source of imports.

By the 1950s New Zealand was an efficient producer of wool, meat and dairy products which could compete successfully in northern hemisphere markets. The success of the export industry allowed New Zealanders to enjoy a similar standard of living to the industrialised countries of Europe and America. The relatively high standard of living attracted a constant inflow of immigrants. In the early 60s, as a result of a worldwide boom in commodity prices, it enjoyed amongst highest living standards in the OECD. However even during this relatively prosperous period, it was recognised that future economic security depended on diversifying the export base, both in terms of markets and of the range of goods being exported. New Zealand's traditional market, Britain, was not growing as fast as other countries and there was the possibility throughout the sixties that it would eventually join the European Economic Community (now known as the EU).

The golden years ended in the 1970s. Several factors were influential such as the entry of Britain into the EEC in 1973 and the first oil price-shock in the same year. Britain's entry into the EEC led to the restriction of access for New Zealand exports and this coincided with the rise in the price of oil which had a severe effect on the New Zealand economy, as it was extremely dependent on importing oil to meet its energy needs. There was a sudden decline in economic performance. The cost of imports rose sharply while exports receipts dropped and the Balance of Payments deficit plummeted to 14% of GDP. Arguably however the effect of these two events only exposed the underlying weakness of New Zealand's economy rather than causing the economic decline. The government of the time decided that the best solution to the problem of New Zealand's dependency on fuel imports was to embark upon a series of major investment projects to develop domestic energy sources. Unfortunately the viability these projects was based on the price of oil continuing to rise more than it did. Most of the so-called 'Think Big' projects turned out to be expensive white elephants.

By the early 1980s, the economy was performing badly. Inflation was high, and at the same time, unemployment was rising rapidly. Subsidies protected inefficient sectors of the economy and discouraged innovation. Years of borrowing to cover the trade deficit and the cost of the 'Think Big' experiment had increased New Zealand's foreign debt. The National government tried to control inflation by imposing a price and wage freeze in 1982. The freeze succeeded in controlling inflation, but money supply continued to grow throughout the two and half years it was in place. In 1984 a Labour government was elected. At the time of the election there was no indication that the new administration would introduce a period of radical economic reform. The Labour party manifesto made no mention of many of the central policy changes they enacted. The programme of economic liberalisation included removal of price and wage controls, deregulation of financial markets, the floating of the dollar, the introduction of a sales tax, the reduction of agricultural and industrial subsidies, the removal of employment protection, and the weakening of the collective bargaining power of unions. This was accompanied by tight monetary policy and the selling of a number of state assets, including the railways, forests, the national airline and the telecommunications section of the post office.

Against these short term swings in government economic policy, a longer term process of economic adjustment has been occurring. New Zealand's export industry has diversified both in product and export markets. A free trade agreement was signed with Australia in 1982 which is now New Zealand's main trading partner, with the balance of trade being slightly in New Zealand's favour. The development of new markets in Asia has been a significant development over the last ten years. Japan is the third largest source of export income after Australia and the USA. Europe, which in the late 1960s provided two-thirds of New Zealand's export revenue, now accounts for less than 20%. The range of exports has also diversified to include forestry, horticulture, wine and manufactured goods. The dependence upon meat, wool and dairy exports has declined considerably as a result. In the 1960s, these three sectors accounted for over 80% of export revenue; they now make up less than 50%. Although the range of products has diversified, the economy as a whole is still reliant upon exporting agricultural and horticultural commodities. As a result the economy remains sensitive to changes in worldwide commodity prices. It is also vulnerable to climatic and environmental factors.

The adjustment process to the restructuring has been long and difficult. Unemployment rose from under 4% in 1985 to over 10% in 1990, levels not seen since the Depression years, as economic activity declined due to tight monetary policy. Farmers' gross incomes dropped by nearly half when government subsidies were removed. A large number of manufacturing industries went to the wall, unable to compete with cheap imports once tariffs were removed. The abolition of financial controls caused a brief speculative boom in the mid-eighties but the stock market crash in 1987 exposed much of the increased activity as paper wealth. The dollar rose as high interest rates attracted overseas investment which reduced returns from exports, critical to the overall health of the economy.

Whether the social costs of economic restructuring outweigh the efficiency gains is still being debated. Some sectors of the economy have adjusted better to deregulation than others. Despite predictions that many farms would not survive the removal of agricultural price supports, there were only a few casualties. The agricultural sector has become more efficient. Manufacturing has not been as fortunate and the shedding of jobs in this sector along with the restructuring of previously inefficient government industries largely accounts for the rise in unemployment. The gap between high and low income earners has grown and poverty has emerged for the first time since the war as a visible social problem. For a country which used to pride itself on its egalitarian ethos and comprehensive social welfare system, these developments have caused much public concern.

Future economic predictions are mixed, as the New Zealand economy is heavily influenced by the economic and political upheavals of South East Asia. Consumer confidence has picked up, but business confidence remains low. Growth in New Zealand's GDP is expected to remain around 2.5% throughout 1998, and pick up in 1999, to reach 3.5% by the Millennium. The economy is also likely to benefit from The America's Cup, Millennium celebrations and the Sydney Olympics. This point of the economic cycle could be an opportune time to invest in the country. The high exchange rate in favour of foreigners and falling house prices (by about 5%) is also encouragement for immigrants.

Government

The system of government in New Zealand is very similar to the British system. It is a parliamentary democracy within the Commonwealth with the Queen as the titular head of state represented in New Zealand by the Governor General. The current inhabitant of Government House is the Right Honorable Justice Michael Hardie Boys, former judge of the Court of Appeal and High Court. New Zealand shows no signs of following the current Australian enthusiasm for republicanism. There is no equivalent to the British House of Lords. The upper House was abolished in the 1950s and there are no plans to reinstate it. Legislation is consequently easier to pass in the New Zealand parliament as it only requires the approval of one body. Parliament used to be dominated by the ruling party and party discipline was the tightest of any Westminster-style parliament.

As a result New Zealand has one of the most centralised systems of executive government in any western country. While levels of local government exist, they do not provide a countervailing force as their powers and responsibilities are comparatively weak. Radical policy programmes can be introduced relatively quickly as is demonstrated by the case of the fourth Labour government, who transformed the country between 1984 and 1990. The problem has been that the electorate has not universally welcomed change as was demonstrated by the electoral backlash against both the major parties in the 1993 election. Neither of the big parties gained the confidence of the electorate, and small parties got a record number of seats. The result on the night was a hung parliament, but a recount in some of the most marginal seats resulted in a narrow victory for the ruling National party.

In conjunction with the 1993 election was a referendum on whether New Zealand should change its method of electing representatives to a proportional representation (PR) system similar to those used in Europe. PR which is the voting system in most European countries, and in fact in democracies with the exception of New Zealand and the UK, uses the percentage of votes a party gains to work out their strength of numbers in parliament or the equivalent legislative body. There are many types of PR and in the referendum, the New Zealand voters were given a choice between a variety of systems. A majority backed MMP, a proportional representation system similar to the one used in Germany. But the support for MMP seems to stem from a reaction against conventional politics and the mainstream parties rather than from any widespread support or even understanding of the consequences of changing the electoral system.

Under the MMP system, you have two votes; the first for the political party ('party vote'), and the second, an 'electorate vote' is for the MP you want to represent your electorate. Parliament is made up of 120 MPs, and the proportion of each party is dependent upon the outcome of the party vote. There are now fewer constituency seats – 31 electorates disappeared and there are now only 65 seats linked to a constituency. Five of these constituency seats are Maori. The remaining 55 MPs are called 'list MPs' and win their place in parliament by making up the proportion of their party according to the 'party vote'. Party lists are the pecking order of MPs for that party. As well as pitting MPs in the same party against each other in the undignified struggle for selection, MMP makes it much easier for small parties to gain representation than is currently the case. The MMP system has also led to the increase in number of women MPs; there are currently 36 women in parliament, with Jenny Shipley as New Zealand's first woman Prime Minister. Some rebel MPs who have struggled in the political wilderness for years also benefit from the MMP system. Two MPs who decided that the best way to get on in the new world of MMP was leave the big parties to found a party in their own image were former National MP Winston Peters who created the New Zealand First party, and Jim Anderton, former Labour MP, who established the Alliance party. Currently, New Zealand First with seventeen seats in parliament holds the balance of power between National (with 44 seats) and Labour (37). Winston Peters has been playing one party off against the other, and both Labour and National consult at length with New Zealand First to try and win them over. Consequently decision making within the New Zealand government is most inefficient. More information concerning MMP can be obtained from The Electoral Commission (39 The Terrace, PO Box 3050, Wellington; tel (04) 474 0670; fax (04) 474 0674; e-mail: elect@netlink.co.nz).

Political Parties

For most of the second half of this century, the New Zealand political scene has been dominated by two major parties, National and Labour. National is a conservative party, traditionally the party of farmers and business people. It has been the dominant political party in New Zealand politics, holding office for the majority of the post-war period. Labour has some elements in common with the British Labour party. Like the British labour party it arose out of the labour movement, but the New Zealand Labour party has subsequently had greater independence from the trade unions. It has often been the innovator of radical social policies, even when these have gone against its own political traditions. The 4th Labour Government which held power from 1984 to 1990 was responsible for introducing anti-nuclear legislation which stopped American warships from entering New Zealand ports. It also deregulated the economy, ran a tight monetary policy along Thatcherite lines and sold off a number of state assets - not exactly socialist policies. For those who like their political spectrum neatly divided into left and right, New Zealand politics currently present a confusing spectacle. Since losing power in 1990, Labour have sacked their old leader, elected a left winger, Helen Clark, the first woman to lead a political party in New Zealand, and are going through a period of rediscovering their social democratic roots, although it remains to be seen if the public will be convinced. National, since being elected to government had a brief experiment with introducing even more extreme free-market policies. Currently, Jenny Shipley is the Prime Minister, sworn into office only five weeks after gaining the allegiance of the National Party power base (whilst Jim Bolger was overseas on business!) and ousting him from his position. She is a formidable politician, committed to lowering taxes and solving the countries' social problems.

Until now, as in Britain smaller parties have been kept out of power by the first past the post electoral system. Parties have been able to gain power holding less than a majority of votes and small parties whose supporters were spread around the country would not even gain sufficient votes in any one electorate to elect an MP to Parliament, even though their overall share of the vote could be substantial. As a result of the 1993 MMP referendum, New Zealand moved to a European style system of proportional representation. One of the results of MMP is that the minor party in the Government can be quite an influence on governmental policy. Five smaller parties now have seats in Parliament, the two main ones being New Zealand First, a populist party led by rebel National MP Winston Peters, and the Alliance, a coalition of left wing parties led by former Labour MP, Jim Anderton. The remaining parties in parliament are ACT, Independent and United.

Geographical Information

Area

New Zealand is an island chain, consisting of two major islands and a number of smaller ones with a total land area of 103,515 sq miles/270,534 sq km, slightly larger than the United Kingdom. It is nearly 1600 km long stretching across 13 degrees latitude from 34 degrees S to 47 degrees S, only 420 km wide at its widest point. Most of the country is mountainous. The snow-capped Southern Alps dominate the South Island dividing the land between the rain forests of the West Coast and the dry pasture lands of the Canterbury, Marlborough and Otago. Fiordland, the south-west corner of the South Island is almost all national park and as its name suggest consists of deep sounds or fiords carved into the bush covered mountains. The North Island still bears the marks of the volcanic activity which formed it. A chain of occasionally active volcanoes runs from White Island sending up clouds of steam off the east coast, through the central volcanic plateau where snow and hotpools coexist, to Mt Egmont on the west coast. There are active thermal areas where mud pools literally bubble and geysers send up streams of boiling water.

National Parks

Thirty per cent of New Zealand's land area is in protected conservation sites, in a network of national, maritime and forest parks. Many of these wilderness areas are untouched by human habitation, although unfortunately the effect of the animals introduced with the arrival of humans has been harder to control. The Department of Conservation which looks after the parks aims to preserve the flora and fauna as far as possible, while allowing people recreational access. They look after an extensive network of tracks and huts for hikers (known in New Zealand as trampers, as in to tramp). There is a small fee for using the huts. The walking tracks vary in difficulty from family strolls of less than half a day to serious two or three day hikes up hill and down. Most New Zealanders go tramping at some point in their lives, whether they are dragged reluctantly along on a school trip or are keen walkers every weekend.

Keep in mind though, that although the New Zealand bush looks welcoming on a warm day, it can be a very hostile environment. The weather can change unexpectedly and in some areas of New Zealand's national parks, you can be far away from any inhabited areas if something goes wrong. It is important to take precautions before venturing into the bush, such as bringing warm clothing and emergency food supplies, and informing someone of your plans.

Regional Divisions and Main Towns

The following regions correspond to the territorial divisions of local government, with the exception of some of the smaller districts such as Gisborne which have been grouped with larger neighbours.
North Island:
Northland, Auckland, Waikato, Bay of Plenty, Gisborne/Hawkes Bay, Taranaki, Manawatu – Wanganui, Wellington.
South Island:
Nelson/Marlborough/Tasman, West Coast, Canterbury, Southland and Otago.

There are five main cities:
North Island:
Auckland, Wellington and Hamilton
South Island:
Christchurch and Dunedin.

Population

At the last census the New Zealand population numbered just over 3.68 million, a half million increase since the early 1970s. Growth rates have been declining since the mid-seventies as a result of downward trends in birth rates, as is the case in most Western countries, the current rate of increase is about 1.1%. The other major factor affecting population change is migration patterns which have been particularly volatile over the last twenty years. New Zealand has a very low population density compared with European countries, at 13.6 people per sq km. (the UK by comparison has 241.5 per sq km and Taiwan has 583.6).

Despite New Zealand's reputation as a largely rural society, 85% live in cities. Auckland, the biggest city, has a population of just under one million, nearly one third of the population. It is a relatively youthful society children under 15 comprise over 22% of the population and those of working age account for over 65% of the population.

Over eighty per cent of the population are of European descent known as Pakeha (from the Maori word for non-Maori). New Zealand Maori make up the next largest group forming about 12% of the population. The next largest group are Polynesians from the Pacific Islands, such as Samoa, Tonga, and Fiji who form nearly 4% of the population. Other ethnic groups represented amongst the population are Chinese and Indian, and more recently, Korean and Japanese.

Climate

New Zealand has an oceanic climate, without extremes of hot or cold. The seasons do not vary as much as in Britain, and are the opposite to the northern hemisphere, January and February being the warmest months and July the coldest. New Zealand's long thin shape results in considerable climatic variation between regions. The far north of the country has an almost sub-tropical climate, with mild winters, hot summers and quite a lot of rain. In the south of the South Island, the country can be frozen over for three months during the winter and the summers are hot and dry. Whatever the region, New Zealand summers are generally hotter than British summers. The sun is also stronger in the Southern Hemisphere resulting in a higher risk of sunburn. Unfortunately the ozone hole over the Antarctic has a tendency to drift north over New Zealand during December, which makes the risk of burning higher. During the summer, a 'burn time' rating is included with television weather reports to warn people of the time it takes to burn between the hottest hours of the day. Along with Australians, New Zealanders have one of the highest rates of skin cancer in the world.

Average Maximum Temperature, Sunshine and Rainfall

City	Mean daily maximum Jan °C/F	July °C/F	Bright sunshine hours	Mean annual rainfall (mm)
Auckland	23/73	14/57	2070	1105
Wellington	20/68	11/52	2025	1270
Christchurch	22/72	11/52	2065	645
Dunedin	19/66	10/50	1600	800

Annual average. Source: NIWA.

Regional Guide

Most New Zealanders live in the North Island, one third of them in the greater Auckland region. The two major North Island cities, Auckland, the largest city, and Wellington, the capital, provide the closest New Zealand equivalent to the culture and lifestyle of big cities in the rest of the world. There is amicable rivalry between the two cities, Auckland being bigger, brasher and more commercial, Sydney for beginners, according to some people. Wellington takes itself more seriously as befits a capital city. It is the headquarters of most national cultural institutions such as the national ballet company and symphony orchestra and the seat of government. The South Island is more sparsely populated but attracts more visitors because of the splendours of the scenery. Christchurch, the biggest city in the south is very English in appearance and has a rather staid, conservative feel, perhaps because of the architecture. In the south of the South Island, the influence of Scottish settlers is very strong. About the only distinctive regional accent in New Zealand is the rolled 'r' of the Southlander. Groups of new immigrants often used to settle in particular regions. The area just of north of Auckland is full of family vineyards run by Dalmatian immigrants who arrived last century from what is now the country of Croatia; and Danes settled in the Wairarapa, the area just north of Wellington. British expatriates are now fairly evenly spread around the country.

Information Facilities

The New Zealand Tourism Board runs a network of Visitor Information Centres throughout the country, where you can obtain maps of the area, information, public transport timetables, and have your queries answered. Information Centres can be found in most large towns. The Tourism board is also beginning an accreditation scheme for the tourism industry. You can recognise accredited establishments by the Taste New Zealand and Kiwihost signs. The address of the national office of the New Zealand Tourism Board is (Level 7, 89 The Terrace, PO Box 95, Wellington, tel (04) 472 8860; fax (04) 472 9494; Website: www.nztb.govt.nz).

Other useful websites for a general overview include Discover NZ at www.discover.co.nz/index and the AA New Zealand Guide at www.aaguides.co.nz/index.

Northland

Visitor Information Centre: Whangarei Visitor's Bureau, Tarewa Park, 92 Otaika Rd; tel (09) 438 1079; fax (09) 438 2943. Useful website: www.northland.ac.nz.
Main city: Whangarei ('wh' in Maori is pronounced like 'f').

Northland is one of the larger regions but is one of the least densely populated with only 142 000 inhabitants, just under 4% of the total population. It stretches from north of Auckland to the very tip of the North Island, Cape Reinga, where according to Maori legend, departing souls in the form of birds pause on the tree at the very end of the land before setting off for the oceans. Northland has a semi-tropical climate, miles of isolated beaches, and undisturbed rainforests. The Bay of Islands on the east coast was one of the earliest sites of European settlement. The Treaty of Waitangi under which the British Crown gained sovereignty over New Zealand was signed at Waitangi on one side of the Bay of Islands, and on the opposite side of the bay is Russell which was the capital of New Zealand for the first twenty years of British rule. These days one of the main areas of economic activity is tourism. It is a popular destination for New Zealand and overseas visitors. Aside from the historical attractions, it is a centre for big game fishing enthusiasts, sailors and divers.

Auckland

Visitor Information: Auckland Visitor Centre, 299 Queen Street, PO Box 7048, Auckland; tel (09) 366 6888; fax (09) 366 6893; also, New Zealand Tourism Board (Auckland Office) P.O.Box 6727 Wellersley St, Auckland; tel (09) 379 7948. Useful websites: akcity.govt.nz, and www.auckland.tourism.co.nz.
Main city: Auckland.

The Auckland region is dominated by the city from which it takes its name, the largest in the country with a population of just under 998,000 and the financial and manufacturing centre. Two natural harbours, one on the Pacific coast, the other on the Tasman, bite deep into the land, and the island consequently is narrow at this point. The city covers the width of the island between the harbours. Although Auckland has the highest population concentration in the country, it is not densely populated by the standards of European cities. Most Aucklanders live in detached single stories dwellings in the suburbs which stretch further into the surrounding countryside each year. The city centre is situated beside the Waitemata harbour and although it has a number of modestly tall high rise buildings, it's not exactly Manhattan. In fact one of Auckland's most attractive aspects is the parks and reserves that are dotted throughout the urban area. Many of these reserves are volcanic hills. There are over sixty extinct volcanoes in the city area. Another attractive feature is the beaches within walking distance of the city centre. Auckland is sometimes resented by the remainder of the country as it dominates New Zealand through its size and concentration of economic activity. There is also a general feeling that Aucklanders don't think there is anything worthwhile 'south of the Bombay Hills', a cluster of hills marking the division between Auckland and Waikato. Nearly one third of the population live in the greater Auckland region and it is likely to be the fastest growing area of economic activity for some time.

Waikato

Visitor Information: Hamilton Visitor Centre, Municipal Building, Garden Place, PO Box 970, Hamilton; tel (07) 839 3580; fax (07) 839 0794. Useful website: the AA regional guide www.aaguides.co.nz.
Main city: Hamilton.

The Waikato region stretches from the Bombay hills, south of Auckland to Lake Taupo in the centre of the North Island. The lake is the source of the river for which the region is named. The Waikato river is the longest in New Zealand. Along its 425 km length there are nine hydro-electric dams which provide a large part of the North Island's electricity requirements. The Waikato is the main dairy farming region in New Zealand. The Coromandel peninsula in the north-east corner of the region is a centre for forestry production. The Coromandel is also a popular holiday destination. Its rugged bush-clad mountains protect almost deserted beaches. Other attractions include the thermal regions around Wairakei, where steam is harnessed to drive turbines producing electricity, and the limestone caves at Waitomo.

Hamilton, the largest city has a population of nearly 159,000 people but the atmosphere of a small town. It has one of the more dynamic universities in the country (whose new vice-chancellor, Bryan Gould is a Kiwi who returned home after a long sojourn in British politics).

The Waikato is also the headquarters of the King movement, one of the Maori cultural and political movements responsible for the renaissance of Maoridom in the 20th century. The King movement is based at Turangawaewae marae (Maori meeting place and cultural centre) at Ngaruawahia, the home of the Maori king. Like many marae, Turangawaewae is open to groups of visitors, by arrangement.

Bay of Plenty

Visitor Information: Tauranga Information & Visitor Centre, Dive Crescent, PO Box 1070, Tauranga; tel (07) 578 8103. Useful websites: nz.com/rotorua/attract/index and the AA regional guide www.aaguides.co.nz.
Main Towns: Tauranga, Rotorua.

The Bay of Plenty is one of the main horticultural regions in the country. It is located on the east coast of the North Island above East Cape. The area around Te Puke is the kiwifruit growing capital of the country. If you are fond of the small, furry, brown fruit, you can find them on sale at roadside stalls at ridiculously cheap prices during the season, sometimes when export cargoes are held up for any reason, growers practically give them away. The Bay of Plenty region is a good place for finding casual fruit picking work in season. Rotorua is famous for its geysers, mudpools, steam rising from the street drains, and distinctive sulphuric smell of the thermal activity, reminiscent of rotten eggs. The beaches around Tauranga and Mount Maunganui are very picturesque and attract crowds (by New Zealand standards) during the summer months.

Hawkes Bay/Gisborne

Visitor Information: Napier Visitor Information Centre, Marine Parade, PO Box 722, Napier; tel (06) 834 1911, fax (06) 835 7219.
Eastland and Gisborne District Information Centre, 209 Grey St, PO Box 170, Gisborne; tel (06) 868 6139, fax (06) 868 6138. Useful website: AA regional guide at www.aaguides.co.nz.
Main towns: Napier, Hastings, Gisborne.

Gisborne and the East Cape region are very sparsely populated with only 46 000 inhabitants, 33 000 of whom live in the main town Gisborne. Dairy and sheep farming are the dominant industries although winemaking is small but growing activity. The East Cape is quite remote, Maori influences are strong and the lifestyle of local Maori is relatively unaffected by European culture. Hawkes Bay, located south of the East Cape, is another primarily agricultural and horticultural region. It has a mild climate with long sunshine hours and low rainfall. The area around Napier and Hastings is particularly known for its vineyards, producing a number of excellent wines, particularly Chardonnay and Sauvignon Blanc. Napier has some of the most striking architecture in New Zealand. Totally flattened by an earthquake in 1931 it was rebuilt in the art deco style then fashionable around the world. Most of the original buildings survive undwarfed by modern tower blocks.

Taranaki

Visitor Information: New Plymouth Public Relations and Marketing Office, Cnr Liardet & Leach St, New Plymouth; tel (06) 759 6080; fax (06)759 6073. Useful website: www.aaguides.co.nz.
Main town: New Plymouth.

According to Maori legend, the North Island of New Zealand was originally a giant fish which the hero Maui hooked from his canoe, the South Island. If you consider the shape of the North Island as a flattish sort of fish, with a fin on each side, Taranaki occupies the western fin. The dominant feature of the Taranaki landscape is Mt Egmont (more commonly known nowadays by its original Maori name, Mt Taranaki), a perfect volcanic cone, topped year round with snow. Taranaki is dairying country and is also the centre of the petrochemical industry. Off the coast of New Plymouth is the Maui natural gas field and a number of small oil fields. The region around Mt Taranaki is a national park and there are a number of hiking paths on the mountain and surrounding area.

Manawatu – Wanganui

Visitor Information: Palmerston North Information Centre, Civic Centre Building, The Square, Palmerston North; tel. (06) 358 5003. Useful website www.aaguides.co.nz.
Wanganui Information Centre, 101 Guyton Street, PO Box 637; tel (06) 345 3286.
Main towns: Palmerston North, Wanganui.

The Manawatu-Wanganui region stretches from just above Wellington up into the centre of the North Island to the central volcanic plateau. The main river in the region is the Wanganui, which is the same name as the town situated on its banks. They should both correctly be known as Whanganui, but established usage prevails. According to Maori myth, the Wanganui was first explored by the great navigator Kupe. The town was one of the earliest established by European settlers who recognised the navigable properties of the river. While other cities have expanded, Wanganui has retained the atmosphere of a quiet country town. Tourist attractions include jet boat rides on the Wanganui river. The main industry is sheep and dairy farming. Tongariro National Park, in the north of the region has within its bounds the highest points in the North Island, the snow-capped volcanoes, Mt Ruapehu, Mt Ngaruahoe and the shortest of the three, Mt Tongariro. Mt Ruapehu is the main North Island skiing destination, although the eruptions of the mountain occurring inconveniently in the winters of 1995 and 1996 has wreaked havoc on recent ski seasons. The whole area is a popular centre for outdoor activities, from climbing to fly-fishing. In the thermal region nearby there are hot springs, and a dip in a naturally heated pool is a popular end to a day's skiing. The largest town is towards the south of the region. Palmerston North, is the home of Massey University, originally one of two specialist agricultural colleges in the country.

Wellington

Visitor Information: Wellington City Information Centre, Cnr Wakefield & Victoria Streets, PO Box 2199, Wellington; tel (04) 801 4000, and the New Zealand Tourism Board, (Wellington); tel (04) 472 8860. Useful website: www.wcc.govt.nz/discwell.
Main City: Wellington.

The Wellington region covers the southern tip of the North Island. It is named for its largest city, Wellington, which has a population of 345,500, and is the capital of New Zealand. Parliament is usually housed in the circular building nicknamed 'the beehive', which is now not big enough to cope with the increase in number of MPs created by the new MMP political system. A very expensive (and most of the population would say, unjustified) enlargement of the parliament building complex is currently underway. The city spreads across steep hills overlooking a harbour shaped like a natural amphitheatre. Wellington is infamous for its winds which must easily rival those of that other windy city, Chicago. A favourite cheap thrill amongst inhabitants is watching airplanes battle their way into Wellington airport on a windy day. Being a passenger on a plane trying to land at Wellington is less fun, as the landing strip is situated on a narrow strip between the harbour and the sea, and often planes abort their takeoff or landing because of high winds and fly to nearby Palmerston North. The city itself is quite small, with a population of around 160,000 in the main urban area but despite its size it is surprisingly lively. There are a host of late night cafés and bars, many of which feature local bands, and a thriving theatre scene. Wellington hosts an arts festival every two years which attracts international musicians and performing artists as well as local artists. Most of the other towns in the region provide commuter fodder for Wellington, and as such lack much personality. The exception perhaps are towns along the edge of the harbour opposite Wellington. Most of these are scarcely more than villages as the steep hills drop almost into the sea at this point leaving only a narrow strip of land to build on. A regular ferry service takes about 25 minutes to cross the harbour to Wellington from Days Bay.

Marlborough/Tasman

Visitor Information: Nelson Visitor Centre, Cnr Trafalgar & Halifax Street, PO Box 194, Nelson; tel (03) 5466338.
Main Cities: Nelson, Blenheim.

The Marlborough and Tasman districts cover the top of the South Island. It is the largest wine making region in the country. The climate is pleasant, hot without being as humid as northern parts, with more sunny days and less rain than Auckland. The area around Nelson is a centre for artisans and craftspeople, particularly potters, which may account for the slightly alternative feel to the town. It is a relaxed, laid-back place (as are most South Island towns) with easy access to some beautiful wilderness areas and beaches. Over the Takaka hills to the west lies the aptly named Golden Bay. There are a number of national parks in the Tasman district. East of the city of Nelson lies the Marlborough district, which boasts the spectacular Marlborough Sounds, a popular yachting and mountain biking destination. Marlborough is also the largest wine making region in the country. Blenheim is the main town in the region.

West Coast

Visitor Information: Buller Visitor & Information Centre, 1 Brougham Street, Westport; tel (03) 789 6658. AA regional website: www.aaguides.co.nz.
Main Towns: Greymouth, Westport.

The West Coast is a wet and wild part of the South Island with its own distinctive breed of New Zealanders. It has the smallest population of the country – there are only 35,000 people in the entire region. The Coast is accessible by a few roads most of which climb up through the Alps in a series of hairpin bends through spectacular scenery. The routes through the centre of the island are occasionally cut off by weather which may account for the remote feeling of the Coast. Or it may be the rugged independence of its inhabitants resulting from the area's historical legacy. Mining, gum digging and possum trapping were the main industries for much of this century and the last; all solitary occupations. Consequently 'West Coasters' are renown for their strength of character and sincere hospitality. There are so few cars on the road that, if driving, you end up waving to every car you pass! Popular tourist industries are as diverse as walking on the Fox and Franz Joseph Glaciers, eco tourism and wildlife tours, to watching glass blowing and gem stone manufacture. The geography of this region is dramatic, from the 'Pancake Rocks' and blowholes on the coast in the north, to the spectacular glaciers and mountains in the south. Mt Cook, at 3,754 metres is New Zealand's highest mountain, but its stature was reduced 10.5 metres in 1991 when the top of the mountain fell off in a landslide. It is a region of extremes; the rainfall is very high and the sandflies are diabolical.

Canterbury

Visitor Information: Canterbury Information Centre, Cnr Worcester Street & Oxford Tce, PO Box 2600, Christchurch, tel (03) 379 9629, and New Zealand Tourism Board (Christchurch), PO Box 3182, Christchurch; tel (03)365 0296. Useful website: is at www.canterburypages.co.nz.
Main City: Christchurch.

The Canterbury region is mostly sheep farming country, miles of pasture land stretching from the foothills of the southern Alps to the coast. The main city Christchurch is the largest in the South Island with a population of more than 331,000. It was founded by an idealistic bunch of Oxford graduates and named for their old college. These days it is known as the Garden City, for its botanic parks, trees and green spaces. It is set on the Avon river and is a popular destination for Japanese tourists who like the slightly English flavour Christchurch retains. The skyline is dominated to the east by the Port Hills, and to the west by the Southern Alps. Mt Hutt, a major ski resort is only an hour's drive from the city. East of Christchurch is Banks Peninsula, a collection of bays and hills jutting out into the Pacific. Lyttleton harbour is the deep water port for the city of Christchurch and is connected to the city by a 1.6 km tunnel running through the Port Hills. Akaroa, the main settlement on the Peninsula was originally founded by the French who had ambitions to colonise New Zealand but were beaten to it by the British. These days the French influence does not extend much beyond the street names and the architecture. The Canterbury plains are prime crop-growing land. Further west on the foothills of the Alps, the land is most used for sheep farming.

Otago

Visitor Information: Dunedin Visitor Information Centre, 48 The Octagon, PO Box 5457, Dunedin; tel (03) 474 3300. The AA regional website: www.aaguides.co.nz.
Main city: Dunedin.

The Otago region covers the south-eastern part of the South Island. Land use is mostly for dairy farming and crop growing. The central Otago basin enjoys surprisingly hot dry summers despite its latitude and is a centre for horticulture, particularly stone fruit orchards. The southern most city, Dunedin was founded by Scottish settlers. Perhaps the most characteristic buildings in Dunedin are those of the University which reflect the importance of education to the early settlers: founded in 1869, the University of Otago is the oldest in New Zealand. Fueled by the discovery of gold in the 1860s Dunedin grew to be one of biggest and most prosperous towns in colonial New Zealand, as can be seen by many buildings, such as the Regent's Theatre. The gold largely ran out after the initial boom, and Dunedin's growth rate fell behind the northern cities. It has remained much the same size since the early days of the 20th century, and many of its historic buildings have been preserved as a result. It has also retained the somewhat austere character of its Presbyterian forefathers, although every year a new intake of students at Otago University tries to reverse this. It is the only truly 'student' town in the country, university life dominating the town during term time while students provide much needed revenue for local businesses. Three and a half hours inland from Dunedin lies Queenstown, a major tourist mecca. Set on Lake Wakatipu and against a spectacular mountain backdrop, it is close to ski resorts and the home of adrenaline activities. Try the 71 metre Skipper's Canyon bungy jump for measure.

Southland

Visitor Information: Gore Information Centre, Cnr Medway and Ordsal Streets, PO Box 1, Gore; tel (03) 208 9908. AA regional website: www.aaguides.co.nz.
Main towns: Invercargill, Gore.

Southland, as the name suggests is the southernmost region of the South Island. Stewart Island at the very bottom of the South Island is the southern most inhabited point of the country. It is off the coast of Southland, below Invercargill, the largest town in the region. At Bluff nearby Invercargill is the country's only aluminium smelter, powered by locally produced hydroelectricity. In the western part of the region is Fiordland national park. It contains some truly awe inspiring scenery: fiords or sounds carved out by glaciers, cut deep channels into the land. The surrounding cliffs are covered in bush and traced by waterfalls. One of the best known parts of Fiordland is Milford Sound, the destination of the Milford track, a popular walking trip for tourists. On the eastern coast of Southland lies the Catlins area, which features abundant wildlife, (seals, sea lions, and Hector's dolphins), native forests, waterfalls and caves. The spectacular Cathedral Caves for example, are only accessible at low tide. Most of Southland is beef and sheep farming country, with some dairying around Invercargill. The people of Southland can be gruff and down to earth, watch out for the rolled 'rr' that can be found around the city of Gore – it's the only regional variation of the New Zealand accent.

Getting There

Travel Agents

If you do not have a regular travel agent, it may be worthwhile considering the advantages of using an agency which specialises in long haul flights or in Australian and New Zealand destinations. They should be in touch with any discounted or cheaper fares that may be available, although the drawback of these deals is usually that the tickets have restrictions and can be very expensive to change once booked. Some antipodean travel agencies offer other services which may be useful, for example, organising temporary accommodation when you first arrive. The cheapest flights are via London, so if you are travelling from another European destination it may be worth checking if it makes sense to go via Heathrow or Gatwick. From London, you can either fly east or west to get to New Zealand, with a refuelling stop either in Asia or the USA. It is slightly quicker to go via Asia, but if you fly via the States, the baggage allowances are much more generous. (see below). Going west also minimises the jetlag because you are following the path of the sun so your body clock is not so disorientated. There are other ways of minimising the effects of jetlag while on the flight. Drink plenty of water, avoid alcohol, and try and stretch your legs every so often. This may sound like boring advice but the jet lag after a thirty-hour flight across twelve time zones is considerable. Avoiding the free airline alcohol is not such a big price to pay for being awake and alive your first few days in your new country. Another idea is to arrive in plenty of time for your flight so you can ask for bulkhead or exit row seats which have extra leg-room.

You are only allowed to take 20 kilos of luggage with you on the aircraft if you travel economy class via Asia to New Zealand. If you travel via America you can take two suitcases, neither of which may exceed 32 kg in weight. Airlines are strict about sticking to these limits and as the excess baggage charge works out at about $72 per kilo you will need to make sure your luggage is within the limits. Should you arrive at the airport and discover that you are over the limit, the best option is unaccompanied baggage. Your luggage will go on the next available flight, and usually reaches your destination a couple of days after you do. You will have to clear it through Customs at the other end and there may be storage charges as well. The usual charge for unaccompanied baggage is about $9 per kilo.

Useful Addresses
Austravel, 50-51 Conduit Street, London W1R 9FB; tel 0171-734 7755; fax 0171-494 1302.
Connections Travel: 93 Wimpole Street, London W1N 8DA; tel 0171-495 5545; fax 0171-495 5704; e-mail: falef@signconnect2_uk.net. Connections brochure gives fares and tours pricing for different seasons and offers ideas as how best to build itineraries.
Cresta World Travel, Cresta House, 32 Victoria Street, Altrincham, Cheshire WA14 1ET; tel 0161-0929 9727; fax 0161-929 7551.
Golden Wings Worldwide, 51 Kent House, Second Floor, 87 Regent Street, London W1R 7HF; tel 0171-734 3070; fax 0171-437 4437.
Journey The World, 1683 High Street, Knowle, Solihull, B93 0LL; tel 01564-777744; fax 01564-777141.
Southern Cross Travel: Best Beech Hill, Wadhurst, TN5 6JH; tel 01892 – 783896; fax 01892 784 866.
Trailfinders, 194 Kensington High Street, Kensington, London W8 7RG; tel 0171-938 3939; fax 0171-938 3305; Website: www.cheapflights.co.uk/agents/trailfinders.html.
Travel Mood: 214 Edgeware Road, London, W2 1DS; tel 0171-258 0280; fax 0171-258 0180, and 61 Reform Street, Dundee DD1 1SP; tel 01382-322713; fax 01382-201079.

Insurance
Working travellers and those on speculative job searches in New Zealand are advised to take out comprehensive travel insurance.

Useful Addresses

Atlas Travel Insurance Service Ltd (ATI): 37 Kings Exchange, Tileyard Road, London N7 9AH; tel 0171-609 5000; fax 0171-609 5011; e-mail: quote@travel_insurance.co.uk.

COE Connections International: 138 Aylesbeare, Shoeburyness, Essex SS3 8AG; tel/fax 01702-587003.

Columbus Direct Travel Insurance, 17 Devonshire Square, London EC2M 4SQ, tel 0171-375 0011; fax 0171-375 0022; Website www.columbusdirect.co.uk

Downunder Insurance: 3 Spring Street, Paddington, London W2 3RA; tel 0171-402 9211; fax 0171-402 9272; e-mail: dunder@globalnet.co.uk.

Golden Wings Worldwide: 29 Kent House, First Floor, 87 Regent Street, London W1R 7HF; tel 0171-437 6379; fax 0171-494 3936.

Residence and Entry Regulations

The Current Position

Throughout New Zealand's history, population growth has been boosted at various points by government policies designed to attract immigrants. The main source of the new arrivals for most of the first century of European settlement was the British Isles. The other major source of European immigrants was the Netherlands. Sadly New Zealand missed out achieving some of the ethnic diversity Australia enjoys by not actively encouraging immigration from other European countries in the post Second World War period. The last major campaign to attract immigrants was in the 1950s. These were the days when the New Zealand government paid for the passage on the condition that the prospective immigrant stayed for two years. When this scheme ended, a more restrictive immigration policy was introduced, based on occupational quotas. Most potential immigrants had to have a job waiting for them before they applied for residency.

The Government operates a points system similar to the Canadian and Australian schemes. Applicants for residency are ranked by the number of points they score for attributes such as age, qualifications, work experience, and an offer of employment (which is worth 20% of the total points). Those who reach the target number set by the New Zealand government automatically receive provisional approval. At time of print, the 1998 target number of immigrants had been increased by 10,000 places to 45,000 migrants per year. The UK is the largest single source of new migrants, followed by South Africa and then South Korea.

New Immigration Policies 1998

In October 1998, new immigration policies were introduced including a revision of the business investor category covering entrepreneurs, investors and those on long-term business visas. Full and detailed information can be obtained from the New Zealand Immigration Service (PO Box 518, Turanga, New Zealand; tel +64 7-578 1883; fax +64 7-578 2555).

Applying for New Zealand Residency

If you qualify for permanent New Zealand residency you are entitled to work in New Zealand without any restrictions. Besides the general category which is based on age and employability criteria, there are four other ways of qualifying for permanent residence: business investment, family, humanitarian, and entrepreneur. Whatever category you are applying under, there is a lot of paperwork involved. You will be required to provide medical certificates and character references. You will not be accepted if you have ever been convicted and served a sentence of five years or more, or a sentence of one year or more in the last ten years. These days, because of the sensitivity of race relations and concerns over the political affiliations of the growing number of South African immigrants, you will also be required to declare that you have never been a member of a white supremacist organisation. Like the American immigration requirement to declare that you have never participated in genocide, the point is not that anyone would declare themselves to be racist but that if you make a false declaration, it is an offence under the Immigration Act and you can be deported forthwith. There are charges for this paperwork: see the table below for the cost of the different types of visas.

Immigration Consultants

You may consider employing the services of an immigration consultant. The number of organisations offering advice on emigrating to New Zealand has grown substantially since the new immigration policy was introduced. Most consultants offer help with all aspects of the immigration process. They will provide general information about New Zealand to help you decide whether you want to make the move. Some consultancies will organise special tour packages to New Zealand so you can visit the country before deciding whether to emigrate. As emigration is a major life step it may be worthwhile to consider a reconnaissance trip and you can make an application for permanent residency while in New Zealand on a visitor's visa or permit if you decide you like the place.

Once you have made the decision, an immigration consultant will guide you through the maze of paperwork and residency regulations which can appear daunting. Geoff Taylor from the Emigration Group says a candidate would maximise their chances of qualifying by using a reputable immigration consultancy, but the final decision rests with the NZ Immigration Service. Consultancies can help in dealing with the red tape and they should make sure you do not omit any vital pieces of information such as previous job experience. You should be wary of any consultancy which appears to promise that they have a special relationship with the New Zealand Immigration Service. All applications are considered equally regardless of whether a consultant has been involved or not. Another useful service consultants provide is help in settling in New Zealand. Most good consultants should provide you with assistance in deciding where to live, looking for jobs, finding a house and other aspects of organising your new life. In choosing a consultant, the most important aspects to consider are the practical help they can offer. Do they have a job search branch in New Zealand? What kind of contacts do they have in promoting your employment chances? According to the New Zealand Immigration Service, the major consultancies they deal with regularly are all above board. If you are uncertain about whether a consultancy is bona fide, you can ask to see testimonials provided by past clients. It is worth shopping around and making sure you get value for money.

Useful Addresses

The Emigration Group: 7 Heritage Court, Lower Bridge Street, Chester, Cheshire CH1 1RD; tel 01244-321414; fax 01244-342288; e-mail theemigrationgroup@ btinternet.com. Professional migration consultants specialising in Australia and New Zealand. Member of the New Zealand Association for Migration and Investment (NZAMI). See advertisement on inside front cover.

Challice Emigration: Freepost (NG6151) Newark NG23 5YZ; tel/fax 01636-525903; email wbce.challice@lineone.net. Professional migration consultants.

Ambler Collins: 59 Fulham High Street, London, SW6 3JJ; tel 0171-371 0213; fax 0171-736 8841; e-mail: amblercollins@compuserve.com

Four Corners Emigration: Freepost NWW 1289, Manchester M22 3FR; tel 0345-419453; fax 0161-498 9889; email UKenquiries@4-corners.com. Professional migration consultants.

Malcom Pacific (UK) Ltd: 1 Hay Hill, Berkeley Square, London, W1X 7LF; tel 0171-607 9700; fax 0171-609 9903.

New Zealand & Australia Migration Bureau: 70 Upper Richmond Road, London SW15 2RP; tel 0181-874 2844; fax 0181-874 1178. European Office: Oranje Nassaulaan 25, 1075 AJ Amsterdam, The Netherlands; tel +31 20 6717017; fax +31 20 6760065; e-mail: info@nzamb.nl.

Useful Publication

New Zealand Outlook published monthly by Consyl Publishing Ltd. (3 Buckhurst Road, Bexhill-on-Sea, East Sussex TN40 1QF; tel 01424-223111; fax 01424-224992). Aimed specifically at migrants and is a useful way of keeping up with NZ migration policy and entry regulations. In the UK six issues cost £6.25 and twelve issues £11.50.

Residence Categories

General residence category

To qualify in this category you must be under 56 years old and have sufficient understanding of English to conduct a conversation, and to read and respond to questions about yourself and your family. Applicants under the general category are assessed through the new points system. Points are awarded in three different areas: employability, age and settlement factors. If your score is above the pass mark then your application is provisionally approved, subject to meeting normal immigration requirements such as a clean bill of health and not having a serious criminal record. The pass mark is subject to change, and at time of print was 25 points. 24 points and below is an automatic fail. You do not get your application fee refunded if you do not qualify.

The system favours young people with tertiary qualifications. However older people with work experience and qualifications can also gain enough points to pass. A job offer adds to your chances; it is currently worth five points. It makes no difference which country you apply from. The points system has the advantage that it is completely neutral: if you have sufficient points your application will be provisionally approved, it is not up to the discretion of an individual officer. You can check your eligibility in these areas by applying for a self-assessment guide from the New Zealand High Commission. To give you an idea of how the system works here is the points table from the most recent self assessment guide:

Employability factors	Factor	Points
1.Qualifications	New Zealand base qualification: a degree, diploma or trade certificate of three years training, study or work experience	10
	New Zealand advanced qualification: a minimum of one years training, study or work experience which builds on the base qualification	11
	New Zealand masters degree or higher	12

You must score a minimum of 10 points for qualifications. Maximum points possible: 12

2.Work Experience	Two years	1
	Four years	2
	Six years	3

Eight years	4
Ten years	5
Twelve years	6
Fourteen years	7
Sixteen years	8
Eighteen years	9
Twenty years	10

You must score a minimum of 1 point for work experience.

3. Offer of Employment Full time, permanent job offer   5

4.Age

18-24years	8
25-29 years	10
30-34 years	8
35-39 years	6
40-44 years	4
45-49 years	2
50-55 years	0

Maximum age limit: 55 years
Maximum points for age factor: 10

4. Settlement factors

NZ $100,000 settlement funds	1
NZ $200,000 settlement funds	2
Family sponsorship	3
Spouse/Partner's base qualification	1
Spouse/Partner's advanced qualification or master's degree	2
1 year work experience in New Zealand	1
2 years work experience in New Zealand	2

Maximum points for settlement factors: 7
PASS MARK: 25

Points to watch out for:
You can only claim points for your highest qualification.
Only one person in a family need qualify. Partners and dependent children under 20 will be granted residence as well.
You do not have to have a job offer although you will score more points if you do.
Years of work experience are rounded down, so if you have nine years and eight months of work experience, that will count as eight years or four points.
You can apply for residence under the general category if you are between 50 and 55 but you will receive no points for your age. You are not eligible if you are 56 years or older.
Medical requirements are not clearly spelled out anywhere but the criteria seems to be whether you would be a burden on the New Zealand health system. Chronic manageable syndromes such as epilepsy would not disqualify you, but having a terminal disease probably would.

If you are just below the pass mark, you should look carefully at the settlement factors to see if you can find the critical extra points. Sponsorship is one area to look into. A family sponsor must be an adult brother, sister, parent or child of the principal applicant or spouse, and must have been a New Zealand citizen or resident who has been living in the country for the three years prior to your application. Securing an offer of skilled employment is worth five points. Skilled employment means that the job must be relevant to your qualification.

Finding the extra points to raise you above the pass mark is an area where a good immigration consultant may be able to help. Some consultants offer a job search service. You could also consider visiting New Zealand and looking in person. Remember you can apply for permanent residency from within New Zealand. First hand experience of any country is still the best way of deciding if you want to live there.

Investor Category

Business investors applying for residence have a simpler points system (from March 1999), more streamlined application processes and a greater incentive to take part in the New Zealand business community.

Investors will need 12 points to qualify in the investor category awarded on The basis of age, business experience and investor funds.
Ages 25 to 29 attract 10 points. Points reduce to zero by age 60. Those aged up to 84 are now eligible, but they will attract minus 4 points.

For business experience 1 point is awarded for 2 years' experience and up to 5 points for 10 years' experience.

The minimum level of qualifying funds is NZ$1 million which attracts 1 point rising to 11 points for $NZ6 million (previously, 10 points were awarded for NZ$3).

Entrepreneur Category

There is a new category of residence for entrepreneurs who have successfully established businesses in New Zealand. To qualify the applicant must demonstrate that their business is benefiting New Zealand in some way. This could be by creating jobs for New Zealanders and/or by revitalising an existing business by providing a new type of product or service.

It is recognised that entrepreneurs do not necessarily have the tertiary qualifications under the General Skills category.

The pathway to becoming a resident is the long-term business visa which is a multiple entry visa available for up to three years and renewable after that for those interesting in establishing a business in New Zealand.

Family Reunification: You are entitled to apply for residence under this category if you have a partner or close family member who is a New Zealand resident or citizen. Spouses, de facto and homosexual partners all qualify but in the case of de facto or homosexual partners you have to go to greater lengths to convince the Immigration Service that the relationship is 'genuine and stable'. The relationship has to have been of at least two years' duration for de facto and four years in the case of homosexual relationships. Approval is not automatic for any of these cases including spouses, and the Immigration Service will probably require an interview with both partners.

You can also qualify under family reunification if you have a close family member who is a New Zealander. Dependent children (under the age of 17, unmarried and childless) may qualify to be reunited with their parents if they were declared on their parents' residence application. Single adults may qualify for reunification with a New Zealand brother, sister or parent. Parents may be reunited with adult children provided all their adult children live outside their country of origin, or if they do not have dependent children, more of their adult children live in New Zealand than in any other country, or if they do have dependent children, they have a greater or equal number of adult children living in New Zealand than in any other country.

To qualify under any of these categories you will need to provide evidence of your relationship to the family member and that they are New Zealand citizens or residents. The sponsor is responsible for accommodation and financial support for the first year of the applicant.

Humanitarian Category: Applicants under the humanitarian category have to be suffering some kind of persecution in their home country and have to have a New Zealand sponsor who is a close family member.

The Application Process

If you are applying under the general category, you will get some idea from the tables of whether you are likely to qualify. Applications for permanent residence should be lodged with the New Zealand Immigration Service. A major cause of delay in having your application considered is incorrect documentation. Make sure for example that you send the full birth certificate (not short birth certificates) for all family members included in an application for residency. Part of the medical requirements are that you have certain blood tests and the results for these must be sent in. Once you have sent the correct documents, your eligibility will be checked by Immigration Service staff. Processing time has been lengthy in the past at the Immigration Service in London. You should begin the application process about a year before your intended date of migration. Using an immigration consultant can save you a lot of time.

Fees:

Visitor's visa	£20	Residence visa (business)	£725
Work visa(temporary)	£45	Student visa	£65
Residence visa	£225		

Citizens from Japan, Iceland and Finland are not charged for any type of visa. Citizens of Greece, Israel, Italy and Turkey are not charged for returning residence and visitor visas. Citizens of Austria are not charged for any residence or visitor visas. Citizens of the USA and Mexico are not charged for Visitor, Work and Student Visas. Citizens of the Philippines and Russia are not charged for visitor visas.

New Zealand Citizenship

If you have resided legally in New Zealand for three years you can apply for New Zealand citizenship. This will entitle you to vote and to carry a New Zealand passport. You will no longer require a returning resident's visa when you travel abroad. Children born in New Zealand to non-New Zealanders are New Zealand citizens. They can have dual nationality and are entitled to a New Zealand passport.

For citizenship inquiries you should contact: The Director of Citizenship (Department of Internal Affairs, PO Box 805, Wellington; tel 04-495 7200; fax 04-495 7222; Website: www.citizenship.dia.govt.nz).

Entry and Work Permits

If you want to visit New Zealand and you are not a citizen or permanent resident then you will need a visitor's visa or permit. You should apply for a visa from the New Zealand embassy in your home country before you travel. The initial period of a visa is usually three months but you can extend it by a further six months once you are in New Zealand by applying to local offices of the New Zealand Immigration Service. It is becoming more common though for travellers not to need to obtain a visa as New Zealand has negotiated visa-free agreements with a number of countries. If you have a passport from one of the countries on the following list, you will not require a visa, you simply apply for a visitor's permit at the airport. You will be required to show that you have sufficient funds to support yourself while you are in New Zealand and a return or onward ticket. Like the visa, the visitor's permit is issued for three months initially and can be renewed by a further six months within New Zealand. Sufficient funding is deemed to be NZ$1000 for every month you intend to stay. If you have a friend or relative prepared to sponsor your visit, and can guarantee your accommodation, the amount is reduced to $400. They will need to fill in a *Sponsoring a visitor* form which they can get from New Zealand Immigration, and which must be sent to you.

Visa-exempted Countries:

Austria, Belgium, Canada, Denmark, Finland, France (this only includes French people living in France), Germany, Greece, Iceland, Indonesia, Ireland, Italy, Japan, Kiribati, Liechtenstein, Luxembourg, Malaysia, Malta, Monaco, Nauru, Netherlands, Norway, Portugal (but only those with permanent Portugese residency), Singapore, Spain, Sweden, Switzerland, Thailand, Tuvalu, USA (excluding certain US Nationals, like American Samoans).

Australia: Australian citizens are free to travel to New Zealand without a passport and can work in New Zealand without requiring a work visa under the terms of the Closer Economic Relations agreement which creates a free labour market across the Tasman.

Britain: British citizens do not need to apply for visas and will be issued visitor's permits for an initial period of six months.

Applying for a longer visa:

If you know before you travel that you want to stay for longer than three months it is worth applying for a visa even if you are from a visa-waiver country. You can apply for a maximum of 12 months, and your application must be made before your current permit expires.

Studying in New Zealand:

In order to study on a course lasting longer than three months, you will need to apply for a student visa before you set off. This can be done at the New Zealand High Commission in London, and will cost £75.00. You will need to provide an acceptance letter from the New Zealand educational institution, receipt for the course fee, evidence of sufficient funds for maintenance, and an outward airline ticket. If you wish to work over the student holidays (November to February), you can apply for a 'Variation of Conditions' to your student permit. If you wish to work following the completion of your course, you can apply for a Work Permit which will allow you to work a maximum of two years. Information about New Zealand universities and polytechnics is available from the Trade Development Board of New Zealand which is in New Zealand House. You must be studying an approved course and have sufficient funds to cover tuition fees and maintenance (see Chapter Four, *Education* for an idea of the cost of New Zealand courses). The Trade Development Board at New Zealand House also has information on tuition fees and maintenance costs. (6th Floor, New Zealand House; tel 0171-973 0380).

Working in New Zealand:
If you wish to work in New Zealand for a short period and you are not a citizen or resident you will need to apply for a temporary work visa. You can either apply for one before you travel if you already have a definite employment offer, or if you find a job while visiting New Zealand, you can apply for a visa there. If you are applying for a work visa before travelling, allow at least four weeks for the application to be processed. Your prospective employer will need to provide details of your job title, responsibilities, qualifications required, conditions and duration of employment and pay, as well as proof that they have unsuccessfully tried to recruit New Zealanders to fill the position. You can apply for a work visa for up to three years, if you have a job offer before you arrive in New Zealand. If you apply for a work visa in New Zealand, the maximum period you will be granted is nine months. The employer will be required to provide the local Immigration Service with the information outlined above. For further information you can get a leaflet called *Getting a Work Visa* from the New Zealand Immigration Service.

Working Holiday Visa: Like Australia, New Zealand has a working holiday visa scheme for young visitors. British, Canadian or Japanese citizens between the ages of 18 and 30 inclusive can apply for the visa which will enable them to take casual work without requiring a separate work visa, while on holiday in New Zealand. The maximum period of the visa is one year and you must be resident in the UK at the time of application. When the scheme started in 1993 only 500 visas were issued; since then the quota has increased to 4,000 per year. The scheme has been extended to Irish Nationals but with a smaller yearly quota of 250. You apply to the New Zealand Immigration Service in London, showing evidence that you have NZ$4200 to support your visit, and a return travel ticket or enough money to purchase one. Allocations are on a first come, first served basis beginning on July 1st.

American students can get a six-month work permit through the Council (CIEE) and similar scheme operates in Canada through Travel CUTS branches.

Useful addresses:

New Zealand Information, Immigration and Visa Inquiries in the UK:
The New Zealand High Commission: Mezzanine, New Zealand House, 80 Haymarket, London, SW1Y 4TQ; tel. 0171-930 8422; fax 0171-839 4580.
The New Zealand Immigration Service: Mezzanine New Zealand House, 80 Haymarket, London, SW1Y 4TQ; tel. 0991-100 100 (calls charged at £1.00 per minute); Website: www.immigration.govt.nz.
The New Zealand Trade Development Board: 6th Floor, New Zealand House, 80 Haymarket, London, SW1Y 4TQ; tel 0171-973 0380.
Information for British Citizens in New Zealand:
British High Commission: 44 Hill Street, PO Box 1812, Wellington; tel (04) 472 6049; fax (04) 471 1974.

Setting Up Home

New Zealand house prices are cheap by British standards. Typical prices can be ascertained from the property section of some New Zealand newspapers. The main New Zealand newspapers can be read at New Zealand House in London (80 Haymarket, London, SW1Y 4TE; tel 0171-930 8422) between 9am and 5pm weekdays. More detailed advertisements can be found in New Zealand real estate magazines. You can order these through *New Zealand Outlook* and *Destination New Zealand* the UK newspapers for intending immigrants. (Pick up copies outside the Visa Enquiries desk on the third floor of New Zealand House or order them from the addresses listed in Chapter Six, *Employment* under *UK Newspapers and Directories*).

Immigration consultants will also offer advice on buying properties. The property market in New Zealand's main cities is currently quite lively as a result of low interest rates and improving economic prospects. Auckland and Wellington are the most expensive places to buy houses. Outside the main cities, property prices are between 30 and 40% cheaper.

Most New Zealand houses are detached, single storey houses on individual plots of land known as 'sections' (The term bungalow to describe such a house is not common). The average New Zealand home consists of three bedrooms, a lounge (usually with an open fireplace) and dining room, kitchen, laundry, bathroom and w.c. Conveyancing is a less complicated business than in the UK because most houses are detached dwellings with no cross leases, and because, with a smaller total population, the house buying 'chains' are typically not as much of a problem as in the UK.

The standard size of the New Zealand section used to be a quarter of an acre, but as urban property prices have risen in recent years, subdivisions have become more common and new houses are being built on much smaller sites. The average size of new houses is just under 170 square metres. Although the vast majority of houses are still separate units, in recent years multi-unit developments have become more common, particularly in the big cities.

Deciding where to live for most people, is influenced first and foremost by employment prospects. The areas where new immigrants are most likely to buy houses are Auckland and Wellington. In both cities the residential areas are mostly suburban and it is most common for people to commute by car into city centre to work. Each suburb has its own particular character and prices can also vary considerably between areas for reasons as diverse as mere fashion or, in the case of hilly areas, related to the amount of sunshine that different parts enjoy, or the view it affords. In Auckland, for example, your property is worth more if it has a view of magnificent Rangitoto Island. It is worth looking at the less fashionable areas; if you are aiming at the cheaper end of the market, you will get more house for your dollar.

If you have children, your choice may be influenced by proximity to schools. The location, however, does not make a lot of difference to the standard of education on offer. Inner city schools perform as well as suburban schools on the whole. Rural schools achieve slightly lower academic results than city schools but have the advantage of smaller class sizes and better pastoral care. The best idea is to go along to schools in the area and see what you think of the atmosphere. Now that school zoning has been abolished, you are free to select the school of your preference, within the limitations of getting the children there every morning.

How do New Zealanders Live?

New Zealand has a high level of home ownership, with nearly three-quarters of dwellings being owner-occupied. (The equivalent figure for the UK is 66%) They tend to be quite house-proud, and spend a lot of time on home improvements and gardening. The average standard of housing is high. Household services such as water, electricity and sewerage are almost universal. Almost all houses have TVs, 75% have videos, and 29% have dishwashers.

Of those who are living in rented homes, a quarter live in state houses rented from the Housing Corporation, while the majority lease housing from private landlords or companies. Rental accommodation is usually provided unfurnished except for ovens, fridges and sometimes, washing machines. Local authorities do not play a major role in providing housing.

The majority of households are made up of just one family. Amongst Maori and Pacific island communities, where extended kinship links are important and because average incomes amongst these groups are lower, households are more likely to include more than one family. Even amongst Maori and Pacific island homes though, one-family households are the most common. The average number of occupants per dwelling is 2.8 people.

Levels of second home ownership are also quite high. Many New Zealand families own what is known as a bach (pronounced 'batch' rather than after the composer) or 'crib'. Bach is the North Island term, and crib, the South Island. It is usually a small holiday cottage on a lake or by the sea. Bachs are a great New Zealand institution. They are unpretentious dwellings usually furnished with furniture and kitchen-ware discarded from the family home, comfortable to live in, not always kept immaculately clean because when the family is on holiday, the chief cook and cleaner needs a holiday too.

Buying a house in New Zealand

Non-New Zealanders can buy property of less than one acre without any bureaucratic formalities, but property purchases over an acre require the permission of the District Land Registrar or the Land Valuation Tribunal. However as most immigrants buy a house once they have been granted permanent residency, this restriction is not normally relevant.

Finding a property

Most people begin by approaching a local real estate agent or searching in free weekly property newspapers in their desired location. A good paper to try is the Property Press (PO Box 99772, Newmarket, Auckland; tel 09-524 0491) which is available in inner city areas. Daily newspapers also carry property advertisements.

There are many types of property on offer, although the variety is not as great as in Europe where architecture of many periods co-exists. European style architecture only has a short history in New Zealand and you do not find many thatched cottages. The typical period house is a wooden Victorian villa. This type is very popular with the do-it-yourself set as a renovation project. Most older houses were made of wood because of the risk of earthquake. The standard New Zealand house of the post War period is a three bedroom, brick bungalow on a large section. Formerly, houses were generally built with a northern hemisphere model in mind and thus did not always make the most of the New Zealand climate. Modern houses are designed to capture the sun and to make the most of outdoor living during the New Zealand summer. Because of rising inner city land prices there is a growing trend towards building town houses and apartment blocks. Town houses are compact units, often multi-level, usually built as part of group on one site. In the suburbs, where land is cheaper you can find modern mansions with swimming pools, en suite bathrooms, separate lounge and dining room, all on a huge site. At the other end of the budget spectrum, you will find houses advertised as 'the handyman's dream' or 'needing TLC' (tender loving care), which is real estate speak for a dwelling in dire need of repair. This type of property is Mecca to the home handyman who seems to lurk under the skin of most New Zealand males and quite a few females. If your acquaintance with nails is confined to those on your digits, then you should probably avoid this type of thing and look for something a more immediately habitable. On the other hand, inner city Victorian villas can still be picked up cheaply if you are prepared to do the work on them and, once renovated, they make charming homes.

Useful Addresses

New Zealand Real Estate Agents:

Auckland
Harcourts Real Estate: PO Box 99549, Newmarket, Auckland; tel freephone 0800 804 805, or (09) 520 5569; fax (09) 524 7059.
L. J. Hooker: 250 Manukau Road, Epsom, Auckland; tel (09) 520 6005.
Ray White United: 251 Symonds Street, Auckland; tel (09) 377 8643; fax (09) 377 6845.

Hamilton
Harcourts Real Estate: 85 Rostrevor Street, Hamilton; tel (07) 839 5085; fax (07) 839 6576.
L. J. Hooker, Challenge Realty: 821 Victoria Street, Hamilton; tel (07) 838 3456.
L. J. Hooker, Accent Realty: 55 London Street, Hamilton; tel/fax (07) 838 3456.

Wellington
L. J. Hooker: 171 Willis Street, Wellington; tel (04) 801 5700.
Guardian First National Real Estate: 20 Johnsonville Road, Johnsonville, Wellington; tel (04) 478 1620; fax (04) 478 4612.
United Realty World: 2 Woodward Street, Wellington; tel (04) 472 9323; fax (04) 473 4902.
Challenge Properties: Level 13, The Terrace, Wellington; tel (04) 495 3030.

Christchurch
Challenge Realty Group: 53 Victoria Street, Christchurch; tel 03-365 0911.
L.J. Hooker: 132 Victoria Street, PO Box 36182 Christchurch; tel (03) 379 6521.
Christchurch United Realty: 235 Stanmore Road, Christchurch; tel (03) 389 2895; fax (03) 351 7665.

Dunedin
Harcourts & Gilchrist Real Estate: 301 Moray Place, Dunedin; tel (03) 477 5334; fax (03) 477 3445.
L.J. Hooker: 599 Andersons Bay Road, Dunedin; tel (03) 455 0770.
Patterson/United Realty: Princes Street, PO Box 221, Dunedin; tel (03) 477 5555; fax (03) 474 0484.

Wayne Graham/Challenge Realty: cnr Wharf and Birch Streets, Dunedin; tel (03) 477 4303; fax (03) 477 5775.

Miscellaneous Useful Addresses

Consyl Publishing: 3 Buckhurst Road, Bexhill-on-Sea, East Sussex TN40 1QF; tel 01424-223111) produce a monthly newspaper *New Zealand Outlook* which is aimed at those planning to emigrate to New Zealand. The newspaper carries details of housing there. A free copy can be obtained by sending a 43p s.a.e..

Emigration Consultancy Services: 8 De Salis Court, Hampton Lovett, Droitwich, Worcestershire WR9 0NX; tel 01905-795 949; fax 01905-795557. As well as helping British emigrants deal with immigration, Emigration Consultancy Services provides help with the practical aspects of migration including accommodation.

Relocations International: 34 Douglas Street, Auckland; tel (09) 378 9888; fax (09) 378 8072 Wellington office: 101-103 Molesworth Street, Wellington; tel (04) 473 9461; fax (04) 473 9404.

Table 1: Average House prices by Region

District	House Price
Northland	$140 000
Auckland	$235 563
Waikato/ Bay of Plenty	$145 000
Hawkes Bay	$126 000
Manawatu/Wanganui	$100 000
Taranaki	$100 000
Wellington	$165 000
Nelson/Marlborough	$147 750
Canterbury/Westland	$145 000
Otago	$92 000
Southland	$70 000
Average for New Zealand	$165 000

Source: Real Estate Institute 1998.

Purchasing and Conveyancing Procedures

Buying a property is less complicated in New Zealand than in many countries. Establishing clear title is generally straightforward because there are fewer complications like cross leasing and lease-hold properties. As a result you do not get chains of prospective buyers waiting for the next person in the chain to organise the sale of their house which is a feature of the market in the UK. Nor are there problems of establishing who actually owns the property in question which can occur in some other European countries.

When you wish to buy a property, you need to obtain the free copy of Real Estate magazine published by the combined local real estate firms. This has a photo of each property, relevant details, and estate agent involved. You may attend an 'open home' (which means you turn up at that address at the time specified), or you can arrange a private visit with the estate agent. The agent is working for the seller, and receives a commission for the sale from them, but must present the property fairly to the buyer. It's possible to deal with several agents at once, as many estate agents have sharing arrangement over the commission for the sale.

It's sensible to have a solicitor check the title details when you come to sign the agreement to buy the property. A solicitor would also be useful as he can arrange to get a Valuer's Report (which costs $300) should you need it, or a Land Information Memorandum Report. A LIM report establishes the town planning requirements and anything which could affect the property, and is available from the local authority. Since the 1984 Reforms under Labour to promote competition, lawyers' fees on the average house sale have decreased from 0.34% to 0.21% of the sale price.

Most homes in New Zealand are owned by the occupier who has a mortgage from a bank or financial institution. Some residential properties are on lease but not a great number. However, most commercial and industrial properties are leased as this provides an annual cost for taxation purposes. You should not let the Estate Agent pressure you into signing a contract, as at time of print, there is a surplus of properties on the market. Your agreement to purchase the property can be subject to obtaining mortgage finance or the sale of your current New Zealand property. Your Solicitor's charge may add $600 to $1000 to the cost of the house but it could save you from making an expensive mistake. The market is not regulated so you can ask around for a reasonably priced Solicitor. A useful magazine published by a network of independent legal firms is *Lawlink* (tel 09-366 0775; fax 09 -309 5113) or found on the internet www.knowledge_basket.co.nz/lawlink.

Finance

Borrowing Money to Buy a Property

Mortgages are the standard method of financing house purchasing in New Zealand. The majority of properties have a mortgage on them. Your Solicitor will help and this should be discussed before you make an offer to purchase a property. Until recently interest rates were about 8% but at the time of printing have increased to between 9.3% and 11% which may reduce the number of people taking out mortgages. Banks are the main lenders. Building societies used to be separate institutions from banks but since deregulation in the 1980s they have been allowed to provide the same services and most have now converted themselves to banks. The banks have responded to the competition over providing mortgages by offering more flexible repayment terms.

Up to 80-90% of the purchase price can be borrowed, but if you borrow more than 80% the bank may require some form of mortgage insurance (see below). The maximum amount you may borrow is not always directly related to your salary but you will be expected to provide information on your monthly income as part of a hypothetical budgeting exercise and repayments would not normally be expected to be more than 30% of your income. If you are borrowing more than 60% of the purchase price, the bank may require a Valuer's Report. For some low income households, mortgage assistance is available from the Housing Corporation if they are unable to get a commercial loan but this is becoming less common.

Mortgage and Associated Costs

Your bank will charge mortgage application costs of around 1% of the value of the mortgage. The Land Transfer Registration fee is $115, although if a lawyer acts on your behalf this fee will come out of general legal disbursements. There are two types of insurance. Mortgage protection insurance is more comprehensive, it repays the mortgage in the event of your death. Mortgage risk insurance will pay the mortgage for a fixed period if you lose your regular income. There is no government benefit to help you pay the costs of a mortgage.

Repayment Conditions

Repayments are usually made on a monthly basis, but can be fortnightly. The usual term of mortgage used to be twenty-five years, but it is increasingly common for people to arrange shorter term mortgages with commensurably higher monthly repayments. Most banks will not approve of a mortgage arrangement which requires you to repay more than one third of monthly income. Interest rates can be either fixed or floating. There are three main types of mortgage: Table, Straight Line or Interest Only. In a table mortgage you pay equal monthly (or fortnightly) payments of interest and capital over the whole term of the mortgage. In a straight line mortgage, monthly payments start high because you pay fixed amounts of principal, plus the amount of interest you have accrued that month. At the beginning, there will be a lot of interest to pay off, but this will decrease as the principle is repaid resulting in decreasing monthly payments.

The third type is an interest only mortgage; you pay a higher rate of interest on a monthly basis, which tends to add up to the same sum, more or less, as a repayment mortgage, but at the end of the whole term the original sum borrowed is effectively written off. The banks are quite flexible about changing the repayment conditions once you have entered into the mortgage, for example increasing or decreasing the size of monthly payments or switching to fortnightly payments. You can even alter the type of mortgage or transfer it to another property.

Renting Property

Most immigrants rent property while they look for a house. You can arrange to rent a furnished apartment before you arrive in New Zealand through an immigration consultant or through some of the newspapers for intending migrants (*New Zealand Outlook* and *Destination New Zealand*, see Chapter Six *Employment* for subscription details). Some travel agents will also provide assistance in finding accommodation. This type of accommodation tends to be more expensive than finding a rental house yourself but has the advantage of being ready and waiting for you as soon as you get off the plane. It will certainly be cheaper than staying in a hotel while you are house hunting.

The cost of rented accommodation is quite moderate, although you can expect to pay more if you want something more than just a run of the mill three bedroomed house. Currently there is a surplus of rental property. They are advertised in the daily newspapers – mainly on Saturdays, but Wednesdays as well. Cheaper houses can be hard to find in towns with a large student population. If you are looking for cheaper accommodation, February/March is a bad time to look as it is the start of the university year and you will be competing with students looking for flats. You can also go to a Real Estate letting agency but you can pay up to one week's rent for them to find you a suitable flat. Most privately let houses are unfurnished. Real estate agents are good places to inquire about furnished property.

Tenancy Agreements

There are two types of tenancy agreements, fixed term and periodic. Most houses are let on a periodic basis. This means that the tenancy runs until either side gives notice. In standard letting contracts, the tenant must give at least 21 days written notice that they want to end the tenancy, and the landlord 90 days notice. The landlord is allowed to give only 42 days notice if they are moving into the house themselves or if they have sold the house. In a fixed term tenancy the duration is fixed at the start of the letting period and cannot by changed except by agreement of both parties. Most tenancy agreements are sorted out between the landlord and the tenant using a standard tenancy agreement available from bookstores. A standard agreement is also available from the Tenancy Services section of the Ministry of Housing. It is not usually necessary to have a lawyer check the agreement. Tenancy Services are there to help in case of disputes between landlords and tenants and they will also give you information about your rights and responsibilities as tenants. The landlord is required to maintain the premises but tenants are responsible for any damage caused by misuse or abuse.

Rental Costs

Tenants are usually required to pay a bond or deposit to the landlord in case of damage to the property. Bonds can be up to four weeks rent, but are usually two weeks' rental. They used to be held by the landlord but as a result of disputes between tenants and landlords over the withholding of bond money, the bond is now passed on to the Bond Processing Centre, part of the Tenancy Services division of the Ministry of Housing. At the end of the tenancy, the bond is refunded to you less any agreed unpaid rent or other amounts owing to the Landlord. Tenancy Services act as arbitrators between tenants and landlords in disagreements over bonds and other disputes such as rental arrears and damage to property.

Tenancy Services, Advice/Mediation & Enquiries
Auckland: Level 11, cnr Customs and Gore Streets, PO Box 90 172, Auckland; tel (09) 357 5450; fax (09) 302 0253.
Hamilton: cnr Bryce and Victoria Streets, Hamilton; tel (07) 834 1569; fax (07) 834 1571.
Wellington: tel (04) 471 6900; fax (04) 472 8828.
*Christchurch:*153 Hereford Street, Christchurch; tel (03) 371 2100; fax (03) 379 8324.
Dunedin: 67 Princes Street, Dunedin; tel (03) 479 3880; fax (03) 477 8884.

Citizens Advice Bureau (National Office): Unit 6, Betty Campbell Community Office Complex, 148 Wakefield Street, PO Box 9777, Wellington; tel toll free 0800 367 222 or (04) 382 8759; fax (04) 382 8647. Citizens Advice offers free confidential advice on housing, health, legal and consumer problems, employment and budgeting. It has over 90 offices throughout New Zealand.

Community Law Centres (National Office): PO Box 2912, Christchurch; tel (03) 366 6870; fax (03) 366 6631. Community Law Centres provides free confidential legal advice and is staffed by solicitors and law students. Contact the Christchurch office to find out your local branch.

Valuation New Zealand (Head Office): Level 5 Vogel Building, Aitken Street, PO Box 5098 Wellington; tel (04) 473 8555; fax (04) 473 8552; e-mail: valnz@valuationnz.govt.nz. Government agency for real estate, mortgage and government valuations.

Rates

Each local council in New Zealand levies a tax based on the value of your property to fund local amenities and services. Road maintenance, sewage disposal, water supply, libraries, park maintenance and street lighting are all paid for by your council rates. The value of your property and hence the amount of rates you pay is decided by Valuation New Zealand. Rates are included in the rent of rental properties.

Insurance and Wills

Wills

If at the time of your death you have a permanent place of residence in New Zealand or you are living in New Zealand for more than half the year, you are considered by New Zealand law to be a resident. This means that any property you own in New Zealand is subject to New Zealand laws if you die intestate. It makes sense therefore make a will, after you have bought a house. Property disposed under a New Zealand will is not subject to inheritance tax. If you are retaining assets in the UK, you should check with your solicitor to see that your New Zealand will is recognised in the UK. Property in other countries is normally subject to the inheritance laws of those countries.

You do not have to use a lawyer or trustee company to draw up a will in New Zealand but it does not cost much and may save problems later. Certain procedures must be followed for a will to be valid, and it must be signed by the testator in the presence of two witnesses who cannot be beneficiaries. Trustee companies (including the Public Trust Office) will draw up a will for free , although you must name them as executors. They will claim a certain proportion of the estate as executors' fees. Alternatively you can get a will drawn up by a lawyer for a fee in the region of $50 to $80.

Insurance

Taking out insurance on a new property is a sensible precaution. Most mortgage lenders will probably require you insure your new house. As in the UK there are different types of cover available. Multi-risk policies (called accidental damage policies) provide blanket cover for all losses unless specifically excluded. Defined risk policies, as the name suggests, list what risks the policy provides cover for. This type of policy is less costly but accidental damage policies are probably a better option. Your house can either be insured for its indemnity value, or replacement value. The indemnity value is the depreciated or current market value of your house, excluding the value of the land. It does not replace with new, nor would it cover the cost of rebuilding but you should be able to buy a similar house. The replacement value can be open-ended or fixed sum. The difference between this and indemnity value is that there is no deduction for depreciation. Open-ended replacement value means the insurer will pay the full cost of repairing or rebuilding as new. Fixed sum replacement value means that the insurer will pay up to the agreed sum. Typical premiums on an accidental damage policy (for accidental loss or damage) range from $300-$400 per annum for an average size house with a replacement value of around $100 000. (Remember, this excludes the value of the land). This premium can be reduced by increasing the excess, or installing a burglar or fire alarm. Premiums are cheaper outside the larger cities.

It makes sense to take out household contents insurance with the same firm as you have your house insurance with. According to *Consumer* magazine, you should get a discount for having both types of insurance with the same company and it will save arguments over who is responsible for a claim. Again you can either get a multi-risk or a defined risk policy for either indemnity or replacement value. If you have a accidental damage policy you can sometimes buy an extension to cover your possessions outside of your house, for example for personal sports equipment.

One unique feature of buying household insurance in New Zealand is earthquake damage insurance. Because New Zealand is prone to earthquakes, a special government scheme exists to provide insurance cover against them. When you take out a household insurance policy that includes cover against fire (i.e. a total replacement policy) you also automatically gain cover in the case of earthquake, landslide, volcanic or tsunami (tidal wave) damage. In fact, it is the New Zealand Government that underwrites the risk of earthquakes because the potential cost of a major earthquake in a big city is too great for commercial insurance companies to handle. Your insurance company will charge you a compulsory disaster insurance premium which they pass on to the Earthquake Commission (PO Box 311, Wellington; tel 0800 652 333). The maximum amount the Commission will pay out is $100,000 or the amount for which you have insured your home, (which ever is lower) and $20,000 for personal belongings or the amount for which you have insured them. (Again they will pay out the lower amount). The premium works out at about 5c for every $100 insured, and the maximum yearly premium is $67.50. The coverage is fairly basic and does not extend, for example, to motor vehicles, boats, jewellery, works of art. Nor will the Commission pay for any indirect costs arising out of an earthquake such as, for example, the cost of having to stay in rented accommodation. It may be a good idea to take out top-up cover with an insurance company. It will cover the items noted above which EQ cover does not include, and will also cover you for the value of your house above the $100, 000 covered by the government. Major earthquakes which cause serious damage are rare.

Utilities

Services such as electricity, telephones, water and sewerage are just about universal in New Zealand. Holiday cottages in some far-flung corners of the islands may not be on mainline electricity and commonly will have a septic tank rather than being on mainline sewerage, but the average family home comes provided with a similar level of services as its UK equivalent. People moving into a house or flat need to arrange for the electricity or gas and telephone to be connected. An agreement for the supply is signed between the supplier and the tenant. Most government departments providing commercial services were turned into State Owned Enterprises (SOEs) in the late 80s. They were set up like commercial companies, although as the name suggests they remained publicly owned, and given commercial targets. The change in performance between the new SOEs and the old government departments was dramatic. When telecommunications were run by the Post Office, average installation time was at least six weeks. Now it seldom takes more than two days. The creation of SOEs has also brought with it some competition in the utilities marketplace. Rival telephone companies are now offering price wars on toll calls, and a more free market exists for some utilities.

Electricity

Most of New Zealand's electricity supply is generated through hydro-electric schemes on New Zealand's main rivers. Hydro energy has the advantage of being cheap, clean and renewable. Most of the power is generated in the South Island on the rivers draining the mountains of the Southern Alps. It is a long standing grievance between South Islanders and the North that despite providing most of the electricity for the country, southerners pay the same. The bills come every two months. An average bill for a three-bedroom house would be around $180-250 for two months supply.

Electricity supply in New Zealand is 230 volts and 50 hertz. Most UK electrical equipment will work in New Zealand. However there is no point bringing televisions or videos as the transmission systems are different. UK video tapes will work in New Zealand video machines. Electricity sockets are three pin but a different shape from the UK so any appliances you bring will need new plugs. Appliances in New Zealand are sold with plugs attached. Electricity is supplied by local electricity companies which are special local companies, some of whom have issued shares to their consumers.

The privatisation of electrical utilities in New Zealand has caused its own problems. The city of Auckland made the international news in February 1998 when the electricity supply to the inner city was cut off for several weeks. The city's power supplier, Mercury Energy, did not sufficiently maintain its cables to the city, and, during the especially hot summer, the four 110 kilovolt cables melted simultaneously. Businesses closed, and residents were evacuated. 60,000 people work, and 5,000 people live in Central Auckland. Although the city retailers claimed they were losing $10 million a day from the power cuts, Mercury Energy would not take responsibility for the disaster, and blamed the collapse of the cables on a freak of nature. The rest of the country, however, seemed to enjoy the plight of the Aucklanders, and Wellington and Dunedin tourist boards advertised the 'power' and 'energy' of their cities in Auckland's newspaper.

Gas

Household gas supply is not universally available. Natural gas is produced off the Taranaki coast and piped to most areas of the North Island. It is available as far north of Auckland as Whangarei, in Wellington and on the east coast in Gisborne, Napier and Hastings. In areas which do not have a household supply, bottled gas is available. In the South Island most gas is of the bottled variety except in Dunedin and parts of Christchurch. The local supply company can be found in the front of the *Yellow Pages* under the useful numbers section. Before they will connect your property the gas company will require you to fill in an application for the supply of gas and to pay a bond of around $100.

Water

New Zealand water is clean and quite drinkable, although it tastes better in some areas of the country than others. In Auckland and Hamilton it has an unpleasant chlorine taste. Most people seem to put up with it, though, as evidenced by the fact that the bottled water market is not particularly large in New Zealand. Water shortages are a not normally a problem, although Auckland has suffered droughts in recent summers, and water conservation during summer is sometimes called for in other cities. In some areas local councils charge for the water supply and your supply will be on a meter, in others the cost of water connection and supply is included in your annual rates bill.

Telephone

Telecommunications technology is relatively advanced as a result of a billion dollar investment programme in the late 80s. Telecom, the state-owned enterprise which took over running telecommunications from the Post Office, was sold off in 1990 to a consortium of two US phone companies and two local companies. The investment programme was part of the process of revamping the company prior to selling it. As a result New Zealand's rather antiquated phone system got a much needed overhaul. Prior to the investment programme, manual exchanges were not uncommon. At the same time the industry was deregulated to allow competitors into domestic supply and provision of phone units. Deregulation has led to improvements in customer service.

After Hong Kong, New Zealand has the highest percentage of digital connections per head of the population. It also has one of the highest densities of telephones in the world, with 468 lines per thousand of the population. The down side of privatisation is that despite being a private company, Telecom, because it owns the network, has an effective monopoly in many areas of telecommunications services. There is no industry regulator to check that the prices Telecom charges consumers are fair. Competition in the long distance calling market exists in the form of Clear Communications, Global One and Worldxchange and as a result toll prices have dropped. However, some industry commentators argue that toll calls are still too expensive.

You are obliged to hire your phone line from Telecom as they retain a monopoly on the provision of the network, but you no longer have to hire the phone itself as well. Despite this, 90% of domestic users still pay $4 a month to hire a Telecom phone. You may find it worthwhile shopping around to see what other models are available. To get your phone connected, Telecom will require proof of who you are, name, date of birth, postal address, physical address of the phone, previous address, employment history and next of kin. It takes about 48 hours to connect a new number. The connection fee is $61.88 to reconnect an existing line, however if you transfer to another property on the same day, the cost is only $30. Telecom has a free call number (called 'freephone') for businesses with a prefix of 0800. This enables customers to call free from anywhere in New Zealand. Freephone numbers for Clear Communications start with 0508.

Local calls are free for domestic customers, but there is a small charge for telephoning directory enquiries. However, Telecom's white pages (alphabetical residents and companies listing) are on the net at www.telecom.co.nz/direct, and the yellow pages at www.yellowpages.co.nz. The costs of toll calls are explained at the start of the phone directory. The ten charging steps depend on distance and the four call rates depend on the time of day. Peak time is 8am to noon Monday to Friday. Long distance calls are slightly cheaper on Clear Communications, the rival long distance calling company. You do not require any special equipment or numbers to use Clear. To route a call through Clear you prefix the number you are dialing with 050. At time of print, there is a special off peak toll rate for international and local toll calls made from 6pm Friday to 8am Monday on both Telecom and Clear. The competition between the telephone companies now gives other special deals at various times also.

Table 2: Useful Phone Numbers

Clear Communications	tel 0800 888 800
Global One	tel (09) 357 3700
Telecom	tel 123
Worldxchange	tel 0800 308 1301

Removals

Packing up your possessions and getting them to the other side of the world is an expensive business. Most household removals are done by sea freight which takes from six weeks to three months. The likely cost of shifting the contents of an average three bedroom house is in the region of £2500-3000, not including insurance. At these sort of prices you will want to think twice about what you really want to take with you. When deciding what to bring, remember that the New Zealand electricity supply is considerably different from a European supply, and slightly different from British supply. It is not just the voltage that differs, the supply frequency or hertz rating in New Zealand is also different. Although electrical goods are more expensive in New Zealand, having your existing appliances adapted to suit New Zealand supply may work out more costly in the end and not worth the trouble. TVs and videos for example, use a different transmission system. Appliances incorporating an automatic timing device, designed to operate on a different supply frequency will require expensive modification. Your removal company should be able to advise you on these points. On the other hand, good quality household furniture, fine china and glass will generally be worth bringing with you. You can get a free hints leaflet about moving abroad by sending a SAE to The British Association of Removers (3 Churchill Court, 58 Station Road, North Harrow, Middlesex, HA2 7SA; tel 0181-861 3331; fax 0181 -861 3332).

Be careful when choosing a removals company. The company who were so helpful when it came to moving you from Swindon to Surrey may not be experts in international removals. Look out for companies that specialise in packing and shipping internationally. If you know of anyone who has had their household shifted, ask them about their shipping company or if you are dealing with an immigration consultancy find out which company other emigrants have used successfully. You should check if they are members of an international removals trade association and if the association offers a payment guarantee scheme if the removals company goes bust while your goods are still in transit. Two well-known ones are the British Association of Removers, and the Association of International Removers. When it comes to comparing quotes from different companies, be sure to get quotes in writing based on the same list of goods. Freighting costs are worked out by volume either on the basis of a shared container, or a full container. In the case of the former, the quote will be based on the cubic volume of your goods, so it is essential to make sure the removals estimator knows exactly what you want to take as any last minute extras will cost more. In the case of a full container quote, the price per container is standard, but you should get a quote for the costs of any excess goods in case they do not all fit in one container. Make sure you know the type of container they are quoting you for, as volumes differ between insulated and non-insulated containers. If the quote is based on a shared container load, make sure it includes an estimate of total volume of your goods. If you have only a small amount of effects to move, it will probably be cheaper to pack them yourself. There are few important points. You should pack your possessions in stout containers, using a material such as woodwool or paper. Most removals companies will provide suitable containers. Goods packed with straw or chaff will not pass New Zealand agricultural quarantine regulations. You should label baggage carefully, inside and out. Most removals firms require about two weeks' advance notice before the date you want your possessions moved.

Insurance for the move

Insuring your possessions during the move is critical. Shipping firms will usually offer marine insurance as part of the service but you need to check the small print carefully. Make sure that the policy is all risks and that it covers any storage period either in the UK or in New Zealand. If the insurance company has offices in New Zealand, any claims are likely to be settled much more quickly than if they have no New Zealand base. There are several different types of marine insurance with varying exclusions so make sure you obtain a copy of the terms and conditions and compare them carefully. The cost of insurance is based on the value of your belongings and is usually around 2 to 3% of their value. If you have a lot of fragile goods, such as china or glassware, the premium may be as high as 4 to 5% of value.

Useful Addresses

Abels International Movers: 3 Hannah Close, Brent Park, Wembley, London NW10 0UJ; tel 0800-626 769; fax 0181-900 9612; e-mail: ray.luck@abels.co.uk.

Avalon Overseas International Movers; Drury Way, Brent Park, London NW10 0JN; tel 0181-451 6336; fax 0181-451 6419.

Brewer and Turnball: The Elephant House, Deykan Avenue, Witton, Birmingham B6 7BH; tel 0500-749 126; fax 0121-326 1900.

DAP International Ltd Overseas House, 209 Manor Road, Erith, Kent DA8 2AD; tel 0181-310 3003; fax 01322-332 518.

Davies Turner: 49 Wates Way, Mitcham, Surrey CR4 4HR; tel 0171-622 4393; fax 0171-720 3897; e-mail: dtwm@msn.com.

Econopak Removals Ltd: Unit K, Abbey Wharf Industrial Estate, Kingsbridge Road, Barking, Essex IG11 0BT; tel 0181-591 3434.

John Mason: 2 Mill Lane Industrial Estate, Mill Lane, Croydon, Surrey CR0 4AA; tel 0181-667 1133; fax 0181-666 0567.

Interpack: 3 Standard Road, London NW10 6EX; tel 0181-965 5550; fax 0181-453 0544.

Personal Shipping Services: 8 Redcross Way, London Bridge, London SE1 9HR; tel 0171-407 6606; fax 0171-407 6704.

Pickfords: 345 Southbury Road, Enfield, Middlesex EN1 1UP; tel 0800 243 687; fax 0181-219 8430.

Scotpac: Containerbase, Gartsherrie Road, Coatbridge ML5 2EJ tel 0141-7767191; fax 01236-449 888.

Vintage Shipping: Unit 36-37, Purfleet Industrial Park, London Road, Aveley, Essex RM15 4YA; tel 0181-591 6929; fax 0181-891 121; e-mail: vintee@btinternet.com.

Customs Regulations

Information regarding the importation of household, personal effects and cars into New Zealand can be found in a series of almost incomprehensible leaflets from New Zealand Customs. New Zealand embassies and high commissions should have copies available. The basic principle is that if you are coming to New Zealand to take up permanent residence, you can import your household goods and car duty free. The goods must be used and not be intended for sale or commercial use. If you are a returning resident, coming back to New Zealand after an absence of more than 21 months, your household goods qualify for the duty free concession, but in the case of cars, you can only qualify for the duty free concession on the first occasion you arrive to take up residence. You are also entitled like any visitor to New Zealand to bring in personal effects duty free. You may not bring plants, fruit and some food into New Zealand.

Import Procedures

Provided that you qualify for the duty free exemption outlined above, importing your household goods ought to be straightforward. The complicating factor is that you and your possessions will most likely be travelling separately, you by plane and your worldly goods by sea, a process taking six weeks at minimum. You can either send off your goods well before your departure and hope their arrival in New Zealand coincides with yours, or send them off when you leave and manage without for your first few weeks in your new country. You should make sure that your insurance policy covers any storage time, either before shipping or delivery at the other end. If your car and possessions arrive in New Zealand before you do, you can avoid paying port storage charges by arranging for a nominee to clear them through customs for you. The Collector of Customs at the port will require evidence of your nominee's authority to act for you and evidence that you are arriving in New Zealand for the first time to take up permanent residence, plus, in the case of a car, documents proving that you have owned it for at least a year, prior to departure (see below for the documentation required). Your nominee will be required to pay a deposit equivalent to the cost of duty on the vehicle and/or goods which will be refunded in full once you arrive.

Whether you are picking up your goods yourself or have authorised a nominee, you need to provide customs with an inventory of your belongings. There are certain imports that are prohibited, most obviously drugs. Firearms require a police permit to be imported. You should be careful to thoroughly clean any garden tools or furniture, hiking boots, or anything else that may have traces of mud or dirt on it as your goods will be inspected by the Ministry of Agriculture and Forestry before being released to you, and they may require such items to be steam cleaned or fumigated to kill off any pests or diseases. MAF inspection charges vary from $100-300 per consignment. If you have any queries about what types of goods you can import and the procedures contact the Collector of Customs at the port of destination, at the addresses below:

New Zealand Customs; tel freephone 0800 428 786.
Auckland: Box 29; tel (09) 377 6655; fax (09) 359 6732.
Auckland International Airport: Box 73003; tel (09) 275 9059; fax (09) 275 5634.
Christchurch: Level 3, Education House, 123 Victoria Street, PO Box 25105
    Christchurch 5.
Christchurch International Airport: Box 14086; tel (03) 358 0600; fax (03) 358
    0606.
Dunedin: Private Bag 1928; tel (03) 477 9251; fax (03) 477 6773.
Invercargill: Box 840; tel (03) 218 7329; fax (03) 218 7328.
Napier: Box 440; tel (06) 835 5799; fax (06) 835 1298.
Nelson: Box 66; tel (03) 548 1484; fax (03) 546 9381.

New Plymouth: Box 136; tel (06) 758 5721; fax (06) 758 1441.
Tauranga: Box 5014, Mt Maunganui; tel (07) 575 9699; fax (07) 575 0522.
Timaru: Box 64; tel (03) 688 9317; fax (03) 688 4668.
Wellington: Box 2218; tel (04) 473 6099; fax (04) 473 7370.
Whangarei: Box 873; tel (09) 438 2400; fax (09) 438 2225.

Importing Pets

Getting your pets to New Zealand is going to cost as much as getting yourself there, and require every bit as much paperwork, and a lot more vaccinations. Requirements for importing animals into New Zealand are extremely stringent. However if you fulfil all the pre-flight veterinary requirements, your animals will be able to go home with you when they arrive in New Zealand without requiring a quarantine period. There are a number of firms who specialise in the air freighting of pets (for names and addresses see below). As this involves organising an IATA approved air travel container which has to be sealed by a vet, as well as an examination immediately prior to departure, it is probably best to hand over your pets to the professionals. You will need to contact a firm at least six weeks before you depart as they will apply for an import permit from New Zealand on your behalf, and it takes at least six weeks for one to be issued and sent over. You will need to organise some of the veterinary procedures yourself as some vaccinations have to be done at least a month prior to departure, and there are a number of tests which have to be done and the results must travel with the animals. Most firms will suggest that you leave the animals with them for the night prior to departure. In most cases they will collect the pet from anywhere in the UK. The cost of all of the above is likely to be around £400-500 for a cat, £1,000 for a small dog, and £2,000 for a large dog.

Useful Addresses

Airpets Oceanic: Willowslea Farm Kennels, Spout Lane North, Stanwell Moor, Staines, Middlesex, TW19 6BW; tel 01753-685571; fax 01753-681655; e-mail: airpets@compuserve.com.
Ladyhaye Livestock Shipping: Hare Lane, Blindley Heath, Lingfield, Surrey RH7 6JB; tel 01342-832161; fax 01342-834778.
Par Air Livestock Shipping Services: Stanway, Colchester, Essex CO3 5LN; tel 01206-330332.
Pinehawk Livestock Shippers: Church Road, Carlton, Newmarket, Suffolk, CB8 9LA; tel 01223-290249; fax 01223-290 449.
Skymaster Air Cargo Ltd: Room 15, Building 305, Cargo Centre, Manchester Airport, Altrincham, Cheshire W90 5PY; tel 0161-436 2190; fax 0161-499 9312.
Transpet: 158 Chingford Mount Road London E4 9BS; tel 0181-529 0979.
Worldwide Animal Travel/Pet Emigration: 43 London Road, Brentwood, Essex CM14 4NN; tel 01277-231611 & 0181-552 5592; fax 01277-262726.
Quarantine Addresses
Ministry of Agriculture and Forestry: Animal Quarantine Division, Box 2526 Wellington; tel (04) 472 7171; fax (04) 474 4132.
Quarantine Stations:
Auckland: Custom House, PO Box 1254, Auckland; tel 09-377 3008; fax 09-307 1024.
Wellington: ASB Bank House, PO Box 12108, Wellington; tel 04-473 8996; fax 04-473 2975.

Christchurch: 14 Sir William Pickering Drive, Private Bag 4718, Christchurch; tel 03-358 1725; fax 03-364 7926.

Importing a Vehicle

If you are considering importing your car, there are a number of firms who specialise in organising the sea freighting of motor vehicles. You will obviously want to consider whether the original value of the car plus the cost of freight, port handling costs and insurance is lower than the replacement cost of the car in New Zealand. In general, European cars cost more to replace in New Zealand than the their original value plus shipping costs, assuming the vehicle qualifies for duty free entry (see below for the conditions). Japanese and Asian cars are cheaper because of the commercial importation of second hand vehicles from Japan. One source of information on second-hand car prices in New Zealand is the classified section of newspapers. You can order New Zealand motor trade magazines from *Destination New Zealand* and *New Zealand Outlook.* Some car shipping companies will also provide lists of recent New Zealand prices for common models of car.

If you are emigrating to New Zealand for the first time, you can import your car into New Zealand free of duty provided you satisfy Customs that you are importing the vehicle for your own use, that you have owned it for at least a year prior to your departure, and that you arriving in New Zealand to take up permanent residence for the first time. You will be required to sign a deed of covenant agreeing that if you sell the car or boat within two years of importing it, you will be retrospectively liable for the duty and sales tax (GST). If your car does not qualify for duty-free entry, duty is levied at 20% of purchase price for UK made vehicles, and 30% of purchase price for other foreign cars, less depreciation. The exchange rate used in calculating the New Zealand dollar value of your car will be based on the current exchange rate at the time you clear your vehicle. The costs of shipping an average size car are between £1200 and £2000 depending on the size of the car and which port in New Zealand your car is being shipped to. It usually takes about six weeks. Some companies offer a cheaper option where the vehicle is not shipped in a container, but the risks of damage or theft in transit are higher. You should arrange insurance for your vehicle, which ever option you choose. Average premiums are around £15 – £30 per £1000 insured value, which should be calculated on the New Zealand value of the car. Most companies advise that you do not pack personal belongings in the car for the journey. There is a risk of pilferage particularly if the car is not containerised during the journey and the contents of the car will have to be declared to customs by the shipping company or you will risk a fine.

Procedures for clearing your car through customs in New Zealand are as follows. The vehicle will be inspected by the Ministry of Agriculture and Forestry (MAF). All used vehicles must be steam cleaned before MAF will pass them. You can have your car commercially steam cleaned before shipping but remember to keep the receipt to show to MAF in New Zealand. Some shipping companies will steam clean your car as part of the service. MAF's object is to prevent any pests and diseases which could endanger livestock being brought in to the country and their standards therefore are stringent. We know of one recent immigrant who was required by MAF to have his car steam-cleaned a second time because the shipping company's clean had not removed mud from under the wheel arches. Your car will be required to comply with New Zealand safety regulations, some of which differ from European standards. Your vehicle must have front and rear seatbelts, and a high mounted rear stop light. It is a good idea to have these fitted before you leave because you will not be able to drive the car in New Zealand until it complies with local safety standards. Left hand drive vehicles require special import permission. Apply to the Land Transport Safety Authority (7-27 Waterloo Quay, Box 2840, Wellington; tel 04-494 8600).

Next you will need to provide documentary evidence to the collector of customs that the car is yours and if you are applying for a duty free entry, that you have owned it for at least one year prior to importing it, in the form of a dated receipt of purchase showing the date delivery was taken, registration papers, odometer details, evidence of the date on which you gave up the vehicle for shipping to New Zealand and passport showing verification of permanent residency.

You cannot drive the car legally until it has a warrant of fitness and is registered, so you will need to arrange for it to be transported from the port to the nearest vehicle inspection test centre to obtain a vehicle inspection certificate. These used to be called warrants of fitness, and in some places testing centres still advertise them as warrants. Once it has passed its warrant, you take the certificate to a post office, along with the ownership documents and the importation documents, and obtain a registration certificate, (from the nearest post office) sticker and number plates. All of this is likely to take a couple of days and cost from $450-$600 depending on whether you need to have the vehicle cleaned.

Useful Addresses

Anglo Pacific Shipping: Unit 1, Bush Industrial Estate, Standard Road, North Acton, London, NW10 6DF; tel 0181-838 8090; fax 0181-965 4954.

Cargo Forwarding Ltd: Unit 96, London Industrial Park, Roding Road, London, E6 4LS; tel 0171-474 7000; fax 0171-474 3000.

Interconti Forwarding Ltd: PO Box 1, Landmark, Main Road, Salcombe, Devon, TQ8 8LB; tel 01548 – 843191; fax 01548-843 414.

Karman Shipping Services: Unit 14, Firbank Way, Leighton Buzzard, Bedfordshire LU7 8YP; tel 01525-851545; fax 0152-5 850 996.

PSS International Removals: 8 Redcross Way, London SE1 9HR; tel 0171-407 6606; fax 0171-407 6704.

In addition, a number of shipping companies will also organise freighting your car. See Personal Shipping, Anglo Shipping, Econopak, and Double E, listed under Removals firms above.

Buying a Car

Having found out the cost of importing your car to New Zealand you may decide that the best option is to leave it behind. New cars are comparatively expensive but the second hand market in Japanese and Asian cars is competitive. In the government budget of April 1988, tariffs on importing vehicles was lifted, further reducing the cost of imported cars (but badly affecting the New Zealand motor assembly industry). European cars tend to be quite pricey and are can be difficult to get parts for. Familiar models may go under slightly different names in New Zealand. There is no domestically owned brand, but most cars are locally assembled. The government is reducing tariffs resulting in less locally assembled cars and more new and second hand imported vehicles. Two New Zealand motor industry websites may be useful in finding a car are www.autonet.co.nz, and www.autovillage.co.nz.

Second Hand Cars

Buying second hand is a viable option. Cars have to be sold warranted as road worthy. A second hand vehicle dealer is required by law to inform the buyer honestly about the vehicle and its history, and the car must be of the model, year, and odometer mileage displayed. The Fair Trading Act operates to protect buyers, and under the act it's not necessary to prove that a certain individual had been misled, only that a typical consumer could have been deceived. There are a number of companies offering pre-purchase vehicle checks including the AA who will check a car without charge if you are a member. A second hand vehicle can be repossessed if that car was used as security for a loan by its previous owner, and the loan not repaid. The Motor Vehicles Security Register (162-164 Grafton Road, Private Bag 92061, Auckland Mail Centre; tel freephone 0800 909 777; fax 09-912 7787) can check that this is not the case with your car.

Car Hire

If you want to organise car hire before you arrive, there are agencies who will arrange your rental for you with a New Zealand company. For example, Visit the World (21 Norman Road, St Leonards-on-Sea, East Sussex; tel 01424-722152; fax 01424-722304). It is also possible to rent a car in advance through an international rental firm, such as Avis, Hertz or Budget. Hirers in New Zealand must be at least 21 years of age and will need a current international, UK or New Zealand driving licence. Useful websites include Avis www.avislease.co.nz, and AA Host Rentals at www.aa.org.nz.

Insurance

You are not legally required to get insurance in New Zealand, however it is sensible to get at least third party coverage. If you are involved in an accident and cause harm to another driver, you will not be personally liable for the injuries you do to them because of the no-faults compensation for personal injury provided by the Government through the Accident Compensation Corporation (See Chapter Four, *Daily Life*). But if you write off their car and you have no insurance then, like anywhere else in the world, you will be paying the bill. The premiums for full insurance coverage vary according to your age (under 25s pay a lot more), gender (some firms offer females a discount because they are statistically less likely to have accidents) and driving history. A no claims record entitles you to discounted premiums. You should bring evidence of your claims record with you because a claim free UK or European insurance record will qualify you for the bonus. Some firms may not be prepared to insure you until you have a New Zealand drivers licence . See Chapter Four *Daily Life* for requirements for getting a New Zealand drivers licence.

Daily Life

One of the disconcerting aspects of emigrating to a country where the locals speak the same language is that there is a tendency to underestimate the cultural differences. New Zealand, for all its superficial reminders of England, is a foreign country. Some of the streets may be named after English counties and the towns after British soldiers, but the daily lives of New Zealanders are very different from the lives of people in the UK. It is obviously not possible to explain all the peculiarities of life in New Zealand in one short chapter and individuals are unlikely in any case to experience any major form of culture shock. This chapter therefore aims to prepare you for some of the main, every day differences between New Zealand and the UK.

The Languages

New Zealanders speak their own distinctive version of English. Newcomers may be forgiven for thinking that New Zealanders use one vowel sound, although locals do not seem to have any problems distinguishing between words. 'New Zealand' as pronounced by the locals sounds like 'Nu Zilind'. As well as the subtle distinctions between vowel sounds, further problems for the newcomer arise from the rapid pace at which New Zealanders speak. Probably more of an obstacle than the accent to understanding New Zealanders is the use of uniquely Kiwi expressions. A 'dairy' is a corner store (open till late and selling most of the essentials), a 'crib' in the South Island or 'bach' in the North is a holiday home on the coast or beside a lake. Being asked to 'bring a plate' to a party means you are being asked to bring a plate of food along to share with others. BYO stands for 'bring your own' alcohol – either to a party or to a restaurant. BYO restaurants have a licence to serve alcohol, but not to sell it. They are usually cheaper than 'licensed' restaurants, but they will charge a corkage fee per bottle (of about $2). To 'charge an arm and a leg' is to demand a high price for something. Some of the slang is similar to Australian, for example 'pommy' for an English person, 'bush' for forest, 'shout' for buying a round in a pub. Additionally, a number of Maori expressions have become part of everyday usage, for example *Pakeha* for a person of European descent.

The *Dictionary of New Zealand English* (published by Oxford University Press 1998), might prove useful to save you any confusion. This Dictionary has been hailed as a celebration of the New Zealand language. However, it carries a £90 price tag in the UK; or it can be bought in New Zealand for $150.

Maori is the other official language although it is not in everyday use in most regions. Official signs are bilingual as are Government documents. The number of Maori speakers is growing and there is an active campaign to preserve this language (*Te Reo* in Maori). Pronunciation of Maori is not difficult to learn even if at first glance some of the place names seem impossibly complex. It is a good skill to master though, as correct pronunciation of Maori is a sign of courtesy and also indicates that as a newcomer, you are prepared to integrate into the local community. The greeting *'Kia Ora'* which extends good health to the other person, may be repeated back with the same words. Generally Maori words have a phonetic spelling. The language had no written form before European settlement.

The most comprehensive attempt to produce a written form was by a missionary, Reverend Williams.

There are five vowel sounds each of which may be short or long:

short a:	like u in 'but'	long a:	like a in 'father'
short e:	like e in 'pet'	long e:	like ai in 'fairy'
short i	like i in 'pit'	long i	like ee in 'meet'
short o	like or in 'port'	long o	like ore in 'pore'
short u	like u in 'put'	long u	like oo in 'moon'

Diphthongs (double vowel sounds) retain the sound of the second vowel clearly. Consonants are as in English with the following exceptions:

wh	is pronounced f; hence 'Whangarei' is pronounced 'Fong – a – ray'
ng	is like ng in the middle of 'singer, ie the g is never hard
r	is slightly rolled

Word stress is rather complicated and you would do better to learn by listening to a Maori speaker. Generally every syllable is stressed evenly. It is worth noting that many Pakeha pronounce Maori words, particularly common place names, embarrassingly badly. Do not follow their example. In recent years radio and TV announcers have been learning to pronounce Maori correctly and in general, their pronunciation is a reasonable guide.

Schools and Education

The New Zealand education system is dominated by the state sector which educates 95% of the population. The Ministry of Education spends $5 billion yearly on education, over 16% of the national budget. Schooling is compulsory from ages six through to sixteen, although most New Zealand children start school at the age of five. The school year has three terms, beginning in early February and running through to December with holidays in May and August. Four term school years are being trialled at some state schools. Schooling is largely free although state schools are beginning to charge 'optional' fees to cover extra equipment and facilities.

There is no tradition of streaming into academic and not-so-academic schools, so while the average standard of education at a New Zealand high school is probably higher than at its equivalent, the British comprehensive school, the academic standards achieved by the brightest pupils are not as advanced. Generally New Zealand students do well in international tests, particularly in reading comprehension. Their mathematics skills compare less favourably particularly with the standards achieved by Japanese and other Asian students. Most schools have good cultural, academic and sporting facilities. Even inner city schools have extensive playing fields. There is a strong tradition of team sports, (not just rugby although soccer used to be banned at some particularly strong rugby schools lest the boys be lured away from chasing the oval ball to 'inferior' versions of football) and many state schools offer outdoor activity programmes where pupils learn abseiling, canoeing, and go hiking in New Zealand's national parks.

Schools are becoming ethnically more diverse particularly in Auckland with its substantial Polynesian population. Increasingly the new immigrants are Asian. As a result foreign language instruction which used to be predominantly in French and German is being replaced by Japanese and other Asian languages, reflecting the change in focus in New Zealand's trade from Europe to the Pacific rim. The language of instruction, except in a few Maori language immersion schools, remains English.

In general New Zealand state schools are safe and well-disciplined learning environments. Nevertheless, some parents choose alternatives to the state system for their children. Most private schools have religious links, either to Anglican or Catholic churches. Many Anglican schools offer a single-sex, English style boarding education and a traditional approach to learning and discipline. They manage to be more English than their models or perhaps just a few decades out of date as they are both stricter and more spartan than independent schools in the UK. Fees for Independent or Private schools vary from $1,800-$7,700 per year for primary schools, and $4,160 to $9,500 for secondary schools. Boarding fees are not included in these fees, and they range from $4,000 to $7,300 per year. A number of state schools also offer boarding facilities. Usually these are rural schools whose students come from a widely dispersed population so boarding is the only practical way of overcoming the distance from home to school. Not all state boarding schools are in the country. Nelson College and Christchurch Boys are city schools with a long tradition of providing a state boarding school education. As state schools their boarding fees tend to be cheaper than the private sector.

At time of print, there is such a dearth of primary and secondary school teachers that a department has been created in the Ministry of Education to encourage teachers to come to New Zealand to work. Contact TeachNZ for more information (TeachNZ, Ministry of Education, PO Box 1666, Wellington; tel +64 4-473 5544; fax +64 4-471 4432).

The Structure of the Education System

Preschool: This is divided into playcentres which tend to be run by volunteer groups of parents, and cater for children from a young age, kindergartens, usually for the over twos, and private crèches catering for anything that walks, waddles or wees. Kindergartens are usually free while playcentres may charge a nominal sum. Crèches on the other hand can be quite expensive, although the government subsidises the running costs of all registered childcare centres with qualified staff. More than 90% of four-year-olds are in some kind of preschool programme. A growing number of children, Pakeha and Maori, attend *Kohanga Reo* or Maori language nests where they learn *taha maori* (Maori language and culture).

Primary: Primary schools cater for children aged five to ten years old. The curriculum includes reading, writing, science, mathematics, and social studies. Teaching standards are high. The teaching of reading skills is particularly strong and New Zealand reading programmes are being copied in British and North American schools.

Intermediate: Most children spend two years at intermediate school between primary and high school. Some primary schools however, are beginning to keep their senior students for a further two years as the interlude is thought to be disruptive rather than helpful. In country regions, 'area' schools have always included years six and seven (usually called forms one and two). At intermediate school pupils begin studying foreign languages (traditionally French, now increasingly Maori), and move between specialist teachers rather than being taught by one person for every subject.

Secondary: Secondary education begins in the eighth year of school, at around age 13. In pre-recession New Zealand when jobs were easy to find it was quite common for students to leave school as soon as it was legal at age 15, but retention rates have improved as the economy has declined. The core curriculum consists of English, Maths, General Science, Music, Arts and Craft, Social Studies and Physical Education, all of which are compulsory for the first two years. Students sit national examinations, School certificate at the end of their fifth form year (the third year of secondary education) and University Bursary or the more academic 'Scholarship' at the end of their final year.

Further Education

Further education is divided into three areas, universities, polytechnics and colleges of education (teacher training colleges).

Universities: New Zealand universities offer degree programmes in a similar range of subjects to British universities. Most bachelor degrees are three year courses with an option of taking a four year honours programme. There are seven universities, located in the four main cities and three smaller regional towns. Standards are uniform, none of the seven being particularly older or more established, Auckland's size probably makes it the leader in more fields but 20,000 plus students on a crowded inner city campus has its downside as well. Teaching in arts subjects is mostly done in large lecture streams with weekly tutorials of about a dozen students. There are now so many students attending universities, that in some of the unrestricted courses, there are not enough seats in the lecture theatres and some students try to take notes sitting on the stairs, or even outside the door. Admission procedures vary depending on the institution and the course. Some high demand courses such as medicine, law and business administration have restricted entry usually based on University Bursary results. Other courses are open to anyone who meets the general university entrance requirement.

Polytechnics: As the name suggests New Zealand polytechnics remain by and large the specialists in technical and applied subjects. There is less cross over with universities in subject area, although some programmes (for example business studies and accounting) can be studied either in a polytechnic for a certificate or diploma or in a longer degree programme at university. The majority of polytechnic students however either study part-time while working or are on short full-time courses.

Student Fees: Tuition fees for New Zealand students, which used to be free, now cost between NZ $2,400-$12,000 for a full time year, depending on the course and the institution. Foreign fees can be five times that of domestic students, and range from $10,000-$25,000 for an undergraduate course. Reductions are available for New Zealand students from low income families. The possibility of fees being doubled in the next few years has been recently mooted by a task force, looking into tertiary education.

Student Allowances: Full time students from families whose annual income is less than $27,872 are eligible for the means tested student maintenance grants, called student allowances. These students must have permanent residency to be eligible. The amount of the allowance decreases on a sliding scale the more a student's parents earn, and the allowances cease with a parental income of over $45,760. Students 25 and over are not subject to the family means test.

Student Loans: Permanent resident students who do not qualify for student allowances may borrow money through the government run students loans scheme to pay for maintenance and tuition. You can either be a full or part time student, but your course must last 12 weeks or longer. For full time students, you may borrow the amount of your compulsory fees, plus $1,000 for course related costs and up to $150 per week. Part time students may borrow the amount of their compulsory fees plus the proportion of the $1,000 course costs (the length of their course as a proportion of a full time course). All loans incur a $50 administration fee each year. You are charged daily interest on the loan; in 1997 the rate of interest was 8.2%. You can pay the loan back at any time, until you earn $14,560, when the unpaid loan becomes a compulsory repayment.

Foreigners at New Zealand Universities

Foreign students (that is, non-New Zealand residents) get hit even harder in the wallet than New Zealand students. Fees vary across courses and by university, from $9500 per annum for an arts or humanities course, to $18,000-25,000 for medicine or dentistry. For information on studying at New Zealand universities or polytechnics as a foreign student, contact the Trade Development Board at the New Zealand High Commission, (2nd Floor, New Zealand House 80 Haymarket, London SW1Y 4TQ; tel 0171-973 0380).

International Schools

There are no schools in New Zealand specifically set up for international students. However some schools offer senior students preparation for the International Baccalaureate which is an entrance qualification for most European universities. To find out more about this contact the Trade Development Board (see address above).

Useful Addresses

Ministry of Education: 45 Pipitea Street, PO Box 1666, Thorndon, Wellington; tel (04) 473 5544.

Schools offering the International Baccalaureate:

Kristin School: PO Box 87, Albany, 1331, Auckland Wellington; tel (09) 415 9566; fax (09) 415 8495; e-mail: kristin@kristin.school.nz. Co-educational private boarding and day school.
Scots College: PO Box 15 064, Wellington; tel (04) 388 0850; fax (04)388 2887. Boys only, private boarding and day school.
Waitaki Girls College: Trent Street, Box 42 Oamaru; tel (03) 434 8429; fax (03) 434 6783. Girls only, state boarding and day school.

Media and Communications

Newspapers

New Zealanders read as many newspapers as the British and a lot more than North Americans. Unfortunately the standard of the newspapers does not justify this dedication to newsprint. Regional papers were established last century when provincial government was more powerful than national government and communication networks between the scattered European settlements were poor. These regional papers have all survived and as a result New Zealand has a high number of daily newspapers, but there is no truly national paper. The apparently national *New Zealand Herald* is not widely circulated in the South Island. Most of the major papers are of the size and quality of a large provincial paper and betray their provincial loyalties by their selection of news stories. There is only one tabloid style newspaper, *The Truth* which appears weekly and does not approach the shock, horror, sheer awful appeal of its British counterparts.

Business news is provided by the *National Business Review*, also a weekly which covers politics and international news as well. A growing trend is giveaway suburban newspapers.

Specialist news agents in the main city stock overseas newspapers but they are expensive and usually arrive some days late, particularly European editions. Anyone wishing to keep up with the news from the UK can do so through the *International Express*, a weekly digest of the London Daily and Sunday Expresses widely available in Australasia. In New Zealand it is obtainable from Gordon and Gotch (2 Carr Road. Mt. Roskill, Auckland; tel 09 625 3000; fax 09-625 3030) and is printed in Auckland. Another alternative for those truly homesick of news from home are the overseas editions of *The Telegraph* or *The Guardian*. These are weekly editions of the major news stories from these and other papers, available either from newsagents or on subscription. Foreign newspapers including British ones can be read on the internet.

Main Newspapers

The New Zealand Herald: Conservative in tone and appearance. Based in Auckland and news content reflects this, despite its name. Circulation 221,047; Website: www.nzherald.co.nz.

The Dominion: Political focus as might be expected a newspaper based in the capital city. Used to be a liberal, unpartisan scrutineer of government, has become a convert to neo-liberal economic dogma. Circulation 70,310.

The Evening Post: Also Wellington based, more regional news than *The Dominion*, surprisingly good comment and arts content. Circulation 63,622; Website: www.evpost.co.nz.

The Christchurch Press: Distributed throughout top half of South Island. Good coverage of Canterbury region news, less so of national and international stories. Circulation 98,071. Website: www.press.co.nz.

The Otago Daily Times: Dunedin based. Circulation 43,352. Website: www.odt.co.nz.

There are two Sunday papers, the *Sunday Star Times* and *Sunday News*, which are published by Independent Newspapers Ltd and are distributed throughout the country.

Magazines

Over 2,300 magazines are available in New Zealand on a regular basis, but only about 60 of these are New Zealand titles. The others include international news magazines such as *Time*, *The Economist*, and *Newsweek*. Local political comment is provided by the *New Zealand Listener* and the *Political Review*. The *Listener* also carries TV and radio listings, as does the *TV Guide*, which has the biggest circulation of any New Zealand magazine. Other very popular magazines are *Woman's Day* and the *New Zealand Women's Weekly*, a venerable survivor found in every doctor's surgery. Its heyday may be over now that putting the British royals on the cover leads to indifference rather than sales. *More* magazine is an upmarket women's magazine which has surprisingly good articles and a no-nonsense practical feminist line. Less mainstream feminist comment can be found in *Broadsheet*. A number of glossy lifestyle magazines have sprung up in the last decade. Of particular note is *Metro*, the Auckland city magazine. Reading *Metro* will help the newcomer understand why the rest of the country can't stand Auckland. Metro's stablemate aimed at readers in the rest of the country is *North and South*. Both are liberal on political issues, conservative on social welfare issues and support the economic liberalisation programme launched by the government in the 1980s. *New Zealand Cuisine* is dedicated to fine food and wine. There are a surprising number of literary magazines, apparently thriving, despite small circulations. The most well established of these is the Christchurch based *Landfall*.

Magazines exist for just about every sporting pursuit. Also popular are do-it-yourself and home improvement magazines. Many New Zealand magazines, including real estate and leisure periodicals can be ordered through Consyl Publishing Ltd. (3 Buckhurst Road, Bexhill-on-Sea, East Sussex TN40 1QF; tel 01424-223111; 24 hour credit card sales tel 01424-223 161).

Television

There are four terrestrial channels available in New Zealand. TV1 and TV2 are publicly owned and run, and are funded through TV licence fees. TV1 broadcasts much sport and current affairs, while TV2 shows more a light entertainment. TV3 and newly established Channel 4 are privately run, and broadcast both factual and entertainment programmes. All the terrestrial channels have advertising. There are a few regional TV channels, and TAB channel, which broadcasts horse-racing. Cable TV is still in its infancy. Satellite TV is represented by SKY, another Rupert Murdoch subsidiary, offering five channels which consist of two movie channels, a documentary channel, and sports and news channels. The news channel includes the BBC and CNN and may be best option for catching up with the world news. The television news on TV1 and TV3 is improving in its coverage of international affairs, drawing on BBC, ABC CNN and other news sources, but still remains quite parochial. New Zealand TV news has unfortunately opted for a poor imitation of American local news programmes. The graphics and visual effects are sophisticated, but the news analysis and sometimes camerawork are not. Unsurprisingly, when the average item does not exceed a minute and half in length, in-depth analysis of stories is rare. On TV1 there are BBC News and other BBC programmes during the night which can be recorded for later viewing. The content of the four terrestrial channels provides a mixed diet of the best of the BBC, popular American sit-coms and Australian and home grown soaps. Every household with a television set must pay the Public Broadcasting Fee (currently set at $110 per household per year). This is collected by New Zealand On Air (freephone 0800 733 000; Website: www.nzonair.govt.nz).

Radio

Radio New Zealand runs a network of local stations which are funded through advertising revenue and offer a mixed diet of middle of the road popular music, talk back, news and sports. It also runs two non-commercial nationally broadcast stations, the National Programme and Concert FM which are funded through the TV licence fees. The National Programme is broadly equivalent to the UK's Radio 4. Its morning news show, *Morning Report*, is an excellent source of news and comment on political and economic issues. The Concert programme broadcasts classical music and information programmes. There is a large local private radio sector: 46 AM and 84 FM commercial stations, including student radio, Maori language radio and community access radio. Local and national radio stations in New Zealand broadcast on 110 AM and 332 FM frequencies, so there is a great choice of radio programmes. There is also a National Radio Sports Frequency. However many stations, especially FM radio, have a limited range due to the mountainous terrain of the country. The BBC World Service is broadcast by an Auckland-based private radio station with frequencies in Auckland and Wellington. It plans to extend its coverage into other main centres in the near future.

Post

Postal services are handled by New Zealand Post which has a monopoly on letter delivery up to 80 grams in weight. Parcel delivery is also provided by private courier firms. Domestic delivery is once daily, usually mid-morning. There is a network of more than 1000 post offices throughout the country, the majority of which are postal agencies which provide other services as well. A further 2900 outlets sell stamps.

There are two classes of mail, Fast Post which promises next day delivery anywhere in the country and ordinary post. The standard cost of a fast post letter is 80c and for an ordinary rate letter, 40c. At time of print, blue aerogrammes to the UK cost $1.00, and an airmail letter to the UK cost $1.80. For customer enquiries and up to date charges, call NZ Post on freephone 0800 501 501.

Post offices offer a poste restante service free of charge, that is, they will hold all letters to you for three months awaiting your collection. However, parcels over 2kg held in this way cost $2.50 per week.

Telephones

For information about having a telephone installed in your house, see Chapter Three, *Setting Up Home*. New Zealand Telecom has been overhauling the phone system since 1990, introducing standard seven digit numbers throughout the country. Most of the chaos caused by the change is now over, although the New Zealand Number Update Desk is still running and can be contacted on 0155. The international code for New Zealand is 64. There are five area codes for the different regions of the country, 09 for Auckland and northwards, 07 for the Waikato and central North Island area, 06 for the southern half of the North Island, 04 for the Wellington region, and 03 for the South Island. As in the UK, free phone numbers start with 0800 (through Telecom) and Clear freephone numbers start with 0508. Phone boxes are well distributed but most are now card phones which can be irritating if you do not have a card handy. They come in $5, $10, $20, or $50 denominations and can be bought from bookshops, dairies or Post Offices. Local calls from a coinbox or card phone cost 50c for the call. Very few coin phones exist as do some of the original model payphones which have a button marked A on the front which you press when the call is connected. In the cities, card and coin phones can usually be found cohabiting, and in some places, credit card phones as well.

Cars and Motoring

Compared with European motorways, New Zealand's highway system is uncongested, although per head of population, New Zealanders own as many cars as the Italians or the Swiss and slightly more than the British. Older models are a common sight, a hang-over from the days when new cars were very expensive so people drove their old car for a long time. Most of the older cars are British or American makes. Modern cars tend to be Japanese makes. Because of the absence of heavy traffic there is not much of a network of multi-lane motorways. Most state highways are single carriageway and there are no tolls. Multi-lane motorways carry traffic into and out of the four main cities and through parts of Auckland and Wellington. Congestion on these stretches during rushhour is occasionally a problem, but nothing compared to traffic jams in European or North American cities. To relieve problems associated with rushhour, many firms use 'glide time', whereby your daily work hours start when you arrive, rather than at a set time.

Driving outside the main cities is usually a pleasant experience. The roads are uncluttered and the scenery superb. The weather is often more of an obstacle to getting to your destination than other drivers. Flooding or heavy snow falls only occasionally block main routes, particularly the roads through the volcanic plateau in the central North Island and the cross alpine routes in South Island. There are signs at the start of tricky stretches of road indicating which routes are open. In general the signs indicating distances and routes on the highway system are less frequent than in Europe (Although to be fair there is usually only one main route to any destination). Junctions are not as well designed, roundabouts are less common and tend to be poorly signposted.

New Zealand drivers have a reputation for being fast and rather aggressive, but the advent of speed cameras and other traffic safety programmes are tending to change this attitude. It is easy to see why you might be tempted to drive well over the speed limit when there is no other traffic in sight, let alone any sign of the law. City drivers are less considerate than in Europe. It is rare for people to give way to allow cars from side roads to join the main stream of traffic, again perhaps because there are usually fewer congestion problems. Nor do New Zealand drivers willingly move over into the slow lane to let faster traffic past. Unfortunately driving in New Zealand is not very safe. It has one of the worst accident records per head of population in the developed world. About 600 people die on the roads each year, and the 'road toll' often appears on the national TV news. The government is trying to improve the statistics by targeting the worst offending group, namely young men who drink and drive, so be aware that the blood alcohol limits are strictly enforced.

Driving Regulations

The maximum speed on highways and motorways is 100 km and in built up areas 50 km. Speed cameras are being introduced at various places in cities and on country roads. New Zealanders drive on the left hand side of the road, and the rules of the road are similar to British driving regulations, but there are several differences; at crossroads traffic turning left must give way to on-coming vehicles turning right, it is illegal to park facing the wrong way, and safety belts must be worn by the driver and all passengers. The sequence of the traffic lights is different from Britain, the lights change straight from red to green, then amber followed by red again. Standard international road signs are being introduced. One sign which may be unfamiliar is LSZ enclosed by a red circle, indicating a limited speed zone in which the motorist should slow down to allow for children or other traffic. This is frequently used when state highways pass through small towns.

As noted above, drink-driving regulations are strictly enforced. The limit is the same as in Britain, 80 mls per 100 mls of blood or less than two pints of beer for the average adult male. Drivers under twenty years old have a lower limit: 30 mls per

100 mls of blood. Police officers are able to stop motorists at random and breath test them. The maximum penalty is a $1500 fine and six months in prison. Repeated offenders can lose their licence. Seat belts must be worn in the front of cars and in the back if fitted. Helmets are compulsory for motor cyclists and bicycle riders.

Breakdowns and Accidents

The annual national road death toll of 600, over twice the number per 100,000 people as in Britain, includes many caused by head on collisions. These are more likely to lead to fatalities and are partly due to the lack of a median strip and crash barriers on New Zealand highways. Another factor, particularly in accidents involving young people, is alcohol. The Government has recently made the driving test much more stringent and introduced restricted licences for the under 20s in an effort to improve road safety.

The New Zealand Automobile Association (POB 1794, Wellington; tel 04-470 9999) runs a similar service to its operation in the UK and can be called at any time (freephone 0800 500 222) to assist with mechanical difficulties or breakdowns. Members of the UK AA and RAC have reciprocal rights to use AA services. It costs around $50 per year to join. The number for AA insurance is 0800 500 213. If you are involved in an accident, you must contact the police. (The emergency number is 111) Unfortunately New Zealand highways are often not well provided with call boxes or emergency telephones.

Driving Licence

A British or International Drivers Licence is valid for 12 months after arrival in New Zealand. At the end of this period visitors must apply for a New Zealand licence which involves sitting a written and oral test, and then an interview with a police officer to obtain exemption from taking the practical test. Drivers under the age of twenty are eligible only for a restricted licence and are not allowed to drive after dark. For more information regarding British licenses, contact the Driver and Vehicle Licensing Agency in Swansea (tel 01792-772 134.)

Car Registration

Cars must be registered with the Post Office and have a current Vehicle Inspection Certificate (VIC). They must also have a Vehicle Identification Number (VIN), an identification scheme to try and cut down on vehicle theft. At the time of writing, the cost of registering an ordinary motorcar was $158.00 per year. First time registration for a new car costs approximately $300 including new number plates. Cars can be registered at any Post Office shop. Re-registration forms are sent out automatically. Most garages offer VIC testing (Warrants of Fitness). It costs about $25. New cars need a warrant every year for the first six years and then six monthly after that.

Useful Addresses
Land Transport Safety Authority Head Office: 4th Floor, 7-27 Waterloo Quay, Box
    2840, Wellington; tel (04) 494 8600; fax (04) 494 8601. For information on
    vehicle warranties, vehicle and driver licensing call freephone 0800 108 809.
The New Zealand Automobile Association: PO Box 1794, Wellington; tel 04-470
    9999 or freephone 0800 500 222.

Transport

Air

As the major population centres are many miles apart, getting between cities by road or rail is time consuming. Air travel is a popular alternative. There are two main internal airlines: the state owned airline, Air New Zealand and the Australian airline Ansett. The two airlines operate out of separate terminals on the same sites in the main cities. The chief benefit from competition was to persuade Air New Zealand to spruce up its terminals which were basic to say the least: Wellington airport was originally a World War Two air hanger, with an appropriately utilitarian atmosphere.

Fare structures between the two airlines are similar. Ansett offers more discounts, while Air New Zealand offers a larger network, incorporating a number of smaller airlines, Eagle Air in the North Islands, Nelson Air, which covers the top of the South Island, and Mount Cook airlines (mostly tourist routes). A variety of discounted fares are available if you book ahead. Air New Zealand offers no frills flights, called City Savers on the main routes. There are also special deals on late night flights or flights during off peak hours. It is worth ringing Air New Zealand or Ansett to find out about what is available. Holders of the International Student Identity Card, can get a 50% discount on standby travel. On the major routes this may entail waiting around in the airport until a flight has spare capacity, but it rarely involves more than a couple of hours delay unless it is a particularly busy period like the start of the school holidays.

If you are visiting New Zealand before deciding whether to migrate permanently, you could look at purchasing a discount air pass. Ansett New Zealand offers a three sector pass for $450 or an eight sector pass for $1140 which can be purchased inside or outside of New Zealand, but if you are buying it inside the country, GST of 12.5% is payable. (The full economy fare per sector is around $250 so the passes offer substantial discounts) Air New Zealand offers a similar air pass as does Mt Cook airlines, but the airpass for Mt Cook must be purchased outside the country.

Trains

The train network is not exactly comprehensive. There are eight train routes around the country and only a few trains to most major destinations each day. Trains cost about the same as the equivalent journey by bus, although there are some faster services which are more expensive. Many of the routes are chiefly designed with tourists in mind, for example the transalpine express from Christchurch to Greymouth, across the Southern Alps. Reservations are advisable during the summer on popular tourist routes. The national reservations telephone number is NZ Rail (0800 802 802), and enquiry line is (0800 801 070).

Coaches

Bus services (usually called coaches) between major cities provide a much more frequent service than the trains. There are three main companies, Newmans, Mt Cook, and InterCity. Mt Cook operates only in the South Island, and Newmans only in the North. InterCity is a subsidiary of NZ Rail. The national reservations numbers are Mt Cook (0800 800 287), Newmans (0800 733500) or (09-309 9738), and InterCity (0800 468 372) or (03-379 9020).

City Transport

Public transport in most of the major cities does not provide a sufficiently comprehensive network to replace the private car as the major method of getting to work. Because urban population densities are lower than in Europe this does not yet produce enormous pollution and congestion problems. However inner city parking is expensive. Commuter rail networks in Auckland and Wellington replace the car for a small percentage of the working population.

Taxis

Taxis in New Zealand can be found at taxi stands or ordered by phone. They do not drive around waiting to be hired, so there is no point trying to flag one down even if it looks empty. The fares are all metered so you do not need to agree a price with the driver before setting off. In many cities minivans run a taxi service from the airport into any destination in the central city. This is almost always a cheaper option than a taxi, although slightly less convenient as you may not be the first person to be dropped off. They are also often referred to as airport shuttles.

The Inter-island Ferry

There are two types of ferry which cross Cook Strait linking the North and South Islands: the Interislander ferry, and a high speed catamaran called The Lynx. The Interislander offers four to five ferry crossings a day, with a roll on, roll off service for cars. The trip takes about three hours. The standard cost for a small family car is $165, although there are discounts (between 15 and 50%) for travelling during the off peak season (non-holiday periods). The fare for foot passengers is $46 standard, and $30 off peak. The North Island departure point is Aotea Quay in Wellington, and in the South Island, Picton Ferry Terminal. The ferries include such amenities as movie theatres, bars and quite adequate cafeterias. If it is a bad crossing though, probably the last thing on your mind will be food. The Cook Strait is a particularly rough stretch of water.

The Lynx catamaran operates three crossings each way daily between December and March, and the crossing time is reduced to one hour 45 minutes. The single fare for adults is $59, and one way cost for cars is $190. The departure points are the same as for the Interislander.

Useful Addresses

Air New Zealand: cnr Customs and Albert Streets, Private Bag 92007, Auckland; tel (09) 366 2400; fax (09) 275 5927; Website: www.airnz.co.nz.

Ansett New Zealand: PO Box 4168, Auckland; tel (09) 3096235; fax (09) 309 6434.

InterCity Coachlines: CPO Box 3625, Auckland; tel 0800 468 372, or (09) 639 0500; fax (09) 639 0503.

Mount Cook Line: Airline/Landline, PO Box 4644, Christchurch; tel (reservations) 0800-800287 or Auckland (09) 309 5395; fax (09) 275 9594; internet:www.clearfield.co.nz/mount_cook/mc_home for flights and www.mtcook.co.nz/landlines for coach trips.

Newmans Route Services: PO Box 90 – 821, Auckland; tel (09)309 9738; fax (09) 302 1614; Website: www.discover.co.nz/Newmans/nwmcoach.

Tranz Rail Ltd: Private Bag, Wellington, tel (reservations) 0800-802 802; Website: www.waikato.ac.nz/nz/rail.

New Zealand Tourism Board: New Zealand House, Haymarket, London SW1Y
  4TQ; tel 0171-930 1662. Information line: 0839-300 900 (calls charged at 49p
  per minute).
The Interislander: Tranz Rail Ltd, Private Bag, Wellington; tel (reservations) 0800
  – 802 802; fax (04) 498 3721 or 0800 101 525; Website: www.aa.org.nz/ferry.
The Lynx: Tranz Rail Ltd, Private Bag Wellington; tel 0800 802 802 or (04) 498
  3000; fax (04) 498 3090.

Banks and Finance

New Zealand's banking system is amongst the most advanced in the world and is
very convenient to use. Many banks either have or are moving towards computer
systems which will allow the overnight clearance of cheques. A visit to the bank
no longer need involve any paperwork as most transactions are done electronically
using money cards with PINs to access accounts. Banking hours are Monday to
Friday, 9.00 am to 4.30 pm, although on Tuesdays some banks start at 9.30am
because of staff training. You can use automatic tellers (cash machines) at any time
to transfer money between accounts, and order statements or cheque books. Your
money card, known as an ATM card (automatic teller machine card), also
functions as a direct debit card for EFT-POS transactions. EFT-POS stands for
Electronic Fund Transfer at the Point Of Sale. It is the equivalent of Switch in the
UK. Most major retailers offer the EFT-POS service. Cheques are still a common
method of payment despite the advances in electronic banking.

   One major difference between New Zealand and the UK is that New Zealand
banks do not issue cheque guarantee cards. The onus is on the receiver of the
cheque to make sure it is not fraudulent. Retailers usually require ID for cheques
in the form of a credit card and often take your name and address when you pay by
cheque. Credit cards are popular in New Zealand, Mastercard and Visa being the
most widely used. Most bills are paid through standing orders (called direct credit)
and your wages will probably likewise be paid into your account directly. Most
banks provide telebanking facilities, in which you can order most banking
transactions by phone.

Banking costs
Account holders pay bank fees for their accounts. There is a monthly transaction
fee of between $2 and $5, but exemptions may apply for students and the elderly.
There is also a fee for individual transactions on top of the monthly fee, but some
banks exempt the first few entries each month. Charges are made for electronic
transfers and automatic payments. The government charges a resident withholding
tax which is currently 19.5% of your interest.

Bank Accounts

Most people open an account with one of the following retail banks: the Bank of
New Zealand, the Australia New Zealand Banking Group (ANZ), the National
Bank of New Zealand, WestpacTrust, (an amalgamation of Westpac Banking
Corporation and Trustbank, which formerly operated as local district trusts), and
Countrywide, (an amalgamation of former building societies). The ASB, formerly
the Auckland Savings Bank, now operates nationwide. Branches of foreign banks
also operate but the banks listed above have an extensive network of banking
outlets developed as result of New Zealand's scattered population.

   Some of these banks have branches in the UK and one option to consider is opening an account with them before you leave for New Zealand. There is a generally a fee for this service and a minimum deposit requirement. An example is the Auckland Savings Bank (c/o Commonwealth Bank of Australia, 85 Queen Victoria Street, London EC4V 4HA; tel 0171-710 3990). Their website is at www.asbbank.co.nz. One advantage of opening an account before you arrive in New Zealand is that it solves the problem of transferring money: you simply arrange for a telexed transfer to your new account. The alternatives to telexing money directly to a New Zealand bank account are outlined in the section on *International Money Transfers* below. Opening an account once you arrive in New Zealand does not take long, but there are a few hitches for the new arrival. Some banks require proof of a regular income before allowing you to open a cheque account, even if you have deposited money with them. You should be issued immediately with an ATM card, which will allow you to withdraw money from a bank or an automatic teller machine. To facilitate opening an account in New Zealand, it is a good idea to bring a letter of introduction from your UK bank. Both the ANZ and BNZ have London offices, but do not open NZ accounts from there. The government transaction duty on credit card accounts (5% of all purchases) was withdrawn on 1 April, 1998.

Investment Advice: Many expatriates tend to seek advice on money related matters such as employee benefits, retirement income funding, personal investments and savings. Companies specialising in providing worldwide financial services include *Brewin Dolphin Securities* of 5 Giltspur Street, London EC1A 9BD (tel 0171-248 4400; e-mail rlindsay-stewart@brewin.co.uk) and *The International Benefits Practice (Aon Consulting)*, Minet House, 66 Prescot Street. London E1 8HG (tel 0171-680 5508; fax 0171 702 1072).

Banking Ombudsman

In New Zealand, there is an independent, neutral person who can investigate complaints relating to banking services, such as mistakes or negligence. There is no charge for the use of the ombudsman. However, people should try to take their complaint direct to the organisation concerned in the first place.

International Money Transfers

There are no foreign exchange controls on shifting money out of New Zealand. Getting money to New Zealand is most quickly achieved through a money wire or a telegraphic transfer. You can either do this through a specialist money-wiring company such as American Express or Western Union, or through the banks. The specialist companies cost more but the process is much faster, less than 15 minutes. Through the banks it usually takes a couple of days but the cost is about half the amount charged by wiring companies.

Money

New Zealand has a decimal money system using dollars as the monetary unit, each dollar consisting of 100 cents. The abbreviation for the dollar is $ and c for cents which stand after the numbers. At the time of going to press the exchange rate was £1 = $3.12.

Cost of Living

Living costs in New Zealand vary, depending on where you live and how you spend your money. Generally, it is more expensive to live in Auckland and Wellington than the rest of the country. The general weekly living costs per household chart below was compiled by Statistics New Zealand:

Food, Dining out, takeaways	$105
Rent/home ownership	$123
Running & equipment for the home	$88
Clothing and footwear	$27
Transport/travel	$106
Total	**$449**

For further details contact Statistics New Zealand, (Head Office, 85 Molesworth Street, PO Box 2922, Wellington; tel 04-495 4600; fax 04-495 4610; e-mail: info@stats.govt.nz).

Taxation

The taxation system was extensively reformed as part of the economic liberalisation in the 1980s. A goods and services tax was introduced, called GST (equivalent to a sales tax), and the philosophy of a 'user pays' policy, resulted in a reduction in personal tax rates. Through the 'user pays' policy, government subsidies have been reduced for certain services like university education, and some medical costs. Some government departments have been sold off to become State Owned Enterprises, and these SOEs also charge out the cost of their services. The Inland Revenue Department (IRD) is the government agency responsible for the collection of taxes, and there are IRD branches in all the cities and major towns. The income tax year runs from 1st April to 31st March of the following year.

Income Tax

1998 personal tax rates:

Annual Income	Tax Rate
$0 – $38,000	graduated up to 19.5 cents in the dollar
over $38,000	33 cents in the dollar

There is a rebate system which means that low income earners may pay about 5% tax. It is then graduated up to 19.5% for $38,000 pa. Most salary and wage earners have income tax automatically deducted from their wages under PAYE (Pay As You Earn). The employer pays the PAYE monthly to the Inland Revenue. Those who are PAYE and paying Resident Withholding Tax (on dividends or interest from a bank account) do not need to file a tax return (since June 1998). Self employed individuals, or those with income from a trust or rents pay three tax instalments throughout the financial year. They receive an IR3 form at the end of the tax year which they may complete by 7th July, but even this is not compulsory.

Prior to 1st April 1988, aged beneficiaries who received National Superannuation had to pay a surcharge of 25% on other income they earned above a certain limit. Following a campaign of protest from the elderly, this surcharge has been wiped.

A Resident Withholding Tax is charged by banks on interest and dividends.

The rate of RWT is currently 21.5%, and it is deducted by the financial institution before sending you payment. When you invest, you are required to provide your IRD number to the firm. You will need to apply for an IRD number before you earn money from any source. If you have a second job, you are taxed at a higher rate (called a secondary rate or SEC). An overall adjustment will take place when you file your annual return. Because most of your income is taxed at the source, some people no longer file tax returns. It is prudent to make your calculations, though, as you may be due a refund.

The IRD will help people complete their tax return at no cost, but the individual must provide all the necessary documents. Tax accountants charge a fee, but this fee can be deducted as an expense on the following year's return. There is no equivalent to National Insurance contributions: all social security and health spending is financed through general taxation. For further details contact your local Inland Revenue Office, or the national office (Inland Revenue Department, 12-22 Hawkstone Street, PO Box 2198, Wellington; tel 04-472 1032; fax 04-478 5801; Website: www.ird.govt.nz).

Local Tax

Local authorities finance their activities by levying rates on land and property. The system is similar to that which operated in the UK until the introduction of the Poll Tax. Some local authorities charge separately for services such as rubbish collection and water supply. Rates are levied on the value of your land plus improvements (that is, the house). Rates vary around the country and depending on the value of the land and improvements. An annual bill of between $900-2000 would be typical for a standard family house. Property is revalued every five years by Valuation New Zealand.

Goods and Services Tax (GST)

GST is an indirect tax on most goods and services, similar to VAT, but on a greater number of items. It is currently set at 12.5%. It is borne by the ultimate consumer but is payable at every stage of producing goods or services. GST is almost always marked in the display price. It applies to most commodities, exemptions include rental accommodation, donated goods and services and financial services. Exports are zero rated. Businesses with a net turnover of greater than $30 000 per annum must be GST registered and complete a GST return every six months. They can claim back the GST content of the goods and services they purchase. However, visitors cannot claim a refund on this tax.

Other Taxes

There is no capital gains tax as such, or death duties in New Zealand. However certain provisions in the Income Tax Act operate so as to tax as income profits which might otherwise be regarded as capital gains.

Gift Duty. Gift duty is a charge on gifts over $2,000 which one person makes to another. The person who makes the gift is liable to pay any duty when nothing is received in return, or the value of the gift given in return is less in value than the gift. Subject to certain exemptions, duty is charged on a sliding scale from 5% of the value of a gift worth over $27,000 to 25% for a gift exceeding $72,000.

Health Care, Insurance & Hospitals
Health Care
Prevailing public health care standards are generally high. Until recently, preventable diseases had been almost eradicated. However, one of the signs of the social distress caused by the economic restructuring of the 80s is that the diseases of poverty such as rickets, scurvy and tuberculosis are on the rise again. Life expectancy is the same as in the UK but there are significant differences between ethnic groups. Overall, New Zealanders smoke less than Europeans.

The provision of health care has been a major political issue over the last ten years. Apart from charges for doctors' fees and some prescription charges, for many years health services were provided free to the user. However, the increasing cost of specialist health services coupled with the reduction in the number of tax paying workers has brought about a partial user-pays service. The criteria for public health funding is being constantly debated by politicians and senior health care workers. Three quarters of what New Zealand spends on health and disability services is paid by the government from taxes. Health spending follows social welfare as a major item of government expenditure. In April 1998 $6.2 billion was allocated for health care – 7.8% of GDP. In addition, the life expectancy of New Zealanders is increasing; currently males are expected to live to age 73, and females to 79 which means that users need health care for longer which also adds to costs.

The general pattern of the public health system in New Zealand is that primary health care (GPs, prescriptions, out-patients visits to hospitals) is paid for by the user, while secondary health care is provided free. Over a third of New Zealanders have supplementary private medical insurance to cover the additional costs of medical care in the public system and to enable them to afford the costs of private hospitals. The costs of health care not covered by the state are between $30 and $40 for a visit to a doctor, prescription charges at $15 per item maximum, optometrists (opticians) and dentists charges at around $80 per visit. People on low incomes can get a Community Services Card which entitles them to cheaper primary care, but not dental care. As in Britain, the GPs provide most basic health care. It is not necessary to register with just one doctor, although for obvious reasons people tend to stay with the same doctor.

Hospitals
Hospital funding and management is currently in a state of upheaval due to the introduction of an internal market system similar to the NHS internal market. Hospitals were named Crown Health Enterprises (which have the unfortunate acronym CHEs, leading to a whole series of cheesy jokes) which lasted until 1998 when it was decided that the 23 CHEs were to be called 'hospitals' again. These 23 hospitals compete for the available funds on a regional basis. The population of each regional area has become a critical factor in this battle, and the more specialised and expensive surgical facilities are being concentrated in the higher populated areas. Even so, hospitals have huge deficits in their internal finance structure – the total of New Zealand hospital deficits in 1997 was $236 million, and a large part of 1998's budget spending on health went to finance these deficits. The Government has so far failed to define what health services it expects hospitals to provide free of charge, but at least the aim of making hospitals profit-making, has been abandoned. The quality of care in the public hospital sector does

not seem to have declined from its previous high standards but more services are being provided on with user-charges, and waiting lists are growing. Public Hospitals still provide no charge operations but the waiting lists are lengthening and if your condition is non-emergency or life threatening, you will find there is a long wait for surgery. Additionally, a points system has been introduced so that people of high priority are dealt with first.

You are generally less likely to be a victim of medical misadventure at the hands of some young doctor at the end of 100 hour shift. Young doctors went on strike in the late 80s and successfully negotiated much better pay and conditions than their counterparts in the UK.

As a result of long waiting lists, a great number of people have taken out medical insurance and elect to go to a private hospital (there are no private beds in public hospitals). Private hospitals cater mainly for elective surgery and for those who prefer a private room and more choice of when they have their operation.

Dental Care

Dental care for adults is not subsidised by the government but is provided free for all primary school children through the school dental system. Most New Zealand primary schools will have a dental clinic on the premises. As a result of receiving free basic care nearly half of New Zealand school children have no fillings by the time they get to high school.

Abortion

Abortion is legal under certain strictly defined conditions. If it is judged that the continuation of the pregnancy would result in serious danger to the life or mental or physical health of the woman, or that there is substantial risk that the child would be born handicapped then an abortion may be approved by two specially appointed consultants. The rate is about the same per 1000 population as the UK and half that of the USA.

Reciprocal Agreements

New Zealand has reciprocal health care agreements with most Commonwealth countries, including the UK. Visitors from these countries are entitled to access to the New Zealand health care system on the same basis as New Zealand citizens and residents. If you are a UK citizen visiting New Zealand to decide whether or not to emigrate, you are entitled to free treatment in the hospital system. You will pay the same as New Zealanders do for doctors' visits, about $30 for a consultation. Further information can be obtained from the Reciprocal Agreements Department of the Department of Social Security (tel 0191-225 9206; fax 0191-225 4215; e-mail: a.moy@new040.dss.gov.uk).

Private Medical Insurance

About 60% of New Zealanders have private medical insurance. The main reasons for buying private insurance seem to be to cover the additional costs of using the public system, such as doctors' fees and prescription charges, and to cover the costs of private hospital care. Getting insurance just to cover the costs of primary care is unlikely to be cost effective. The average annual costs for doctors' visits and prescriptions charges may be less than the premiums even for a budget insurance deal which only covers primary care. Premiums for this type of package are around $200 per year for an individual and between $400 to $900 for a family.

A comprehensive insurance deal which covers everything from routine primary care to major surgery in a private hospital will cost anything from $500 upwards annually or an individual or $1500 for a family. However policies vary widely depending on the amount of cover and the exclusions. The main advantages of private hospital care are greater choice over the timing of an operation, and private rooms. You can get hospital only cover which is usually cheaper than a comprehensive policy.

Remember though, the public hospital system provides the full range of care. The advantages of having private insurance are mostly the convenience factor. It is not yet necessary to have private medical insurance in New Zealand. Check that there is a repatriation clause in your policy if this is important to you.

It is also possible to arrange private medical insurance in advance. One of the best known UK companies is BUPA International; tel 01273-208181; fax 01273-866583; e-mail advice@bupa-intl.com; Website www.bupa-intl.com.

The Accident Compensation Corporation (ACC)

New Zealand has a unique system of state protection in the case of personal injury or accident. The government pays out compensation for loss of earnings due to accidents in the workplace, at home or on the sports field. This is a no fault cover for residents and visitors of New Zealand for accident, medical misadventure or certain behaviour for which criminal proceedings may be brought. Consequently, there is no right to sue for personal injury. The cost of ACC is met through payroll levies on employers and employees. It is another area of welfare provision which has suffered from retrenchment in recent years, and the original 1972 ACC system has been reduced. Lump-sum compensation according to a fixed scale depending on the injury has been abolished, and all assistance is made on a case by case basis. However assistance is available for a wide variety of costs including medical treatment, private hospital treatment, loss of earnings, loss of potential earnings, home help and child care, house modification in the case of permanent disability and training for independent living. The ACC places great emphasis on aiding people back to the workforce with rehabilitation treatment. The cost of non-work related accidents is met through the earner's premium which is collected through the tax system and the cost for work related accidents is collected through the employer's premium or levy. In the latest budget, firms are now allowed to take out accident insurance for their employees through private firms, instead of ACC if they wish.

ACC also covers visitors to New Zealand for certain personal accident injuries. Claims are started when you go to doctor or hospital, and ACC contributes towards treatment costs, transport (getting to the treatment) costs, and rehabilitation assistance. Visitors may only get this assistance while in New Zealand.

Social Welfare & Unemployment Benefits

Access to the social welfare system in New Zealand does not depend upon establishing a contribution record: benefits are available to all who meet the residency and income criteria. Although entitlement criteria are generous, benefit rates are not: most benefits are worth less than 50% of the average weekly wage (which is approximately $580). Increasingly prospective claimants face income and asset tests, for example high income earners who become unemployed may face a stand down period before they are entitled to unemployment benefit and may have to demonstrate that they have used up their own savings before qualifying for state aid. Benefits are available to those who fit the criteria and are legal residents of New Zealand, but in some cases you need to have lived there for several years. There is a reciprocal social security agreement with the UK which entitles UK residents who move to New Zealand to qualify for New Zealand benefits under the same criteria as New Zealanders. Some UK benefits are payable in New Zealand and in some circumstances it may be advisable to keep paying British National Insurance contributions. Immigrants from other countries will have to satisfy residence criteria before they become eligible. Most benefits are taxed before payment and the net amount is paid to the beneficiary, usually directly into a bank account.

Unemployment benefit: Payments are not related to previous earnings and the weekly rate is very low. The single rate is currently about $147.34 per week, and for married couples, $245.56 per week. Anyone under twenty-five years old is paid a lower rate. The unemployment benefit is payable to New Zealand citizens and residents only. The applicant must be actively looking for work, and ready for work or be involved in a training course. The Income Support Service also helps people with finding work experience (which is called 'Joblink') and seasonal jobs. Such work is in the tourist business, or in the farming, fishing, or horticulture industries. There is also a wage subsidy available to employers who offer you full time work. This is called 'Job Plus'. UK unemployment benefit is not payable in New Zealand.

Enterprise Allowance: The New Zealand Employment Service offers a monthly allowance to help with the living expenses of people establishing a business. It can be paid up to a year.

Invalid Benefit: Available to people aged 16 years or more who are severely restricted in their capacity for work due to accident, illness or congenital disability. It is not available to those who have enough money to live off themselves.

Sickness Benefit: This is available those over 16 who are incapacitated for work through sickness or accident. It also includes women who are over 28 weeks pregnant. The level of the sickness benefit is the same rate as the dole.

UK Sickness and Invalidity Benefit: This benefit is payable in New Zealand only if you are absent from the UK temporarily and your absence is for the specific purpose of obtaining treatment for your disability. However, these regulations can change at any time, and it is strongly recommended that you contact the Overseas Benefits Branch of the Department of Social Security (tel 0191-213 5000) for up to the minute information.

Domestic Purposes Benefit (DPB): The DPB is available to a parent caring for a child without the support of a partner. The parent needs to be over 18 years of age, (16 if you are married) and have a dependent child under 18. For a parent with one child the rate is $211.04 weekly. If your youngest child is over 6, the beneficiary must be actively looking for part time work. People over 16 caring for someone sick or frail who would ordinarily need hospital care can also be eligible for the DPB.

Family Support: Family support is cash assistance for low income families. The IRD calculates the amount due, based on the applicant's income and the number and age of children in the family. Family Support is paid to the main caregiver of the children, and children are can be counted up to the age of 18.

Child Support: Parents who are not living with their children make payments to support those children through the Child Support Agency, a division of the IRD. Child support is paid for children not living with a parent up to 19 years of age, unless the young person becomes self supporting. The amount paid in child support is based on the income of the parent paying support. The IRD passes on the payment made to the parent with whom the children are living. Other benefits available include the transitional retirement benefit, War Pensions, Young Job Seekers Benefit, Training Benefit, Widows Benefit, Childcare Subsidy, Accommodation Supplement, and Emergency Benefit. For more details on any of these, enquire at the local Income Support Service office or call (freephone 0800 559 009). For residents on low and middle incomes, Income Support provides a Community Services Card which reduces the costs of health care. Permanent legal residents can apply to the National Community Services Card Centre (PO Box 5054, Wellington; freephone 0800 999 999).

Crime and the Police

Unfortunately New Zealand's reputation for being a peaceful country with few social problems is not entirely deserved. The crime rate has been rising in recent years and the days when people would regularly go out without locking their front doors are over. It has a slightly higher rate of murders than the UK, but many times lower than the US rate. However although you should not have an unrealistically rosy picture of New Zealand society, it is important to keep it in perspective. Violent crime is sufficiently uncommon as to be newsworthy. In general, New Zealand cities are safe places to walk around and the police force are not yet routinely armed. A lot of the crime in New Zealand is domestic violence. Firearms are strictly controlled in the country and gun carriers must have a special permit from the Police Arms Office. The current government policy is committed to providing sufficient police numbers.

Local Government

Local government in New Zealand is very much subordinate to central government. Its powers and functions are set by parliament. There are two levels, regional councils which have responsibilities broadly for the environmental and land use, including control of pests and noxious plants. They also have some responsibilities over civil defence in the case of flood or earthquake. The next level are territorial or local councils. Both are directly elected, and have the power to set rates. Their responsibilities are not as wide ranging as local councils in the UK. They mostly provide services such as rubbish collection and disposal, parks, swimming pools, cemeteries, and libraries. They are responsible for a variety of regulatory measures for example, building consent, health inspection and control of noise, pollution and parking.

Official Information

Information held by the government and its ministries, education and health institutions, state owned enterprises and local government is called official information. There is legislation governing the availability of this material, and members of the public can write in to the organisation concerned to find out certain facts and figures.

Social Life

Meeting people & Making Friends

New Zealanders are very easy to get to know. They are relaxed about opening up a conversation with complete strangers. In fact if you walk into a country pub and fail to say hello to the locals, it would be considered quite rude. People are welcoming in inviting you back to their homes. New Zealanders do not make such invitations out of politeness, they mean it, so never feel you are taking advantage. It is a less formal country than the UK. It is considered quite normal for example to call round without a specific invitation. Neighbours will often drop in and introduce themselves to new people moving in, and perhaps take them some baking. For all the immediate friendliness, New Zealanders can be quite reserved in some respects. They are not likely to tell you much about their feelings or values until you get to know them well.

Social Attitudes

Perhaps as a result of their pioneering forebears, New Zealanders are an independent people. There is a great tradition of self-reliance, whether it comes to building an extension on the back of the house, or cutting off ties with the rest of the Western alliance during the Cold War period by refusing American nuclear armed ships access to New Zealand ports. Innovation is respected. Finding an ingenious, low-cost solution to a problem was obviously an asset in pioneering days. There is even a phrase for it: 'Kiwi ingenuity' which describes a pragmatic, imaginative approach to problem solving.

Despite approving of innovative and non-traditional approaches to problem solving, rural New Zealand remains quite conservative in outlook. Innovative lifestyles are not generally approved of. However tolerance is also a New Zealand characteristic, perhaps because the independent streak in the average New Zealander leads them to respect the right of others to live their lives as they choose. Urban New Zealand is more liberal in outlook. Green issues receive quite a lot of support, perhaps because New Zealanders are aware they live in one of the last largely unspoilt wilderness areas in the world and they have some responsibility to hand it on to their children without ruining it. There is strong support for bicultural and multiculturalism in theory. However Pakeha New Zealanders can increasingly be heard complaining that the Maori are treated more favourably by government. In fact positive discrimination programmes of the type common in the USA are more perceived than actual. There are however, special grants for Maori business and for educational purposes. Few institutions run a formal quota system although all are required to have an equal employment policy. Maori leaders acknowledge that Maori society is increasingly dependent on welfare benefits and Maori workers are more likely to be unemployed than Pakeha. They were more severely affected by the economic restructuring of the last decade because job losses were predominantly in the unskilled area the Maori have tended to have lower skills levels required for jobs, than the Pakeha.

Like the Welsh and the Scots before them, New Zealanders feel the need to assert their own identity to prove that they are different from the English and the colonial power which shaped the early period of settlement and hence became the original model for New Zealand culture. The need to assert themselves usually manifests itself as a fairly critical attitude towards English life, culture and climate, on the part of those who have visited that country. This criticism is usually not intended to be rude, rather it functions as a form of commiseration for the English for having had the misfortune to have been born there rather than in New Zealand. Reciprocal ruthless honesty about the drawbacks of living in New Zealand is unlikely to be welcomed however. In fact they tend to be defensive about New Zealand, even though they think its merits ought to be self-evident.

Smoking. Smoking is a lot less socially acceptable in New Zealand than it is in Europe. Public buildings are smoke free zones by law. Most restaurants provide a smoke free area with some even banning smoking completely.

Useful Address
Settlement Information Programme: New Zealand Immigration Service, Freepost Number 95124, PO Box 3705, Wellington; tel (04) 915 4010.

Entertainment and Culture

New Zealand may not be as well-known overseas for its musicians and artists (opera diva Dame Kiri Te Kanawa excepted) as it is for its sports men and women, but in fact there is a lively local cultural scene. Increasingly, performers from New Zealand are succeeding internationally. Kiri Te Kanawa, is respected throughout New Zealand, not so much because every household worships opera, but because like the All Blacks she is a New Zealander succeeding internationally. She therefore attracts huge audiences, when she returns home to perform.

There are three fully professional orchestra companies, based in Auckland, Wellington and Christchurch, and there are a number of semi-professional and amateur regional orchestras. International soloists and chamber groups visit frequently, and every two years the Wellington festival of the Performing Arts attracts some top rate orchestras and ensembles from all over the world.

Other types of performing arts thrive, particularly in Wellington which has a number of professional theatres, the Royal New Zealand Ballet, a several modern dance companies and the New Zealand Symphony Orchestra. The New Zealand film scene is currently enjoying a lot of success both at home and overseas. *The Piano:* made by New Zealander Jane Campion is one of line of internationally acclaimed films which includes *Heavenly Creatures*, *Once Were Warriors*, and *Angel at my Table*.

Sport

What can you say about a country where a former Prime Minister gets involved with the choice over the coach of the rugby team? New Zealanders are intensely nationalistic when it comes to identifying with the successes of their national teams, particularly the All Blacks rugby team. Losing a rugby match can cast a gloom over the entire nation. It is about more than just losing a game. New Zealand is such a small player in the international political and economic order, that the fact that the country's elite sports teams are capable of taking on the big guys and winning becomes a matter of national pride.

Cricket runs a close second in the interest of New Zealanders, although most New Zealanders bemoan the poor performance of their national team. However, test matches are followed closely on the television, even when broadcast from the other hemisphere in the middle of the night. In fact, television news bulletins always cover cricket and rugby – from watching New Zealand TV, you could be mistaken for thinking there are only two sports played in the country. Much less coverage is given to the Silver Ferns, the women's netball team, although they are more consistently successful on the world stage. For a brief and glorious period the soccer team (the 'All Whites') were in the limelight when they qualified for the World Cup.

New Zealanders are not just enthusiastic about watching sport. A large number of people participate in their spare time. Nearly 50% of the population belong to some kind of sport, fitness or leisure club. The most popular activities are aquatic sports such as swimming, diving, rowing, or water polo. As well as team sports such as hockey, netball, rugby and football (usually called soccer), an increasing number of New Zealanders are involved in individual sports like mountain biking, climbing, skate boarding, triathalon competitions, or trail bike riding. Adrenaline sports are on the increase in the country, as thrill seekers risk challenges presented by the mountains and rivers around them. From the birthplace of bungy jumping, adventures such as black water rafting (rafting in caves) rap jumping (abseiling face-down on a building) and river sledding (going down white water rapids on a boogie board) are on offer for large sums of money. New and more terrifying sports emerge each year. But if you do not count yourself among the the yahoos there are plenty of more rational sports and outdoor activities available including scuba-diving, whale watching and swimming with dolphins in the open sea.

Recreational Fishing Restrictions

Fishing is a popular sport in New Zealand, and there is an abundance of clean rivers and fish life. However, there are regulations concerning New Zealand fishing in order to protect the resource. Amateur fishermen are not allowed to take more than the daily limit, sell or trade what they caught, or catch undersized fish. There are also restrictions on the minimum size of shellfish and lobsters. Fishermen who operate commercially are required to have a fishing permit. For more information, contact the Ministry of Agriculture and Forestry (101 The Terrace, PO Box 2526, Wellington; tel 04-474 4100; fax 04-474 4111; e mail: comms@fish.govt.nz).

Maori Culture

The Maori have been in Aotearoa (New Zealand) for approximately 1000 years, a long time compared to the 150 years of Pakeha (European) settlement. Maori culture remains distinct from the rest of New Zealand culture, although each influences the other.

Maori Social Customs

The Marae

The distinctive and central focus of Maori culture is the *Marae* or meeting place. A *marae* consists of a *wharenui* (meeting house), a *wharekai* (eating house) and *wharepaku* (ablution block). To the Maori however, it is not the presence of the buildings that is significant, but the spiritual importance of the location, the discussions and exchanges between people and events ranging from marriages to funerals that take place on the *marae*. It is customary to welcome visitors onto the *marae* in a ceremony called a *powhiri* (welcome).

The Powhiri

Visitors (called the *manuhiri*) will gather outside the gate of the *marae*. It is considered improper to walk onto the *marae* uninvited. The visitors will be 'called on' by the host people (the *tangata whenua*). This is called the *karanga* and is usually performed by a woman from the host side. The *manuhiri* will proceed slowly onto the marae as one group. Usually the women are to the front of the group. One of these women will answer the welcoming call with a *karanga* of her own. The group will pause in silence to *tangi* (remember the dead) and then will move slowly to the seating provided. The front row of seating is reserved for those men who wish to *whaikorero* (speak).

Whaikorero (speeches) are to welcome manuhiri, to remember those who have died, to thank *tangata whenua* and always mentions the reason for the visit. Each speech is followed by a *waiata* (song), sung by the speaker's group to show their support of him. The final speaker for the *manuhiri* will lay down the *koha* (gift). Today *koha* are mostly monetary to contribute to the cost of the *hui* (gathering). The final speech is usually made on the host side.

At the conclusion of the *whaikorero* it is customary for the visitors and the hosts to *hongi* (press noses). This is usually done by shaking right hands, bracing your left hand on the other person's right arm and pressing your nose into theirs twice whilst looking them in the eye. Today some people will shake hands instead. It is best to follow the lead of the *tangata whenua*. After the formalities, hosts and guests share a meal together. It is at this point that the *manuhiri* become *tangata whenua* and the *pohiri* is concluded.

Points to Remember
The *wharenui* is for gatherings and for sleeping. You should always remove your shoes before entering the *wharenui*. Never walk on mattresses or sit on pillows.Certain places are reserved for the elders (*kaumatua*) to sit and sleep in. You should never eat in the *wharenui*.

In the *wharekai* (eating house) be careful not to put hair clips, scarves, combs, glasses or anything to do with the head, on the table. This is because the head is sacred (tapu). Tables are also tapu, so do not sit, or put your feet any tables. A *hangi* is a delicious feast whereby the food is cooked by rocks heated by fire in a hole in the ground, and the food baskets are placed on the rocks and are covered with earth. When serving yourself, it is polite to take small helpings (and quite acceptable to have several of them) rather than one large plateful. Before meals there will usually be grace. It is good manners to allow the *kaumatua* to eat first, and after the first meal once you have become part of the tangata whenua, to offer to help with the dishes or preparation of the next meal.

Do not smoke in any of the buildings on the *marae* and do not use cameras or tape recorders unless given permission. Never be afraid to ask what protocol you should be following. Part of Maori culture emphasises the importance of welcoming guests and making them feel at home, so if you are prepared to be respectful of the culture and traditions, then nobody will mind explaining points of protocol to you. A useful book on Maori culture is *Te Marae – A Guide to Customs and Protocols* (Hiwi and Pat Tauroa, Heinemann Reed, 1986). If you want to find out more about Maori culture during a visit to New Zealand, the New Zealand Tourism Board publishes a leaflet called *New Zealand Maori Cultural Heritage Guide* which lists a number of tourism operators who provide visits to marae and other cultural experiences (*New Zealand Tourism Board:* New Zealand House, 80 Haymarket SW1Y 4TQ, London; tel 0171-930 1662.) The New Zealand Immigration Service publishes a leaflet called *The Treaty of Waitangi* which explains the relevance of the treaty to new immigrants.

Shops and Shopping

Most types of shops in New Zealand will be familiar to the UK immigrant, and in some cases even the names are the same. (Although chains with the same names as

UK shops often sell different goods in New Zealand which can be disorientating. For example *Woolworths* is one of New Zealand's largest supermarket chains and *Boots* is just a pharmacy, not a general department store as well). Shops are open from 8.30 am until 5pm, five days a week, and 8.30 am until midday on Saturday. Sunday shopping began in 1989 and is now well established. Most shops also have one late night when they are open until 9pm, usually Thursday or Friday. In some larger towns suburban malls and superstores are taking business out of the city centre. Auckland is a case in point, Queen Street, once the focal point of the city centre is almost deserted on a Friday night. In other cities, councils have made determined efforts to revive the town centres. Christchurch's Cathedral Square and Wanganui's Victoria Avenue are good examples.

Food Shopping: Most people buy their weekly groceries from supermarkets. The large supermarkets with the biggest range tend to be out-of-town which makes access difficult for non-car owners. You will find the same types of food, as you would find in British supermarkets, but most of the stock will be made in New Zealand as imported goods are expensive. There are probably more distinctions between different types of supermarket chains than in Britain. Some offer a cheap no-frills service with minimal overheads. These tend to be warehouse style places where you pack your own bags and there is not a great range of goods, just all the basics sold very cheaply. Other chains are aiming at the high-income end of the market. They will offer a greater level of customer service, with a range of speciality departments in-store, bakery, butchers, delicatessen, etc. but are comparatively expensive. Most supermarkets are open seven days a week and will usually have at least one late night when they are open until 9pm.

Local shops have not yet disappeared but are threatened by the convenience of supermarket shopping and the cheaper prices. Most city neighbourhoods have a convenience store (called a dairy). Dairies stock practically everything and are usually open late (until 9pm or 10pm), but charge higher prices than a supermarket. Some neighbourhoods still have their local butcher, greengrocers and bakery but these are becoming less common.

Serious foodies will probably miss the range of European and speciality foods available in the UK. Delicatessens stock a range of imported foods but at a price. On the other hand, most staple foods are cheaper than in the Europe. The good news is that European style specialities are now starting to be made locally. For example Italian breads such as *foccacia* and *ciabatta* are baked locally in the big cities, and fresh pasta can be found in most towns. A New Plymouth company is producing French style cheeses, although they seem to cost nearly as much as the real thing. New Zealand's varied climate provides suitable conditions to grow a wide range of fruit and vegetables, but you will find that what is available in the shops depends on the season, as it is mostly locally grown. Produce with a short shelf life cannot be imported to cover the off-season because the distances involved are too great. On the other hand you can buy exotic produce common to the area: Pacific Island specialities such as taro (a root vegetable), coconut and plantains are one type of imported produce that is commonly available in the bigger towns. Fresh fish and shellfish are another New Zealand speciality. Green lipped mussels, pacific oysters, local salmon, smoked eel, trout, are all popular. Because export demand drives up the prices, seafood is not cheap.

Local wines are also generally of good quality. New Zealand white wines were 'discovered' by UK wine writers in the late 80s which had an enormous galvanising effect on the New Zealand industry. The number of vineyards multiplied, and everybody started producing Sauvignon Blanc as that was in demand. New Zealand wines are no cheaper at home than they are in Europe, but the range is greater. There are over 2000 labels produced every year. You can buy not just the ubiquitous Sauvignon Blanc but also some seriously good Chardonnay, and even some respectable red wines – several New Zealand Pinot Noirs have won international acclaim.

Australian wines are readily available and are generally cheaper than New Zealand wines because their industry does not face the same crippling taxes which hit New Zealand producers.

Non-food Shopping: Most consumer goods are readily available in New Zealand. Imported goods are cheaper than they used to be as a result of tariffs being lowered in the 1980s. However it is probably not the shopping that attracts most visitors or immigrants. There is no equivalent to Regent Street or Fifth Avenue even in the big cities. Department store chains such as Deka and DIC sell most of the essentials from clothing through to household goods and white goods in rather unimaginative surroundings. Clothing is comparatively cheap although design standards are not particularly high in the chain stores. Independent designers flourish in the larger cities selling well-made and reasonably-priced clothing.

Hire Purchase: More expensive consumer durables are often available in New Zealand under hire purchase. Once the buyer signs a hire purchase agreement and pays a deposit they can take the goods home to use, and pay the remainder of the price by regular instalments. If the instalment demands are not met, however, the goods can be repossessed.

Tipping and Service Charges: gratuities are not necessary in New Zealand, and service charges are not added onto hotel or restaurant bills. However, a tip as reward for extra service or consideration would be appreciated.

Food and Drink

The New Zealand diet is mostly derived from the eating patterns of the British immigrants, influenced by the relative abundance of dairy products and cheap mutton and beef. New Zealanders tend to consume far too much cholesterol and saturated fat and as a result have one of the highest rates of heart disease in the western world. This is changing slowly as a result of government campaigns promoting healthier eating styles and a new interest in the diet and food of Asian countries. But despite the best attempts of the healthy lifestyle lobby, the traditional Sunday lunch in many a New Zealand home remains roast lamb with all the trimmings. during the week the main meal is usually the evening meal, which confusingly, New Zealanders call 'tea'.

Eating out isn't quite the let-down it once was, now that the country is less fixated with 'traditional' British cooking. The quality of restaurants in the main cities is very high. Restaurants are constantly seeking to define a distinctive 'New Zealand cuisine', and come up with delicious combinations of fruit and meat.

The improvement in the domestic wine industry has helped to turn the New Zealanders into more discerning gastronomes. There is a lot of interest in European food trends. Many New Zealand restaurants have what is called a BYO (BYO stands for Bring Your Own) licence. They are not allowed to sell alcoholic beverages, instead the customer brings their own wine which the restaurant opens. They usually make a small charge called corkage for this. The advantage of BYO establishments is that you avoid the huge mark up restaurants usually put on wine and you have a much wider choice of what to drink. BYO restaurants tend to be cheaper than fully licensed places, at $25 to $45 a head for a three course meal, not including what you paid for the wine. A three course meal at a licensed restaurant is more likely to be in the $45 to $60 range, not including the cost of wine. The cheapest and sometimes the most interesting food can be found at the fashionable espresso bars which are mushrooming in the big cities. You can eat in these sorts of places for less than $20.

The situation in small towns can be grim. Chinese takeaways are probably your best bet anywhere from north of Wellington to the Bombay Hills, and in the hinterlands of Canterbury and Otago. Good local restaurants exist in small towns New Zealand but unless a friend you trust (and wants to keep your friendship) has recommended a restaurant, you might be better off with takeaways. Indian restaurants are less common as they are in the UK, but other Asian food establishments, especially Japanese and Malaysian, are becoming more prolific. New Zealand fish and chip shops used to be run by Chinese immigrants, hence the term 'Chinese takeaway', as most sell cheap, reasonable quality Chinese food as well. Nonetheless, the fish and chips in takeaways are surprisingly good as instead of frying chips and other goodies in advance and letting them dry out under hot lamps, they fry your order up individually. They still come wrapped in newspaper in most places too, with no European health regulations to interfere. No one has yet died in New Zealand of newsprint poisoning.

Public Holidays

1 January	New Year's Day
2 January	Day after New Year's Day
6 February	Waitangi Day (formerly New Zealand Day)
April	Good Friday
April	Easter Monday
25 April	Anzac Day
June	Queen's Birthday
October	Labour Day
25 December	Christmas Day
26 December	Boxing Day

However, the only days that almost all shops are closed on are Good Friday, Easter Sunday, Anzac Day and Christmas Day.

Time

New Zealand is twelve hours ahead of Greenwich Mean Time. During Daylight Saving the clocks are put forward by one hour, from the first Sunday in October to the third Sunday of the following March.

Metrication

New Zealand uses the metric measuring system for distances, weights and measures, with a few imperial hangovers. For example beer usually is sold by the pint or half pint. Road signs are all in kilometres as are speed limits. To convert kilometres into miles, multiply by five and divide by eight. Temperatures are in degrees Celsius. As a rough guide, convert to Fahrenheit, double the degrees and add 30.

Retirement

Background Information

There are more than 33,000 British people of retirement age living in New Zealand and a large number from other European countries. Undoubtedly for many older people, the chance to be reunited with children who have already migrated to New Zealand is a major attraction. Having adult children in New Zealand will also make it easier to get permanent residency. Otherwise migration may be difficult for people of retirement age, as New Zealand's immigration policy is aimed at attracting people into the workforce.

New Zealand offers many advantages for those considering a change of scenery upon retirement. The standard of living is high and the exchange rate is favourable so your savings should go a long way. British and American retirees will not have to learn a new language and the culture is sufficiently similar to that of Britain to make it seem familiar. The climate in most parts of New Zealand is warmer than Northern Europe. There are the attractions of living in a less crowded country, with in general, fewer social problems and a lower crime rate. New Zealand's population is an ageing one, so there are a lot of clubs and services to cater for older people's interests and needs.

Although doctors' visits cost about $30-40 per consultation, hospital care is still free for New Zealanders and immigrants from countries with reciprocal social security agreements. In general the New Zealand health system is less under-resourced than the NHS. On the other hand, certain types of specialist medical care may be better provided in the UK and other European countries simply because New Zealand is too small to have the range of expertise in these areas.

The drawbacks of emigrating have to be considered as well. You will be far away from friends and family in the Northern hemisphere and you may find life a little lonely at first. Many retirees mention that one of the hardest aspects of their new life is not being able to afford to return home for family events such as weddings. New Zealand is twenty five hours away from London by plane and the trip is not cheap. Most British migrants report that they find it easy to get to know New Zealanders, and although new friends are not a substitute for old, you need not fear being isolated for long in your new country.

The Decision to Leave

Making a permanent move to another country is a very different matter from just visiting it, particularly when you will be adjusting to all the lifestyle changes retirement brings as well. It may be a good idea therefore to spend a longer period in New Zealand before deciding whether to make a permanent move there. Many people make the decision to move after a visit to New Zealand to see family or friends. If you have a British passport you are entitled to visit New Zealand for up to six months without requiring a visa. A visit may be a good opportunity to explore different parts of the country before deciding where you would most like to settle. A number of companies arrange coach and train tours with itineraries that cover most of New Zealand in a short period. Some companies will also arrange farm and home stay tours which will enable you to experience the lifestyle of New

Zealand families. One such company is Leisurerail (PO Box 113, Peterborough, PE3 8HY; tel 01733-335599; fax 01733-505 451).

As has been noted elsewhere, rental accommodation is generally easy to find, so you may like to try living in your prospective retirement locality for a while. It will also give you a chance to assess the real costs of living in New Zealand. Financial considerations are an important factor when you are living on a fixed income. You can use a visit to assess the property market in order to find out what kind of housing you will be able to afford. In general if you have sold property in the UK, you should be able to afford a New Zealand house of at least an equivalent if not better standard, particularly if you choose to live outside the main cities.

Residence and Entry Regulations

Because the general migration category is not open to people aged 55 or above, the most likely route to New Zealand residency for an older person is the family reunification or business development categories. Under the family reunification category, you can apply for residency if you have an adult child or children living in New Zealand and no adult children living in your own country, or alternatively if you have children living in your home country and you have more children living in New Zealand than any other country including your own. Alternatively if you have sufficient capital you can apply under the business investment category. The minimum amount required is NZ$750, 000, and you must meet the passmark which is currently 12 points. (See Chapter Two, *Residence and Entry*).

Applying for Residence

To qualify for residency under the family reunification category, you will need to provide evidence of the family relationships, and the citizenship or residency status of your New Zealand children, and of children living in other countries. You will need to submit birth and marriage certificates and copies of residency permits. Additionally you will have to satisfy the health and character requirements as outlined in Chapter Two for general residency applications.

Possible retirement areas

Popular retirement areas for New Zealanders are in the warmer regions on the east coast of the North Island and the north of the South Island. Many New Zealanders move to the coast when they retire, often to their beach house or bach. Some communities have a higher proportion of older people than others which you may consider an advantage. One consideration to bear in mind, is that in remoter areas you will certainly need to own a car or to live close to local services as public transport is not convenient enough to rely on. A population retirement option for New Zealanders is the 'ten acre block' or 'lifestyle block', a house in the country with a large plot of land. Ten acres may be the size of farm in Europe, but by the standards of New Zealand farms, these are hobby plots, for city folk who want to try the rural lifestyle. Some people cultivate their land, others just enjoy the extra space.

Tauranga and the Bay of Plenty: On the east coast of the North Island, the Bay of Plenty has a pleasant climate and is one of the main horticultural regions as a result. In the summer time, the white sandy beaches and gentle waves of Mt Manganui beach attract many families.

Hawke's Bay: Known for its sub tropical climate and easy pace of life, Hawke's Bay makes an ideal spot for retiring. There is a wealth of orchards and vineyards here, as Hawke's Bay is one of the premier wine making regions in the country. Lovers of architecture will enjoy the buildings of Napier, the 'art deco capital of the world'.

Kapiti Coast: Just north of Wellington, on the west coast of the North Island, the coast is a popular retirement destination for locals. It is dotted with small towns, from Paraparaumu, up to Otaki, many made up largely of holiday homes for Wellingtonians to escape to for the weekends. There are a large number of permanent residents as well, many of retirement age. Transport networks are good, there is a commuter train service into Wellington city, as well as a local bus network. The coast itself can be quite rough, but just down the coast, Pirogue harbour provides more sheltered waters for boating or fishing.

Banks Peninsula: Over the Port Hills to the south of Christchurch, the peninsula was called Bank's Island on the first map of New Zealand after Captain Cook's navigator, Joseph Banks who thought its deep inlets cut it off from the main land. In contrast with the flat sweeping plains of Canterbury, the peninsula is all hills and valleys divided by deep harbours. Further east over the hills is Akaroa, with its echoes of the first French settlers. Streets are called 'Rues' and the building code specifies that new houses are built in the style of the homes of the original French settlers with steeply raked roofs. You would certainly need to be a car owner to live on the peninsula as the bus service to Christchurch is infrequent and the remoter valleys lack local services.

Hobbies and interests

New Zealand offers many opportunities for using your new leisure time. The country is full of keen gardeners and the climate is well suited for those who like to spend time outdoors. If you are planning an active retirement, there is a lot of beautiful countryside to be explored. There are sporting opportunities to suit just about everybody. Golfing is a popular activity. There are public golf courses in most towns and cities. Bowls and croquet are also popular with older people. If you are interested in cultural pursuits, you will probably consider settling near one of the main cities. Fortunately one of the advantages of living in New Zealand is that you can combine proximity to major cities with the semi-rural lifestyle if that is what appeals to you. For example, Banks Peninsula is only 40 minutes away from the centre of Christchurch. Every town has a senior citizens club, equally open to the recent immigrant as to the native New Zealander. These provide a chance to meet other older people as well as social facilities. Many older people use their new leisure time to go back to study, either through night classes or by enrolling at a university part-time. Most New Zealand universities exempt mature students from formal entrance qualifications and instead will assess your ability to study and enrol you at the appropriate level. You can often get used to being a student again by taking a pre-degree certificate in liberal arts which have less rigorous assessment procedures. Night classes are offered in a wide variety of subjects from foreign languages through to car maintenance at local high schools or polytechnics. The following are just some of the clubs available for European and American ex-pats.

Useful Addresses

Age Concern NZ (Inc): 3rd Floor, Riddiford House, 150 Featherston Street, PO Box 10 688, Wellington; tel (04) 471 2709; fax (04) 473 2504. Promotes quality of life and well being for older people.

Anglican Church Friendship Group: Overseas Settlement Secretary, Board for Social Responsibility, Church House, Great Smith Street, Westminster, London SW1P 3NZ.

British Isles Club of Wellington: 66 Kauri Street, Mirimar, Wellington; tel (04) 388 1597.

Citizens Advice Bureau (National Office): Unit 6, Betty Campbell Community Office Complex, 148 Wakefield Street, PO Box 9777, Wellington; tel toll free 0800 367 222 or (04) 382 8759; fax (04) 382 8647. Citizens Advice can advice on local social clubs and interest groups. It has over 90 offices throughout New Zealand.

Community Advisory Services: For information about community groups, contact the Department of Internal Affairs, tel (04) 495 7200; fax (04) 495 7222.

New Zealand American Association Inc.: PO Box 2957, Wellington; tel (04) 801 8960.

Ministerial Advisory Council for Senior Citizens: Social Policy Agency, Department of Social Welfare, Private Bag 21, Wellington; tel (04) 916 3750; fax (04) 916 3778; e-mail: natalie.lavery@dsw.govt.nz.

Victoria League for Commonwealth Friendship (London branch): 55 Leinster Square, Bayswater, London W2 4PU; tel 0171-229 3961.

YWCA (national office): tel 04 384 8117; fax (04) 384 3301. There are 10 local YWCA associations, which organise programmes and activities for women.

Pensions

New Zealand Pensions

New Zealand has reciprocal social security arrangements with a number of countries including the UK, Ireland and the Netherlands. The general principal of these reciprocal arrangements is that people migrating from one country to the other are treated like citizens of their new country with regard to social security arrangements and are entitled to the same range of benefits. However the particular arrangements differ between countries. In the case of UK citizens, if you are entitled to receive a British retirement pension, you can continue to receive it in New Zealand. The level of the British pension is frozen from the point you leave the UK, and is not inflation adjusted. If you become eligible for the pension while in New Zealand, it will be paid at the rate which applies in the UK when you are first entitled to a pension. Under the reciprocal agreement you are entitled to qualify for the New Zealand state retirement pension, National Superannuation if you have been resident in the UK and New Zealand for at least ten years in total. If you qualify, the New Zealand Government supplements the your British pension so that it is at the same level as National Superannuation. National Superannuation pays $510 per week before tax for a single person living alone, and $382 per week each, before tax for a married couple. It is paid fortnightly.

If you come from a country which does not have a reciprocal agreement with New Zealand you are not entitled to receive the New Zealand pension until you have been a resident for ten years.

British emigrants who settle in New Zealand are entitled to a UK pension when they reach the qualifying age – 60 for a woman, 65 for a man. The amount of the pension is dependent on the number of years in paid employment in the UK. The UK pension can be directly credited to a New Zealand bank or building society account every 4 or 13 weeks. When you become entitled to NZ National Superannuation, you will receive the full New Zealand pension, made up of the UK pension plus the balance being paid by the New Zealand government. To apply for the UK pension, write to the Contributions Agency International Services, Department of Social Security (Pensions and Overseas Benefits Directorate), Newcastle Upon Tyne, NE98 1BA.

The agreement between New Zealand and the UK gives equal treatment and protection of benefit rights when you move from one country to the other. The amount of the UK pension you receive is taxable income in New Zealand.

Receiving Your Pension Abroad

Pension arrangements for expatriates vary. In some countries if you have established entitlement in your own country then you can continue to receive your pension in New Zealand. As was noted above, some countries have reciprocal agreements with New Zealand which entitle you to the same range of benefits as a local. You should contact your local Department of Social Security for further information.

Taxation

Once you are a New Zealand resident, you pay New Zealand income tax on your world wide income, including income from any overseas based pension schemes. Residency for taxation purposes has nothing to do with your immigration status. You are deemed to be New Zealand resident for tax purposes if you have a permanent place of abode in New Zealand, regardless of whether you also have one in another country. Having a permanent abode in New Zealand is not limited to owning a dwelling, the courts will also take into account social, personal, and financial ties as evidence of where your permanent abode is. If you are in New Zealand for more than 183 days in any 12 month period you are also regarded as a New Zealand resident for taxation purposes whether or not you have a permanent abode in New Zealand. New Zealand has double tax treaties with twenty-four countries including the USA, Canada, the UK, France, Germany, and the Netherlands. These treaties limit the tax liability for citizens of one country resident in the other, so that an individual does not in theory pay tax twice on the same income.

New Zealand Health Care

One of the drawbacks of the New Zealand health care system for a retired person is that although hospital care is free, doctor's visits are not, nor are prescriptions. For those pensioners on low incomes from countries with reciprocal social security arrangements, there is the Community Services Card which reduces the costs of health care. Permanent legal residents can apply to the National Community Services Card Centre (PO Box 5054, Wellington; freephone 0800 999 999). There is also a cap on the total amount you will be charged annually for prescriptions so if you need a lot of medication, you do not pay anything for it after a certain point.

Private medical insurance is one option to consider to cover the additional costs of health care in New Zealand. See Chapter Four, *The Health Care System* for further details. Private insurance will cover the cost of treatment in private hospitals which may give you more choice about the timing of operations. But as is indicated in Chapter Four, the annual cost of premiums is likely to make full private insurance costly, unless you frequently use primary health care services.

Wills and Legal Considerations

You should draw up a will in New Zealand if you are considering buying property and settling there. Dying intestate complicates matters sufficiently for one's heirs without doing so in a foreign country. In the event that a non-New Zealander dies intestate the laws of their own country will apply. As it is more likely that you will be a New Zealand citizen or at least domiciled there in the eyes of the law, New Zealand intestate laws would apply. Under New Zealand intestate laws, your estate would be divided between a surviving spouse and your children, with your spouse getting the major share. This would be the case even if you had separated from but not divorced your spouse.

In New Zealand, a will does not have to be drawn up by a lawyer. However, there are obvious advantages to having your will drawn up by a lawyer or trust company. If there are any mistakes in the way the will is drawn up they can invalidate it, and the lawyer or trust company chosen to draw up your will can administer your estate. This may be a good idea, particularly if you have no close relatives in the country. In the UK, people often nominate a relative or friend(s) as executor of the will. However, it is better to have a trust company or solicitor as your Executor. It also saves problems if your nominated executor predeceases you. Many New Zealand lawyers do not charge for drawing up wills, and if you nominated the solicitor or trust company that drew up your will, you will either pay no fee or a minimal fee for the execution of the will.

Death

In the event of a friend or relative dying in New Zealand, there are certain formalities which have to be attended to, as is the case in the UK. A death must be certified by a doctor. You should consider as well what you would like your friends or relatives to do in the event of your death, and perhaps leave written instructions with your will. The cost of shipping a body back to Europe to be buried is extremely high.

SECTION II

Working in New Zealand

Employment

Business and Industry Report

Regional Employment Guide

Starting a Business

Employment

The Employment Scene

With a labour market similar to the United Kingdom's, the same language and a similar level of economic development, New Zealand has long been a good place for those wanting to emigrate from the UK to look for jobs. In the past the country enjoyed very low unemployment with the average level throughout the 1970s being less than 2%. However the situation in the last decade has been less favourable. Throughout the 1980s unemployment in New Zealand increased rapidly. A large number of jobs were lost throughout manufacturing industries during the radical economic reforms of the 1980s. Some of the job losses can be attributed to long term trends in the labour market and reflect the same kinds of changes that have occurred in other western countries where manufacturing industries have been unable to compete with cheaper labour costs in the newly industrialised countries of Asia. There has been a similar shift in New Zealand's industrial structure from manufacturing to service industries as has been evident in the United Kingdom. Other job losses can be traced to the lowering of tariff barriers as a result of New Zealand's conversion to neo-liberal economic policies. Tight monetary policy aimed at squeezing inflationary pressures out of the economy also contributed to the economic downturn. Employment in the manufacturing sector dropped by a quarter during the 1980s from 316,000 jobs to 235,000. This sector now employs just over 18% of the workforce, compared to 23% ten years ago. Although the primary sector (agricultural, horticulture, fishing) has always been the basis of New Zealand's economic prosperity, it is a comparatively small source of jobs, employing about 10% of the workforce. There are approximately 161,000 people employed in the primary sector.

The only sector to have experienced constant growth is the service sector which now accounts for 70% of employment. Within the service sector, the fastest growing source of jobs has been in business and financial services which employs around 10% of the workforce. The biggest employment area in the service sector is wholesale, retail, restaurants and hotels, which employs just over 21% of workforce. The increase in service sector jobs in the last decade has not been sufficient to make up for the loss of jobs in the manufacturing and primary sectors. Overall the total number of people in employment declined by 7% between 1981 and 1991.

The current employment situation is more encouraging than the above may suggest. The number of people in employment has been growing at a faster rate every year for the last decade, although because more people are looking for work, the rate of unemployment has not dropped substantially since the recession ended. The total number of people in employment increased 15% between 1991 and 1995, when the labour force participation rate numbered 1,621,500 people. A recent survey of companies by a Wellington economic research agency showed that 20% of companies were considering increasing their workforce in the short term. Most of this demand is likely to be for skilled labour with some firms shedding unskilled workers to take on workers with skills.

Future economic predictions are mixed, as the New Zealand economy is heavily influenced by the economic and political upheavals of South East Asia. Business confidence remains low, but consumer confidence has picked up. Growth in New Zealand's GDP is expected to pick up in 1999, to reach 3.5% by the millennium. A useful publication with the up-to-date state of New Zealand's economy and exports is *Export News* published by Headliner Publishing Company for TradeNZ, is available from the Trade Development Board in New Zealand House (80 Haymarket, London SW1Y 4TQ).

Residence and Work Regulations

New Zealand requires that foreign nationals working in New Zealand whether for local or foreign companies obtain work permits for the period of employment which in most cases may not exceed three years. Permission from the New Zealand Immigration Service must be sought prior to arrival and it must be shown that the worker has skills not readily available in locally. If you are visiting New Zealand and have found a job, you may apply for a work permit within the country, but the maximum period for which it will be granted is nine months. The same restrictions on skills applies. For further details see Chapter Two, *Residence and Entry*.

Skills and Qualifications

In general British qualifications are recognised and well regarded in New Zealand. New Zealand's university education system derives its structure from British, particularly Scottish universities, so the types of qualifications available from universities are similar in title and content to UK ones. Trade and vocational qualifications have different titles. You can apply to the New Zealand Qualifications Authority, the government agency that oversees the qualifications system, to have the equivalence of your UK qualifications assessed. In some cases you may have to do this as part of the application for residency under the General Category. The necessary forms can be obtained from the New Zealand Immigration Service at New Zealand House in London, or you can write to the Qualifications Authority directly. (New Zealand Qualifications Authority, 79 Taranaki Street, PO Box 160, Wellington; tel 04-802 3420; fax 04-802 3112). The Qualifications Authority charges a fee for this service. British school qualifications are accepted as entry requirements for New Zealand universities. Details of entry requirements are available from the Trade Development Board.

Professional Qualifications

Professional employment in New Zealand is regulated by the relevant professional bodies. In order to work in these areas you must register with these organisations. In most cases this will involve an assessment of qualifications and experience and you may be required to take further examinations. In some professions you can arrange for these exams to be taken in your own country. It is important to contact the relevant professional body in good time because applications usually take several months to be considered and qualifying exams are held only once or twice a year in foreign countries. As an example of the type of procedure you have to go through, the following are required for foreign lawyers intending to practice in New Zealand:

Legal Practitioners seeking assessment should write to:
The Executive Director, New Zealand Law Society (26 Waring Taylor Street, Wellington, tel 04-4727837; fax 04-4737909; Website: www.nz_lawsoc.org.nz).

You will be required to include the following information:
Documentary evidence of tertiary educational standing and attainment,

including academic record, showing courses completed and grades.

Documentary evidence of admission as a lawyer in your own country.

A curriculum vitae giving names, dates, and places of practice.

A copy of your law school's handbook showing the structure of the degree and the content and length of each course.

A statutory declaration verifying identity and certifying the accuracy of the above information.

Where applicable, a demonstration of proficiency in the English language.

Two bank drafts in payment of application fees:

– One for NZ $100 payable to the New Zealand Law Society.

– One for NZ $720 payable to the Council for Legal Education.

Not all professional bodies have such complex registration procedures. Membership of the New Zealand Society of Accountants is automatically granted to any member of the three British Associations of Chartered Accountants, that is, the Institute of Chartered Accountants of England and Wales, the Institute of Chartered Accountants of Scotland, and the Chartered Association of Certified Accountants. However, any person in New Zealand is able to call themselves 'an accountant'. It is only when they want to call themselves 'chartered' that they will need to join the New Zealand body.

Teachers do not have to join a professional body, but overseas qualified teachers do have to have their qualifications assessed by the Teacher Registration Board. (PO Box 5326, Wellington; 04-4710852; fax 04-4710870).

Addresses of Professional Bodies

New Zealand Institute of Chartered Accountants: Cigna House, 40 Mercer Street, PO Box 11, 342 Manners Street, Wellington; tel (04)474 7840; fax (04) 473 6303.

New Zealand Institute of Architects: PO Box 438, Wellington; tel (04) 4735 346; fax (04) 472 0182.

The Dental Council of New Zealand: PO Box 10448, Wellington; tel (04) 499 4820; fax (04) 499 1668.

Institute of Professional Engineers NZ (inc): 101 Molesworth Street, PO Box 12-241, Wellington; tel (04)473 9444; fax (04)473 2324.

The Medical Council of New Zealand: 139 – 143 Willis Street, PO Box 11-649, Wellington; tel (04)3847635; fax (04)3858902.

The Nursing Council: 97-99 Courtney Place, PO Box 9644, Wellington; tel (04)385 9589; fax (04)801 8502.

Veterinary Association of New Zealand: 69 Boulcott Street, Wellington; tel (04) 471 0484; fax (04) 471 0494.

Finding a Job

Newspapers

Most New Zealand jobs are advertised in newspapers most of which have a daily situations vacant section which tends to be larger on one particular day of the week; usually Saturdays. Some professional jobs will be advertised in specialist publications and at executive level jobs are usually filled through recruitment agencies sometimes without being advertised.

The starting place for your job-hunt therefore, is the major New Zealand newspapers. A small number of jobs are advertised directly in the UK in the newspapers listed below. The types of jobs that tend to be advertised directly are in areas where there is a shortage of skills locally, for example in computers and information technology or accountancy.

The major daily newspapers can be read at New Zealand House in London (80 Haymarket SW1Y 4TQ) 9am-5pm weekdays).

Subscriptions to New Zealand newspapers can be obtained by contacting their media agent in the UK: Kevin Millyard, (TNT, Unit 6, Spitfire Way, Spitfire Estate, Hounslow, Middlesex TW5 9NW; tel 0181-848 1111; fax 0181-813 5232). In some cases it may be cheaper to contact the newspapers directly.

Useful Addresses

The Main New Zealand Newspapers

The New Zealand Herald: 46 Albert Street, Auckland; tel (09) 379 5050; fax (09) 373 6434 (Distributed throughout the North Island; Circulation 221,047). Internet www.nzherald.co.nz.

The Dominion: PO Box 3740, Wellington; tel (04) 474 0222; fax (04) 474 0490 (Distributed in lower North Island; Circulation 70,310).

The Evening Post: PO Box 3740, Wellington; tel (04) 474 0444; fax (04) 474 0237 (Distributed in lower North Island; Circulation 63,622). Website: www.evpost.co.nz.

The Press: Private Bag 4722, Christchurch; tel (03) 379 0940; fax (03) 364 8492 (Distributed in Canterbury and Nelson/Tasman region; Circulation 98,071). Internet:www.press.co.nz.

The Otago Daily Times: PO Box 181, Dunedin; tel (03) 477 4760; fax (03) 474 7423 (Distributed in lower South Island; Circulation 45,352). Website: www.odt.co.nz.

The above circulation figures are from the Newspaper Publishers Association, Wellington 1998.

Specialist Publications

Some types of jobs tend to be advertised in specialist magazines. These publications are also useful sources of information about the current job scene in their particular field. Another option would be to place a employment wanted advert with them.

Useful Addresses

Architecture New Zealand, Private Bag 99915 Newmarket, Auckland 1031, tel (09) 846 4068; fax (09) 846 8742.

Commercial Horticulture Magazine: cnr Aitken Terrace and King Street, Kingsland, Auckland; tel (09) 358 2749.

GP Weekly: Adis Press Ltd, Browns Bay Road, Browns Bay, Auckland, tel (09) 478 2268.

Horticulture News: PO Box 4233, Auckland; tel (09) 520 9451; fax (09) 520 9459.

Hospitality Magazine, PO Box 9596 Newmarket, Auckland, tel (09) 5293000; fax (09) 5293001.

Management: PO Box 5544, Auckland; tel (09) 630 8940.

Marketing Magazine: 72 Dominion Road, Mount Eden, Auckland; tel (09) 630 5626.

Mercantile Gazette: Suite 8, 200 Victoria Street, Auckland; tel/fax (09) 302 4892.
New Zealand Business: Level 2, 72 Dominion Road, Mount Eden, Auckland; tel (09) 630 5626.
New Zealand Farmer: PO Box 4233, Auckland; tel (09) 520 9451; fax (09) 579 9589.
New Zealand Manufacturer: Published by the New Zealand Manufacturers Federation Inc., 3-9 Church Street, PO Box 11543, Wellington; tel (04) 473 3000; fax (04) 473 3004; e-mail: manfed@manufacturers.org.nz.

Professional Associations

Many professional vacancies are carried in specialist magazines, which are usually published by the relevant professional associations. In some cases all vacancies appear in these publications, for example all permanent teaching jobs are advertised in the *Education Gazette*. They will also usually carry employment wanted adverts. Sometimes it is possible to subscribe just to the employment wanted pages. You can contact the professional bodies listed above for further information. Jobs with the New Zealand Government appear on the internet at www.jobs.govt.nz.

Useful Addresses

Chartered Accountants Journal of New Zealand: PO Box 11-342, Wellington; tel (04) 473 8544; fax (04) 472 6282.
Education Gazette: Legislation Services, GP Print, PO Box 3293, Thorndon, Wellington; tel (04) 471 5532; fax (04) 472 6444.
Law Talk: New Zealand Law Society, PO Box 5041, Wellington; tel (04) 472 7837; fax (04) 473 7909; e-mail: inquiries@nz_lawsoc.org.nz.
New Zealand Engineering: 101 Molesworth Street, Wellington; tel (04) 495 2399; fax (04) 473 4108.
The New Zealand Medical Journal: The New Zealand Medical Association, 26 The Terrace, PO Box 156, Wellington; tel (04) 472 4741; fax (04) 471 0838.
The New Zealand Dental Journal: PO Box 3016, Wellington; tel (04) 801 6187; fax (04) 801 6261.

Trades and Skilled Craftspeople

As is the case with the professional associations, in order to work in New Zealand as a trades or craftsperson, you must join the relevant association or society. If you have qualifications and experience in your own country you will not normally be required to fulfil any additional requirements. You should contact the organisations listed below for further details. Most of these organisations publish a trade magazine which may be a useful source of information about job prospects.

Useful Addresses

The New Zealand Society of Master Plumbers & Gasfitters Inc: 180 Taranaki Street, Wellington; tel (04) 384 4184; fax (04) 384 2456. Also publishes *The New Zealand Plumbers Journal:* address as above.
The New Zealand Master Builders Association, Willis Street, PO Box 1769, Wellington; tel (04) 384 9787. Also publishes: *Building Today:* 26 Prosford Street, PO Box 37-390, Parnell Road, Auckland; tel (09) 378 7959; fax (09) 308 9690.

New Zealand Institute of Surveyors: 171 Lambton Quay, Wellington; tel (04) 471 1774; fax (04) 471 1907. Also publishes *New Zealand Surveyor:* address as above.

The New Zealand Painting Contractors Association: 63 Mirimar Avenue, Mirimar PO Box 15-137, Wellington, tel/fax (04) 388 1516. Also publishes: *New Zealand Painter and Decorator:* address as above.

New Zealand Institute of Valuers: PO Box 27-146, Wellington; tel (04) 385 8436; fax (04) 382 9214. Also publishes: *New Zealand Valuers Journal:* address as above.

UK Newspapers and Directories

As noted above, the trend for the international advertising of jobs has not generally caught on with New Zealand employers because of the obvious difficulties with labour mobility to such a remote country. Only a small percentage of jobs are advertised directly in the UK. For example university lectureships are advertised in the *Times Higher Education Supplement.* The fortnightly publication *Overseas Jobs Express* advertises full time jobs in a variety of areas for many countries including New Zealand. As well there are two newspapers available in the UK for intending migrants to New Zealand, *Destination New Zealand* and *New Zealand Outlook.* These occasionally carry advertisements for jobs and usually carry advertisements for job-search agencies based in the UK which will help you look in New Zealand. The weekly paper for New Zealanders in London, *New Zealand News UK*, is a good source of job advertisements for positions in New Zealand. *New Zealand News UK* is distributed free in London outside central city tube stations and all three papers are available beside the Immigration Service visa inquiry desk on the third floor of New Zealand House or can be obtained on subscription from the addresses below.

Useful Addresses

Destination New Zealand: Outbound Newspapers, 1 Commercial Road, Eastbourne, East Sussex, BN21 3XQ; tel 01323- 412001; fax 01323-649249; e-mail: outbounduk@aol.com.

New Zealand News UK: PO Box 10, Berwick Upon Tweed, Northumberland, TD15 1BW; tel 01289-306677; fax 01289-307 377; or at Royal Opera Arcade, Haymarket, London SW1Y 4UY; tel 0171-930 6451; fax 0171-930 8780; e-mail: nznlondon@aol.com. Free weekly found in most London tube stations.

TNT Magazine: 14-15 Child's Place, Earls Court, London SW5 9RX; tel 0171-373 3377; fax 0171-341 6600. Free weekly again found in most London tube stations.

New Zealand Outlook: Consyl Publishing Ltd, 3 Buckhurst Road, Bexhill-on-Sea, Sussex TN40 1QF; tel 01424-223111. Published monthly. In the UK six issues cost £6.25 and twelve issues £11.50.

Overseas Jobs Express: Premier House, Shoreham Airport, West Sussex, BN43 5FF; tel 01273-440220; fax 01273-440229; e-mail: editor@overseasjobs.com. Published fortnightly.

Approaching Employers Direct

As in the UK, a large number of jobs are filled without ever being advertised. Advertising and screening applicants is lengthy and expensive. A well written CV which lands on the personnel manager's desk at the right time could save them time and money, and find you the type of job you want. It is also a way of exploiting personal contacts. You can begin your research by finding out the New Zealand companies working in your area of expertise. One place to start is the Yellow Pages which you can consult at the front desk of New Zealand House between 9am and 5pm weekdays. The Information Office on the Second Floor of New Zealand House has business directories and is open 2pm to 4pm weekdays. It is not a job search service however. You can obtain a copy of the *New Zealand Export Yearbook* from the Trade Development Board on the second floor of New Zealand House, which lists New Zealand companies involved in the export market and what range of products they sell. There is a list of major New Zealand employers at the end of this chapter. Two useful books are *Finding a Job in New Zealand* by Joy Muirhead (£9.99), and *A Wife's Guide to Living and Working Abroad* by Robin Pascoe (£8.95). These can be ordered through Consyl Publishing Ltd. (3 Buckhurst Road, Bexhill-on-Sea, East Sussex TN40 1QF; tel 01424-223 111).

Chambers of Commerce & Professional Institutes

Chambers of Commerce exist to serve the interests of their members, local businesses, not as job search agencies but they are usually prepared to help with information. Local chambers of commerce should provide you with a list of their members for a small fee. A list of Chambers of Commerce in the main cities can be found in the *Regional Employment Guide* below. Another type of organisation which will have details of member companies are the professional institutes. Also listed below are the NZ-UK Chamber of Commerce and the American Chamber of Commerce which publish directories of British and American companies respectively with branches, affiliates or subsidiaries in New Zealand.

Useful Addresses

Chambers of Commerce:
American Chamber of Commerce: PO Box 106 002, Auckland; tel 09-4727549.
New Zealand Chambers of Commerce: PO Box 11-043, Manners St, Wellington; fax/tel (04) 4723376.
Australasian-UK Chamber of Commerce: 393 The Strand, London WC2R 0LT; tel 0171-379 0720; fax 0171-379 0721.

Professional Institutes and Registration Bodies:
Architects Education and Registration Board: PO Box 438, Wellington; tel (04)473 5346; fax (04) 472 0182.
New Zealand Bankers Institute: PO Box 3043, Wellington; tel (04)472 8838; fax (04) 473 1698.
Electrical Works Registration Board: PO Box 10156, Wellington; tel (04)472 3636; fax (04) 473 2395.
Insurance Institute Of New Zealand: 111-115 Customhouse Quay, PO Box 1368, Wellington; tel (04)499 4630; fax (04) 499 4536.
New Zealand Institute of Management: 1-5 Ghuznee Street, PO Box 67, Wellington; tel (04) 473 7737; fax (04) 471 1926; e-mail: nzim@central.co.nz.
Nursing Council of New Zealand: PO Box 9644, Wellington; tel (04)385 9589; fax (04) 801 8502.
Pharmaceutical Council of New Zealand: PO Box 11640, Wellington; tel (04)385 9708; fax (04) 384 8085.

Plumbers, Gasfitters and Drainlayers Board: PO Box 11422, Wellington; tel (04)384 2751; fax (04) 384 7468.

Real Estate Agents Licensing Board: PO Box 5570, Wellesley Street, Auckland; tel (09) 520 6949; fax (09) 379 8471.

Teachers Registration Board: PO Box 5326, Wellington; tel (04)471 0852; fax (04) 471 0870.

Veterinary Council of New Zealand: PO Box 10563, Wellington; tel (04)473 9600; fax (04) 473 8869.

Placing Employment Wanted Adverts

Another approach is placing an employment wanted advert with the newspapers and publications listed above. Contact the newspapers directly for advertising rates.

Employment Agencies

UK-based Organisations

There are a number of organisations in the UK which can help you find a job in New Zealand. Some companies specialise in finding jobs for intending migrants, others recruit on behalf of employers and sometimes have New Zealand assignments. The latter type operate on behalf of employers and do not search on behalf of prospective workers, however they will fill some vacancies from people they have on their books so it may be worthwhile sending them a CV and a speculative application. As has been mentioned elsewhere, help with job seeking is one of the services which immigration consultancies provide.

Recruitment and Job Search Agencies for intending emigrants:

Taylor & Associates (Head Office): PO Box 99122 Newmarket, Auckland; tel (09) 520 0765; fax (09) 520 0764; e-mail: nzjobs@tayassc.co.nz. UK Representative Office: PO Box 1401, Chester, Cheshire, CH1 1FF; tel 01244-321414; fax 01244-342288. Professional migrant job search consultants specialising in Australia and New Zealand. Member of the New Zealand Association for Migration and Investment (NZAMI). See advertisement on inside front cover.

Emigration Consultancy Services: 8 De Salis Court, Hampton Lovett, Droitwich, Worcestershire WR9 0NX; tel 01562- 755998; fax 01905-795557.

Grays Recruitment Services: 3c Church Road, Berwick, Scotland EH39 4AD; tel 01620 892 609; fax 01620 895 320.

Hewitson-Walker Group: New Zealand House, 80 Haymarket, London SW1Y 4HW; tel 0171-321 2999; fax 0171-839 5919.

International Jobsearch: 5 College Street, St Albans, Herts, AL3 4PW; tel 01727- 865533; fax 01727-846751.

Morgan and Banks International: Telephone Luan Skelland 0171-240 1040, or Leigh Efferion in New Zealand 09-367 9000. For work in the banking, insurance or commercial sectors.

Parker Bridge Recruitment Ltd: 1st Floor, Marlborough Court, 14-16 Holborn, London EC1N 2LE; tel 0171-464 1550; fax 0171-464 1999. Auckland branch: tel 09-377 3727; fax 09 – 3031496. Financial sector.

Prime Recruitment Contracts: 105a East Street, Southampton; SO14 3HH; tel 01703-233277.

Two useful websites for job listings are at www.nzjobs.co.nz and www.apl.co.nz.

New Zealand Employment Service

The Department of Labour in New Zealand provides job-search assistance through the New Zealand Employment Service, a network of 75 offices advertising local vacancies. They carry a wide range of vacancies for casual, skilled and unskilled work, and offer advice and information on training for job seekers. There is no fee to use the Employment Service, but you have to be a New Zealand resident or citizen. Contact the *New Zealand Employment Service:* freephone 0800 808 222 for an office near you.

Employment Agencies in New Zealand

There are a large number of private employment agencies in New Zealand. As in the UK, these agencies charge the employer when they make a successful placement and are free for the job seeker, although they will offer other services such as career assessment and advice on preparation of CVs for which there may be a charge.

Useful Addresses

Computing/Information Technology
Aacorn International Ltd: PO Box 105-355, Auckland Central; tel (09) 309 7862; fax (09) 309 9034; Website: www.aacorn.co.nz.
Enterprise Staff Consultants Ltd: 3rd Floor, Ferry Building, 99 Quay Street, Auckland, PO Box 1799, Auckland; tel (09) 309 4349; fax (09) 307 1285; e-mail: office@enterprise.co.nz.
Information Technology Recruitment (ITEC): PO Box 6798, Wellesley Street, Auckland; tel (09) 302 5304; fax (09) 373 2968; e-mail: itec@xtra.co.nz.
Mercury Consulting Group: PO Box 10 – 605, Wellington; tel (04) 499 2624; fax (04) 499 1655; e-mail: inquire@mercuryrecruit.co.nz.
Panda Computer People: 20 Pukerangi Crescent, Ellerslie, PO Box 11-011, Auckland; tel (09) 525 7420; fax (09) 525 7430.
Qube Associates Ltd: EDP Personnel Consultants, PO Box 1849, Auckland; tel (09) 307 3852; fax (09) 366 7171.

Farming
Agfirst Consultants Ltd: PO Box 1261, Hastings; tel (06) 876 9200; fax (06) 876 9225; e-mail: hawksbay@agfirst.co.nz.
Agriculture New Zealand: First Floor, 127 Keith Street, Box 1345 Palmerston North; tel (06) 350 1720; fax (06) 351 7901; e-mail: radfordd@agnz.co.nz.
Marvin Farm Services: 95 Awara Street, PO Box 248, Matamata, Waikato; tel (07) 8886025; fax (07) 888 6023.

Finance/Accountancy
Clayton Ford: Level 6, Clayton Ford House, 132 The Terrace, PO Box 10083, Wellington; tel (04) 473 6223; fax (04) 471 2100; e-mail: clayton.ford@xtra.co.nz
Opal Consulting Group: POB 7067, Auckland; tel 09-379 0200; fax (09) 377 4127; e-mail: opal@opalconsult.co.nz

Professional/Managerial/General
Advanced Personnel Services Ltd: First Floor, 829 Colombo, Christchurch; tel (03)3654322; fax (03)3657356.
Drake International: 10th floor Scollway House 5-7 Willeston Street, PO Box

10063, Wellington; tel (04) 472 6972; fax (04) 473 4930.
IDPE Consulting Group: Level 13, Dalmuir House, 114 The Terrace, PO Box 4191, Wellington; tel (04) 472 2212; fax (04) 472 2211.
Lampen Group: PO Box 2155, Wellington; tel (04) 472 4157; fax (04) 471 0958. Auckland branch; PO Box 2438, Auckland; tel 09-357 9800; fax 09-357 9801.
Wheeler Campbell Consulting Ltd: PO Box 205 Wellington; tel 04-499 1500 (24 Hours); fax 04-499 160;. Website: www.wheelercampbell.co.nz.

Hotel/Catering
Artisan International NZ Ltd: PO Box 56 159 Auckland; tel (09) 358 0500; fax (09) 358 5111; e-mail: artisan@xtra.co.nz
Kelly Staffing Services: PO Box 10151, Wellington; tel (04) 499 2825; fax (04) 499 2821.

Medical/Nursing
Acorn: PO Box 74-385, Auckland; tel (09) 630 8300.
Auckland Medical Bureau: 469 Parnell Road, PO Box 37753, Auckland; tel (09) 377 5903.
Healthlink: Suite 1 Level 1 72 Dominion Road, and PO Box 5393, Wellesley Street, Auckland; tel (09) 303 3122.
Nightingale Nursing and Homecare Ltd: PO Box 54-137, Plimmerton, Wellington; tel (04) 239 9230.
Wheeler Campbell Consulting Ltd: PO Box 205 Wellington; tel 04-499 1500 (24 Hours); fax 04-499 1600. Website: www.wheelercampbell.co.nz
Internet job vacancies for health professionals can be found at www.hospitals.co.nz

Secretarial
Opal Consulting Group: PO Box 2209 Wellington; tel (04) 385 4011; fax (04) 385 6704; e-mail: wgtn@opalconsult.co.nz; Auckland Branch: POB 7067, Auckland; tel 09-379 0200; fax 09 377 4127; e-mail: opal@opalconsult.co.nz.
Alectus Recruitment Consultants: Level 6, Ports of Auckland Building, Quay Street Auckland; tel (09) 366 3866.

Company or Organisation Transfers

One alternative to finding work yourself in New Zealand is to find work with a company with prospects of being transferred to New Zealand. Unfortunately few companies recruit staff with the promise of being posted to a particular country, however if you choose a New Zealand company to work for, your chances are obviously greater. Still this process is likely to be a long term route into New Zealand. The Australasian-UK Chambers of Commerce publishes the *Australasian British Business Directory* which is available for £35.00 and covers New Zealand companies operating in the UK and vice versa. The American Chamber of Commerce in New Zealand publishes a similar directory of American companies operating in New Zealand. (See the addresses above). The big multinationals also have subsidiaries in New Zealand, sometimes under different names. For example Levers trades in New Zealand as Unilever.

Job Application

The job application process in New Zealand is similar to that in the UK. A typical application will comprise of a letter of application or covering letter and a curriculum vitae (CV). Companies short-list on the basis of CVs and interview the selected candidates before making a decision.

Application Letters and CVs.

If you are sending off speculative letters it is worth taking the time to ring up the company and find out who the personnel or general manager is. A personally addressed letter is much more effective than one which is clearly a copy of one sent to a dozen other companies. Letters, whether applying for a specific vacancy or inquiring about possible future vacancies, should be formal in tone, brief (one side of an A4 sheet), and should outline why you are particularly qualified to work for the company. Curriculum Vitaes are expected to cover much the same sort of ground as CVs in the UK, education, qualifications, work experience, skills and personal details. In New Zealand CVs list jobs and qualifications in reverse chronological order, ie the most recent job first and the earliest last. Try to keep it to two pages and make sure it is clearly laid out. This is particularly important if you are faxing applications to New Zealand as fax machines blur copy slightly and if the typeface on your CV is too small, some important details may be lost. It is worthwhile getting some professional advice on the preparation of your CV; services which assist with CVs can be found under Employment Agencies in the Yellow Pages. Do not send original documents with applications.

Interview Procedure

If you are applying for a job in New Zealand from the UK, and the company wishes to interview you, in most cases they will not be prepared to pay your travel costs. Some companies will arrange interviews by video link or telephone. Another option to consider is to arrange a number of job interviews to coincide with a visit to New Zealand, or your arrival in New Zealand if your residency has been approved. There are job search companies in the UK who specialise in lining up job interviews before you set off for New Zealand. See the section *UK Employment Agencies*, above.

Job interviews in New Zealand are practically no different to those you might expect in the UK. They tend to be quite formal and you should dress appropriately for a work situation, although the dress code in the New Zealand work place is slightly more casual than in Britain. If you wish to brush up your job search and interviewing skills, most bookshops stock 'how to' guides for finding work.

It is illegal for employers to discriminate on the basis of sex, race, colour, marital status or sexual orientation. Firms will usually have an Equal Employment Opportunity (EEO) policy in their Mission Statement and will have a quota set of the proportion of their workers who are from minority groups.

Aspects of Employment

Salaries

You should not expect a New Zealand salary to be the same as a salary in your home country once the exchange rate is taken into account. Salaries in New Zealand are lower than those for equivalent positions in Europe. On the other hand, living costs are considerably lower. Primary produce, fruit and vegetables, and clothing are all quite cheap. It is difficult to make a direct comparison of living standards between Europe and New Zealand because so many factors are hard to compare. For example, going overseas for an annual holiday becomes very expensive when the nearest country is three hours away, and that is only Australia. On the other hand, you have easy access to great beaches and can enjoy much better climate than northern Europeans, year round. As a generalisation it would be fair to say that living standards are equivalent for most middle income earners. Despite New Zealand's egalitarian attitudes and equal employment policies, there is still some pay disparity between men and women. The average weekly earnings were listed by the Department of Statistics as $744.94 for males and $556.03 for females. The following salaries for different occupations will give you an idea of relative earnings.

Accountant:	$55,000+
Accounts Clerk:	$30,000-$40,000
Engineer:	$50,000+
General middle management:	$85,000+
Secretary in an office:	$25,000-$30,000
Stockbroker:	$50,000+

The minimum wage is set out below:

	Youth Rate	Adult(over 20 years old)
per hour	$4.20	$7.00
per day (8 hours)	$33.60	$56.00
per week(40 hours)	$168.00	$280.00

Working Conditions

Standard conditions of employment used to be a forty-hour week, 8.30am-5pm, five days a week. However with the introduction of more flexible working arrangements under the new industrial relations legislation, variations on this theme, such as glide time, are becoming increasingly common. For example Fisher & Paykel, New Zealand's largest manufacturer of kitchen and laundry appliances has shifted to ten hour shifts, four days a week, in some of their divisions. Rates for overtime are another area changing due to the impact of new legislation. Whereas under the old award system (the equivalent of British collective agreements) overtime in most industries was one and half times the standard rates, in many sectors now particularly for casual workers and in the service sector, overtime rates are being cut back or disappearing entirely. Longer working hours are also becoming a feature of many industries. Holiday provision is still protected by law under the Holidays Act. After twelve months' continuous employment, the employee is entitled to three weeks paid leave. In addition there are 11 paid public holidays. Employees do not have to work on public holidays unless they agree or their contract provides for this. The compulsory retirement age is 65, although this is to be progressively phased out by the end of the decade.

Parental Leave

Parental leave is available to employees who have worked for 12 months or more with the same employer, either part-time (for more than ten hours per week) or full time. Employees adopting a child under five years old are also entitled to parental leave. The types of leave are all unpaid and the conditions are as follows:

Special Leave: Up to ten days during pregnancy for women to have ante-natal checks.

Maternity Leave: Up to 14 continuous weeks for the mother which can start up to six weeks before the expected date of birth.

Paternity Leave: Up to two continuous weeks for the father around the expected date of birth.

Extended Leave: Up to 52 continuous weeks, excluding any maternity leave taken available in the 12 months after the birth. Extended leave may be shared by both parents but may not exceed 52 weeks in total.

Job Protection
If you take less than four weeks parental leave, your job must be kept open. If you take more than four weeks, the employer may decide that the job cannot be kept open, but you have a right to challenge that decision. If you accept this decision then you are entitled to a preference period of six months when the employer must offer you a job substantially similar to the one you have left. You may not be dismissed for becoming pregnant or for applying for parental leave.

Trades Unions

Prior to the Employment Contracts Act of 1991, New Zealand unions enjoyed a monopoly over workplace representation and union membership in many industries was compulsory. The resulting system of wage determination was highly centralised and inflexible. If unions and employers negotiating in each industry at a national level could not agree, the dispute would be settled through compulsory arbitration by a tribunal made up of members from both sides. As a result of this system, employment conditions were guaranteed at some minimum level in just about all industries, and the disparity between the high paid and the low paid was not very great.

The Employment Contracts Act of 1991 removed union monopolies over bargaining in the workplace, abolished compulsory membership, and the Arbitration Tribunals. Wage fixing is now in theory completely decentralised, although some of the bigger unions still negotiate at national level. Employers and employees negotiate employment contracts which may be either collective or individual. Employees may nominate someone to act as their bargaining agent. Employers are obliged to recognise whoever an employee nominates as their bargaining agent although this does not mean they must negotiate or settle with that agent. Now that trade unions no longer have a protected legal status, total membership has fallen from approximately 683, 000 in 1985 to approximately 339, 000 in 1996, which is approximately 20% of the labour force. The number of employees on collective agreements has also fallen sharply: 75% of the workforce are now employed on individual contracts. Flexibility has brought benefits to some employees and industries but has weakened the position of others. Part time workers, those in workplaces with only a few employees and the service sector generally all have less job security, fewer employment protections and in some cases have seen a real reduction in pay. The current coalition government plans to make amendments to the act, but isn't in agreement as to the direction of the changes needed; National wants to tighten the act in such ways as removing personal grievance rights for new workers, and change the way the Employment Court operates, while New Zealand First wants to relax the act by strengthening the protection available to workers.

Most New Zealand unions belong to the national body: The New Zealand Council of Trade Unions (PO Box 6645, Wellington tel (04) 3851 334; fax (04)

385 6051; e-mail: ctu@hq.nzctu.union.org.nz; website www.union.org.nz). The NZCTU publishes a comprehensive directory of all trade unions in the country.

Employment Contracts

At the beginning of your employment you will negotiate an employment contract with your employer. You can be covered under an existing collective contract if it provides for new workers to join and if your employer agrees. Otherwise you will negotiate an individual contract. Individual contracts can be either written or oral but it is desirable to have a written contract. If you wish to have a bargaining agent represent you, you have a choice between joining a union or employing a private bargaining agent. Remember though that though your employer must recognise your bargaining agent they are not obliged to settle with them. An employment contract must by law have certain provisions. There must be an effective personal grievance procedure and disputes procedure. The minimum conditions outlined above, wages and holiday provision and the parental leave provisions, cannot be overridden. A good checklist for individual employment contracts can be obtained from the magazine published by a network of independent legal firms called *Lawlink* (tel 09-366 0775; fax 09-309 5113), or found at their website http://knowledge_basket.co.nz/lawlink.

Employment Tribunal & Employment Court

Two institutions for resolving disputes were set up under the Act, the Tribunal, which mostly mediates in disputes, either personal disputes or grievances arising from breach of employment contracts, and the Employment Court which deals with matters referred on by the tribunal, and more serious issues such as disputes involving strikes and lockouts. There is no right to strike while an employment contract is current.

Women in Work

Over 55% of New Zealand women over the age of 15 work in either full or part time jobs. This figure has been steadily increasing since the 1960s, although it seems to have plateaued in recent years and even dropped off slightly in the late 80s, which may reflect the effects of the economic downturn. The participation rates for women are considerably lower than the corresponding figures for men across all age groups and particularly in the 25-34 age group, reflecting the fact that women are still the primary care givers for children. About a third of the female workforce work part time, a much higher figure than for men.

Despite still bearing more family responsibilities than men, New Zealand women are moving into previously male dominated areas, particularly the professions. Female students outnumber men in areas such as medicine and law, although this is a recent development and men still dominate at senior levels in these professions. Equal pay for the same work was established under the Equal Pay Act of 1972, and other forms of discrimination in the workplace based on gender, race or any other non relevant factor is illegal under the Human Rights Commission Act of 1972. If you believe you have been discriminated against unlawfully, you can either use the personal grievance procedures in your employment contract or you can make a complaint to the Human Rights Commission. Despite the effects of the Equal Pay Act, women's ordinary time earnings remain about 25% lower than men's. Women are still concentrated in a narrower range of occupations which in general, pay less well. Equal pay claims are also harder to establish in the new environment of individual contracts. Discrimination in individual cases is much harder to prove than in a situation where everyone receives the same rate of pay for a job. Despite these negative influences, the attitude towards women in employment in New Zealand is generally positive. Childcare is becoming more affordable now that the government subsidises pre-school care centres. Some of these advances have been achieved through the efforts of women politicians. Women have a high profile in New Zealand public life. A third of the members of parliament are women and currently, Jenny Shipley is New Zealand's first female Prime Minister.

Permanent Work

Executive Employment Prospects

Although New Zealand is currently in a recession, prospects are good for executive employment as the local labour market is unable to provide enough suitably skilled applicants for the demand. However, the executive vacancies are for people with a high level of technical and interpersonal skills.

Information Technology

There is always a demand for skilled programmers particularly with university level qualifications. New Zealanders qualified in these areas tend to be attracted overseas by the comparatively higher salaries. Currently the types of positions being advertised are for software developers with skills in C, C++, Unix, Dos and OS2.

Medical

The numbers of foreign doctors registering with the Medical Council has increased in recent years and the Council is now worried that there may be soon be an oversupply of medical personnel. The increase in numbers seems to be the result of an increase in numbers of skilled immigrants, particularly from South Africa which has resulted in a reverse 'brain-drain'. The situation in New Zealand has usually been the opposite with trained New Zealanders going abroad leaving opportunities for qualified migrants. You should contact the Medical Council for an accurate assessment of employment opportunities. As has been noted already, you must register with the Medical Council in order to practice as a doctor in New Zealand. Doctors from Australia, Britain, Ireland and South Africa who have been registered in their own country are usually accepted for registration without requiring further qualifications. Doctors from other countries will usually have to sit registration exams.

Nurses must apply to be registered with the Nursing Council of New Zealand. The current employment situation is not particularly good for general nurses although the Council notes that there are opportunities for experienced nurses and midwives with specialist skills. Psychiatric, renal, orthopaedics, general surgical are other areas where vacancies are currently being advertised.

Teaching

There are currently excellent work opportunities within the New Zealand education system. At time of print, there is such a dearth of primary and secondary school teachers that a department has been created in the Ministry of Education to encourage teachers to come to New Zealand to work. Contact TeachNZ for more information (TeachNZ, Ministry of Education, PO Box 1666, Wellington; tel 04-473 5544; fax 04-471 4432).

As noted above, immigrants intending to teach require to have their qualifications approved by the Teacher Registration Board. There is a particular demand for qualified science and mathematics teachers. The *Education Gazette* is published fortnightly and advertises all permanent teaching positions in state and independent schools. You can read copies of the Gazette at the Information Office, second floor New Zealand House, or by subscribing directly to the address above. (See *Professional Associations*).

Short-term Employment

Short-term employment prospects are improving as the economy picks up after some rather lean years. However, as already noted in Chapter Two, *Residence and Entry* unless you are a New Zealander or have residency you will have to get a work visa to work while in New Zealand, even for a short period. One of the conditions of these visas is that you are doing jobs for which there are no appropriately qualified New Zealanders. Given that the types of jobs most people obtain while travelling are unskilled labouring jobs, your chances of working legitimately are not great. There is a lot of paperwork for your employer to get through, (see Chapter Two) just to hire a fruit picker.

Alternatively, if you are a British citizen aged between 18 and 30 you can apply for one of the 500 working holiday visas issued each year, before you leave for New Zealand. (See *Residence and Entry* chapter) If you do not have a work permit, many farmers may not be too concerned as they have many short term jobs, particularly seasonal jobs in rural areas and often cannot find locals interested in doing them. Under these circumstances you may find that employers are more interested in whether you are keen on working than whether you are legal. But be careful because in recent years the Immigration Service has been doing sweeps of picking gangs in remote areas to check whether they have work permits. You may endanger your chances of staying in New Zealand if you try to bend the rules on working.

Agriculture

There are a lot of opportunities for keen workers in orchards, even if you have little or no experience. However, since the work is unskilled you will find that pay rates are far from high. Fruit picking tends to be paid at what is called piece rates (rates per kilo or bin filled). Obviously as you get better at the work, your pay rates improve but you may find it discouraging going, as well as back-breaking depending on the crop; asparagus picking is reputed to be the worst. It is possible to follow the different harvests around the country as each type of produce comes into season and to find work virtually year round. In the main horticultural areas during the harvest, work will not be hard to find. Farmers advertise locally, sometimes contacting local youth hostels or backpackers' accommodation, or simply putting a sign up at the gate. They will often provide accommodation, albeit of a rather basic kind, and sometimes even fresh fruit and vegetables or dairy products. Generally the remoter the area, the more difficulty the farmers have in attracting local labour, so the better your chances. However this is no guarantee that they will be able to pay more, they are just more likely to provide non-wage perks such as accommodation or food in order to get the workers. For details of the timing and locations of various harvests see *Work Your Way Around the World* available from Vacation Work Publications (9 Park End Street, Oxford OX1 1HJ; tel 01865-241978; fax 01865-790 885; Website: www.vacationwork. co.uk).

Unlike fruit picking, working on farms usually requires some experience. For example you will see almost daily advertisements in the Waikato papers for milkers, but they require people with the skills already. Some unskilled work is available in shearing sheds, for example the job of rousie (the person who picks up the shorn fleeces) does not require much beyond a strong pair of arms. If you have at least two years practical farming under your belt and want to get experience of working on a New Zealand farm, you can contact the International Farm Experience Programme, (YFC Centre, National Agricultural Centre, Stoneleigh Park, Stoneleigh, Warwickshire, CV8 2LG; tel 01203-696584; fax 01203-696559; e-mail: ifep@yfc_web.org.uk).

The majority of grapes produced in New Zealand are used to make wine. Wine production is one of New Zealand's fastest growing industries – over the years 1995-1996 the 6000 hectare area of grape vines increased ten per cent. The major export market for New Zealand wine is Britain, which buys 68% of the volume of total wine exports. New Zealand has sought a wine agreement with the European Union to gain access to valuable European markets. Further expansion in the industry is expected also because the number of vineyards in the country are increasing.

Au Pair/Nannying

There is some demand for nannies and au pairs in New Zealand. The term au pair is uncommon, and the generic term child-carer is more usual. Posts are advertised in the daily papers or on local notice boards. There are agencies who can be found in the Yellow Pages. Wages are quite low, around NZ$7 per hour, or $290-310 per week.

Useful Addresses

ABC Superior Nanny Agency: PO Box 10555, The Terrace, Wellington; tel (04) 499 9839.

Karitane Nurses and Nannies Bureau: PO Box 292, Albany, Auckland; tel (09) 575 7174.

Auckland Nanny Company: PO Box 142 Greenhithe, Auckland; tel (09) 413 8336.

Teaching English

New Zealand is a popular destination for Asian students wanting to learn English, because of its reputation as a safe and friendly country. As an employment prospect you will almost certainly need the appropriate TEFL qualifications or experience in order to get a work permit, because as has already been noted above, the Immigration Service has to be satisfied that you have skills not possessed by New Zealand job seekers. Speaking English as your first language is not enough to qualify you, however much you may dispute whether Nu Zilindish as spoken by the natives is actually English at all. There are more than 40 public and private English-language schools. Some of the bigger ones are listed below.

Useful Addresses
Aspiring Language Institute: 242 Papanui Road, Christchurch; tel (03) 355 3231.
Capital Language Academy: Level 9 The Breeze Plaza, 65 Manners Street, PO

Box 1100, Wellington; tel (04) 472 7557; fax (04) 472 5285.
Dominion English School: 47 Customs St, Auckland, PO Box 4217, Auckland; tel
   (09) 377 3280; fax (09) 377 3473; e-mail: study@dominion.co.nz.
Dominion English School: 4th Floor, 116 Worcester Street, PO Box 3908,
   Christchurch; (03) 365 3370; e-mail: study@dominion.co.nz.
Garden City English School: cnr Hereford Street and Oxford Terrace,
   Christchurch; tel (03) 377 0091; fax (03) 377 1251.
International Language Academies: 20 & 50 Kilmore Street, PO Box 25 – 170
   Christchurch; tel (03) 3795452; fax (03) 3795373.
Languages International: 27 Princes St, PO Box 5293, Auckland 1; tel (09) 309
   0615; fax (09) 3772806; e-mail: success@langsint.co.nz.
Seafield School of English: 1/99 Seaview Road, Christchurch; tel (03) 388 3850;
   fax (03) 388 4970.
Southern English Schools: 69 Worcester Bvd, PO Box 1300, Christchurch; tel/fax
   (03) 365 6022.

Tourism

Over a million tourists visit New Zealand each year and as a result there are a lot
of opportunities for casual workers in the tourist regions. Hotel and catering staff
positions in tourist destinations are a good place to start looking. Working hours
are long and the pay low, but on the other hand, the location may make up for the
working conditions. Tourists tip better than locals as New Zealanders traditionally
do not tip serving staff. If you can ski and have the relevant qualification, there are
a lot of opportunities on New Zealand ski fields for ski instructors or ski patrol
personnel. Other types of skills which may help you find employment are aquatic
sports skills such as scuba diving, water skiing, or life saving skills. New Zealand
beaches are patrolled by mostly by volunteer surf life savers who have specialist
skills in rescuing people from the often turbulent waters so you are more likely to
finding employment looking after hotel or private pools. Qualified aerobics
instructors should find opportunities at the many private gyms around the country.

Voluntary work

If you want to avoid work permit hassles and still be legal, there are voluntary
schemes whereby you can work in exchange for food and lodgings. The most well
known scheme goes under the name of WWOOF, which stands for Willing Workers
on Organic Farms. There are many organic farms in New Zealand so potentially you
could see quite a lot of the country without paying for your accommodation. Usually
you do about half a day's work in exchange for your board and lodgings. The work
can be quite varied and you should be prepared for strictly vegetarian rations Send a
s.a.e. to the UK branch of WWOOF (PO Box 2675, Lewes, Sussex BN7; tel 01273-
476286), who will send you a membership application form; membership costs £10
per year for UK residents and £15 per year for non UK residents, and after you have
volunteered for two weekends in Britain you can request the list of WWOOF
headquarters around the world. Alternatively you can write directly to New Zealand
and request the list of WWOOFer farms from Andrew and Jane Strange, (PO Box
1172, Nelson, New Zealand) for a fee of NZ$15.

   The New Zealand Wilderness Trust is another organisation which offers
volunteer work. Based in Hamilton, the NZWT provides practical conservation
work for volunteers, and their address is (PO Box 19300, Hamilton; tel 07 839
6767; fax 07 838 1184).

Business and Industry Report

The New Zealand economy again seems to be facing a period of uncertainty, as it faces the fallout of the economic and political upheavals of South East Asia. The value of the dollar has plummeted, as have petrol and house prices (which is a good thing for immigrants wishing to come to New Zealand) Consumer confidence has picked up, but business confidence remains low. Growth in New Zealand's GDP is expected to pick up in 1999, to reach 3.5% by the Millennium. At this stage in the economic cycle could be a good time to invest in New Zealand. Factor costs are already 20-25% lower than in Australia. The weakened economy is expected to drag down inflation which was only 1.3% in 1998. The Asian crisis has caused falling commodity prices in certain export sectors, such as the agriculture, mining, chemicals and minerals sectors. However, the wood and pulp and paper sector has not been so badly affected by Asia.

Agriculture

Agriculture contributes over $4.3 billion annually to the New Zealand economy and accounts for 60% of its export earnings. It is one of the major agricultural exporting countries in the world and is the largest exporter of lamb and mutton, providing over half the world's exports of these products. The New Zealand agricultural industry is highly mechanised and is a low employer of labour as a result. The average family farm employs the farmer, spouse and perhaps one farmhand. It is also one of the most efficient agricultural sectors in the world and has the lowest level of subsidies of any OECD country. The removal of supplementary minimum payments in 1984 was predicted by many in the farming sector to be a disaster. Instead although some farmers were forced to sell up, the sector responded by becoming more efficient and although farm land prices have not yet recovered to their pre-SMP prices, farm profitability is once again favourable. Farmers are now vulnerable to world prices in agricultural commodities and as a result many have diversified in order to spread their risk. Reliance upon traditional production areas has declined: sheep numbers are at their lowest since the 1950s as a result of low wool prices. New production areas such as venison are being developed. Farmers are experimenting with diversification of land use, planting land for forestry while still grazing it, for example. Despite the uncertainty of trading at world prices, the removal of subsidies seem to have done the industry good. The diversity of output has helped the country expand its export markets.

The main products are still sheep meat, dairy products, wool and beef. New Zealand has a natural advantage in agriculture due to its climate which is ideal for grassland farming. The land itself was not originally suited for this purpose being heavily forested and quite hilly. It has been brought under cultivation by lot of effort and the application of grassland management techniques developed in New Zealand's specialist agricultural research stations. Some of this agricultural expertise is being exported overseas in the form of sales of farm machinery, developed in New Zealand, agricultural consulting services, and New Zealand breeding animals. New Zealand is a world leader in animal and plant breeding technology. There were hopes some years ago that 'agri-tech' might double its contribution to export earnings, but this seems to have been an optimistic assessment. On the other hand this sector is primarily responsive to local demand and as farm profitability improves, it is likely investment in agricultural production techniques will increase.

The impact of the 1994 GATT agreement improved market access for New Zealand's agricultural exports. Under the Uruguay Agreement the European Union will have to lift the current restrictive quotas which prevent access for New Zealand butter and lamb into European markets. however, the current outlook for the agricultural industry is not good. Agricultural commodity prices have suffered badly from the Asian crisis and low global inflation.

Banking and Finance

Banking and financial services was one of the fastest growing employment sectors between 1986 and 1991. In part this was a one-off boom as a result of the deregulation of the financial sector as part of the programme of economic reform instituted by the Labour government in the 1980s. As a result of deregulation there was a rapid growth in money market activity, particularly in the areas of foreign exchange, where all restrictions over transfers were lifted. New Zealand's relatively undeveloped financial industry enjoyed a boom. A range of new financial instruments was introduced such as forward contracts, options and exchange rate futures and secondary markets such as in government securities grew. The share market soared due to the increase in money supply resulting from deregulation. The boom was short-lived however and the inevitable collapse came in October 1987 when the main share price index, the Barclays share index dropped to below its 1984 level. It has not recovered to pre-crash levels.

The second stage of deregulation in the financial sector occurred in the late 1980s. The regulations governing the supervision and registration of banks was relaxed under the Reserve Bank of New Zealand Act of 1986, and as result most building societies registered as banks and a number of foreign banks established New Zealand subsidiaries. Two further acts in 1987 and 1988 further removed distinctions between trading banks, trustee banks and building societies. The increase in the number of financial institutions and the range of activities they were involved in resulted in a rapid growth of employment in this area. Activity has levelled off recently and it seems likely that employment growth will as well.

Construction

Construction is another industry affected by the downturn in New Zealand's economy. Residential construction has fallen, and commercial construction remains steady, but no major growth is expected. When looking for employment, generally it is easier for skilled tradespeople; carpenters, fitters, welders and joiners to find work in this sector. New Zealand construction companies have particular expertise in building to earthquake proof standards. The construction industry employs more than 6% of the workforce.

Energy, Coal and Petrochemicals

Coal is New Zealand's largest energy resource, with nearly nine billion tons potentially recoverable according to the Coal Resource Survey programme. New Zealand produces just under three million tons of coal annually, mainly sub-bituminous coal from North Island fields. The West Coast of the South Island is the biggest source of bituminous coal most of which is exported to Japan, India and China. The quality of New Zealand coal makes it ideal for use in the chemical and steel industries. Industrial usage consumes nearly three-quarters of the remaining production. Coal is no longer a feed stock for thermal power stations as gas is becoming more competitive. In the future dual process stations such as the power station at Huntly, north of Hamilton which can use either gas or coal may go back to using coal as domestic gas supplies decline. The petrochemical industry is concentrated around the natural gas and oil fields off the coast of Taranaki. Six fields produce crude oil, condensate and natural gas which provide about 50% of New Zealand's energy needs. Natural gas is the major product. Around a third of natural gas produced is used to make synthetic petrol at a processing plant near Motonui.

Seventy to 80% of New Zealand's electricity supply is produced by hydro-electric generators on major rivers. The generating authority currently is the Electricity Corporation of New Zealand (ECNZ), a state owned enterprise. It runs 31 operational hydro-electric stations and 9 thermal power stations. The most recent investment in electricity generation was the Clyde Dam project opened in 1992, providing 432 megawatts. However, the largest generator of energy is still the Manapouri Dam, at 600 megawatts. The government has plans to break up ECNZ to allow for competitive generation. Distribution of final consumers is currently handled by energy companies owned by a mixture of consumer, local authority and private interests. A Maori trust plans to build another geothermal power station near Taupo.

Major Companies:
BP New Zealand, Fletcher Challenge, Dominion Oil Refining, Mobil Oil New Zealand, Caltex NZ, Electricity Corporation of New Zealand.

Fishing and Aquaculture

Another growth export commodity is fresh fish and shell fish. New Zealand's clean waters provide fish of exceptional quality. Fisheries exports were worth NZ $1.1 billion in 1995. New Zealand's exclusive economic zone, wherein all fishing is controlled by the Ministry of Agriculture and Fisheries extends for 200 nautical miles from the coast line, and is one of the largest in the world. MAF runs a system of transferable quotas which has been in place since 1986, and more recent legislation has further tightened the procedures operated by the 'Quota Management System' (QMS). Assessments are made about the size of the fishstock and the sustainable commercial catch for each species is estimated. The total catch is allocated between fishing companies through individual quotas which companies can buy or sell. Twenty per cent of quotas for new species are allocated to the Maori under a deal between the tribes and the government settled in 1992.

There is a sizable fish and shellfish farming industry. The main export products are pacific oysters, green lipped mussels, and salmon. Increased diversity is expected in the next decade. Paua (a large New Zealand shellfish) farms and Seaweed trial projects have already been established. This industry like much of New Zealand's agricultural and horticultural output is vulnerable to disease which can wipe out an entire season's crop, as happened in the summer of 1992-3 when toxic algae bloom resulted in shellfish harvesting being suspended. The other major threat to the seafood industry comes from trade barriers. About 85% of the revenues of the industry come from exports but most of the markets New Zealand trades with have volume restrictions (quotas) on imports. New Zealand currently has just over 1.2% of world seafood trade and could expand this if the quotas were increased. One target is increasing sales to Europe which currently takes about 12% of New Zealand exports. However the EU usually negotiates market liberalisation in return for access to fishing grounds. This would be difficult to grant directly in the case of the New Zealand industry because of the system of transferable fishing quotas described above. Given the current fierce competition over EU fishing grounds, and the charges being levelled at various countries of over-fishing, leasing the rights to fish in New Zealand waters could be a possible opening to European markets.

Forestry

Forests cover 7.8 million hectares, or 29% of New Zealand's land area. The bulk of this is native rainforest which is no longer a major source of timber for export. Pressure from conservation groups and the increasing profitability of other plantation species has restricted the harvesting of native forests. Just under 3% of native forests are still being logged under strict conditions. Production forests cover 1.3 million hectares and are a renewable resource. The bulk of these forests are planted in introduced species, mainly radiata pine with a small percentage of Douglas fir and a few other species. The forestry industry is concentrated in the centre of the North Island where the main production forests are located. There are smaller plantation forests in the South Island, mainly in the Tasman area and on the West Coast. The forestry industry is New Zealand's third largest export earning sector after the meat and dairy industries, earning over $1.6 billion annually. Future prospects for growth are encouraging as restrictions on the importing of tropical hardwoods spread. Although export volumes are predicted to keep growing, prices have proved volatile. In the future competition from radiata pine suppliers in other southern hemisphere countries may depress prices.

The state used to own half the total area of commercial forests but as part of the privatisation move in the last decade, management and cutting rights were sold to the private sector. The private sector now manages 80% of plantations. Major companies involved in the buying of state forestry assets were Carter Holt Harvey, Fletcher Challenge and Rayonier New Zealand who now own half the planted forest resource. Several other overseas companies made significant investments. The wood and pulp and paper industries do not seem to have suffered from the economic crises in Asia, and the wood industry especially is expected to benefit from the growth in Australia and the United States.

Major Companies
TT Rayonier, Juken Nissho, Ernslaw One, Forestry Corporation of New Zealand, Wenita Forestry, Carter Holt Harvey, Fletcher Challenge, NZ Forest Products.

Manufacturing

The government has been encouraging competition and efficiency in the manufacturing sector with a programme of tariffs on imported goods. During the last round, all ad valorum tariffs would be decreased to either 15%, 10% or 5%, and in July 1998, the five per cent tariff rate becomes duty free. Tariffs have also resulted in lowering the cost of imported materials, as well as increasing competition by opening up the country to more imported goods. After a period of instability and threatened jobs, companies in the industry have become more streamlined and innovative. An example of local success stories in manufacturing exports is Mercer Stainless Ltd, whose Auckland food service division has a contract with MacDonalds worldwide to produce kitchens for their food outlets in 17 countries. It also handles rivals KFC, and expects to expand into Asia. The manufacturing sector currently employs 290,000 people, over 18% of the working population.

Automotive: There is no New Zealand owned car manufacturing industry. The majority of vehicles are imported unassembled, mainly from Japan, and assembled locally. The industry suffered a major decline with the lowering of tariffs between 1988-90 and the downturn in the domestic economy which reduced the demand for new cars. Business and consumer confidence have improved, and there have been moves in the industry to rationalise production across the Tasman with Australia. There is a small but significant export market for components manufactured in New Zealand. The current export value for components such as tyres, alloy wheel springs and windscreens totals $180 million.

Major Companies: Ford NZ, General Motors NZ, Toyota NZ.

Textiles: Australia is the major market for the New Zealand textile and apparel industry. It was one of the last industries to retain quotas on the importation of competing foreign goods and still has a higher tariff regime than many other manufacturing sectors. More tariff reductions are proposed which may result in further job losses. Exports are increasing however, particularly to the major market, Australia. The industry is largely made up of specialised small firms.

Steel and non–ferrous metals: Steel and aluminium are the only metals produced in any quantity in New Zealand. Unwrought aluminium from the Comalco smelter near Bluff is a major export earner using raw bauxite imported from Australia. The New Zealand steel works at Glenbrook produces steel by a unique direct reduction process using local ironsands. Gold is a small but fast growing export industry. Employment opportunities are decreasing in this sector because of capital upgrades by firms to increase efficiency, and the decreased demand from Asian countries which has cut export prices.

Major Companies: BHP New Zealand Steel, Pacific Steel, Comalco-CHH Aluminium.

Electronics: Electronics is one of the surprising success stories of the restructured New Zealand economy. Under the old regime of protected domestic industries the sector was predominantly involved in the manufacture of consumer electronics. Now most of these goods, TVs, videos, etc are imported from Asia where costs are cheaper. The major exception is the domestic whiteware industry (the local term for fridges, dishwashers, ovens etc.) where New Zealanders show a strong preference for long established local brands such as Fisher and Paykel. The electronics industry, instead of declining with the reduction in tariffs, has diversified and found niche markets in high tech commercial and industrial products. For example one Christchurch based company, Dynamic Controls is the world's main manufacturer of controllers for power wheel chairs and scooters. Software is another area where New Zealand firms have developed specialist markets. New Zealand exports $100 million worth of software annually, only half of a per cent of world trade in this area, but a good performance for a country better known for exporting dead animals. Job prospects for skilled workers in the industry are good. There is currently a skills shortage from assembly workers through to engineers and software designers. The size of the New Zealand industry has limited the numbers being trained so that it has been unable to keep up with the current leap in demand for its products.

Major Companies: AWA New Zealand, Fisher and Paykel Electronics, IBM New Zealand.

Food and Beverages: The major destination for food manufacturing exports is Australia. Food and beverages enterprises employ just over a quarter of the total manufacturing workforce. Large enterprises dominate the industry and employ the majority of the workforce but there are a number of small businesses producing high quality luxury goods such as smoked seafood, speciality cheeses and wines.

Major Companies: Bluebird Foods, DB Group, Cerebos Gregg, Goodman Fielder, Kraft General Foods, Nestle New Zealand, Lion Nathan, Abels, Montana Wines, Villa Maria Wines.

Tourism

Tourism is now the single biggest earner of foreign exchange, earning $13.2 million a day and employing around 171,000 people, making it one of the largest industries in New Zealand. Despite being hit hard by the crisis in Asia, numbers are predicted to resume double digit growth by the end of the century. On average there are over a million foreign visitors each year – more than one visitor for every three New Zealanders. Overseas visitors make up nearly two thirds of hotel guests. New Zealand is promoted to overseas visitors by the New Zealand Tourism Board which coordinates the visitor information centre network. The Tourism Board also coordinates a number of quality assurance schemes for hospitality services, KiwiHost and the Qualmark scheme. The main attractions for most overseas visitors are the clean environment and beautiful scenery, but a growing number of tourists are after a more active holiday, skiing trips, jet-boat rides, white water rafting, even bungy jumping. This has lead to the growth of a new type of tourism, called 'adventure tourism'. One area which should take off in the future is 'green tourism' or 'eco-tourism'. Often thought to be a contradiction in terms because the impact of visitors upon the environment is usually harmful, green tourism aims to combine sharing the environment with tourists and protecting it. Activities such as whale watching off the Kaikoura coast above Christchurch, and visiting bird sanctuary islands already attracts the eco-sensitive.

Transport

As a small exporting economy on the edge of the world, the New Zealand economy is highly dependent on maintaining its external transportation links. Internal transportation networks are also important as its small population is spread over two islands, nearly 2,000 kilometres in combined length. Early transport developments were largely the result of government investment. The rail network, harbours, and road building were all extensively developed under a programme of major public works during the 1870s. State ownership and investment was the pattern for transportation development over the next century. The government owned and ran the railways, a shipping line, and eventually the national airline. State ownership of transportation links diminished under the programme of state asset sales begun by the Labour Government in the 1980s. Now private sector investment is behind most new transport projects, with the exception of road building which remains the responsibility of Transit New Zealand, a government authority. Road transportation was deregulated during the 1980s as was public transport in most cities. New Zealand Rail was sold to a consortium made up of a Canadian, an American and a New Zealand company in 1993. Port authorities were set up as companies, largely owned by local authorities, with two partly privately owned. Further private ownership is encouraged by the government.

Regional Employment Guide

THE UPPER NORTH ISLAND

Northland and Auckland
Major Cities: Auckland (pop. 998,000), Whangarei (pop. 45,800).
Newspapers: *The New Zealand Herald* (PO Box 32, Auckland), *Northern Advocate* (PO Box 210, Whangarei).
Chambers of Commerce: Auckland Chamber of Commerce and Industry: 100

Mayoral Drive, Auckland; tel (09) 309 6100; fax (09) 309 0081. Chamber of Commerce of Northland, 115 Bank Street, Whangarei; tel (09) 438 4771.

Industry/Other Comments: The Auckland region is the main business and industrial centre and employs nearly one third of the total workforce. 50% are employed in the services sector, comprising wholesale, retail, community, social and personal services. The Auckland region provides most of the jobs in manufacturing, construction, business and financial services. Auckland has a container port and an international airport. Employment prospects in the area are good and getting better. The region is predicted to be the leader in economic growth over the next few years and this is reflected in the number of businesses looking to expand their workforce. Numbers of job advertisements continue to increase, and growth industries in the future are likely to be construction and manufacturing. The recently opened Sky Tower Casino has been a large employer. North of the greater Auckland area, job prospects are likely to be associated with the growth of tourism and the expected improvement in agricultural export volumes. New Zealand's only crude oil refinery is located at Marsden Point near Whangarei in the east coast. South of Auckland, at Glenbrook is the BHP New Zealand Steel factory which uses a unique production process based on the reduction of local ironsand. West coasts beaches in New Zealand are characterised by the high proportion of iron ore in the sand which results in black coloration.

THE CENTRAL NORTH ISLAND

Waikato, Bay of Plenty, Gisborne and Hawkes Bay

Major Cities: Hamilton (pop. 159,000), Tauranga (pop. 83,000), Rotorua (pop. 57,000) New Plymouth (pop. 49,000) Hastings (pop. 59,000), Napier (pop. 55,000) .

Newspapers: *The Waikato Times* (Private Bag 3086, Hamilton), *Bay of Plenty Times* (108 Durham Street, Private Bag 12002, Tauranga), *Hawkes Bay Herald Tribune* (113 Karamu Road North, PO Box 180, Hastings) *Daily Telegraph* (49 Tennyson Street, PO Box 343, Napier).

Chambers of Commerce: Waikato Chamber of Commerce, 554 Victoria Street, Hamilton; tel (07) 839 5895. Bay of Plenty Chamber of Commerce, Commerce Centre, 195 Devonport Road, Tauranga, (07) 577 9823. Hawkes Bay Chamber of Commerce: Clifton Buildings 119 Queen Street East, Hastings; tel (06) 876 5938.

Industry/Other Comments: The Waikato is one of the main dairy farming regions in the country. Horticulture, particularly citrus fruit and kiwi fruit, is the predominant industry in the Bay of Plenty on the east coast. The Hawkes Bay region is a major wine making district, and has some of the oldest established wineries in the country: the Mission vineyard run by Catholic monks first started producing wine last century. Hamilton, the fourth largest city in the country is home to a number of manufacturing enterprises, a university, and a large wholesale and retail sector. Most light industry in the region is based on the processing of agricultural and forestry raw products. The central region of the North Island is the main centre for the pulp and paper making industry. Large plantation forests of radiata pine provide the raw materials for the production of newsprint, wood pulp, paper and paperboard. The Waikato is the largest coal producing region in the country, with 17 mainly open cast mines producing 1.3 million tons of sub-bitumous coal, over half the total annual output of the country. Gas is main product of the petro-chemical industry based on the Taranaki coast near New Plymouth. The region is also a tourist destination. Major attractions include the thermal region around Rotorua and the network of limestone caves near Waitomo.

Economic prospects in the region are favourable particularly for horticulture and forestry, and associated industries, although growth is not predicted to be as high as in Auckland.

THE LOWER NORTH ISLAND

Taranaki, Manawatu-Wanganui and Wellington
Major Cities: Wellington (pop. 335,000), Palmerston North (pop. 74,000), Wanganui (pop. 41,000).
Newspapers: *The Dominion* (PO Box 3470, Wellington), *Manawatu Evening Standard* (PO Box 3, Palmerston North) *Wanganui Chronicle* (59 Taupo Quay, PO Box 433, Wanganui).
Chambers of Commerce: *Wellington Chamber of Commerce:* 109 Featherston St, PO Box 1590, Wellington; tel (04) 472 2725; fax (04) 4711767. Wanganui Chamber of Commerce, Commerce House, 39 Victoria Ave, Wanganui tel (06) 345 0080; fax (06) 345 0246.
Industry/Other Comments: The capital city Wellington is the headquarters of central government. Most major law firms, accountants and management firms have their base in Wellington as well, although some firms prefer to have their head office in Auckland reflecting that city's commercial dominance. Wellington is the centre of the performing arts, as the national orchestra and ballet, and there is an abundance of dance companies, opera groups and professional theatres in the city. It also plays host to an international festival of the Arts every two years. Business, government and retail enterprises dominate the main urban area. Manufacturing industry is concentrated in the outlying suburbs and on the Petone seafront at the northern end of the Wellington harbour. Outside the urban area, to the north, the Wairarapa district is dairy and sheep farming country. Martinborough, north of Wellington, is a newly emerging major player in wine production.

THE UPPER SOUTH ISLAND

Nelson-Marlborough, West Coast and Canterbury
Major Cities: Christchurch (pop. 331,000), Nelson (pop. 52,000).
Newspapers: *The Christchurch Press* (Private Bag 4722, Christchurch), *The Nelson Mail* (15 Bridge Street, PO Box 244, Nelson).
Chambers of Commerce: Canterbury Employers Chamber of Commerce: 57 Kilmore St, Christchurch; tel (03) 366 5096. Nelson Chamber of Commerce, 54 Montgomery Square, Nelson; tel (03) 548 1363.
Industry/Other Comments: Christchurch and the Canterbury region are predicted to be one of the fastest growing local economies. Improvements to market access for New Zealand lamb resulting from GATT should boost the Canterbury region which is the largest sheep farming region in the country. It has a container port nearby at Lyttleton and the second busiest international airport in the country. As well as agricultural industry, Christchurch is the largest region for manufacturing employment after Auckland. It has a number of high-tech electronic and software firms. Canterbury is to be the site of a new 'Hard Business Network' supported by the Ministry of Commerce through the Canterbury Business Development Board. Networks are intended to be partnerships between small businesses which individually would have difficulty in promoting themselves overseas. Tourism is the other major source of economic activity in the region. Tourist attractions are the scenery and the skiing. Christchurch is only an

hour away from the ski fields of Mt Hutt. The first legal casino opened in the former Christchurch railway station in 1994. Further north, the Nelson/Marlborough region is a major wine growing district, and a centre for forestry and fishing. Exports of timber through Port Nelson are predicted to quadruple over the next five years. Growth in regional GDP, employment and exports for the West Coast region for 1998-2000 is expected to be twice that of any other region in the country. The West Coast is benefitting from its recent deep water port, and the development of three new coal mines, which is expected to boost its already healthy coal exports.

THE LOWER SOUTH ISLAND

Southland and Otago
Major Cities: Dunedin (pop. 112,000), Invercargill (pop. 49,000).
Newspapers: *The Otago Daily Times* (PO Box 181, Dunedin) *The Southland Times* (67 Esk Street, PO Box 805, Invercargill).
Chambers of Commerce: Otago Chamber of Commerce: 2 Stafford Street, PO Box 5713, Dunedin; tel (03) 479 0181. Chamber of Commerce Southland Inc., PO Box 856, Invercargill; tel (03) 218 7188.
Industry/Other Comments: The agricultural base of the rural economy in Otago and Southland is mainly concentrated on sheep farming with smaller numbers of dairy and beef farms. Horticultural activity in the region is based on stonefruit orchards. Vineyards are relatively new to the region. Until recently the climate was thought to be too cold for grape growing, but several local wineries have established an enviable reputation. Manufacturing in the region is concentrated around the cities of Dunedin and Invercargill with the exception of the Comalco Aluminium smelter located at Tiwai point near Bluff. Bluff is also known for its production of oysters. American forestry company Rayonier is currently looking at siting a fibre board plant somewhere in Southland which should boost employment prospects in that area.

Directory of Major Employers

Accountancy
Arthur Anderson: Arthur Anderson Tower, National Bank Centre, 209 Queen St, PO Box 199, Auckland; tel (09) 302 0280; fax (09) 302 0370.
BDO Hogg Young Cathie: 166 Harris Road, East Tamaki, Auckland; tel (09) 274 9340; fax (09) 274 0863.
Coopers & Lybrand: Coopers & Lybrand Tower 23-29 Albert St, Auckland, PO Box 48, Auckland; tel (09) 358 4888; fax (09) 358 3300.
Ernst & Young: National Mutual Centre, Shortland Street PO Box 2146, Auckland; tel (09) 377 4790; fax (09) 309 8137.
KPMG Peat Marwick: KPMG Centre 9 Princes St Auckland; tel (09) 367 5800; fax (09) 367 5871.
Price Waterhouse: Price Waterhouse Centre 66 Wyndham St PO Box 748, Auckland; tel (09) 309 3421; fax (09) 309 4166.

Banking
ANZ Banking Group (New Zealand) Ltd: 215–229 Lambton Quay, PO Box 1492, Wellington; tel (04) 496 7000; fax (04) 473 6919.
Bank of New Zealand: BNZ Centre, 1 Willis Street, Wellington, PO Box 2392, Wellington; tel (04) 474 6000; fax (04) 474 6531.

Citibank: 11th Floor, Citibank Centre, 23 Customs Street East, PO Box 2805, Auckland; tel (09) 379 9922; fax (09) 302 1681. Customer Service tel 0800 445 051.

Countrywide Banking Corp. Ltd: PO Box 5445, Wellesley Street, Auckland; tel (09) 309 8900; fax (09) 377 9550.

CS First Boston: 282 Lambton Quay, Wellington; tel (04) 474 4448; fax (04) 474 4432.

National Bank of New Zealand: National Bank House, 170-186 Featherston St, Wellington, PO Box 1791, Wellington; tel (04) 494 4000; fax (04) 474 4013.

Reserve Bank of New Zealand: 2 The Terrace, PO Box 2498, Wellington; tel (04) 472 2029; fax (04) 473 8554.

Westpac Banking Corporation: Westpac House, 318-324 Lambton Quay, Wellington, PO Box 691, Wellington; tel (04) 498 1199; fax (04) 498 1786.

Business and Management Services

Datacom Systems Ltd: PO Box 6376, Wellington; tel (04) 460 1500; fax (04) 460 1511; Auckland branch: 106 Vincent Street, Box 6041 Auckland Central; tel (09) 303 1489; fax (09) 3033375.

Deloitte Touche Tohmatsu (Management Consultants): 32 Oxford Tce, Christchurch; tel (03) 379 7010; fax (03) 366 6539.

Fuji Xerox New Zealand Ltd: 17 Hargreaves Street, Ponsonby, PO Box 5948, Auckland; tel (09) 377 3834; fax (09) 356 4444; Website: www.fujixerox.co.nz

Opal Consulting Group: PO Box 7067, Auckland; tel (09) 379 0200; fax (09) 377 4127; e-mail: opal@opalconsult.co.nz

Morgan and Banks: Level 6, Ports of Auckland Building, CPO Box 579, Auckland; tel (09) 367 9000; fax (09) 367 9001; Website: www.morganbanks.com.au

PA Consulting Group: 1st Floor, 1 Nelson Street, Auckland; tel (09) 303 2743; fax (09) 303 1276.

Unisys New Zealand Ltd: 3 Owens Road, Epsom, PO Box 5144, Auckland; tel (09) 630 1333; fax (09) 638 7650.

Wang New Zealand: Wang Terraces, 9 City Road, PO Box 8804, Auckland; tel (09) 306 4600; fax (09) 309 3960; Website: www.wang.co.nz

Forestry, Pulp and Paper

Carter Holt Harvey Ltd: 640 Great South Road Manakau City, Private Bag 92-106 Auckland; tel (09) 262 6000; fax (09) 262 6099.

Forestry Corporation of New Zealand: Mount Shipping Office, 101 Hewletts Road, Mount Maunganui; tel (07) 575 9818; fax (07) 575 9811.

Juken Nissho Ltd: 101 Customs Street East, PO Box 1450, Auckland; tel (09) 309 1750; fax (09) 309 0326.

Ministry of Agriculture and Forestry: 101 The Terrace, PO Box 2526, Wellington; tel (04) 474 4100; fax (04) 474 4111.

Hotel Chains

Best Western: 190 Great South Road, Remuera, Auckland; tel (09) 520 5418.

Quality Hotels: 150 Anzac Avenue, PO Box 3272, Auckland; tel (09) 379 8509, or freephone 0800 808 228; fax (09) 379 8582.

Southern Pacific Hotel Corporation: Level 14 Westpac Tower, 120 Albert Street, PO Box 3921, Auckland; tel (09) 309 4411; fax (09) 309 3577.

Insurance Companies

AMI Insurance: 63 Albert St, Auckland; tel (09) 377 4640; fax (09) 309 5943

AMP Insurance: 300 Great South Road, Greenlane, Auckland tel (09) 524 3500; fax (09) 524 3502.

Commercial Union Travel Insurance: Level 7, 205 Queen Street, Auckland; tel (09) 524 3500; fax (09) 524 3502.

NZI Insurance: 3-13 Shortland Street, Private Bag 92-130 Auckland; tel (09) 309 7000; fax (09) 309 7097.

State Insurance: Cnr Wakefield & Rutland Streets, Auckland; tel (09) 827 5789; fax (09) 358 4033.

Law Firms

Russell McVeagh McKenzie Bartleet & Co; The Shortland Centre 51-53 Shortland St, Auckland; tel (09) 309 8839; fax (09) 377 1849; e-mail: rmmbakl@rmmb.co.nz

Rudd Watts & Stone: 125 Queen St, Auckland, PO Box 3798, Auckland; tel (09) 353 9700; fax (09) 353 9701.

Simpson Grierson: Simpson Grierson Building, 92 Albert St, Auckland; tel (09) 358 2222; fax (09) 307 0331.

Bell Gully Buddle Weir: The Auckland Club Tower, 34 Shortland St, Auckland, PO Box 4199, Auckland; tel (09) 309 0859; fax (09) 309 3312; Website: www.bgbw.co.nz

Manufacturing and Marketing

Aspak Foods (formerly Abels) Ltd: 92-98 Harris Road, East Tamaki, Auckland; tel (09) 274 5099; (09) 274 4891.

Radiola Corporation (formerly AWA) New Zealand Ltd: Wineera Drive, Porirua, Wellington, Private Bag, Porirua, Wellington; tel (04) 237 0159; fax (04) 237 1264.

Bayer New Zealand Ltd: 3 Argus Place, Glenfield, Auckland, PO Box 2825, Auckland; tel (09) 443 3093; fax (09) 443 3094.

BHP New Zealand Steel: Private Bag 92121, Auckland; tel (09) 375 8999; fax (09) 375 8959.

Bluebird Foods Ltd: 124 Wiri Station Road, Manukau City, Auckland, Private Bag 76903, Manukau City, Auckland; tel (09) 262 8800; fax (09) 262 8898.

Cadbury Confectionery Ltd: 280 Cumberland Street, Dunedin, PO Box 890, Dunedin; tel (03) 467 7800; fax (03) 467 7811.

Cerebos Gregg Ltd: 291 East Tamaki, Auckland, PO Box 58095, Auckland; tel (09) 274 2777; fax (09) 274 2775.

Colgate Palmolive Ltd: 415 Church Street, Penrose, Auckland; tel (09) 525 2300, Fax (09) 525 2353.

Comalco: Head Office, 2 Hunter Street, Wellington, tel (04) 471 1527; fax (04) 4728041.

DB Group Led; Citibank Centre, 23 Customs Street East, PO Box 1659, Auckland; tel (09) 379 7980; fax (09) 358 0506.

Fisher and Paykel: 78 Springs Road East Tamaki, Auckland, Private Bag 14917, Panmure, Auckland; tel (09) 2730600; fax (09) 273 0609.

Ford Motor Co. Ltd: Private Bag 76912, Manakau City, Auckland; tel (09) 277 8400; fax (09) 278 5741.

Holden (formerly General Motors) NZ Ltd: PO Box 40413, Upper Hutt; tel (04) 528 1200; fax (04) 528 1125.

Goodman Fielder Ltd: Goodman Fielder House, Level 3, 7 Springs Road, East Tamaki, PO Box 58090, Greenmount, Auckland; tel (09) 272 1216; fax (09) 272 1203.

IBM New Zealand Ltd: 171 Featherston Street, PO Box 38993, Petone,

Wellington; tel (04) 576 5999; fax (04) 576 5529.

Kraft Foods Ltd: 15 Weka Street. PO Box 22340 Otahu, Auckland; tel (09) 276 4955; fax (09) 270 1152.

Lion Nathan Ltd: PO Box 190, Auckland; tel (09) 303 3388; fax (09) 303 3307.

Montana Wines: 171 Pilkington Road, Glen Innes, Auckland, PO Box 18293; tel (09) 570 8400; fax (09) 570 8440.

Nestle New Zealand Ltd: 1 Broadway, Newmarket, Auckland, PO Box 1784; tel (09) 367 2800; fax (09) 367 2819.

Procter and Gamble: PO Box 5861, Wellesley Street, Auckland; tel (09) 356 1800; fax (09) 356 1818.

Toyota NZ Ltd: Private Bag 13909, Johnsonville, Wellington; tel (04) 478 4149; fax (04) 478 9090.

Villa Maria Estate Ltd: 5 Kirkbridge Road, Mangere, Auckland, PO Box 43046, Auckland; tel (09) 275 6119; fax (09) 275 6776.

Oil and Petrochemicals
BP Oil NZ Ltd: PO Box 892, Wellington; tel (04) 495 5000, fax (04) 495 5400.

Fletcher Challenge Energy: Level 3, James Fletcher House, 581 Great South Road Penrose, Auckland; tel (09) 525 9212; fax (09) 525 9379.

Mobil Oil NZ Ltd: PO Box 1709, Auckland; tel (09) 302 4700, fax 0800 808 112.

Shell NZ Ltd: 96–102 The Terrace, PO Box 2091, Wellington; tel (04) 472 0080; fax 0800 743 553.

Telecommunications and Utilities
AT&T: 3 Ferncroft Street, Grafton, Auckland; tel (09) 358 0303; fax (09) 358 0848.

Coalcorp: PO Box 439, Wellington.

Electricity Corporation NZ: 23 Lambton Quay, PO Box 930, Wellington; tel (04) 472 3550; fax (04) 4734.

NZ Post Ltd: Private Bag 39990, Wellington 1; tel (04) 496 4999.

Transport, and Shipping
Air New Zealand: cnr Customs and Albert Streets, Private Bag 92007, Auckland; tel (09) 366 2400; fax (09) 275 5927.

Apex International Forwarding Ltd: 9A Mahunga Drive, Mangere Bridge, PO Box 2427, Auckland; tel (09) 6343616; fax (09) 622 2264.

Beacon Chartering and Shipping Ltd: Level 8, 44 Anzac Avenue, Auckland, PO Box 418, Auckland; tel (09) 379 7994; fax (09) 309 3427.

Columbus Line NZ Ltd: 52 Symonds Street Auckland, PO Box 3551, Auckland; tel (09) 377 3460; fax (09) 309 3003.

DHL Worldwide Express: 49 Mahunga Drive, Mangere, Auckland, PO Box 13509, Onehunga, Auckland; tel (09) 636 5000; fax (09) 636 7634.

Tranz Rail Ltd: 39 Johnson Street, PO Box 593, Private Bag, Wellington; tel (04) 4995 935; fax (04) 4995 792.

Pacific Forum Line (NZ) Ltd: 49-55 Anzac Avenue, Auckland, PO Box 796, Auckland; tel (09) 356 2333; fax (09) 356 2330.

Shipping Enterprises: Barneys Building, 15 Totara Street, Mount Maunganui; tel (07) 575 9684; fax (07) 575 9222.

Starting a Business

In principle, it is quite feasible for foreigners to set up a business or to buy part or all of an existing business in New Zealand. The prevailing attitude towards business ventures, whether started by New Zealanders or immigrants is positive and helpful. To make a success of the venture requires, of course, the same blend of careful planning, energy and luck that you need in any country. More than anything, you need to research your chosen potential market or markets to ensure that the products or services that you offer are geared to meet a real demand at an appropriate price. Much of your groundwork can be done in advance, but there is no substitute for visiting and seeing for yourself the environment in which you wish to try the venture. It may be worth considering spending substantial time living and working in New Zealand before making a final commitment to a particular enterprise.

In most cases therefore, it is likely that you will have obtained New Zealand residency before setting up a business on your own. If you are not a New Zealand citizen or resident and you are investing substantial sums of money (more than NZ $10 million) in New Zealand shares or assets, or you are investing in certain areas of the economy such as broadcasting, you will require the permission of the Overseas Investment Commission (*OIC:* 2 The Terrace, PO Box 2498, Wellington; tel 04 471 3838; fax 04 471 3655). Permission is dependent on the extent to which the projected business will contribute to the economy. Similarly permission is required if you are not a New Zealander and you are the principal of a business with a turnover of greater than NZ $10 million or it is particular restricted areas of the economy. However these restrictions will not affect most immigrants considering setting up a small business in New Zealand.

If you are organising your application for New Zealand residency with the intention of setting up a business there you should note that a special scheme exists to attract business investors. (See Chapter Two, *Residence and Entry*). The sums required to qualify for the Business Investment category are fairly substantial. If you do not have the necessary capital to qualify under this category, then you will need to apply under the General or Family categories.

In recent years, regulations governing setting up business in New Zealand have been relaxed. The Companies Act was substantially amended in 1994 to make the process of incorporating a company simpler. There are a number of government agencies set up to help small businesses and the attitude towards entrepreneurs is positive. The operating environment for businesses is quite similar to the UK. Telephone, computer systems, and financial services are advanced. The workforce has a similar level of qualifications to UK workers. As part of encouraging individual initiative and competitive economic environment, the government is trying to cut down on the amount of red-tape involved in doing business, and to encourage small businesses to set up. The result is that it is a good time to be starting up a new business in New Zealand. This chapter will look at what is involved in buying a business in New Zealand or in starting your own.

Preparation

Choosing a Business

Since in broad terms, New Zealanders engage in similar business, cultural and social activities to Europeans, there are similar potential markets for anyone contemplating setting up a new enterprise. The differences need to be borne in mind, however, not the least of which is that the comparatively small total population and its distribution will have a significant effect on the structure of potential markets. For example if you are considering setting up in the restaurant industry you will find that in the larger cities restaurants and wine bars abound: the market is pretty well saturated and thus very competitive. Such businesses are stretched to find some new competitive advantage and that is often manifested as gimmickry which of course has a short-lived novelty appeal. In the rural areas, there are fewer restaurants and wine-bars, however, there is less population to support them as New Zealand is not particularly densely populated. An opportunity, yes, but maybe one that requires a lot of 'up front' investment in marketing and publicity. Given that moving to a new country is going to be pretty challenging in itself, it may be wise to opt for a safer bet such as selecting an enterprise for which there is a known or an established market, or one in which you have particular skills and experience. Obviously there is an advantage in buying an already established business in this respect, however before you buy you should research the track record of your chosen enterprise. Remember that the majority of businesses succeed not on the uniqueness of the concept but on the application of sound and careful management techniques.

Researching Your Business

Whether it is your intention to buy a business or to set up from scratch, researching the potential market for that business is essential. The specific information that you need to determine whether there is a viable market will depend greatly upon the type of business, the services or the products you have in mind. There are companies specialising in market research in the major cities in New Zealand, which would be able to provide data on most aspects of the market or would offer to conduct specific enquiries, for a fee, in areas of the market which were less well researched. This type of service is usually beyond the budget of those setting up a small business. There are some companies offering research services specifically tailored for small businesses and you can do some of the research work yourself. One of the first places to start looking for information is the local public library. Most public libraries run an information service for local businesses and for those intending to set up a business. They will have information on market trends, local suppliers, possible competitors, planning and development strategies. Some libraries offer a contract research service and will do a lot of the legwork by investigating the feasibility of a project for you. This may be a cost-effective option simply because they will be familiar with the sources of information and will be able to find out quickly what you need to know. Information on businesses and commerce in specific regions can be obtained from the local Chamber of Commerce. Chambers of Commerce in the main cities are listed below. The Department of Statistics, now called Statistic New Zealand, runs a professional consultancy service for data on imports, prices, population etc. They publish the *Quarterly Economic Survey* of various sectors of the economy. Predominantly this is income and expenditure data, although they also collect investment data. Each year this is gathered into the more detailed *Annual Enterprise Survey*. More general data on the New Zealand economy is published in the monthly *Key Statistics*. They also publish the *New Zealand Year Book* (see below). If your business is involved in the export market, the Ministry of Foreign Affairs and Trade can help with economic and political information about your target markets.

Researching market opportunities in New Zealand from Europe is naturally more difficult than doing the ground work once you arrive. There are companies which offer an information gathering service specifically for intending immigrants, in areas ranging from business opportunities to education prospects. (see 'Business and Market Research Organisations' listed below). Other sources of information are the *New Zealand Year Book*, which provides a highly detailed picture of social, demographic, and economic trends in New Zealand. It is a useful introduction to the structure of the economy and the main business sectors. The disadvantage of the yearbook is that the information is based on five yearly census data, so while it is very detailed, it is not always up to date. Copies of the yearbook can be bought at the Kiwifruits shop (6 Royal Opera Arcade, London SW1Y; tel 0171-930 4587), which specialises in New Zealand products, or can be found in some libraries. The Information Office at the New Zealand High Commission has a copy of the yearbook as well as individual chapters on specific topics.

Useful Addresses

Chambers of Commerce

New Zealand Chambers of Commerce: PO Box 11–043, Manners Street, Wellington; fax/tel (04) 472 3376.

Auckland Chamber of Commerce and Industry: 100 Mayoral Drive, Auckland; tel (09) 309 6100; fax (09) 309 0081.

Canterbury Employers Chamber of Commerce: 57 Kilmore St, Christchurch; tel (03) 366 5096.

Otago Chamber of Commerce: 2 Stafford Street, PO Box 5713, Dunedin; tel (03) 479 0181.

Wellington Chamber of Commerce: 109 Featherston St, Wellington; tel (04) 472 2725; fax (04) 471 1767.

Business and Market Research Organisations

Business Research Centre:, Anderson Consulting Tower, 45 Johnson Street, PO Box 10617, Wellington; tel (04) 4993088; fax (04) 499 3414.

Business Information Service: Wellington Public Library, PO Box 1992, tel (04) 8014059; fax (04) 8014088.

New Zealand Institute of Economic Research: 8 Halswell Street, Box 3479, Wellington; tel (04) 472 1880; fax (04) 472 1211; e-mail econ@nzier.org.nz.

Business and Economic Research Ltd: Level 5, 108 The Terrace, PO Box 10277, Wellington; tel (04) 470 5550; fax (04) 473 3276.

Government Departments

Ministry of Foreign Affairs and Trade: 40 The Terrace, Private Bag 18901, Wellington; tel (04) 474 8500; fax (04) 472 9596; Website: www.mft.govt.nz.

Statistics New Zealand (Head Office): 85 Molesworth Street, PO Box 2922, Wellington; tel (04) 495 4600; fax (04) 495 4610; e-mail: info@stats.govt.nz.

Statistics New Zealand: Information Consultancy Groups:
Auckland: 70 Symonds Street, Private Bag, 920003, Auckland; tel (09) 357 2100; fax (09) 379 0859.

Christchurch: Winchester House, 64 Kilmore Street, Private Bag 4741, Christchurch; tel (03) 374 8700; fax (03) 374 8864.
Dunedin: Civic Centre (4th Floor) The Octagon, Private Bag 1935, Dunedin; tel (03) 477 7511; fax (03) 477 5243.

Choosing an Area

Having decided on your line of business, the next logical step is to decide where to locate it. Obviously the type of business will determine this in many cases, for example choosing where to site a horticultural enterprise will largely be determined by climate. The tourism industry has until recently been concentrated in the geothermal area around Rotorua, and the South Island more generally, with most visitors staying in Christchurch or Queenstown. Auckland is attempting to attract visitors for longer stays and is likely to be a growth area for tourism in the future. Another growing sector is adventure tourism, with the south of the Waikato region around Waitomo caves, Nelson and the West Coast likely to benefit. Export manufacturing is strongest in Auckland and Christchurch. Forestry, another export sector predicted to grow is likely to benefit the region around Rotorua, Taupo and Turangi. Overall according to *Metro* magazine, Auckland is likely to enjoy the highest economic growth over the next few years with the Bay of Plenty, Canterbury and Otago following behind.

Useful Publications
The Small Business Book, a New Zealand Guide: Robert Hamlin and John English, Bridget Williams, 1993.
Your Successful Small Business: A New Zealand Guide to Starting Out and Staying In Business: Judith Ashton, Viking Pacific, 1992.
ABC Directory of Business and Commercial Opportunity: PO Box 9087, Newmarket, Auckland; tel (09) 307 0598; fax (09) 309 3076.
Business Development News: Ministry of Commerce, PO Box 1473, Wellington; tel (04) 472 0030-extension 8057; fax (04) 471 2658.
The National Business Review: Level 26, BNZ Tower, 125 Queen Street, PO Box 1734, Auckland; tel (09) 307 1629; fax (09) 309 7878; Website: www.nbr.co.nz

Small and Medium Enterprises

Specific assistance for people wanting to set up their own business is available from the Small Business Agency. (35 Woburn Road, PO Box 11-012 Manners Street, Wellington; tel 04-472 3141; fax 04-499 5545). The agency provides advice to individuals as well as running courses on how to set up a small business. There are a number of community based enterprise and employment centres involved with developing new employment and small business initiatives. The national co-ordinator for the Small business Enterprise Centre of New Zealand is Raewyn Weller, (SBECNZ, Box 563 Te Puke; tel 07 573 8888; fax 07 573 8891). The Inland Revenue Department also runs a small business advisory service which provides help with working out your tax obligations. They can be contacted at local IRD offices.

Buying a Business v Setting up from Scratch

The decision between buying a business or setting up your own is basically about the degree of risk you are prepared to take and what kind of capital you can raise.

Buying a business requires much more money, but on the other hand, you will be buying a going concern which will provide an immediate source of income. Setting up from scratch can be done on a shoestring, but if you underestimate your financial needs at the beginning, your enterprise may not last long. Your first years in business may be difficult for cash flow and unanticipated expenses so it is important not to miscalculate the size of the budget you can realistically manage on. You may also find that the stress of changing your country of abode is enough to cope with during your first years in New Zealand and the move to set up your own operation may be easier after you have acclimatised to New Zealand in other ways. If you do decide to go ahead and buy an existing business, the place to start looking is the daily newspapers classified sections. Specialist business estate agencies can be found by looking in the Yellow Pages. To give you some idea of the types of opportunities and the prices, the following businesses were recently advertised for sale: Auckland: Freehold Superette with two bedroom accommodation for sale, 675 square metres commercial section, $300,000; North Canterbury, Restaurant on State Highway 1, $75,000; Nelson: twelve unit motor lodge on main road, $525,000.

Raising Finance

Banks & Business Plans

There are various sources of loans for small businesses available, the most common being the banks. However, any lender or giver of grants will expect some reassurance of serious commitment from the person or persons asking for help. This means in most cases, evidence that they are committing a significant amount of their own capital to the venture. As was noted above, the major reason for small business failure is bad financial planning so in order to convince a bank that you are a worthwhile investment you need to produce a business plan. Without going into too much detail here, your business plan should include:

A summary containing a broad outline of your vision of the business.

A brief CV of each person involved in the business, highlighting skills and expertise relevant to the scheme.

A description of the main services or products that you intend to offer.

Evidence that a viable market exists for your services or products.

An outline of your marketing communication strategy (how you intend to contact your potential customers).

Financial information

Expenditure: Start-up costs, cash flow projections, salaries, running (operating) costs including materials, production, heating, lighting, premises (rent) etc., other expenses (Remember to make a generous allowance for contingencies).

Projected income: (Sales).

Remember that you are trying to present a positive case to your audience; the more professional and credible the plan, the more chance you have of success: clarity and a realistic rather than optimistic view will enhance your proposal and if realism tells you that the idea is not sound, then you must review it or even come up with another idea.

A final comment on business plans: there are people who can offer advice on how to write your plan; listen to that advice; there are also people who will write it for you, but if you prepare it yourself, then you will be that much closer to an understanding of your projected business.

Investment Incentives

There are very few investment incentive schemes available directly from central government. The main sources of funding are local Business Development Boards funded by the government which offer grants and incentive funds to attract businesses into their regions. (see below) The one exception is tourism where government loans are available through the Tourist Accommodation Development scheme. The New Zealand Employment Service offers a monthly 'Enterprise Allowance' to help with the living expenses of people establishing a business. It can be paid for up to a year.

Regional Investment Offices

The Ministry of Commerce's network of local Business Development Boards provide information and assistance for existing businesses and to intending business people. Unfortunately grants for business development were discontinued in November 1997. However the government approved money in the 1998 Budget for assisting businesses, and the upskilling of management and staff. Contact the Ministry of Commerce (tel 04-472 0030; fax 04-473 4638) for more information.

The Ministry also publishes *Business Development News*, a monthly publication providing information about business initiatives. If you want further information about how regional development boards decide to allocate grants, you can contact the *Business Development Board Network:* (Ministry of Commerce 33 Bowen St, PO Box 1473, Wellington; tel (04) 472 0030; fax (04) 473 4638).

Addresses of Business Development Boards

Aorangi Business Development Board: Stafford and Sefton Streets PO Box 779, Timaru; tel (03) 688 8106; fax (03) 688 1712.

Auckland Business Development Board: 47 Wakefield St PO Box 7040, Auckland; tel (09) 308 9141; fax (09) 308 9138.

Bay Of Plenty Business Development Board: Cameron Rd & First Ave, PO Box 568, Tauranga; tel (07) 577 6000; fax (07) 577 6010.

Canterbury Business Development Board: 109 Cambridge Tce, Christchurch; tel (03) 365 1918; fax (03) 379 0697.

East Coast Business Development Board: 151 Grey Street, PO Box 517, Gisborne; tel (06) 867 9744; fax (06) 867 9183.

Hawkes Bay Business Development Board: 40 Niven Street, PO Box 3344, Onekawa; tel (06) 843 1099; fax (06) 843 8099.

Kapiti/ Horowhenua Business Development Board: 29 Queen St, PO Box 673 Levin, tel (06) 367 9669/(04) 298 8207; fax (06) 368 1925.

King Country/Taupo Business Development Board: King and Taupiri Streets, PO Box 44, Te Kuiti; tel (07) 878 8685; fax (07) 878 6740.

Manawatu Business Development Board: 1st Floor, The Square Centre, cnr The Square and Main Street, Palmerston North; tel (06) 350 1805.

Marlborough Business Development Board: 3 Main St, PO Box 652, Blenheim; tel (03) 578 2313; fax (03) 578 7343.

Nelson Bays Business Development Board: 37 Bridge St, PO Box 840, Nelson; (03) 548 8622; fax (03) 546 6455.

Northland Business Development Trust: 25 Rathbone Street, Whangarei; tel (09) 438 1700.

Otago Business Development Board: 282 Moray Place PO Box 5558, Dunedin; (03) 477 6528; fax (03) 479 0649.

Southland Business Development Board: 27 Kelvin Street, PO Box 979, Invercargill; tel (03) 218 9860; fax (03) 214 4654.

Taranaki Business Development Board: 1st Floor, AA Building, 49 Powderham Street, New Plymouth; tel (06) 759 9080; fax (06) 759 9145.

Thames Valley/Coromandel Business Development Board: Normanby Road PO Box 86, Paeroa; tel (07) 862 7423; fax (07) 862 7421.

Waikato Business Development Board: Lincoln Street, Frankton, PO Box 960, Hamilton; tel (07) 846 0200; fax (07) 846 0205.

Wairarapa Business Development Board: cnr Smith and Dixon Streets, PO Box 251, Masterton; tel (06) 378 2705; fax (06) 378 9548.

Wanganui Business Development Board: 259 Victoria Avenue, PO Box 7045, Wanganui; tel (06) 345 0949; fax (06) 345 0666.

Wellington Business Development Board: 249 High St, Lower Hutt; tel (04) 566 9192; fax (04) 566 9191.

West Coast Business Development Board: 100 Mackay St, PO Box 361, Greymouth; tel (03) 768 6334; fax (03) 768 5408.

Business Structures and Registration

Businesses in New Zealand can take similar forms to those in the UK, namely: Public Limited Company, Partnership, Joint Venture, Trust, or Sole Trader. The three most common forms for small businesses are sole trader, partnership or public limited company. The form of your business determines who benefits from it but also who is liable should something go wrong. It is not uncommon for businesses to start up in one form then change into another as they expand so you don't have to make a once and for all decision before you start.

Sole Trader: In this structure, you are the sole owner and controller of your business. This is the simplest form of business structure to start up: you simply tell the IRD you are becoming self-employed. If your business has a turnover greater than $50,000 you will also need to register for Goods and Services Tax, but these are the only legal formalities required. The disadvantage of the simple structure is that as a sole trader you are personally responsible for any debts incurred by your business and your personal assets can be taken as payment.

Partnership: Partnerships are formed by private agreement between the partners and their form is quite flexible, dependent upon the terms of that agreement. It is a good idea, although not legally necessary, to have the agreement drawn up or checked by a lawyer. Juliet Ashton in her book *Your Successful Small Business* suggests that the agreement should cover the name of the partnership and the business, the date of the agreement and an indication of how long the partnership is intended to last, as well as how much capital has been invested by each partner in the firm and the interest on it, the way the profits will be split and who is responsible for management and control of the business, arrangements about holidays, illness, division of responsibilities and what will happen if one of the partners dies. There is a tendency to assume you will work things out as you go along, particularly if you are going into business with a friend, However there are many pitfalls in this approach, and although it may seem legalistic it is a better idea to have written clearly who is responsible for what aspect of the business rather than put your partnership under strain by not having a clear understanding from the beginning. You should in any case think twice before going into business with a friend. You need to assess objectively their strengths and weaknesses as a potential business person, as well as how you will get along with them under pressure. As with a sole trader structure you are personally responsible for any debts incurred by your business, even if your partner made the decisions that led the business into difficulties.

Limited Companies: As distinct from partnerships and sole-trading operations, if you own a company you are not personally responsible for its debts. The company has a separate legal existence and your liability is limited to the extent of your share ownership. However it is worth noting that if you have to borrow money to set up your company, banks will commonly require personal guarantees from the directors, so you will not be protected by the company's legal status. You can either buy a company off the shelf from one of the businesses that specialise in selling shelf companies (advertised in the *Yellow Pages*) or you can set one up yourself. Company incorporation in New Zealand has been simplified. There is now only one type of company and there is no longer any minimum or maximum number of directors or shareholders required. To set up a company you require the following:

1. A name
2. At least one shareholder
3. At least one director
4. At least one share
5. A registered office and an address.

The director and shareholder can be one and the same so in fact it only needs one person to set up a company. You begin by registering the name you have chosen with the Registrar of Companies. Obviously you have to pick a name which no-one else has used already. Once the name has been approved you can apply to have your company registered. Along with your application (which must be signed and must state the company's name, registered office and address) you must include signed consents from all directors to act as such and certificates stating that they are not disqualified from acting, consents by shareholders to take the stated number of shares, notice from the Registrar reserving the company's name, and the constitution of the company if there is one. Companies need no longer state their objects in a constitution. Once he receives a properly completed application the Registrar will issue a certificate of incorporation. The current cost of incorporation is $300. The Commercial Affairs Division of the Ministry of Commerce registers companies, and maintains public records on all companies. It also deals with the finances and assets of bankruptcies. The local offices of Commercial Affairs are listed below:

Auckland: Level 7, Departmental Building, 3 Kingston Street, Private Bag 92-513 Wellersley Street, Auckland; tel (09) 309 8411; fax (09) 377 2723.
Christchurch: Level 4, Cardinal House, Cnr Gloucester Street and Oxford Terrace, Private Bag 4714, Christchurch; tel (03) 366 4354; fax (03) 365 6445.
Dunedin: Level 4, MLC Building, Cnr Princes and Manse Streets, Private Bag 1927, Dunedin; (03) 477 3722; fax (03) 477 5932.
Hamilton: ASB Building, 500 Victoria Street, Private Bag 3090, Hamilton; tel (07) 839 5055; fax (07) 839 4348.
Napier: Level 2, 26-28 Bower Street, Private Bag 6001 Napier; tel (06) 835 7588; fax (06) 835 7421.
Wellington: Level 9, Boulcott House, 47 Boulcott Street, Private Bag 5901, Wellington; tel (04) 471 1028; fax (04) 473 2921.

Ideas for New Businesses

Most new immigrants will need a chance to look around once they arrive in New Zealand before deciding what line of business to take up. There are a lot of established avenues for the first time business person as you will see when looking at the businesses for sale section in the papers. Should you want to consider trying something different, the following suggestions may give you some ideas.

Accommodation: As long as the tourist boom continues, providing accommodation is likely to be a reasonably safe bet. B&Bs are not as common in New Zealand as they are in the UK although the idea is beginning to catch on, as an inexpensive accommodation option. However you will need to research the potential market carefully. Many tourists arrive on package deals with accommodation organised through the large hotel chains. On the other hand, many Asian tourists travel to New Zealand, particularly Christchurch because of its English associations. You could market your B&B as a real English experience. Another relatively undeveloped type of accommodation in New Zealand is the country house hotel. While there are a number of luxury country lodges at top prices, the market is by no means oversupplied at the high end.

Publishing: There is no newspaper aimed at European expats, although the size of community could support one. The main cities (apart from Wellington) lack a weekly arts and events magazine. There are a number of give-away newspapers providing a listings service but production standards are not high. There is an opportunity for a well produced magazine covering the music scene, arts, leisure and general listings.

Tourism: The most recent development in tourism is so-called adventure tourism, not just taking pictures of the scenery but actively getting into the environment, through for example jet boat rides, white water rafting, bungy jumping, big game fishing, and helicopter or balloon rides. Some of these areas are already well catered for and in some cases, where the rides take place in Department of Conservation lands for example, only a few operators may be licensed. Other areas could be developed, for example the increasingly popular eco-tourism, or horse trekking.

Running a Business

Employing Staff

As an employer you negotiate individual contracts of employment with your staff, who can either nominate a bargaining agent in the negotiations or represent themselves directly. While there is a lot of flexibility over negotiating terms and conditions relevant to your workplace, Certain statutory protections remain for workers. There is a legal minimum wage of NZ $280 for an adult working a 40 hour week. (The minimum wage is set out under *Aspects of Employment* in chapter 6.) This does not apply to people under the age of 20, apprentices and other trainees. There are eleven paid public holidays, and after 12 months employment, employees are entitled to three weeks paid annual leave. There are also provisions for special leave in the case of bereavement, and parental leave (both maternity and paternity, although new dads get less time off than new mums). See under *Working Conditions* in Chapter Six for further details.

Contracts: Employment contracts must contain a section on dispute settlement, and there are standard procedures for dealing with personal grievance cases against employers for unjustified dismissal.

Wages & Time Record: You are required to keep a wages and time record for each employee.

Taxes: Your other legal obligations as an employer concern taxation. You are required to deduct payroll taxes (known as PAYE) from your employee's wages and make returns of the same to the Inland Revenue Department. You must get all your employees to fill out a tax deduction certificate called an IR12, and you must pay an accident compensation levy for each employee, yearly. If you provide any perks for staff as part of their employment package, then you have to pay fringe benefit taxes on them. (See *Taxation* below for more details.)

Accountants

As has been noted, the major reason for small business failure is poor management, usually poor financial control. You would be well advised to consult an accountant who specialises in dealing with small businesses to help you look after this important area. Your local small business advisory service should have a list of local accountants. In the case of companies there are certain statutory requirements you must fulfill with regard to financial reporting. Every company is required to keep full, true and complete record of its affairs and transactions including providing a Profit and Loss Account and a Balance Sheet. Accounting practice is regulated by the Institute of Chartered Accountants of New Zealand (Cigna House, 40 Mercer Street, PO Box 11-342 Manners Street, Wellington; tel 04-474 7840; fax 04-473 6303) which provides mandatory standards for company financial reporting called Statements of Standard Accounting Practice (SSAPs). Any material departure from these has to be disclosed in financial statements. The standards are intended for use by other types of business though not compulsory.

Taxation

The Inland Revenue Department publishes a guide for small businesses on their tax obligations. You can obtain copies from any IRD office. They also run the Small Business Advisory Service which advises beginning business people about what taxes they need to know about, what records to keep, how to complete tax returns and when to file returns and make payments. To get in touch with the service, you simply indicate when you register for GST or as a new employer that you would like an advisory consultation. You can either come into an IRD office for an appointment or an advisor will come and visit your office. They also run regular seminars.

Applying for an IRD number
One of the first requirements of any type of business operation is an Inland Revenue Department number. (IRD number) If you already have a personal IRD number and you are a sole trader, then you can continue to use this number. If your business location is different from your home address and you are registering for GST or as an employer then you may obtain another number for your business. Companies and partnerships must have their own numbers. You apply by contacting the nearest IRD office and filling in a form. You will need a passport or birth certificate as identification for a personal IRD number. In the case of a partnership, you must provide the IRD numbers of the partners, and for a company IRD, a copy of the certificate of incorporation.

Types of Taxes
There are four major types of taxes which you will have to deal with when doing business in New Zealand; income tax and company tax, Goods and Services Tax (GST), Accident Compensation Levies and Fringe Benefit Tax.

Income Tax and Company Tax: Income tax is payable by all persons or business entities. Individuals are taxed on a progressive rate system whereby 19.5% is payable on earnings up to NZ$38,000, and 33% over that figure. Resident companies are taxed at a flat rate of 33% on income earned, whereas non-resident companies are taxed at 38%.

Goods and Services Tax (GST): All businesses with an anticipated turnover of greater than $30,000 per annum are required to register for GST. GST is not a tax on your own business, it is a tax on sales to your customers which you collect on behalf of the IRD. It is similar to VAT, but the threshold is comparatively lower for GST so more small businesses are covered by it. Under the $30,000 threshold you can choose whether or not to register. If you deal with other registered businesses it may be worthwhile because they will be charging you GST which you will not be able to claim back. You pay GST on all your business inputs, supplies etc. You then add GST to all the sales you make. You make GST returns every six months.

Fringe Benefit Tax and Accident Compensation: If you provide any extra benefits to your employees such as a company car then you must pay fringe benefit tax. Even if you do not provide any perks, you must send in a yearly return. ACC is a fixed levy on each member of your workforce, however, from June 1998 there is a provision for work place accident insurance to be arranged through private insurance firms. The company could even provide an in-house insurance arrangement for its employees if the firm is large enough.

Annual Tax Returns
Different returns will be required depending on whether you are a sole trader, a company or a partnership. The tax year runs from 1st April to 31 March, and although businesses can use different year end dates for reporting purposes, the balance date will be related to the nearest 31st March for tax purposes. Sole traders must complete an IR3, the return for self employed people. In a partnership, each partner must fill in an IR3, plus an IR7 must be filled in for the partnership as a whole. A company must fill in an IR4, and each shareholder must also file an individual return. Included with each return must be a copy of the accounts. For more information contact your local Inland Revenue Office, or the national office (Inland Revenue Department, 12-22 Hawkstone Street, PO Box 2198, Wellington; tel (04) 472 1032; fax (04) 478 5801).

Useful Publications
Doing Business In New Zealand: free from Ernst & Young, Publications Department, Beckett House, 1 Lambeth Road, London SE1 7EU; tel 0171-931 6581; fax 0171-931 4458.
Running a Small Business? – A guide to your tax obligations: Inland Revenue Department, available from local IRD offices.

Appendix – Personal Case Histories

Katie Da Gama (Australia)

Katie Da Gama, aged 24, decided to take a working holiday in Australia after completing a demanding law degree at Cambridge University. She wanted a 'gap year' between her finals and the commencement of the her year in bar school (she is training to be a barrister). Katie saw the trip as an opportunity to widen her experience of the world and eventually spent a whole year in Australia.

Katie applied for a Working Holiday Maker visa at Australia House, opting not to apply by post, and was surprised by how quick and easy it was. She made sure that she took all the appropriate supporting documentation and waited only half an hour before she was granted her visa. She applied in December for a planned February departure on a charter airline Britannia (on a one-way ticket costing £175). Katie was fortunate in having family connections in Perth, and arranged to fly to Western Australia where she was met by her godmother. 'I was glad that I had somewhere to go,' she says, 'and would advise anyone undertaking this trip to have accommodation arranged. It can be very daunting arriving in a completely strange environment after such a long flight'.

Katie decided to look for temporary work in the field of office administration and registered with as many agencies as she could. She took multiple copies of her CV with her to Australia, and found that being prepared in this way made the whole process less stressful. 'It would have been helpful if I had made sure that I had references as well, though,' Katie adds. 'Almost every employee wants evidence that you are reliable and of good character, and references from previous employers, tutors or landlords are invaluable.' Katie found work within two weeks at the University of Western Australia, which she loved, and after that was never without work during the period of her stay. She also found that the contacts she made helped her with accommodation; eventually she ended up house-sitting which enabled her to save more money for her travels.

After spending approximately nine months working in Perth, Katie set off on a round-Australia trip, taking in Uluru and other outback regions. She also travelled to New Zealand and Fiji. The highlights of the trip she considers too numerous to mention, but summarises its essential quality as one of welcome. 'I was amazed by the hospitality,' she said. 'Everywhere I went people welcomed me and went out of their way to help me. I couldn't believe the level of genuine friendliness and know that I have made lifelong friends.'

Katie recommends that anyone planning a working holiday in Australia should join the Youth Hostel Association before leaving and, if possible, obtain an International Student Identity Card (ISIC), available from STA Travel. These are cheaper to organise in your home country and offer very favourable discounts. She also suggests setting up a web-based e-mail address, such as HotMail, which can be accessed from Internet terminals anywhere you travel. 'The State Libraries in every state in Australia have free Internet access.' Katie says, 'and if you have an email address organised you can keep in touch instantly and for free.'

On returning to the UK in February, Katie worked for a few months before starting bar school. She enjoyed her Australian experience so much that both she and her brother have now applied to migrate there.

Sally Starling (Australia)

Sally is a part of history as she went to Australia in 1971 as a 'ten pound Pom' – one of the thousands of UK immigrants lured down-under by promises of sunshine and prosperity. 'In those days,' Sally remembers, 'they *paid* you to go. I was living in London at the time, and was fed up with the cold and endless minor winter illnesses. When I saw a poster in the tube advertising the £10 scheme, I made up my mind to go on the spot, and within weeks I was on my way.' Sally arrived in Melbourne and soon moved to Sydney where she quickly found work as a secretary. She remembers that the difference in her health and general well-being improved very rapidly after she arrived, and her overwhelming impression was one of good fortune.

Sally lived in Sydney for four years, during which time she saved money to travel abroad. Unfortunately, whilst living in Canada, she let her immigrant status lapse, and when she decided it was time to go back to Australia she found herself having to apply anew to migrate. 'Luckily, it was still relatively easy at that time to move to Australia, and I was absolutely convinced, after spending a few years travelling, that Australia was the country where I wanted to spend the rest of my life. To me, it had become home.' Her application was accepted and she returned to Perth where she has since made a permanent home.

When asked to describe any difficulties in adjusting to her new environment, Sally mentioned the language barrier! 'When I first arrived I just couldn't understand what people were saying,' she said. 'I found it quite intimidating when I was out in a group of people, and it took me a while to feel comfortable socially.'

Sally now owns her own highly successful business which she established, and enjoys a relaxed and prosperous lifestyle. She and her husband have recently successfully sponsored her mother-in-law's application to migrate as a retiree, and they have also attempted to sponsor Sally's brother, although this application was turned down on age grounds under the points system. Sally maintains strong links with the UK and returns for holidays and family visits regularly.

Jonathan Young and Gillian Webster (New Zealand)

Jonathan Young is 37 and met New Zealander Gillian Webster, 28 in London. They settled in Auckland in 1995. After spending two years working in London, Gillian wanted to return home to enjoy a quality of life she felt she could not attain in England. Jonathan was working as an equity analyst in an investment bank in London, but enjoyed playing a lot of sport and wanted to spend less time commuting and more time on his windsurfer.

Why did you decide to move to New Zealand?
My partner was homesick and wanted to be near her parents in Auckland as they got older. I wasn't enjoying the treadmill of working in London and decided it was time for a change. I travelled home with Gillian for a couple of Christmases and really liked the country and the lifestyle. After London, I really appreciate leaving my job at 5.30 and being at the beach in twenty minutes.

How did you go about preparing for the move?
First of all we bought airline tickets to New Zealand which went through the US, as the luggage allowance is much more generous – you are allowed 64kg of luggage rather than only 20kg when you fly via Asia. Also, a couple of Gillian's friends were at the end of their OE (overseas experience) in London and were shipping all their belongings home, so we decided to send all our belongings in the same consignment. It lowered the cost for all of us because the first box is the most expensive. It was lucky they were going to the same city, as only one person's address can go on the shipment.